D0568980

Crime and Insecurity

Crime and Insecurity

The Governance of Safety in Europe

Edited by Adam Crawford

WILLAN
PUBLISHING

Published by

Willan Publishing
Culmcott House
Mill Street, Uffculme
Cullompton, Devon
EX15 3AT, UK
Tel: +44(0)1884 840337
Fax: +44(0)1884 840251
e-mail: info@willanpublishing.co.uk
website: www.willanpublishing.co.uk

Published simultaneously in the USA and Canada by

Willan Publishing
c/o ISBS, 5824 N.E. Hassalo St
Portland, Oregon 97213-3644, USA
Tel: +001(0)503 287 3093
Fax: +001(0)503 280 8832
website: www.isbs.com

First published 2002

ISBN 1-903240-48-4 Hardback

British Library Cataloguing-in-Publication Data

A catalogue record for this book is available from the British Library.

Printed by T J International Ltd, Trecerus Industrial Estate, Padstow, Cornwall,
PL28 8RW
Typeset by PDQ Typesetting, Newcastle-under-Lyme, Staffordshire

Contents

Acknowledgements

This book emerges out of a stimulating one-day colloquium entitled 'Insecurity and Safety in the New Millennium', held at the University of Leeds on 23 March 2000. Most of the chapters in this book were presented in preliminary form at the colloquium. The subsequent deliberations helped to sharpen the focus of analysis and to encourage debate and coherency of the various contributions. I would like to thank all the delegates who participated in, and contributed to, the colloquium. In addition, I would like to thank Geradine Craven for the enthusiasm with which she assisted in the preparation and realisation of the colloquium itself. Finally, I am grateful to Susan Flint for her editorial assistance and comments with regard to a number of the chapters.

Notes on contributors

Hans-Jörg Albrecht is Director of the Max Planck Institute for International Law at Freiburg. He is co-editor of *Drug Policies in Western Europe* (1989) and *Crime and Criminal Policy in Europe* (1990).

Zygmunt Bauman is Emeritus Professor of Sociology at the Universities of Leeds and Warsaw. He is one of the leading contemporary commentators on the changing conditions of social and political life, having published numerous books including more recently *Postmodernity and its Discontents* (1997), *Globalization: The Human Consequences* and *Liquid Modernity* (2000).

Adam Crawford is Professor of Criminology and Criminal Justice at the University of Leeds. He is author of *The Local Governance of Crime* (1997), *Crime Prevention and Community Safety* (1998) and co-editor of *Integrating a Victim Perspective within Criminal Justice* (2000).

Jo Goodey is Lecturer in Criminology at the Centre for Criminal Justice Studies, University of Leeds. She is on secondment to the United Nations International Centre for Crime Prevention in Vienna on a Marie Curie Fellowship. Her research interests lie in the fields of victimisation, race and crime and human trafficking in the EU. She is co-editor of *Integrating a Victim Perspective within Criminal Justice* (2000).

Juliet Lodge is Professor of European Integration and Director of the Jean Monnet European Centre of Excellence at the University of Leeds. She has written widely on the European Union, notably on matters of internal and external security. Her most recent book is an edited collection entitled *The 1999 Elections to the European Parliament* (2000). She heads an EU funded transnational research project on sustainable democracy and tolerance.

Martina McGuinness is Lecturer in Risk Management and Strategy at the Management School, University of Sheffield. She completed her PhD at the University of Leeds, where she worked (together with Clive Walker) on a project entitled 'Political violence and commercial victims', funded by the Airey Neave Trust, from which their chapter is drawn.

Leslie J. Moran is Reader in Law at Birkbeck College, University of London. He has written extensively on matters relating to gay issues in the law. He is author of *The Homosexual(ity) of Law* (1996) and co-editor of *Legal Queeries* (1998, with D. Monk and S. Beresford). He is completing a book provisionally entitled *Queer Violence*.

Tim Newburn is the Joseph Rowntree Professor of Urban Social Policy and Director of the Public Policy Research Unit at Goldsmiths' College, University of London. He is the author of numerous books including *Permission and Regulation* (1991), *Crime and Criminal Justice Policy* (1995), *The Future of Policing* (1997, with R. Morgan) and *Private Security and Public Policing* (1998 with T. Jones).

G. Wyn Rees is Senior Lecturer in International Relations in the Politics Department at the University of Leicester. His recent publications include *Reforming the European Union: From Maastricht to Amsterdam* (2000, co-edited with P. Lynch and N. Neuwahl) and *Britain and Defence 1945–2000: A Policy Re-evaluation* (2001, co-authored with S. Croft, A. Dorman and M. Uttley).

Sebastian Roché is senior CNRS research fellow in the Institute of Political Studies (CERAT) at the University of Grenoble. He has written numerous books on the politics of insecurity and juvenile delinquency in France, including *Le Sentiment d'Insécurité* (1993), *La Société Incivile* (1996) and *La Délinquance des Jeunes (2001).*

Clive Walker is Professor of Criminal Justice Studies and Head of the Law Department at the University of Leeds. He has written extensively on police powers, criminal justice, human rights and terrorism and the law. His earlier publications include *Political Violence and the Law in Ireland* (1989, with G. Hogan), *The Prevention of Terrorism in British Law* (1993) and he is co-editor of *Miscarriages of Justice* (1999, with K. Starmer) and *The Internet, Law and Society* (2000, with Y. Akdeniz and D. Wall).

Sandra Walklate is Professor of Criminology in the Department of Sociology at Manchester Metropolitan University. She has published extensively in the fields of victimology, gender and crime and community safety, including *Critical Victimology* (1994, with R. Mawby), *Understanding Criminology* (1998) and *Gender, Crime and Criminal Justice* (2001).

David Wall is Senior Lecturer and Director of the Centre for Criminal Justice Studies at the University of Leeds, where he conducts research and teaches in the fields of policing, criminal justice processes, crime and information technology. His previous publications include *The Chief Constables of England and Wales* (1998). He is co-editor of *The Internet, Law and Society* (2000, with Y. Akdeniz and C. Walker) and editor of *Crime and the Internet* (2001).

Mark Webber is Senior Lecturer in Politics in the Department of European Studies at the University of Loughborough. He is the author of *The International Politics of Russia and the Successor* (1996), editor of *Russia and Europe: Conflict or Cooperation?* (2000) and co-author of *Foreign Policy in a Transformed World* (2002, with M. Smith).

Figures and tables

Figures

Tables

Introduction: governance and security

Adam Crawford

Concerns about crime and insecurity have become essential aspects of the political and social discourse of individuals, communities, non-governmental organisations, businesses, governments and international bodies. We are increasingly governed through crime and insecurity. Public issues are increasingly defined in terms of their potential crimogenic qualities or adverse implications for safety and security. Crime and insecurity have come to occupy a prominent place in political discourse, the construction of social order and cultural representations of the times in which we live. They are at the forefront of the public imagination, influencing so much of the activities and talk of ordinary citizens. Moreover, crime and insecurity are on the move; they circulate in novel ways, penetrating public and private spheres, seeping through new technologies and turning apparently benign and taken-for-granted aspects of contemporary life – such as shopping, travel, working and using the Internet – into potential threats. In a 'liquid' modern world (Bauman 2000) they simultaneously invade local and transnational arenas. Just as crime and insecurity appear to be shifting, so too responses to crime and insecurity are on the move. They are being refocused and extended just as the criminal justice complex and the modern nation-state itself are the subjects of transformation. As crime and insecurity have become unbounded so too policing is becoming cut free from its association with the modern state to incorporate a diversity of actors.

This book brings together different disciplinary approaches to concerns around contemporary insecurities and responses to them across Europe. It explores the sources of insecurity, alarm and risk both at transnational and local levels. The 'threats to security' addressed in this book relate both to macro threats to the security of nation-states, as well as to countless micro challenges to personal safety presented by a host of less precise threats, and include transnational organised crime, human trafficking, migration, terrorism, interpersonal violence, personal safety, anti-social behaviour and disorder. On closer inspection, as a number of the contributors to this collection note, many of these constitute 'ideological categories'. The rise of new 'insecurity' is associated, by various commentators, with a number of recent developments in late modernity: the collapse of communism in Eastern Europe, globalisation, the rearticulation and 'hollowing out' of the modern state and the growth of new forms of risk, particularly those inspired by technological advancements. Recurring themes within this collection revolve around the conceptual diptych of 'governance' and 'security'.

Governance

There is little doubt that the continuing consolidation of the EU and the devolution of powers within states, as well as the greater involvement of diverse non-state actors in the process of governing different areas of social and economic life, have challenged traditional conceptual understandings of relationships between state and civil society. Hence, 'governance' evokes and seeks to describe a shift in the modes of governing. More particularly for the purpose of this book, the governance narrative alludes to the changing nature, form and location of responses to crime and insecurity in terms of the way in which these are governed, regulated and ordered. This theme reflects the shifting terrain between, and within, state and society. Rod Rhodes sets out a useful definition, in which 'governance signifies a *change* in the meaning of government, referring to a *new* process of governing; or a *changed* condition of ordered rule; or the *new* method by which society is governed, (1996: 652–3), emphasis in orginal). The term governance suggests the recalibration of powers and responsibilities across and between the state, market and civil society. It evokes a rupture with a state-centred approach to government which had come to dominate political thinking, policy and practice (Rhodes 1997).

At one level, commentators on the development of the EU have sought to develop a framework for analysing the relationships between EU institutions, nation-states and subnational governments. At another level, commentators have tried to make sense of multisectoral and interorganisational networks, be they regional developments, urban and rural coalitions or neighbourhood and community-based organisations. The terminologies 'policy communities', 'partnerships' and 'joined-up government' have all been used to refer to networks that transcend the traditional competencies of state bureaucracies; these incorporate non-state actors and stakeholders (particularly from the business and voluntary sectors) that bridge the public and private spheres; they aim to produce holistic solutions that are 'problem-orientated' rather than defined according to the organisations most readily available for their solution; and they connect through horizontal relations of interdependencies, rather than vertical relations of control. As such, governance reflects a process through which public and private actions and resources are co-ordinated and given common meaning.

According to Rhodes, governance refers to 'self-organising, inter-organisational networks' (2000: 346). He suggests (*ibid.*) these exhibit the following characteristics:

- Interdependence between organisations – extending beyond government and incorporating non-state actors and organisations – with the resultant blurring of boundaries, responsibilities and functions between public, private and voluntary sectors.

- Continuing interactions between network members, on the basis of the need to exchange resources and negotiate shared purpose.

- Interactions rooted in trust and regulated by game-like rules negotiated and agreed by the participants.

- A significant degree of autonomy from the state.

Moreover, the concept of governance has application below, above and beyond the nation-state. As such, it can help us make sense of highly localised networks and regulatory orders as well as transnational and European-level developments (Pierre 2000). It affords an understanding of 'multi-level governance' (Pierre and Stoker 2000) whereby the relations between systems of governance reorder traditional notions of top-down control. Relations between levels of governance are not necessarily ordered hierarchically but have more complex, contextually specific relationships. In the EU context, for example, transnational institutions frequently target subnational institutions, hence side stepping the level of the nation-state.

The shift from state-centred government to networked governance has particular implications in the fields of crime control and security. Crudely put, the modern state defined its sovereign authority and, hence itself, primarily in terms of its monopolistic capacity to defend its populations from external and internal threats to security and order. To this end, it sought to govern (in)security through its military and its police. 'Policing' became associated with the direct activities of state agencies. The policing of 'internal security', after the establishment of the modern police in England in 1829, became defined in terms of the activities of the police. Where once 'policing' had been seen as an aspect of political economy and good governance, it increasingly took on a very much narrower meaning and became synonymous with what the police actually do.

The contemporary age has seen a reversal of this conceptual narrowing and quest for monopolistic control by the state. Instead, more recently, we have witnessed the policing of security and order being increasingly directed by multiple auspices other than the state and conducted through a plurality of agencies other than public police services. We have a complex array of networks, partnerships, interlaced alliances of organisations and active citizenry that transcend the 'public' and 'private' spheres constituting hybrid mixes of plural agencies, places and functions. Recent changes in social organisation suggest that definitions of policing need to be cut free from their territorial and state-centred bindings. As Peter Manning suggests: 'while quite distinct national, international and transnational police mandates exist (the map), legally constituted policing organisations and the actual ground to be controlled (the territory), are simultaneously shifting. Nation states and associated police forces may not map, much less control, the territory they claim governance over' (2000: 178). The policing of new social spaces such as the Internet – as David Wall demonstrates in his chapter – reflects this challenge in particularly acute ways.

Recent years have witnessed the pluralisation of responsibility for crime prevention and public safety (Garland 2001). The relationship between government and the governed is now one in which the language of 'partnership' has become integral (Crawford 1997). We are now all cast as 'partners against crime' in a new corporate approach, involving a fundamental rearticulation of the role of the state, individual and group responsibilities and professional 'expertise'. Where once the public was told to 'leave it to the professionals', now they are enjoined to active participation in a more obviously 'self-policing society'. This fragmentation has itself been state sponsored: encouraged by the introduction of privatisation and quasi-markets through purchaser–provider splits. We can no longer speak (if we ever could) of a state monopoly in crime control and policing. They have become shared, as diverse agencies, organisations, groups and individuals are implicated in these tasks.

However, it is easy both to overestimate the capacity of governments in earlier times to govern with more or less absolute control and to underestimate the role of governments in contemporary governance. Government and governance are not dichotomous concepts but are better understood as points along a continuum (Pierre and Peters 2000: 29). The modern state remains an important actor and power container and has proved reasonably resilient in adapting to external pressures.

Governance describes features of a framework and process of co-ordination but does not necessarily tell us much about outcomes. Whilst it can help provide a new way of looking at things, as well as describe a new set of things to look at, it begs a series of unanswered questions. With regard to the new relationship between government and govern-ance, what is the role of the state? To what extent and through what mechanisms do states seek to steer governance? More broadly, what are the constellations of power relations within the new networks of governance? Do they represent a marketisation of policy processes in which public policies are captured by private interests? There is a tendency on the part of commentators to emphasise the benign and consensual nature of negotiation within networks of governance. And yet, network processes are infused with both conflicts over purposes and ideologies as well as differential power relations in which the more powerful players are likely to dominate. Hence, in practice, which interests actually dominate the goals and desired outcomes of specific networks of governance?

With regard to outcomes, we need to ask: how effective are the new forms of governance? To what extent is the governability of certain social fields under contemporary conditions as important as the governing capacity of new networks and regulatory orders? Moreover, what are the implications for participation, transparency and inclusion of these new forms of governance? The manner in which networks operate are often anti-democratic processes. Joint and negotiated decisions tie the diverse actors into corporate outcomes, but often fail to identify lines of responsibility and accountability. Institutional complexity – in multi-level governance – further obscures who is accountable to whom, and for what. Rigid frameworks of law and due process often get in the way of fluid negotiations and informal relations of interdependence. Informality may foster inequality. As such, we need to ask: upon what notions of legitimacy do forms of governance rest? And, to what extent are these new political orders authorised by, and subjected to, democratic accountability?

5

The chapters in this book go some way towards understanding the ways in which forms of governance through crime and insecurity have produced new modes of regulation with new narratives and ideologies. Whilst in some instances this can be participatory and open, the dark side of 'governance' – particularly notable around issues of crime control and order – is exclusion and the demonisation of 'others' as new 'folk devils' (Young 1999). It is perhaps unsurprising that new networks of governance have required new discourses through which quests for legitimacy have been sought. Security and order have been at the forefront of these.

Security

Despite its omnipresence in much policy debate, there is considerable lack of clarity about the meaning of 'security' and hence its negative inflexion, namely, 'insecurity'. It would appear that understandings of security vary according to different disciplines. The concept appears to have a different resonance within the field of international relations and European studies than it does within a sociological or criminological sense. This is reflected, in part, by some of the different contributions to this book. Not only does the term operate at both a macro and micro level – relating to mass threats of warfare and political terrorism as well as to small-scale, localised disorders, anti-social behaviour and affronts to quality of life – but it also relates, on the one hand, to complex public institutional orders and, on the other hand, to parochial informal social relations.

Security occupies a tense relationship with freedom – there is a trade-off between the two, such that more freedom demands less security and more security demands less freedom. Bauman notes: 'The perfect balance between freedom and security is perhaps a logical incongruence and practical impossibility, but this by itself is a most powerful reason to seek ever better formulae for trade-off' (2001: 42). As such, security connects with ideals of happiness and order. It is bound up with people's hopes and fantasies as well as their fears and anxieties; it informs people's sense of self; their notions of collective and personal identity; their grasp of and relation to the world around them. It is imagined and reimagined, damaged and reconstructed. It therefore may not be very surprising that concerns over 'insecurity' and the process of 'securitisation' have been at the heart of the European project.

The open-textured nature of security stems, in part, from the fact that it is understood in relation to an *absence* in time and space. It is the negative corollary of insecurity: fear, risk and danger. Conceptually, security embodies no necessary positive attributes but rather lacks contrary ones. Security is the quest for a situation or moment in which something undesirable does not exist or does not occur. And yet, as Lucia Zedner has argued, 'increasingly, the pursuit of security appears to require not merely an absence of threats but the positive reinforcement of public perceptions of their safety' (2000: 201). As such, it is bound up with quality-of-life issues and nostalgic quests for genuine human identity, connectedness and reciprocity precisely at a moment in time at which these appear most absent. This is particularly to be found in debates about 'community safety', which Zedner refers to as security's 'fashionable analogue' (*ibid.*). Hence, security embodies elements of subjectivity but is also subject to manipulation on the back of public anxiety. This is not to suggest that all anxieties about crime or fear of crime are not grounded in reality. On the contrary, many anxieties about crime are a negotiated aspect of everyday life. Nor is this to suggest that levels of crime do not have direct and corrosive effects upon the social psyche. Rather, it is to suggest that the impact and experience of this (social as well as individual) harm is (increasingly) unevenly distributed throughout society. It is socially situated. Consequently, it has different cultural inflexions and referents.

Nevertheless, there has been a blurring and merging of international, communal and personal security – not least in the light of the terrorist attacks in the USA on 11 September 2001. The local and the global are intricately connected. The idea of 'securitisation' suggests a process whereby significant political, financial and technological investments are being made in security itself. It has become a commodity in a blossoming market. Despite the rationalistic tones of much security discourse, security is intrinsically related to complex individual and collective sentiments about threats to established order, anxieties and fears, all of which are connected to wider, subjective and non-rationalistic elements of social identity and well-being (Sparks 1992: 124). Danger has many meanings for people, including, but extending far beyond, crime. It connects not only with experience (both personal and vicarious), local knowledge, tradition and folklore, but also with unconscious desires and traumas.

At the heart of security debates has been the nation-state's mission for monopoly of public power and coercion. Policing and crime control have come to represent pre-eminent and central symbols of state sovereignty. This has the implications that, particularly with regard to transnational concerns, security has been fundamentally linked to the development and capacity of the nation-state. Statehood and the quest for security have been intertwined. However, as suggested earlier, more recently the myth of the sovereign state – with security as its central mandate – has become increasingly exposed, decoupling the security–state dualism. At both transnational and subnational levels there has emerged a recognition of the incapacity of the state to guarantee security in diverse ways and in different contexts. The void produced by this acknowledgement increasingly has been filled by both an internationalisation and a marketisation of security.

The notion of 'security as commodity' provides consumers with real choices enabling them to confront and manage their sense of insecurity. As such, a sense of security informs tangible decisions people make regarding where they go, live, shop, the nature of their leisure activities and so on. However, investments in security as a commodity are at best tentative attempts to control an unknowable, unpredictable and risky social world. This requires an investment of trust, one which is always subject to being undermined by new developments or shifts in feelings of (in)security. Purchasing 'security' may be a way in which actors can attempt to situate and interpret themselves and the world around them as stable, coherent and manageable despite, or maybe because of, the realities of uncertainty, fragmentation and a loss of collective identity. As such, it may represent a quest for an unattainable and imaginary ideal in which comfort, reassurance and order are sought. And yet, security speaks to those seeking it through assurances and guarantees as to its objective effects.

Consequently, the commodified notion of 'private security' may itself be an unachievable goal: 'a new form of "magic" within a system that eschews the invisible and the unknowable' (Spitzer 1987: 47). The acquisition of, and quest for, ever greater 'security as commodity' may serve to undermine feelings of 'security' by institutionalising anxiety. Security itself may be insatiable, as more demands more. Furthermore, the marketisation of security challenges individuals and groups to act as 'responsible' rational choice actors in weighing up the risks and security dimensions of social interaction. And yet, the individualistic quest for personal security may impact adversely on others and on collective experiences and sentiments of safety. Hence, in a regime of choice in which security is a continually pursued commodity, there may be an inherent antagonism between *feeling secure* and *being social*. Private security is not only in large part exclusive but its quest may also increase the unequal distribution of public safety through displacement, concentration and compounding effects of reputation (Crawford 1998).

A common theme throughout this collection is the expansion, broadening and changing form of 'insecurity', both perceived and real. This transformation of insecurity and what it is taken to mean raises a number of questions: is heightened insecurity a product of increases in risks to security or is it a product of raised perceptions of such risks? In other words, are we witnessing a period of greater objective insecurity or greater subjective concerns over security? If the former, where are these new threats coming from? If the latter, why are we so concerned about insecurity? Or is insecurity a metaphor or trope for some other phenomenon? Moreover, how does this transformation of (in)security relate to wider economic and socio-political changes?

These questions inform a number of recurring concerns that run throughout the various chapters in this book, most notably: the internationalisation and, more particularly, the Europeanisation of certain forms of crime; the apparent 'convergence' of criminal justice practice and the emergence of a common criminal justice policy; the interconnectedness of transnational and local responses to crime; questions about the conceptualisation of crime, insecurity and fears; and changing cultural sensibilities and levels of tolerance of crime, disorder, 'otherness' and difficulty.

The confluence of the two themes of security and governance – as indicated by a number of commentators to this volume – sees a blurring of a number of traditional distinctions and an erosion of conceptual dichotomies (albeit these were rarely ever hard and fast in previous times) between:

- internal and external security;
- civil and military policing;
- the regulation of public and private spaces;
- the nature of public policing and commercial security;
- the role of state and civil society in matters of governance with a pluralisation of responsibility beyond the nation-state;
- the distinction between crime and social problems; and, hence, a cross-disciplinary and intersectorial approach to governance fusing (and confusing) criminal and social policy.

This confluence also suggests an ambivalence about the residual capacity of the nation-state to assert its sovereign authority, thus producing a volatile mix of criminal justice policies which are at one moment assured, expressive and morally toned, and at the next moment hesitant, rationalistic and instrumental. There are tensions between the techno-cratic urge to manage crime and insecurities and expressive responses to fears and anxieties. The limitations of traditional criminal justice are recognised in certain instances only to be discounted or ignored in others. This dualistic denial and recognition produces volatile shifts in the state's presentation of its own capacity for effective action in crime control (Garland 1996). Moreover, state-sponsored initiatives also produce new, and potentially rival, sites of governance, both at supranational and subnational levels, within which nation-states have a different relationship with non-state actors. The preoccupation with security and order documented in this book reflects simultaneously the limited capacity for state action and problems of state sovereignty and legitimation as much as it reflects rational responses to crime and insecurity, as well as attempts to reassert new forms of control over shifting territories and peoples.

Organisation of the book

This book advances a multidisciplinary understanding of major changes in the nature and form of governance at interstate and local levels with regard to insecurity and safety. It brings together leading commentators from diverse disciplines to consider a number of issues raised by, and the implications of, the new governance of insecurity and safety at pan-European and local community levels. These are issues that simulta-neously transcend and reconfigure traditional disciplinary boundaries. The book draws upon and connects debates within the fields of criminology, sociology, politics, European studies and international relations.

The book is divided into three parts. Part 1 begins with two introductory contributions that sketch out some of the broad issues and terrain of debate. Part 2 considers cross-national and pan-European developments and debates concerning security, safety and governance, notably with regard to policing and migration. From differing perspec-tives, it examines the supranational and international institutional infrastructures of governance that have been constructed in recent years around concerns over crime and insecurity. Part 3 focuses upon local expressions and meanings of safety and insecurity and the manner in which these feed into and affect local understandings and practices as well as modes of governing and regulating such sentiments. It draws upon the increasing salience given to local issues of community safety both in France and, more generally, in Britain among different population groups and within divergent social contexts and places.

Part 1 begins with an overview of some recent developments and debates both at local and supranational levels by Adam Crawford (Chapter 1). At the local level he considers and seeks to explain the rapid rise of community safety and analogous trends. He then goes on to highlight some of the broad developments at the European level and the manner in which these are interconnected. 'Community' formation at the European level reflects similar dynamics as those found in local community development, particularly with regard to the role insecurity plays in the construction of communal identity through processes of inclusion and exclusion that constitute boundaries of insider and outsider: of 'us and them'. The chapter then goes on to explore the manner in which local governance issues have increasingly come to occupy a European-wide position through a convergence of approaches, which is the product of both trans-European co-operation and competition. The chapter also examines the involvement of the commercial security sector within European developments and raises a number of questions about the implications of a new and developing territory of the policing of crime and insecurity which is, simultaneously, public and private as well as local, national and transnational.

Next, Zygmunt Bauman (Chapter 2) offers a compelling account of our contemporary social condition and the place that concerns about safety and security have come to occupy therein. The late modern condition, he suggests, is one in which security is sacrificed day by day on the altar of ever-expanding freedom. Governments increasingly can do little to guarantee security or certainty and, in some cases, promote insecurity and uncertainty through flexible and unstable labour patterns and the corrosion of long-term commitments. As a consequence, governments increasingly invest in one of the few arenas in which they may be able to affect change: in the production of symbols of 'orderly environments', ostensibly to entice nomadic capital and a sentiment of 'safety' among domestic populations. As such, the rise of concerns over safety and security may tell us more about the weaknesses of the contemporary state than about genuine changes in public safety. Bauman's focus, therefore, is less upon whether safety has itself become more precarious – given difficulties of objective quantification of change over time (albeit that certainty, in the sense of biographical continuity, has clearly fragmented, particularly in the 'flexible' labour market as long-term 'careers' are replaced by short-term 'jobs') – than with the manner in which insecurity and unsafety are stimulated and maintained. Looking closely at the 'figures of fear' around which contemporary panics are structured, he suggests we can learn more about the character of uncertainty and insecurity than we can about the intrinsic nature of their 'nuisance power'. This is a theme to which other authors return throughout the book, notably with regard to the manner in which immigration, insecurity and crime have become interwoven in much political discourse across Europe and the extent to which immigrants have become poignant contemporary 'figures of fear'. For Bauman, it is precisely because of their mobility that these individuals are cast as the bearers of insecurity.

Part 2 opens with a chapter by Rees and Webber (Chapter 3) in which they explore the governance of insecurity across Europe from a perspective of international relations. They highlight the broadening of the concept of security and the blurring of the boundaries between internal and external security, particularly in the post-Cold War period. They suggest that economic restructuring in former Soviet bloc countries has presented new opportunities for criminality with particular implications for transnational organised crime. This has seen an increased 'interdependence of security' across Europe to the extent that developments in one part of the continent often have repercussions elsewhere. 'Securitisation', they suggest, has seen the emergence of new threats, and 'external enemies' replace the ideological and military fears of Soviet communism. This process, however, has been a hesitant and contested one that extends far beyond security and into the fabric of the politics of identity in Europe. This theme, connecting security with identity through the contrast of 'self' and 'others' – 'insiders' and 'outsiders' – in different ways, is to be found permeating various chapters in this collection.

In outlining some of the different modes of governance that have emerged in the shift from external security to internal security, Rees and Webber note some of the complex issues to which this has given rise, notably at the level of the EU. A prominent issue is that of national sovereignty. The historic association of responses to crime as expressions of national sovereignty has meant that states have often been reluctant to cede monopolistic control in this field. Crime control has often been seen to be the last bastion and pre-eminent symbol of state sovereignty. And yet, as various chapters in this volume testify, the late modern era is one in which challenges to this image of monopolistic control have come from both above and below the nation-state. The development of supranational – political, legal and economic – institutions has questioned state sovereignty within its own borders. In clinging on to the notion of national sovereignty over internal security matters in the face of increasing pressures from migration and transnational organised crime, not only have the two concerns become ideologically linked but also there has been an unwillingness to recognise and address the manner in which these are issues beyond the capacity of individual states. Such that some states, notably the UK, have been reluctant to relinquish national control over internal security matters, for fear this will inadvertently accelerate the process of European integration and the transfer of more wide-ranging powers to the institutions of the EU.

Juliet Lodge (Chapter 4) gives a detailed account of the growth and elaboration of a European institutional infrastructure and the concern around issues of insecurity within the EU – notably the development of intergovernmental Pillar III on justice and home affairs, dedicated to the realisation of an EU of 'freedom, security and justice'. Her chapter begins by outlining the main provisions of the Amsterdam Treaty and the Pre-Accession Pact on Organised Crime. It then goes on to explore some of the unresolved problem areas that may imperil the realisation of 'freedom, security and justice' to which the EU is committed. Lodge highlights some of the difficulties and challenges posed by Pillar III for the process of EU enlargement. It is argued that unless steps are taken to ring-fence and protect the 'internal security *acquis*' of the EU, then enlargement might become an excuse to postpone and, hence, jeopardise, the attainment of freedom, security and justice in the expanded EU. In this regard, she highlights the crucial future role of the European Commission. A precondition for success of internal security and of expansion, she concludes, is the need to render existing mechanisms more effective.

Jo Goodey (Chapter 5), by contrast, challenges some of the taken-for-granted assumptions concerning, what she calls, the ' "migration, crime, security" continuum' upon which the EU's institutional infrastructure is premised. She questions 'whose insecurity' is of primary concern in these developments and, hence, by default, 'whose insecurity' is marginalised or deemed 'undeserving'. Rather like Bauman, she suggests that by scrutinising the 'figures of fear' around which present panics and institutions are constructed, we can discover more about the nature of insecurity and the processes of 'othering' that are often involved in the demonisation of contemporary scapegoats. She questions the extent to which the images of organised crime, criminality and victimisation, which infuse EU developments, rely upon stereotypes of certain non-EU citizens as 'outsiders'. She goes on to contrast this with the insecurity and personal threats to safety for vulnerable non-EU citizens who are the subjects of victimisation and abuse. To this end, she examines the case of victims of human trafficking as the 'flipside' of what is perceived to be the dominant security threat. She suggests that the 'human security problem' posed by migration has become synonymous with a 'national security threat'. As a consequence, the EU has conceived itself as the victim, neglecting the real personal victims of transnational organised crime who are often the most vulnerable and marginalised people in the EU.

Hans-Jörg Albrecht (Chapter 6) takes up a number of themes raised by Bauman and Goodey in assessing the role of immigration into and across Europe within policy discourses and debates concerning crime and insecurity. He suggests that migration and immigration have become intrinsically bound up with contemporary 'folk devils' and 'folk dangers', to the point that we are witnessing increased outbreaks of violence and hate crime directed against asylum seekers, immigrants and guest workers across Europe. This fixation upon immigrants as the embodiment of insecurity and unsafety reflects real changes in modern societies, notably increased mobility, the fact of large-scale migration and immigration, the existence of significant minority groups that can be scapegoated and the fact that states have lost substantial powers to regulate and govern their own populations, specifically their failure to solve social and economic crises by way of traditional forms of governance.

Albrecht suggests that it is not enough merely to berate the lack of reliable data on immigration and crime (despite the obvious difficulties), as some critical commentators do. Rather, his analysis takes us behind the rhetoric and explores in detail what it is we know about changes in patterns of migration and immigration in Europe over time, as well as the involvement of different migrant populations in criminal activity. Despite the fixed dominant assumption about immigrants and insecurity, he suggests that the evidence shows different experiences of immigration across countries and historical contexts, as well as divergent involvement of immigrants within criminal activities. First, he identifies the impact of migration upon different generations of immigrants as the social and economic context has changed from one of labour-related immigration (often based on post-colonial relationships) in the 1950s and 1960s to one of predominantly 'unwanted immigration', prompted by military conflicts, civil wars and processes of rapid economic and social dislocation in poorer countries. Secondly, whilst some immigrant groups exhibit much higher participation or involvement in crime than do majority groups, this is not uniform but differs across generations and within different ethnic minority populations. Some immigrant groups have similar or even lower levels of involvement in criminal activities than does the majority group within the society in which they live. Moreover, he suggests that where there are higher levels of immigrant involvement in crime these tend to be explained by their position within the society. However, in addition, cultural differences between similarly situated social groups can result in somewhat different crime patterns, both in terms of the nature and extent of involvement in criminal activity. To illustrate this he identifies a number of groups of immigrants involved in crime and suggests their involvement is largely a product of their precarious and marginal position within the host economy, as well as the availability of illicit opportunities, namely, their relationship to external and internal black markets or shadow economies.

According to Albrecht, except for crimes which are themselves the direct and indirect product of immigration laws and regulations (together with some limited 'subsistence crime' where asylum seekers are excluded from the labour market), the evidence suggests no direct relationship between immigration and crime. Where immigrants and foreign nationals do participate in forms of criminal activities involving illicit markets, these largely reflect the precarious economic and social position immigrants have come to occupy – largely replacing a domestic 'underclass'. Albrecht argues that the tenor of recent policy debates has resulted in a more punitive response to immigration. This is reflected in both prison statistics and in the introduction of 'tougher', more coercive, administrative and criminal legislation. Collectively, these developments indicate a general shift from a liberal concept of labour immigration in the 1960s towards a conception of migration and immigration as a – maybe *the* – major contemporary social problem.

Whilst the mobility of people pervades much contemporary public anxiety discourses and presents certain direct challenges to safety, so too does the movement of information and the access to communications. Recent developments in communication technologies have substantially transformed social, cultural and economic activities and relations, none more so than the Internet. Technologically driven developments, such as the Internet, also present acute anxieties, particularly where they have the potential of reaching into the previously perceived safe havens of private space. The Internet, simultaneously, presents new opportunities for communication – some of which are quite radical – and also presents new risks and threats. Moreover, these opportunities and risks can be accessed from, and may flood (back) into, the privacy of one's home, thus increasing its salience as a fear-inducing medium. For Ulrich Beck, the contemporary 'risk society', which developments such as the Internet herald, is 'an epoch in which the dark sides of progress increasingly come to dominate social debate' (1995: 2). The transnational reach of the Internet and the manner in which it transforms the relationship between time and space have both generated new fears and anxieties about 'unbounded threats' and created new opportunities for crime. Moreover, the amount of information that passes across the Internet presents significant challenges to regulation.

Much of the state-driven effort and activities put into transnational policing, as Johnston (2000: 110) has noted, has focused upon 'terrestrial crime': related to the relaxation of physical border controls across the emergent EU. This effort has often ignored or failed to address criminal activities that are conducted through non-territorial spheres such as cyberspace, as David Wall documents in Chapter 7 on 'Insecurity and the policing of cyberspace'. Wall charts the fears and realities of cybercrime and its regulation. He demonstrates the manner in which the Internet presents new challenges to traditional regulatory bodies, as well as to our understanding and conception of policing and criminology. He suggests that much of the debate, to date, about policing cyberspace has developed against a background of little rigorous data and much unreliable media speculation on the back of a small number of celebrity cases. By contrast, Wall outlines the parameters of contemporary knowledge about cybercrimes. In so doing, he explores the manner in which and the extent to which they are contiguous with, and depart from, more established forms of criminal activity.

Wall argues that cyberspace, far from being an unregulated 'free-for-all', is actually the site of multi-level governance involving divergent actors with different regulatory purchase over the Internet environment. These include, first, Internet users and user groups engaged in forms of 'self-policing', some of which resonate with forms of terrestrial 'community self-regulation' involving active citizens. Internet service providers are a second-level regulatory body. Here, access providers simultaneously regulate those who use the Internet, creating a certain tension between the service they provide and external forces. Corporate security departments offer a third level form of governance, largely serving to protect the interests of large commercial, telecommunications and other related organisations. Fourthly, state-funded non-police agencies contribute to the governance map as do, finally, state-funded public police organisations. Interestingly, these different tiers of regulation, collectively, cut across traditional notions of 'public' and 'private' regulation and transcend national boundaries. Policing, here, is seen in its broadest sense as a variety of activities aimed at the promotion and maintenance of order and security. Some of these activities are more or less complementary, as differing definitions of order and security vie with each other and differing models of justice are deployed. The complex networks of regulation also raise questions about differing justice outcomes, principles of competency and forms of accountability, all of which Wall reviews. It is clear that traditional notions of state-centred policing do not apply well to cyberspace and that the future of regulating the Internet necessitates plural forms of multi-level governance.

Part 3 focuses upon the local governance of crime and insecurity. It begins with a chapter by Sebastian Roché (Chapter 8) that connects pan-European issues over safety with transformations to the governance of crime and security in France. He explores the way in which the French state's discourse on crime has been transformed in the last quarter of the twentieth century. Furthermore, in this new discourse the role of the police has changed. 'Insecurity' has emerged as a symbolic representation of a new politics. This has seen debates about crime disconnected from debates about class struggle and instead related to problems of disorder. It has also seen the emergence of a new lexicon used to present the issues. This has coalesced around 'insecurity', 'incivilities' and 'urban violence' and has become focused upon the *banlieues* – generally, large peripheral public housing estates built in the 1950s and 1960s – which have become the new terrain of political action. Moreover, the *banlieues* are localities in which France's recent immigrant populations are housed. And yet, debates about 'race' or 'ethnicity' are hidden from public discourse – they are 'silenced' in the name of the egalitarian ideals of French nationhood. As Roché suggests, there is clearly an ethnic dimension to insecurity in France, but there is no formal expression of this. Rather, broad 'social questions' have become territorialised around particular localities.

Roché highlights three principal sites of tension in the unfolding new governance. The first exists between central and local government. France's traditional highly centralised state apparatus has been the subject of significant decentralising reforms since the early 1980s. However, in the field of crime and insecurity these reforms have left a paradox in that some important local structures have been established, notably those advancing a logic of local interagency partnerships, whilst key agencies (the police and the judicial system) have remained the subject of national control. Hence, social issues (such as crime and insecurity), which transcend the competency of single agencies, have become the sites of internecine conflict between central government and local municipal authorities. Most notably, the police have become caught up in the tension between calls for local policing and central control. The second tension lies between public and private sector organisations. France, like other countries, has seen the significant growth of a private security industry, fanned by concerns over security and an apparently incapable state. The third tension Roché highlights exists between professionals and the public. Public participation is extolled in policy discourse, only to be rendered all but redundant in practice by countervailing forces of managerialisation and professionalisation.

The French experience acts as a fascinating lens through which to consider the changing governance of crime and insecurity. This is so, not only because in the field of crime prevention France developed an avowedly 'social approach', hailed by many British commentators, but also because its republican tradition highlights – in very profound ways – many of the transformations in governance that are referenced in recent developments (albeit in a less acute manner) in other countries around Europe (Duprez and Hebberecht 2002). The fact that France has a tradition of state-centred solutions to social problems means the contemporary recognition of the limitations of the capacity of the state to guarantee social order has extensive ramifications. In France, where the state through its laws is the 'purveyor of identity', the current ambivalence in political responses to contemporary limitations of state governance is particularly acute. Moreover, the French example serves as a contrast – albeit also with profound similarities – to British developments (Crawford 2001). These are the subject of the remaining chapters in this volume.

Clive Walker and Martina McGuinness (Chapter 9) connect pan-national issues of risk and insecurity with problems of governance over a particular place, which brings together global capital and transnational political violence. In this case, their focus is upon commercial risks and insecurity presented by terrorism and political violence as affecting the regulation and policing of the 'square mile' of the City of London. This atypical locale produces – or demands – atypical modes of regulation. The City of London is at particular risk of political violence and terrorism precisely because it is a place in which international capital and exchange are concentrated. As Walker and McGuinness document, it is also the subject of very tangible risks resulting in potentially extensive destruction, destabilisation and damage. Responding to insecurity in novel and far-reaching ways becomes a political imperative. The fear capital may relocate away from London to some other financial centre demands that security is paramount. Creating a 'safe environment', or at least one in which risks are mitigated, is fundamental in maintaining and attracting investors and traders. Here, security demands not only policing in a traditional sense or crime prevention through environmental design – by erecting barriers and blockades, enhancing surveillance and so on – but also entails a response through insurance – or in this case reinsurance – as a means of spreading risk.

Walker and McGuinness analyse the nature of the response to the bombings in the City of London in 1992 and 1993 (plus the London Docklands and Manchester bombings in 1996). Political violence – unlike other crimes – seeks or provokes a response. They connect an analysis of the response to debates about the 'risk society' (Beck 1992). The political nature of such acts – targeted at the political economy – and the political responses to them, they suggest, allow for an analysis that opens up the social matrix surrounding the environment in which they occur. They use the IRA bombings as a case study, explaining why commercial targets were selected at the particular moment in time and the nature of the strategies involved. The most direct response concerned the issue of insurance. Walker and McGuinness outline the complex legislative response in the form of the Reinsurance (Acts of Terrorism) Act 1993. They then go on to explore how this strategy connected with wider socio-political considerations and how it operated in practice.

The reinsurance legislation treats crime – political violence – as a risk to be calculated and managed. It reflects an instrumental rationality – which is much more concerned with pacifying markets than with moral condemnation or expressive punishment. The reinsurance legislation reflects what Garland (1996: 450) has called, 'the new criminologies of everyday life'. Crime – even as spectacular and destructive as political violence – is normalised alongside other 'harms' as part of our contemporary condition. Moreover, there is an actuarial and future-orientated logic to the legislation with similarities to other (less tangible) risks and insecurities. The reinsurance legislation also reflects a blurring of public and private spheres, notably in the 'publicness' of private affairs as the state is bound up in the reinsurance market. It constructs a complex web of governance enmeshing state and business interests. And at a time when the capacity of the state is under question, it reminds us of its enduring importance. Moreover, the response itself is a legislative one, the traditional instrument of state action. It also brings a highly politicised form of insecurity and, as such, a highly politicised response, which is particularly 'late modern' in its need to accommodate the demands of global capital within localised contexts. In the light of the attack on the World Trade Center and the Pentagon on 11 September 2001, the insights provided by Walker and McGuinness shed valuable light on the manner in which global risks affect local modes of regulation.

One of the themes which unites a number of chapters in this collection relates to the impact of technological change and the manner in which new technologies facilitate and foster safety or encourage, sustain and institutionalise a climate of insecurity. One of the most tangible and physical expressions of a politics of insecurity has been the rapid (almost exponential) expansion of technologies of surveillance – notably CCTV cameras – which have proliferated in public and private spaces. This proliferation has often occurred in the perception that these symbols of trust create 'safe havens of territoriality' and offer 'environments of security'. They are consummately 'the physical expressions of a social fabric that defends itself', in Newman's terms (1972: 3). As such, they assuage fears and anxieties as much as they directly prevent or assist in the detection of crime. To date, much of the analysis of CCTV cameras has been restricted to public or quasi-public spaces such as shopping areas and malls.

Tim Newburn, in Chapter 10, considers the introduction of CCTV cameras in a very different context, namely, a police custody suite. Newburn reflects upon criminological understandings of CCTV in the light of research into its use in a police station in Kilburn, London. As such, he poses some challenging questions about the objectives of technologies of surveillance; their location in hybrid spaces (such as a custody suite); the balance of privacy and protection afforded by CCTV; and the nature of any impact, notably with regard to the manner in which social relations within locations governed by CCTV may be affected. In so doing, Newburn sounds a caution as to the dangers of dystopianism, which is vividly present in many criminological accounts of the contemporary and future governance of insecurity, particularly the role of technology. In this case study, the supervisors (namely, the police) are themselves also the supervised: the subjects of surveillance. Newburn suggests the technology of CCTV – in this instance at least – offers certain possibilities of police governance, whereby the citizens watch the state. This potential affords a very different imagery to that of 'Big Brother' or the 'maximum security society' and allows us to begin to think more critically than hitherto of the possibilities as well as the potential dangers of technological change in an insecure world.

Leslie Moran (Chapter 11) explores the experiences and meanings of safety and insecurity among other (but altogether different) marginalised groups within traditional criminological research, namely, lesbians and gay men. He examines the connections between experiences and anxieties over violence among lesbians and gay men in the context of sexuality and space. In so doing, he draws upon focus group research data from lesbians and gay men living in two locations in the north of England. Of particular concern, for Moran, is the ambiguous place 'home' occupies within talk about insecurity and safety. Drawing upon feminist criminological research on fear of crime and victimisation, he suggests the 'myth of the safe home' that preoccupies much (police-inspired) safety advice for women also has a similar sway over advice proffered to lesbians and gay men where the threat of 'stranger violence' dominates. Moran suggests that whilst feminist research reminds us to proceed with caution to avoid perpetuating the 'myth of the safe home', he also uses the focus group data to suggest it would be wrong merely to invert the logic of such a proposition. Not only does 'home' occupy an ambivalent position in the understandings and conversations of lesbians and gay men with regard to safety and insecurity, but also 'home' is used as a referent and metaphor beyond the private space of domesticity. The 'home' and 'comfort' are meanings and practices that have significance in private spaces and in the public realm. Using the 'home' as a lens of analysis, Moran goes on to consider the problematic relationship between gender and space and draws upon the focus group data to offer critiques of current safety policy and practice. The aesthetics of comfort – notably environmental improvements often implemented in the name of enhancing feelings of security – which promote the removal of 'disorder' and 'dirt' and in their place seek to offer visibility, cleanliness and purity may be at odds with experiences and imaginings of 'home'. Such strategies draw upon 'home' merely as a place of exclusion and as such may end up institutionalising anxiety. The ambivalent experience of 'home' for lesbians and gay men defies any attempt to construct policies that seek to reduce the home to a place of safety or unsafety.

Finally, in Chapter 12, Sandra Walklate explores local understandings of community safety within the broader context of late modern society. She takes up the question posed by Bauman regarding the fragmentation of social life in late modern societies and asks: for whom is social life fragmenting? In so doing, she frames her analysis through the lens of the contemporary nature of relationships of trust. She offers a critique of the assumptions within community safety that stress the importance of community as a source of moral authority. She shows how kinds of trust that exist and operate in communities may actually not always be necessarily about creating 'regular honest behaviour' but may also be about creating 'regular dishonest behaviour'. She suggests it is the regularity or otherwise of the behaviour that sustains or threatens social trust relationships rather than its moral authority. Walklate provides, first, a review of the literature on trust and its relevance for criminology and, secondly, an analysis of a particular rural case study. She explores issues of trust in place-based community safety developments drawn from her own earlier research into urban communities. As such, she questions the extent to which issues relating to trust and community safety share similarities (and divergences) between very different settings: on the one hand, two inner-city deprived areas and, on the other hand, an affluent rural locality.

Consequently, Walklate considers the transferability of conceptualisations drawn from one place-based context to another and the implications. In so doing, she presents a case study of rural Cheshire in late 1999 and 2000. She charts the manner in which local people mobilised around the withdrawal of police patrols as an expression of their anxieties. The affective response of local people sits awkwardly alongside the seeming rationality of the policing response to crime-related issues. What emerge are the expressions of concerns of people in secure economic positions – a far cry from the urban 'losers' from recent economic restructuring. And yet, these affluent people also have common interests in maintaining a sense of security, but who have seen the traditional means of managing these taken from them. A patrolling police presence or rather the lack of it, in this context, means much more than the rational managing of declining resources or simply the nostalgic reimagining of the past through the eyes of the present. The case study offers a fascinating micro analysis of the salience of place, feelings of insecurity, expectations of policing and understandings of social change as well as its impact upon rural areas. It affords an insight into the concerns and anxieties of populations traditionally ignored by criminological research.

This book draws together a diversity of case studies and approaches to the common theme of insecurity in the contemporary age. It explores the origins and ideologies around modern fears and insecurities and examines the multi-level responses to crime risks and perceptions of unsafety. Despite its explicitly diverse and eclectic composition, numerous recurring themes reverberate throughout the collection as a whole. It represents an attempt to chart and analyse the shifting meaning and terrain upon which social life is increasingly governed through crime and insecurity. In so doing, the various chapters from their divergent vantage points and through their different intellectual lenses take stock of and reflect upon a phenomenon with significant implications for future governance.

References

Bauman, Z. (2000) *Liquid Modernity*. Cambridge: Polity Press.

Bauman, Z. (2001) *The Individualized Society*. Cambridge: Polity Press.

Beck, U. (1992) *The Risk Society*. London: Sage.

Beck, U. (1995) *Ecological Enlightenment*. Atlantic Highlands, NJ: Humanities Press.

Crawford, A. (1997) *The Local Governance of Crime*. Oxford: Clarendon Press.

Crawford, A. (1998) Community safety and the quest for security: holding back the dynamics of social exclusion. *Policy Studies*, 19(3/4): 237–53.

Crawford, A. (2001) The growth of crime prevention in France as contrasted with the English experience: some thoughts on the politics of insecurity. In G. Hughes, E. McLaughlin and J. Muncie (eds) *Crime Prevention and Community Safety: New Directions*. London: Sage.

Duprez, D. and Hebberecht, P. (eds) (2002) *The Politics of Crime Prevention and Security in the 1990s across Europe*. Brussels: VUB Press.

Garland, D. (1996) The limits of the sovereign state: strategies of crime control in contemporary society. *British Journal of Criminology*, 36 (4): 445–71.

Garland, D. (2001) *The Culture of Control*. Oxford: Oxford University Press.

Johnston, L. (2000) *Policing Britain: Risk, Security and Governance*. Harlow: Longman.

Manning, P. (2000) Policing new social spaces. In J.W.E. Sheptycki (ed.) *Issues in Transnational Policing*. London: Routledge.

Newman, O. (1972) *Defensible Space*. New York: Architectural Press.

Pierre, J. (ed.) (2000) *Debating Governance: Authority, Steering, and Democracy*. Oxford: Oxford University Press.

Pierre, J. and Peters, B.G. (2000) *Governance, Politics and the State*. Basingstoke: Macmillan.

Pierre, J. and Stoker, G. (2000) Towards multi-level governance. In P. Dunleavy, A. Gamble, I. Holliday and G. Peele (eds) *Developments in British Politics* (6th edn). London: Macmillan.

Rhodes, R.A.W. (1996) The new governance: governing without government. *Political Studies*, 44: 652–67.

Rhodes, R.A.W. (1997) *Understanding Governance: Policy Networks, Governance, Reflexivity and Accountability*. Buckingham: Open University Press.

Rhodes, R.A.W. (2000) The governance narrative. *Public Administration*, 78(2): 345–63.

Sparks, J.R. (1992) Reason and unreason in 'Left realism': some problems in the constitution of the fear of crime. In R. Matthews and J. Young (eds) *Issues in Realist Criminology*. London: Sage.

Spitzer, S. (1987) Security and control in capitalist societies: the fetishism of security and the secret thereof. In J. Lowman, R. Menzies and T. S. Palys (eds) *Transcarceration: Essays in the Sociology of Social Control*. Aldershot: Gower.

Young, J. (1999) *The Exclusive Society*. London: Sage.

Zedner, L. (2000) The pursuit of security. In T. Hope and R. Sparks (eds) *Crime, Risk and Insecurity*. London: Routledge.

Part I
Crime and insecurity

Chapter 1

The governance of crime and insecurity in an anxious age: the trans-European and the local

Adam Crawford

Introduction

Across European countries, nation-states appear to be confronting a major crisis under the dual pressures of globalisation and localisation. The march of global capital and finance, together with ever-closer European integration, has encouraged the international flow of business, trade and information. However, alongside this process of *delocalisation* – in which social systems are stretched across time and space – exists an apparently contradictory process of *relocalisation*. Here forms of control are increasingly inscribed into the fabric of local territorial and spatial interactions (Robert 2000). In the process, many traditional forms of place-based authority and social control have been torn up. Global flows of capital and culture have significantly affected and recast territorial communities.

This has resulted in what some commentators have referred to as the 'hollowing out of the state' (Rhodes 1994): the erosion of the nation-state's capability to exercise political control. The modern state – the self-proclaimed monopolistic guardian of social order and crime control – is being restructured and its powers rearticulated both from above and below. This 'hollowing out' of the state is expressed in, and stimulated by, governmental strategies of privatisation, diverse forms of 'state rule at a distance' and the emergence of public–private partnerships and 'policy networks' (Crawford 2001a). As a result, there appears to be an increasingly profound relationship between globalised conditions and local circumstances. This constitutes a fundamental hallmark of late modernity. And yet these tendencies are uneven: whilst capital and information flow freely, politics and labour remain decidedly local (Castells 1996).

The impact and implications of these trends have been differently experienced in divergent European countries. In France, for example, the 'shock of globalisation' has been particularly acute as the French state has been forced to come to terms with its own limitations under external pressures (Garapon 1995). This is particularly so given the shortcomings of traditional French legal culture in responding to the tasks of contemporary social life: notably the flexible and pragmatic demands of global markets and the local demands of the recognition of diverse social identities. Both of these appear to be at odds with the rigidity, idealism and universalising symbolism of French legal and political discourse (Wieviorka 1997).

Across Europe, contemporary social life is one in which increasing uncertainty, insecurity and diversity co-exist with concerns about safety. Traditional forms of acquaintance and trust (often borne of localised relations organised in terms of place) upon which security and safety have been founded are increasingly fragmenting through processes of 'detraditionalisation'. In its place we must increasingly place trust in disembedded and abstract systems as well as in the expertise of others. Structural changes in the labour market have been significant elements in 'ontological insecurity'. The uncertainty of modernity – in the sense that self-identity is no longer embedded in biographical continuity – produces the absence of a psychic protective cushion of security, as a consequence of which trust necessitates taking risks. As Giddens notes: 'The experience of security usually rests upon a balance of trust and acceptable risk' (1990:36). This risk-taking imperative of modern life etches 'ontological insecurity' into the fabric of modern social existence. Moreover, this imperative is 'individualised' in the sense that individuals must produce and reconstruct their biographies and life trajectories themselves (Giddens 1991: 70–88).

New sources of harm appear to present themselves as a result of the dangers and opportunities presented by new technologies and as populations become more mobile. Dangers and risks stretch across time and space, unbounded by nation-states, but potentially invading our environment, our living-rooms and our kitchens (as anxieties over BSE and its human variant CJD remind us), let alone jumping out at us as we walk home at night through the anonymous metropolis. The new prominence of risk connects individual autonomy with the influence and role of scientific innovation and technological change. Science is central to the identification, amelioration and creation of hazard and risk. It is *'one of the causes, the medium of definition and the source of solutions* to risks' (Beck 1992: 155, emphasis in original). Moreover, risks are not bounded by nation-states. Risks embody both opportunities and dangers; as such, they represent a rupture with tradition and nature. Hence, we are witnessing both a growing sensitisation to risk and the problematisation of risk itself. Experts and publics disagree as to risks. For Beck then, the 'risk society' is 'by tendency also a self-critical society' (1994: 11).

Consequently, concerns with 'safety' have become saturated with anxieties generated by other elements of contemporary existence, namely, insecurity and uncertainty. Responses to (in)security and (un)safety appear increasingly to inform decisions made by governments, organisations and ordinary people in their social interactions. Increasingly, towns and cities vie for new positions of influence and wealth in the reorganised national and international economy. The ability of cities to reposition themselves in a global economy depends upon their capacity to attract investors, both capital and people, which in part is determined by the attractiveness of a city as a 'safe place', particularly the inner-city business districts. At the level of the individual, insecurity and uncertainty can cause withdrawal into the 'safe havens of territoriality', producing a market in security that places increasing emphasis upon creating and offering 'environments of trust' where symbols of security and safety, as well as strategies of control, are inscribed into the architecture and surroundings.

On one level, these security concerns have been dispersed into new arenas – beyond the nation-state. At another level, the response of modern governments has been to identify new fields in which security can be reasserted 'at arm's length' from the nation-state. Europe and the local community have provided different but inter-related outlets for this rearticulation. The focus of this book is to consider some of the interconnections between these two fields in diverse settings. In this chapter, I outline some of the broad contours to the debates around, first, the local governance of crime and insecurity and, secondly, the governance of crime and insecurity at a European level. I then go on to consider the manner in which local governance issues are increasingly securing a European-wide presence and the involvement of the commercial security sector within European developments.

The localisation of crime and insecurity

The resulting importance of locality and the salience of 'place', within an increasingly globalising economy and culture, have often been ignored or underplayed by commentators in debates concerning globalisation. However, it is precisely the interplay between these two processes which means that global pressures are refracted through local meanings, identities and sensibilities. The importance of a 'sense of locality' – what Taylor *et al.* (1996: 13) call the 'local structure of feeling' – can produce resistance or adaptation to global transformations. The communal identities produced can often be defensive or particularistic reactions against 'the imposition of global disorder and uncontrollable, fast-paced change' (Castells 1997: 64). This defensiveness to the 'juggernaut' of globalisation can often give rise to a nostalgia: a retrieval and reimagining of tradition.

Moreover, globalisation does not have uniform or homogenising effects. Rather, it has encouraged segmentation, social differentiation and dislocation. Structural changes in the economy have seen the erosion of the importance of social class replaced by other indicators of difference. And yet a person's social position and where he or she lives remain fundamentally important with regard to that person's 'life chances'. Economic polarisation takes on a positively social and spatial form. This produces a distinct unevenness in local economic development both between, and within, cities in late modernity. At a cultural level, social diversity reproduced locally collides and fuses with a global culture. Globalisation, as Bauman suggests, 'divides as much as it unites; it divides as it unites' (1998: 2). The contemporary world, therefore, is more like a patchwork or mosaic of contrasting colours and fabrics than a uniform pattern.

The anxieties produced by the endemic insecurity and uncertainty of late modernity tend to be conflated and compressed into a distinct and overwhelming concern about personal safety. This localised concern finds its clearest expressions in the rise of discourses about 'community safety' across the Anglo-Saxon world (Crawford 1998a) and its closest equivalents across continental Europe: *la justice de proximité* and *les contrats locaux de sécurité* in France (Wyvekens 1996) and *justitie in de buurt* and the policy of *integraal veiligheidsbeleid* in The Netherlands (Boutellier 1997). This politics has given birth to an emerging institutional infrastructure and new forms of governance. This politics has been born out of crises of efficiency, effectiveness, economy and legitimacy in the institutional apparatus of criminal justice, which have fuelled, and simultaneously been fuelled by, an increasing politicisation of crime. In response, Europe has witnessed the growth of converging public policies concerned with (in)security (Hebberecht and Sacks 1997; Duprez and Hebberecht 2002), which combines a cluster of central themes:

1. A focus upon proactive *prevention* rather than reactive detection.

2. An emphasis upon *wider social problems* than merely crime, including broadly defined harms, people's fears, low-level quality of life issues, anti-social behaviour and disorder.

3. A focus upon modes of *informal social control* and local normative orders, as well as the manner in which they relate to, and connect with, formal systems of control.

4. Implementation through decentralised and *local* arrangements for the delivery of this politics, in that local problems are deemed to require local solutions.

5. Delivery through a *partnership* approach, drawing together a variety of organisations and stakeholders, in horizontal networks incorporating local municipal authorities, major public services, the voluntary and business sectors, as well as relevant community groups and associations.

6. All of which are aimed at producing holistic solutions that are 'problem orientated' rather than defined according to the means or organisations most readily available to solve them.

The resultant politics calls for a reconfiguration of the traditional policy process – which is both hierarchical and departmental – through the development of cross-cutting policies that combine the synergy of the various actors and partner organisations. It seeks to co-ordinate national and local policies and practices, as well as to synchronise private and public provision of security services.

'Community safety', in so far as it is concerned with 'quality of life' issues, is saturated with concerns about safety and 'ontological insecurity'. It evokes a 'solution' to crime, incivility and disorder, thus enabling the (local) state to reassert some form of sovereignty. Symbolically, it reaffirms control of a given territory, which is visible and tangible. Moreover, the increasing internationalisation of economic, political and cultural life and governance problems experienced by national governments has left the latter 'casting about for spheres of activity in which they can assert their sovereignty' (Zedner 2000: 201). The current governmental preoccupation with petty crime, disorder and anti-social behaviour reflects a source of 'anxiety' about which something can be done in an otherwise uncertain world. At the same time, concerns about safety connect with people's everyday experiences of contemporary social life over which individuals and groups seek some form of control. This preoccupation with local safety – particularly with low-level incivilities and subcriminal categories of 'disorder' – also reflects the limited capacity for state action.[1] It reflects a dramatic narrowing of the horizons of state 'sovereignty'. As Bauman suggests:

> In the world of global finances, state governments are allotted the role of little else than oversized police precincts; the quantity and quality of the policemen on the beat, sweeping the streets clean of beggars, pesterers and pilferers, and the tightness of the jail walls loom large among the factors of 'investors' confidence', and so among the items calculated when the decisions to invest or de-invest are made. To excel in the job of precinct policeman is the best (perhaps the only) thing state government may do to cajole nomadic capital into investing in its subjects' welfare; and so the shortest roads to the economic prosperity of the land, and so hopefully to the 'feel good' sentiments of the electors, lead through the public display of the policing skill and prowess of the state.'
>
> (1998: 20)

The recent globalising appeal of 'zero tolerance' policing mirrors this dominant concern with policing 'signs of disorder' and locality. The idea of 'zero tolerance' offers a strategy through which to reassert sovereignty, impose discipline and order and reclaim the streets from the deviant. 'Zero tolerance' policing evokes a nostalgic reassertion of moral authority through more aggressive and assertive strategies. As such, 'zero tolerance' serves to act as an emblem of a new form of authority. In so doing, it produces new 'folk devils' and 'deviant others' who, surprisingly, are not the contemporary mass murderers or rapists but are the victims of globalisation: the economically marginalised, socially excluded and alienated.

In addition, by claiming a link between incivilities and serious crime 'zero tolerance' allows for the collection of low-level information of use in risk-based techniques for analysing and targeting potential offenders and crime 'hot spots'. It feeds into future-orientated strategies. Moreover, as with 'community safety' generally, 'zero tolerance' raises the danger that crime and disorder increasingly come to dominate concerns about 'quality of life', urban renewal, inequalities and social policies more generally, such that social problems are increasingly redefined in terms of their crimogenic potential. This is a development that increasingly infects and affects diverse European cultures (van Swaaningen 1997; Wacquant 1999). This is evident in the manner in which 'community safety' has refigured certain social problems in terms of their crime and disorder implications and drawn resources into crime prevention and order maintenance in England and Wales.[2] It is also apparent in the manner in which *la prévention de la délinquance* has become fused and confused within *la politique de la ville* in France (Lazerges 1995; Wyvekens 1997).

The preoccupation with community safety and order maintenance reflects the limited capacity for state action. In Garland's (1996, 2001) account, punitive rhetoric and policy are as much a product of problems of state sovereignty and legitimation as they are a rational response to the problems of crime. As such, oscillation and ambivalence are products of late modern conditions which produce dilemmas for state governance. Bauman (1999: 16–18) has eloquently argued that the rise of concerns around disorder and safety can be located in what he calls 'the cauldron of *unsicherheit*'. This German term translates into three different English concepts: *insecurity*, *uncertainty* and *unsafety*. The late modern condition, he suggests, is one in which security is 'sacrificed day by day on the altar of ever-expanding freedom' (*ibid.*). Governments increasingly can do little to guarantee security or certainty and, in some cases, promote insecurity and uncertainty, through flexible and unstable labour patterns and the corrosion of long-term commitments (Sennett 1998). As a consequence, governments invest in one of the few arenas in which they may be able to affect change: in the production of symbols of 'orderly environments' to entice nomadic capital and a sentiment of 'safety' among domestic populations. The rise of community safety may tell us more about the weaknesses of the contemporary state than about genuine changes in public safety.

The Europeanisation of crime and insecurity

Crime control remains one of the fields of public policy least touched by European law. Law and order is one of the ultimate (residual) regalian aspects of the modern state. Criminal justice has jurisdictional boundaries. In a fluid and moving world criminal justice is rooted to territorial confines; to nations. As a consequence, individual nation-states have jealously guarded their control over criminal matters, as crime control and punishment have traditionally been integrally interwoven with the integrity of the nation-state. Despite the establishment of the EU and subsequent pressures for convergence, criminal law and procedure remain significantly varied across the member states. There persists significant friction between member states which serves to undermine international police and judicial co-operation in the EU. These 'bottlenecks' are diverse in origin but broadly fall into three categories: diverging legislation; different modes of trial; and the violation of sovereignty (Tak 2000: 343).

As a number of contributors to this volume note, much of the European-level activity around responses to crime and its prevention has been premised upon the assumption that there has been an internationalisation of certain types of crime which by their very nature demand European-level responses. The driving force here is that of globalisation. Globalisation has produced new opportunities in the form of greater movement of goods, capital and people and through new technologies and systems of information exchange. Terrorism, the trafficking of drugs, arms, goods and people, fraud, money-laundering, computer crime and football hooliganism are the usual examples given. These crimes, it is believed, breach territorial boundaries and extend beyond the capacity for regulation and control of the single nation-state. These are the crimes, often incorrectly, lumped together under the label 'transnational organised crime'.

Moreover, anxieties over 'transnational organised crime' have been sharpened by the removal of frontier controls within the EU, highlighting the opportunities for the free movement of illicit goods and illegal immigrants. Not only has this encouraged a 'fortress Europe' mentality through the erection of higher and tighter external borders around the perimeters and initial entry points into the EU, but it appears also to have fostered an increased sensitivity and anxiety over what we might refer to as 'the dark side of free movement', to the point that – as Bauman (this volume) argues – 'mobility' itself has become problematised.

In this regard, crime, safety and insecurity have become central themes in the European debate on immigration, migration and asylum seekers, as well as with regard to immigrant and ethnic minority groups within most European countries, a trend that is set to continue (Tonry 1998: 60; Albrecht this volume). Whilst generally crime amongst these groups reflects their social and economic status within given societies, this is amplified by the identification of significant involvement of specific groups with particularly visible (and/or targeted by policing authorities) forms of criminal activity (Melossi 2000). Moreover, the tendency of public debate to homogenise diverse migrant and immigrant populations into an aggregate alien and 'ideal enemy' ignores differences within and between immigrant groups. Nevertheless, debates about immigration and migration are increasingly filtered through a crime and insecurity lens (see Goodey this volume). Dominant assumptions embody powerful beliefs that connect criminality and unsafety with the alien 'other'. In this, economic and social marginality, ethnic segmentation, discrimination, exploitation and criminal victimisation become refracted and transformed into 'danger' and 'threat to public safety'.

And yet the scale, scope and nature of any Europeanisation of crime are debatable. The extent to which there has been either a significant, empirically measurable, growth in these activities over recent years or whether they constitute a significant departure from other forms of criminality over which nation-states' capacity for regulation is severely limited remains contentious. First, there is the problem of comparison across Europe. Different countries operate with divergent definitions of criminal activities, a problem exacerbated by linguistic differences. Dutch drug laws and Belgian firearms legislation are obvious examples, but this lack of equivalence also extends to more mundane forms of criminality. Despite attempts to construct ideas of a common definition of 'Eurocrimes' considerable difference remains. Secondly, there is little reliable official information about the extent of transnational crime. Systems for collecting information are unreliable and obtained on the basis of different criteria in different countries. Thirdly, organised European crime is by no means a new phenomenon (Sheptycki 1998). For some commentators, the novelty and scope of the European response exceeds and is far more extensive than, the novelty or scope of the actual threat. Furthermore, the notion of 'European crime' strictly speaking only has relevance with regard to crimes committed against European institutions, most notably fraud (Anderson *et al.* 1995: 15), but also future concerns over Euro-counterfeiting with the introduction of the European single currency in 2002.

However, it would be wrong to deny that anything has changed. The compression of time and space in late modernity has increased the opportunities for illegal trade. The liberalisation reforms introduced by recent governments (notably the UK) have facilitated entrepreneurs to exploit new illicit and 'clandestine markets' (Sheptycki 1998). Moreover, this liberalisation has been encouraged by transnational financial regulators, such as the World Bank, the World Trade Organisation and the Organisation for Economic Co-operation and Development as well as by the EU as a criterion for entry for any aspiring member states. This has been particularly evident in the former Communist bloc countries in the light of the breakup of the USSR and former eastern European satellites.

European-level responses and developments

Numerous commentators in this volume (notably Lodge and Rees and Webber) outline the growing European infrastructure around policing and the governance of insecurity. A considerable momentum has developed from Trevi through Schengen and the Amsterdam Treaty[3] to the establishment in 1998 of Europol[4] and beyond to Eurojust, the European Police Academy and the greater convergence of various registration and surveillance systems (Mathiesen 2000: 186). The introduction by the Treaty of Amsterdam of an 'area of freedom, security and justice' was proclaimed at the 1999 Tampere European Council as the next great project of the EU. This programme, whilst couched in general terms in the Treaty of Amsterdam, possibly has far-reaching implications in its effects on sovereign jurisdictions. Unlike the single market and the single currency, the 'area of freedom, security and justice' developments potentially transcend all three pillars of the European project in ways that may be potentially subversive to the established institutional order of Europe and raise particular sensitivities about sovereignty.

Nevertheless, the emergent new order is a complex (sometimes contradictory) mix of institution-building and intergovernmental structures that combines (and confuses) *inter-* and *intra*-national anxieties over policing and the governance of insecurity. It conflates transnational concerns *between states* with those *by states* and *within states'* boundaries and populations. Taken together, the resultant governance architecture is an ensemble of developments that are unparalleled, yet uneven: a paradox Neil Walker describes as 'delicately poised between classic intergovernmentalism and supranational polity building' (2000: 91). He identifies three discourses in which debates for and against recent developments have been framed, thus influencing the resultant shape of developments to date (*ibid.*: 92–5).

The first discourse is one of *internal security* – based upon the identification of a range of common interests and threats as well as 'security-orientated' responses to them. The realisation of a 'common space of freedom, security and justice' has often taken a pragmatic form, which has seen the adaptability of institutions to a space and territory that is not national. Most usually, this has developed through intergovernmental co-operation. And yet the emergence of a European space constructed through security alludes to the idea of the EU as a self-contained 'security community' with its dual inclusionary and exclusionary logics. On the one hand, notions of a 'European identity', a 'European way of life' and 'European citizenship' appeal to the common interests to which the European security community aspires. As Ian

Loader notes with regard to policing:

> There now exists, nonetheless, a powerful institutional motor driving the formation of both stronger ties between Europe's police forces, and a transnational police elite oriented to forging common 'solutions' to common 'security' problems. This elite has, in turn, come to form part of an opaque, thinly accountable policy network increasingly organized around an ideology of *European* security.
>
> (2002:133, emphasis is original)

On the other hand, this commonality is premised upon, and defined in terms of, an external 'other' – poor, dangerous and unsafe – against which community and commonality are forged. Security may be a way in which people and institutions can attempt to situate and interpret themselves and the world around them as stable and manageable despite, or maybe because of, the realities of uncertainty and insecurity.

The EU with its initial central emphasis upon 'freedom' has, latterly, concentrated upon 'securitisation'. The inevitable trade-off now sits at the heart of the European agenda. If we ask what it is to be a member or a citizen of the EU, we may discover as many answers as there are languages. Security, the internal fashioning of order, offers a vehicle through which to construct an image of the European ideal in relation to the common threats it is perceived we confront. What we share is fashioned increasingly by our fears and concerns. We share our insecurities. The production of common security threats against which we can define ourselves collectively has become a major element of the construction of the ideology and institutions of European security. Here, European community building parallels other forms of community formation. Threats are often viewed as presented primarily by 'outsiders' against whom the 'community' is perceived to need to defend itself. As I have suggested elsewhere with regard to local communities,

> this vision tends to assume an 'us versus them' attitude, which feeds into, and is reinforced by, the existence of an 'ideology of unity'. Here, crime and criminals are external 'others' and 'community' becomes something under attack from the outside... This insider/ outsider dichotomy taps deep-seated fears about social identity and otherness, particularly given the tendency of crime to bifurcate the 'rough' from the 'respectable'. Given the anxieties that crime evokes it can feed fears. The external threat, whether actual or imagined, can become both the reason for, and the means of sustaining,

'community'. Its collective past and future can be defined by reference to a perceived external threat. (Crawford 1998b: 245)

As such, there are clear resonances between 'community' formation at the European level and local community development particularly with regard to the role insecurity plays in the construction of communal identity through processes of inclusion and exclusion that constitute boundaries of 'insider' and 'outsider'.

The second discourse Walker highlights (2000: 93) is that of *functional spillover*, which has been at the heart of much EU institution building and expansion. Here, the logic is that developments in one field or one sector require adjustments in related or adjacent policy arenas. Hence, efficient and effective programmes and developments across Europe – originally related to the common market – necessitate modifications and corrections in external but connected domains, primarily to ensure some form of equivalence across nations under the auspices of the construction of a 'level playing-field'. This functionalist argument is particularly powerful given its technocratic and managerialist appeal: namely, that interventions in spillover arenas are required in the name of administrative efficiency rather than political desirability. As Weiler (1999) suggests, the elites driving European integration have sought to stress the managerialist concerns of rational management and technocratic expertise in the quest for regulatory solutions.

Aside from the attraction and expediency of this discourse, it has especial validity with regard to matters of insecurity. Security, crime control and policing have a residual, yet crucial, role to play in such arguments. Not only do policing and crime control connect with a wide range of other policy arenas (albeit sometimes indirectly) but also they act as a domain of last resort that sucks in the problematic and difficult issues deflected or displaced from other policy arenas. Rather like the flotsam and froth from overflowing drainage systems crime control serves the purpose of a sewer, which draws down the spillovers from other policy fields. It is a place of last resort: an authoritative solution, one which can exert a pull over and dominate distant, but loosely connected, arenas through its residual and reductionist quality. The increasing governmental appeal of joined-up government, policy networks and partnerships only serves to amplify this sway. Hence, policy debates initially conceived at some distance from questions of security – such as migration, asylum and technological change (like the Internet) – can become drawn into and enmeshed in concerns over insecurity, disorder and crime.

The third discourse mentioned by Walker (2000) is that of *European integration*, which is concerned with the explicit elaboration of a European-level polity as a supranational regulatory order, rivalling the nation-states of which it is composed. For those articulating such a discourse, on the horizon there are proposals for the creation of a European public prosecutor, the definition of common offences such as terrorism (given greater emphasis recently), the recognition of 'Euro-crimes' and the development of European substantive criminal law and criminal procedure. And yet there are also significant objections to such a perspective – most acutely articulated in fields as sensitive as crime control and policing, where critiques of European-level developments are seen as undermining state sovereignty. As Walker notes:

> this discourse does not operate in a manner generally favourable to the expansion of an EU policing capacity ... inasmuch as policing is seen as one of the crucial building blocks of statehood, the continuing emphasis upon state sovereignty as the bottom line of political commitment within the international order has acted as a brake upon the development of a European police capacity. (*ibid*: 94)

Some commentators suggest that this has become an unspoken discourse in the fields of policing, justice and home affairs, where 'we are constructing a federal judicial capacity without speaking its name' (Domenach 2001). The implementation of the Tampere programme through greater integration – harmonisation and mutual recognition – raises both technical and political difficulties and gives rise to considerable tensions and strains. This is not only due to the diversity of nations making up the EU, especially with enlargement pending, but also because managing interstate relations often requires high levels of 'trust, flexibility, co-ordination and efficiency', all of which are not particularly well developed in the fields of policing and criminal justice (Anderson 2001).

To date, there has been greater progress in the realm of police co-operation than judicial co-operation. In part, this is due to the more territorially bounded nature of criminal justice as well as a longer tradition of policing networking in Europe (Bigo 1996). Nevertheless, the policing and security developments at a European level are limited in terms of their operational functions. By and large these developments are predominantly concerned with what Ericson (1994) refers to as 'knowledge work'. Crime control and policing, at this level, are largely 'communications policing' in which organisations and individuals concerned constitute 'information brokers': collating, analysing and disseminating information in liaison with other regional, national and supranational contact points (see Bigo 2000). Sharing knowledge, experience and good practice is a recurring theme (for example the Working Group of Chiefs of Police and the High Level Group on Immigration and Asylum), whilst legal, jurisdictional and police organisational factors at the national level (and below in some countries) create certain obstacles to operational synchronisation. Nevertheless, the advent of Europol does raise certain new possibilities with regard to operational matters and, as Rees and Webber suggest (this volume), we are likely to see a greater fusing of internal and external security organisations, despite domestic/national obstacles. Given the historic linkage of policing with the political project of state-craft it also raises questions about the future shape of European integration.

The symbolic association between crime control and sovereignty has meant not only that developments in this field have lagged behind others, but also that they have sharpened debates over any loss of sovereignty and concerns about mechanisms of accountability and associated democratic deficit (McLaughlin 1992). Any notion of sovereignty as an unrivalled, indivisible or exclusive form of public power is now largely redundant (although it is questionable whether it ever had empirical salience rather than rhetorical force). Walker (2000: 85) notes that it is important to see European-level developments as part of a much wider trend 'towards the relocation of political authority in multiple levels of governance and in non-state sites, in which altered configuration policing and its regulation is no longer securely domiciled within the nation-state'. Interestingly, there are important similarities in developments at a European level with those at the level of nation-states.

As the chapters in this volume testify, around the inter-related issues of insecurity, order maintenance and social identity considerable new challenges have presented themselves from above and beyond, as well as below and within, the territories of the nation-state. The development of supranational – political, legal and economic – institutions has questioned state sovereignty within its own borders (Sheptycki 1995). The very meaning of personal and public security has become problematised as have the modes of governing and responding to conditions of insecurity.

From 'transnational organised crime' to 'urban safety'

As Rees and Webber, Lodge, Goodey and Albrecht all note in their contributions, the principal focus of pan-European level developments and common concern, of recent years, has been with regard to cross-border organised crime or 'transnational organised crime'. This has been the – often ill-defined – demon against which a variety of national and international initiatives have been launched and institutions constructed. More recently, however, the EU has begun to broaden its interest and concern beyond 'transnational' or 'organised' forms of criminality to localised and less serious – more 'ordinary' and 'petty' – forms of crime, and even beyond this to 'anti-social conduct', 'fear of crime' and 'insecurity'. The 'common security problems' which increasingly define the securitisation of Europe are to be found emerging also in relation to the transnationalisation of highly localised forms of crime and disorder. Thus we have seen develop over recent years what we might refer to as an emerging European approach to urban safety premised upon a specific ideology of insecurity.

In part, this can be accounted for through the growth of greater trans-European contacts and networks born of co-operation in the broad arenas of policing and urban regeneration. Police co-operation has encouraged the cross-fertilisation of ideas, strategies and developments in other forms of policing (Sheptycki 2000). In addition, security has become an important commodity within the competition of cities in a global economy. Logan and Molotch (1987) identified the importance of 'local growth coalitions' in repositioning cities within a competition for financial inward investment. As they suggest, this is dependent upon capacities of certain urban areas to perform specific roles in respect of the global, and in our case the European, market. This reorganising of urban fortunes can take different forms. But a central element of this reimagining has been the capacity to present a city as a 'safe place'. As such, local growth coalitions have increasingly focused upon the policing of urban safety, order maintenance and the presentation of cities as secure havens for capital investment. Competition, as well as co-operation, within Europe in this field has stimulated interest in strategies used in different cities to police urban security.

Since 1987 the European Forum on Urban Safety has been at the forefront of promoting exchange of information and practice particularly among local and municipal authorities. Driven by a number of prominent cities across Europe, the forum has sought to develop and elaborate an understanding of 'urban safety' that emphasises city-level coalitions of diverse agencies drawn mainly from the public sector, but latterly also including the private sector, with the aim of improving the quality of life in, and image of, European cities through the 'governance of safety'. The forum has argued there are strong links between the promotion of an inclusive approach to community-based prevention and safety and the preservation of democracy itself (European Forum for Urban Safety 2000). The driving force behind the forum has been through the involvement of local elected representatives which has also ensured that debates within it have been highly politicised. Moreover, it has remained committed to a largely 'French model' of 'social crime prevention', in part influenced by the fact that its first president was Gilbert Bonnemaison, the principal author of the landmark report on crime prevention, *Face à la délinquance, prévention, répression, solidarité* (1982) (see Crawford 2001b), which had a major impact upon subsequent French policies. The work and deliberations of the forum have had significant impact upon the EU. In 1998 the Council of Europe granted consultative status to the forum as an international non-governmental organisation.

The Tampere European Council of 15 and 16 October 1999 concluded there was a need to develop crime prevention measures, to exchange best practices and to strengthen the network of competent national authorities for crime prevention as well as co-operation between national organisations specialising in this field. It identified the chief priority as being urban crime, particularly juvenile and drug-related crime.

In May 2001 the Council of Europe agreed to set up a European Crime Prevention Network, with a secretariat to be located in the Directorate General of Justice and Home Affairs of the commission. Its primary aims are to contribute to the development of crime prevention at the level of the EU and to support crime prevention activities at local and national levels. This it will do by facilitating co-operation, contacts and exchanges of information and experience; providing expertise to the council and to the commission; as well as collecting and analysing information on existing crime prevention activities. In addition to its work with member states the network will develop co-operation with applicant countries, 'third countries' and international organisations.

One of the more interesting potential implications of the adoption and development of local crime prevention issues at a European level, as proposed by the commission, is the 'evaluation of existing or planned legislative instruments against the yardstick of crime proofing' (European Commission 2000: para. 4.2). This evaluation or 'crime impact statement' would be made when any new legislation or decision is drafted, both in the EU and in the member states:

> The Commission will be at pains to evaluate the possible impact of its legislative proposals in terms of opportunities for crime, particularly in sensitive areas .... There should also be a similar

evaluation when the Member States take initiatives for the preparation of national legislation, including subordinate legislation .... Existing legislation should also be evaluated, both community instruments and international instruments to which the Community accedes (*ibid.*).

This would allow European and national authorities to anticipate the potential crime consequences of their policies and decisions. As such, it could give crime prevention a dynamic new focus across a wide range of activities, services and policy arenas. It may place crime considerations on a new centre stage at the heart of policy formation and decision-making. As such, it offers the opportunity to move beyond a few fragmented initiatives to ensure that a preventive culture takes a firmer hold within mainstream policies. Moreover, it would resonate with (in a diluted form) the statutory duty imposed on local authorities in England and Wales (under s. 17 of the Crime and Disorder Act 1998) to consider the crime and disorder implications of their various functions and the need to do all they reasonably can to prevent crime and disorder in their area. Furthermore, it would impose upon domestic governments a process tantamount to that proposed – but never enacted – by the Morgan Committee in its report on *Safer Communities* in the UK (Morgan 1991: 35). However, this increased centrality accorded to crime and insecurity at the heart of policy-making could also result in priority being given to crime and disorder consequences of given policies and activities where there is conflict with other areas of social or public policy. It may accord to crime and insecurity an over-riding role in public policy.

In its decision, the council defined 'crime prevention' as covering 'all measures that are intended to reduce or otherwise contribute to reducing crime and citizens' feelings of insecurity, both quantitatively and qualitatively, either through directly deterring criminal activities or through policies and interventions designed to reduce the potential for crime and the causes of crime' (European Council 2001: Article 1.3).

The EU recognises that, by definition, prevention relates to offences that have not yet been committed and appeals to heightened vigilance, all of which could entail security measures that might impose excessive constraints on citizens (European Commission 2000: para. 3.2). As a consequence, prevention needs to be balanced against – and close attention and respect accorded to – the fundamental rights and freedoms of individuals.

The European Commission, in its communication to the council proposing the establishment of the network, went further in defining 'general crime' as distinct from 'organised crime'. The former, it suggested, covers four separate realities (*ibid.*: para. 2.2.1):

- crime in the strict sense, i.e. offences defined as such in national criminal laws;

- less serious offences that are actually more frequent;

- violence in various contexts; and

- anti-social conduct which, without necessarily being a criminal offence, can by its cumulative effect generate a climate of tension and insecurity.

This reflects two logics. The first is the perceived interconnectedness of transnational developments and highly localised activities: the manner in which globalised conditions infuse local circumstances and simultaneously the locality becomes the primary lens through which sense is made of global trends. The classic illustration of this is the question of illicit drug use, whereby the movement of drugs across borders feeds into local networks with implications for crime and its control.

The second logic is that of 'defining deviance up' (Krauthammer 1993), whereby crime prevention and community safety policies, by focusing energies and attention upon incivilities, anti-social behaviour, disorder, quasi or subcriminal activities and early intervention with young people 'at risk' of offending, previously 'normal' behaviour becomes considered 'deviant'. This appears to mirror, but is simultaneously conjoined to, a contrasting process of 'defining deviancy down' (Moynihan 1993), whereby when there are extremely high crime rates, societies relax their notions of deviance and allow previously deviant behaviour to become 'acceptable' or even 'normal', thus limiting the level of demand placed upon criminal justice systems.

These European-level developments reflect a certain degree of convergence of national experiences – to the extent we may be able to speak of a 'European model' of crime prevention. And yet despite the many similarities at the level of practice brought by the homogenising and converging influences of the EU, the debates about insecurity versus safety, solidarity versus exclusion take rather dissimilar forms in different countries and amongst divergent groups within populations. As Roché (this volume) demonstrates, the experiences of both France and England suggest points of convergence and departure (see Crawford 2001b). They highlight the interconnectedness of cultural difference and strategies of crime control and prevention. Moreover, they remind us that we should neither over-exaggerate the differences between cultures, nor their separateness from pan-European trends.

Private security and commercial policing

Most EU countries have seen a significant expansion of the private security industry and commercial policing over the last decade or so (Jones and Newburn 1998; Ocqueteau 1998). In this, Britain leads the way in terms of private security personnel per inhabitant, closely followed by Germany (de Waard 1999: 153). Estimations as to the size of the private security industry are inevitably subject to considerable limitations, notably due to the lack of official data. Some estimations in Britain suggest the number of personnel in the private security industry has surpassed the number of public police officers (Johnston 2000: 126). At a European level there are considerable variations between countries. However, de Waard (1999: 168) suggests that by early 1997 almost 600,000 employees worked in the industry in the 15 EU countries. This equates to an average of 160 per 100,000 inhabitants. Compared with an EU average of 375 per 100,000 inhabitants for the police, this suggests a ratio of less than half the number of security officers to police officers. Whilst this figure is relatively small compared to North America it is clearly growing and, as an aggregate figure, ignores considerable variations.

Outside the EU in some central and eastern European countries, there is evidence security is increasingly becoming more a private or commercial matter and less a governmental responsibility. Legislative provisions for regulation of the private security industry in these countries are particularly weak as they are in a number of EU countries. Where controls do exist there are considerable divergences as to scope and depth of regulatory systems. Some of the key commercial firms providing private security are themselves transnational, extending within and beyond Europe.

The pluralisation of security has incorporated the private sector into a much broader definition of policing. They have become part of a wider order that includes diverse organisations and crime prevention systems. Local community safety partnerships have encouraged the involvement of private and voluntary sector interests. This is apparent in France (see Roché this volume) and the UK. The community safety partnerships spawned by the Crime and Disorder Act 1998 encourage and entrench a pluralisation of service delivery and service providers at a local level. The logic of the Act, and accompanying guidance (Home Office 1998), is to encourage a pluralisation of local service providers and networks. It does so, not only by transcending the traditional workings of particular local agencies, but also by opening up new policy arenas, facilitating networks across and between the public, voluntary and private sectors. In addition, the emphasis upon locally grounded, problem-solving methodologies has persuaded new local players to enter the field. The unintended but logical consequence of this, however, is to exacerbate co-ordination and undermine the effectiveness of steering mechanisms.

The growth of commercial security has also had implications for the nature and direction of policing and prevention policy more broadly. The increasingly significant position of the commercial sector – particularly its control over large spaces of 'mass private property' – along with greater connections between public and private police through new networks and partnerships has had implications for the nature and experience of 'policing itself'. Ideas and developments from within the private sector have increasingly influenced public policing both directly and indirectly. As Shearing and Stenning (1987) have noted, the strategies of private security are more instrumental than moral: they offer a more proactive rather than reactive approach to problem-solving. They tend to be concerned with loss prevention and risk reduction rather than with law enforcement or the detection and conviction of criminals. As a consequence, we have seen a cross-fertilisation of such ideas within the public provision of policing, resulting in a wider shift towards instrumental, future-orientated and risk-based thinking that transcends and informs the public provision of policing as well (Johnston 2000). As such, the growing involvement of the private security industry has dovetailed with and advanced crime prevention policy.

As well as challenges to the public interest and loss of democratic control, private 'zones of governance' also offer potentially positive social opportunities for crime control in semi-public spaces. First, as mentioned above, they tend to emphasise the instrumental rather than the moral elements of control and policing (Shearing 1992). Secondly, they tend to place less emphasis on detection and punishment and more on the prevention of future offences. Symbolic and ritualistic punishments are not a moral imperative. However, ensuring that the risk of an offence recurring is reduced is an instrumental and financial imperative. As such, they are inclined to invest in a future orientation. Thirdly, they tend to inscribe incentives for conformity and orderly conduct – a 'rewards infrastructure' (Kempa et al. 1999: 206). Finally, they tend to operate consensual forms of control rather than coercive ones, as traditionally associated with state regulation. With regard to the role of the market and the increased role of commercial interests, the challenge is to ensure that marketisation of security accords with, or at least does not undermine, the 'public good'. Commercial interests have injected a dynamism into policing and crime control that both offers opportunities and dangers in the late modern age. The privatisation of security offers real choices with which to confront 'ontological insecurity', albeit these are by no means uniformly distributed. The danger is that security differentials may become defining characteristics of inequality as security becomes an exclusive 'club good' (Hope 2000).

Conclusion

The new governance of safety across Europe involves not only the interconnections between different levels above and below the nation-state – some of which refigure traditional top-down hierarchies – in tiers of multiple governance, but also sees a fusing of public and private interests as non-state actors (including the commercial sectors) are drawn into new networks of control. The territory of the policing of crime and insecurity is simultaneously public and private as well as local, national and transnational. Consequently, we need to move beyond the notion of a unity of law and crime control tied to the nation-state towards an understanding of a plurality of legal orders and modes of regulation: a legal pluralism that connects with, and taps into, other regulatory systems and reflects the increasing polycentric nature of European social life.

The involvement of the private sector as well as other non-state actors in the fields of crime control, prevention and policing also returns us to questions regarding the lack of democratic oversight and accountability of these forms of governance to the public. We need to ask: does transnational (European-wide) crime prevention and the policing of insecurity represent the supranationalisation of governance or transnational regulatory regime with its own techniques and styles of governance? Does it represent the demise of the nation-state? Or does it signify certain supranational tendencies that duplicate or complement the activities of the state, leaving them with a significant, albeit it rearticulated, role in governance? Does transnational policing indicate the decline in the relevance of the nation-state in matters of everyday governance? Or, rather, does it signal the reinvention and rearticulation of its role in more nuanced networks of regulatory processes? If the state is to remain a prominent actor, how might the state – local or national – retain a position as 'power container' without slipping back into pretensions of monopolistic authority? How might the state adapt to a new-found role and status as a 'partner' in the promotion of security and simultaneously steer partnerships and networks in the 'public interest'? Moreover, how might questions of authorisation and legitimation of these modes of governance be addressed in ways that reinvigorate and strengthen democratic controls?

The developments outlined here and in Part 2 of this book show that the national character of criminal justice has become more fragile. There has been a Europeanisation of security and crime concerns at a number of different levels. Moreover, this has occurred not merely with regard to pan-European crimes but also highly localised concerns and anxieties that have seen the appearance of common European responses. These responses have emerged through loose intergovernmental co-operation, the development of common institutional frameworks and a degree of supranationalism, all of which are likely to continue. The complex resulting infrastructure and new modes of governance – with their own tensions and ambiguities – echo and have been constructed through dominant concerns over crime and insecurity. More fundamentally, this suggests not only an institutional convergence but also an ideological one.

Notes

1. The Crime and Disorder Act 1998 in England and Wales strikingly reflects this shift through its focus upon 'disorder', broadly defined. This is exemplified by the controversial 'anti-social behaviour order' which fuses and confuses civil with criminal remedies as well as evening 'curfews' for children under the age of 10.
2. This is particularly apparent in the increasing priority accorded to crime and disorder in Single Regeneration Budget outcomes (Audit Commission 1999: 18) and the use of matched funding by central government in initiatives, such as neighbourhood wardens, which have consequently drawn local authority resources away from other priorities. More broadly, the implementation of s. 17 of the Crime and Disorder Act 1998 has a similar logic.
3. The treaty brought into being Pillar III on justice and home affairs – the intergovernmental pillar now dedicated to the realisation of an EU of 'freedom, security and justice' – but also acknowledged the right of the UK and Ireland to retain border checks.
4. Europol became operational on 1 July 1999.

References

Anderson, M. (2001) The stakes and prospects in EU police and judicial co-operation in criminal matters. Paper presented to the conference 'L'Action publique en matiére de sécurite intérieure: prévention et répression', Association Française de Science Politique, Paris, 18–19 October.

Anderson, M., den Boer, M., Cullen, P., Gilmore, W.C., Raab, C.D. and Walker, N. (1995) *Policing the European Union: Theory, Law and Practice.* Oxford: Clarendon Press.

Audit Commission (1999) *Safety in Numbers: Promoting Community Safety.* London: Audit Commission.

Bauman, Z. (1998) *Globalisation: The Human Consequences.* Cambridge: Polity Press.

Bauman, Z. (1999) *In Search of Politics.* Cambridge: Polity Press.

Beck, U. (1992) *The Risk Society.* London: Sage.

Beck, U. (1994) The reinvention of politics: towards a theory of reflexive modernization. In U. Beck. A. Giddens and S. Lash (eds) *Reflexive Modernization.* Cambridge: Polity Press.

Bigo, D. (1996) *Polices en réseaux, l'experience européenne.* Paris: Presses des Sciences Politiques.

Bigo, D. (2000) Liaison Officers in Europe. In J.W.E. Sheptycki (ed.) *Issues in Transnational Policing.* London: Routledge.

Boutellier, H. (1997) Right to the community. *European Journal on Criminal Policy and Research,* 5(4): 43–52.

Castells, M. (1996) *The Rise of the Network Society.* Oxford: Blackwell.

Castells, M. (1997) *The Power of Identity.* Oxford: Blackwell.

Crawford, A. (1997) *The Local Governance of Crime: Appeals to Community and Partnerships.* Oxford: Clarendon Press.

Crawford, A. (1998a) *Crime Prevention and Community Safety: Politics, Policies and Practices.* Harlow: Longman.

Crawford, A. (1998b) Community safety and the quest for security: holding back the dynamics of social exclusion. *Policy Studies,* 19(3/4): 237–53.

Crawford, A. (2001a) Vers une reconfiguration des pouvoirs? Le niveau local et les perspectives de la gouvernance. *Déviance et Société,* 25(1): 3–32.

Crawford, A. (2001b) The growth of crime prevention in France as contrasted with the English experience: some thoughts on the politics of insecurity. In G. Hughes, E. McLaughlin and J. Muncie (eds) *Crime Prevention and Community Safety: New Directions.* London: Sage.

de Waard, J. (1999) The private security industry in international perspective. *European Journal on Criminal Policy and Research,* 7(2): 143–74.

Domenach, J. (2001) La construction judiciaire de l'Union européenne sans législateur. Paper presented to the conference 'L'Action publique en matiére de sécurite intérieure: prévention et répression', Association Française de Science Politique, Paris, 18–19 October.

Duprez, D. and Hebberecht, P. (eds) (2002) *The Politics of Crime Prevention and Security in the 1990s across Europe.* Brussels: VUB Press.

Ericson, R.V. (1994) The division of expert knowledge in policing and security. *British Journal of Sociology,* 45(2): 149–75.

European Commission (2000) *The Prevention of Crime in the European Union: Reflection* on *Common Guidelines and Proposals for Community Financial Support*. Communication from the Commission to the Council and the European Parliament. Brussels: Commission of the European Communities.

European Council (2001) *Council Decision Setting up a European Crime Prevention Network*. Brussels: Council of the European Union.

European Forum for Urban Safety (2000) *Security and Democracy: A Decade*. Paris: European Forum for Urban Safety.

Garapon, A. (1995) French legal culture and the shock of globalization. *Social and Legal Studies*, 4(4): 493–506.

Garland, D. (1996) The limits of the sovereign state: strategies of crime control in contemporary society. *British Journal of Criminology*, 36(4): 445–71.

Garland, D. (2001) *The Culture of Control*. Oxford: Oxford University Press.

Giddens, A. (1990) *The Consequences of Modernity*. Cambridge: Polity Press.

Giddens, A. (1991) *Modernity and Self-Identity*. Cambridge: Polity Press.

Hebberecht, P. and Sacks, F. (eds) (1997) *La prévention de la délinquance en Europe: nouvelles stratégies*. Paris: l'Harmattan.

Home Office (1998) *Guidance on Statutory Crime and Disorder Partnerships*. London: Home Office.

Hope, T. (2000) Inequality and the clubbing of private security. In T. Hope and R. Sparks (eds) *Crime, Risk and Insecurity*. London: Routledge.

Johnston, L. (2000) *Policing Britain: Risk, Security and Governance*. Harlow: Longman.

Jones, T. and Newburn, T. (1998) *Private Security and Public Policing*. Oxford: Clarendon Press.

Kempa, M., Carrier, R., Wood, J. and Shearing, C. (1999) Reflections on the evolving concept of 'private policing'. *European Journal on Criminal Policy and Research*, 7(2): 197–223.

Krauthammer, C. (1993) Defining deviancy up. *The New Republic*, 22 November: 20–25.

Lazerges, C. (1995) De la politique de prévention de la délinquance à la politique de la ville. In C. Fijnaut, J. Goethals, T. Peters and L. Walgrave (eds) *Changes in Society, Crime and Criminal Justice. Vol. 1. Crime and Insecurity in the City*. The Hague: Kluwer.

Loader, I. (2002) Policing, securitization and democratization in Europe. *Criminal Justice*, 2(2) 125–53.

Logan, J.R. and Molotch, H. (1987) *Urban Fortunes: The Political Economy of Place*. Berkeley, CA: University of California Press.

Mathiesen, T. (2000) On the globalisation of control: towards an integrated surveillance system in Europe. In P. Green and A. Rutherford (eds) *Criminal Policy in Transition*. Oxford: Hart Publishing.

McLaughlin, E. (1992) The democratic deficit: European unity and the accountability of the British police. *British Journal of Criminology*, 32(4): 473–87.

Melossi, D. (2000) The other in the new Europe. In P. Green and A. Rutherford (eds) *Criminal Policy in Transition*. Oxford: Hart Publishing.

Morgan, J. (1991) *Safer Communities: The Local Delivery of Crime Prevention through the Partnership Approach*. London: Home Office.

Moynihan, D.P. (1993) Defining deviancy down. *American Scholar*, 62 (Winter): 17–30.

Ocqueteau, F. (1998) La sécurité privée en France: état des lieux et questions pour l'avenir. *Les Cahiers de la Sécurité Intérieure*, 33: 105–28.

Rhodes, R.A.W. (1994) The hollowing out of the state: the changing nature of the public service in Britain. *Political Quarterly Review*, 65: 137–51.

Robert, P. (2000) Les territoires du contrôle social, quels changements? *Déviance et Société*, 24(3): 215-35.

Sennett, R. (1998) *The Corrosion of Character*. New York: W.W. Norton.

Shearing, C. (1992) The relation between public and private policing. In M. Tonry and N. Morris (eds) *Crime and Justice: A Review of Research. Vol. 15*. Chicago, IL: University of Chicago Press.

Shearing, C. and Stenning, P. (1987) Reframing policing. In C. Shearing and P. Stenning (eds) *Private Policing*. London: Sage.

Sheptycki, J.W.E. (1995) Transnational policing and the makings of a postmodern state. *British Journal of Criminology*, 35(4): 613–35.

Sheptycki, J.W.E. (1998) Policing postmodernism and transnationalisation. *British Journal of Criminology*, 38(3): 485–503.

Sheptycki, J.W.E. (ed.) (2000) *Issues in Transnational Policing*. London: Routledge.

Tak, P.J.P. (2000) Bottlenecks in international police and judicial cooperations in the EU. *European Journal of Crime, Criminal Law and Criminal Justice*, 8(4): 343–60.

Taylor, I., Evans, K. and Fraser, P. (1996) *A Tale of Two Cities*. London: Routledge.

Tonry, M. (1998) A Comparative perspective on minority groups, crime and criminal justice. *European Journal of Crime, Criminal Law and Criminal Justice*, 6(1): 60–73.

van Swaaningen, R. (1997) *Critical Criminology: Visions from Europe*. London: Sage.

Wacquant, L. (1999) Ce vent punitif qui vient d'Amerique. *Le Mode Diplomatique*, Avril (541): 24–5.

Walker, N. (2000) Transnational contexts. In F. Leishman, B. Loveday and S. Savage (eds) *Core Issues in Policing* (2nd edn). Harlow: Longman.

Weiler, J. (1999) *The Constitution of Europe: 'Do the New Clothes Have an Emperor?' and Other Essays on European Integration*. Cambridge: Cambridge University Press.

Wieviorka, M. (1997) *Commenter la France*. Marseille: Éditions de l'Aube.

Wyvekens, A. (1996) Justice de proximité et proximité de la justice: les maisons de justice et du droit. *Droit et Société*, 33: 363–88.

Wyvekens, A. (1997) *L'Insertion locale de la justice pénale*. Paris: L'Harmattan.

Zedner, L. (2000) The pursuit of security. In T. Hope and R. Sparks (eds) *Crime, Risk and Insecurity*. London: Routledge.

Chapter 2

Violence in the age of uncertainty

Zygmunt Bauman

'Violence' could well serve as a paradigmatical sample of the large family of Austin's 'performatives' – the words which, by the act of naming, create the realities they name. In addition, 'violence' is an essentially contested concept that cannot be otherwise since the descriptive and evaluative assertions it implies mix, melt and blend, and cannot be separated. The contest of which the concept of violence is an object concerns the *legitimacy* of force. 'Violence' is illegitimate coercion: more precisely, a coercion that has not gained, or has been denied, legitimacy.

In all order-building and order-maintenance endeavours legitimacy is, by necessity, the prime stake. The battles are waged around the borderline proposed to divide the proper (that is, un-punishable) from the improper (that is, punishable) coercion and enforcement. The declared end of the 'war against violence' in the name of 'law and order' may be social peace and civility, but the aim and the eventual spoils of war are not the elimination, but the *monopoly of coercion.* The 'elimination of violence', the declared objective of such war, is visualised as a state of affairs in which *monopoly is no more contested* and only the duly authorised agencies resort to coercion. In other words, the 'non-violence' presented as the attribute of civilised life does not mean the absence of coercion, but only the absence of *unauthorised* coercion. These are the prime reasons for which war against violence is likely to be waged without end while staying stubbornly, irreparably unwinnable. For all practical purposes, a 'non-violent' social order is a contradiction in terms.

Two important conclusions follow. First, contrary to the declarations of intent that accompany the promotion of 'civilised order', a consistent and determined stand against violence is unlikely to be taken by any of the protagonists and would rather remain as half-hearted and above all as inconclusive in practice as it is grandiose and confident in words. Censure of violence would be cohesive only were it extended to coercion as such; but this is, simply, not on the cards. Order-builders and order-guardians cannot but be in two minds when it comes to the question of usefulness and need of coercion.

Secondly, it is impossible to say with any degree of objectivity whether modern history is a story of rising or receding violence – as it is quite impossible to find the way of unambiguously separating violence from coercion and so measuring 'objectively' its overall volume.

Who is afraid of crime?

This second conclusion acquires particular importance whenever an attempt to make sense of 'crime statistics' is undertaken, and gains further in importance when one wishes to comprehend the recurrent popular (and all too often authoritatively abetted) alarms about rising levels of violence and the message conveyed by the popular selection of the carriers of danger. In the perception of rising violence three different factors, exceedingly difficult to disentangle and virtually impossible to separate neatly, interact.

First, whenever alarms about rising violence are voiced, we may suppose that the notoriously blurred line separating 'natural' coercion (that is, the unavoidable and 'justified' coercion, the 'we can do nothing about it' and 'this is how things are' kind of coercion, the indispensable part of the daily routine one has no choice but to bear without complaint) and violence (that is, the coercion perceived as 'excessive', unjustifiable, uncalled for or deployed by the wrong kind of people) has become yet less legible than it usually tends to be. The acts previously placidly and meekly suffered without resistance are being recast as illegitimate coercion.

Secondly, at a time when habitualised and firmly institutionalised norms that separate the legitimate coercive constraints from violence (let me repeat; a coercion that it is right to resist and which ought to be punished) are fast losing their hold and seem therefore to be reopened for negotiation, we may expect numerous tugs-of-war in the course of which all sides would resort to actions lacking a recognised normative support and so bound to be perceived as violent by the perpetrators, the victims and the bystanders alike. Both the defence of habitual entitlements to exercise coercion and the counter-actions aimed at overcoming that resistance are likely to be widely (though again contentiously) perceived as acts of violence.

Thirdly, the perception of rising violence reflects all too often a sharp rise in general insecurity which only marginally, if at all, can be blamed 'objectively' on the swelling volume of violent acts and actors. Uncertainty about the future and painfully felt insecurity of livelihood and social standing generate great anxiety that more often than not cannot be faced point-blank and confronted directly since its roots are stuck in the areas far beyond the sufferers' reach. Short of the rational solution to the trouble, anxiety generated in ever larger quantities by existential insecurity and fears of an uncertain future seeks more tangible, close-to-hand estuaries – and so it tends to converge on the 'issues of safety' (of the body, property, home, neighbourhood). Looking closely at the 'figures of fear' on which panics focus we can learn less of their intrinsic 'nuisance power' than about the nature of uncertainty and insecurity that haunt the panic stricken.

It so happens that ours are times of profound and rapid change; no wonder that we all, in some degree or other and for one reason or another, feel insecure. Even those among us who, thus far, sit firmly in our respective saddles have no way of knowing what tomorrow will bring. Jobs, factories, whole companies disappear without warning and so does the demand for skills meant to serve the whole of working life, while the governments left or right call us to be more 'flexible' and so promise more change and yet more agonising uncertainty. Neither are the family homes the shelters of confidence and tranquillity we once expected them to be. Few people can be sure to live all their lives in the company of the same partners. Neighbourhoods change too; familiar signs vanish without trace and new ones – unknown, unheard of and barely legible – appear in their place.

Insecure people may be excused for wanting the world to be less opaque and life to be more predictable than it is. There is nothing new about that. What is new is that in the past such a wish used to prompt people time and again to think of a 'good society', better fit for decent and dignified human life, and to join forces in order to bring such a better society about, this is no more the case. These days, the government of the country can do little to strike at the roots of its subjects' insecurity. Hands of state governments are tied by 'global trends' – those faceless, anonymous 'market forces' of which no one is in charge. As Richard Rorty sadly observed 'an attempt by any one country to prevent the immiseration of its workers may result only in depriving them of employment' (1988: 85). And so, short of the means of collective defence and no more sure about the prudence of building them from scratch, we all, each one of us on his or her own, are left to find the way out of trouble using our own wits and muscles. As Ulrich Beck famously quipped, we are told to seek 'biographical solutions to systemic contradictions' (1992: 137).

Sooner or later we are bound to find out that whatever we may individually do, the pain of insecurity will not go away. It seems, however, that whatever our governments can do will not remove it either. And so anxiety seeks other outlets. If a good society in which everyone feels secure is unattainable, then at least we can take more care of the safety in places in our reach. At least we will feel a bit better if we do so. We will not deprecate ourselves nor be derided by others for taking the blows lying down. Like the hero of *One Flew Over the Cuckoo's Nest*, we would at least be able to say that we have tried to do something – tangible, visible – to fight the dangers back and keep them away.

No wonder the impression of 'living in violent times' is so widespread. It would be wrong, however, to take that feeling for proof that the volume of violence is indeed on the rise. Let me repeat that if the routine, repetitive and monotonous coercion has little chance to draw attention, raise alarm and resentment – it is when routine is broken that the coercion which used to sustain it day in and day out hits the eye. It is then that coercion begins to be seen as violence, an unjustified use of force and assault against personal safety, integrity and dignity. But, as it has been suggested before, this is but one part of the story. The rising frequency with which people nowadays resort to *illegitimate* use of force is not just a matter of misperception.

Once the customary rules of cohabitation fall apart, new rules tend to be sought and imposed through 'reconnaisance by battle' (in military practice, this term refers to engaging the enemy in order to reveal how large its defensive capacity is and how far back it can be pushed). Much of contemporary violence – from the family skirmishes through neighbourhood confrontations to intercommunal and inter-ethnic wars – has the nature of such 'reconnaisance by battle', only to be expected in times of transition; of shaky and protean standards, hotly contested borders between normality and abnormality and uncertain routines.

Suspicion of violence is itself an ample source of anxiety, and with the problem of legitimacy unsolved hardly any demand likely to arise from sharing space, home or life is free from such suspicion. Renegotiation of *modus vivendi* is fraught with risks – and so the strategy of *disengagement* (refusal to negotiate and decision to keep one's distance) seems a safer, and for that reason more attractive, bet. This strategy is manifested in the desperate attempts to erect impermeable barriers serving territorial separation – from 'gated communities', closed circuit TV and vigilante patrols, through the replacement of a 'till death us do part' marriages with 'until further notice' cohabitation, up to the ghettoisation of the undesirables and ethnic cleansing.

Fear of violence may be ambient, but is not evenly distributed between the strata of the emergent global hierarchy, which renders a universally shared conception of violence (let alone a 'united stand' in resisting it and fighting it) all the more difficult to achieve. Given that, the display of Houdini skills, the ability to move fast and to opt out, as well as the practice or the threat to escape and disengage, tend to be substituted in the 'liquid' stage of modernity for the pernickety normative regulation of yore and the tight and close policing as the principal strategies of domination and power struggle. Given that this struggle is increasingly waged between speed and slowness – exterritoriality and 'local bonds', freedom to move and necessity to stay – the degree of actual, but above all of the potential, mobility fast becomes the paramount factor of the new hierarchy of global and intrasocietal stratification.

Girling *et al.* (2000), who investigated the perception of endemic violence and criminality in several areas of east Cheshire, felt obliged to refute the widespread assumption that the 'fear of crime' could be ascribed in equal measure to human agents independently of their sharply differing social conditions. For instance, notorious 'teenage disorders' do not

> invoke a blanket response. Individuals (and whole communities) remain differently positioned with respect to the gathering of 'disorderly' youths and vary markedly in how they make sense of and handle the problems such youths appear to cause.... In some instances ... such disorder seems disconnected from other important and valued aspects of people's lives. This generally occurs where a community of place is neither the only nor the most significant repository of meaning and security for people ... [which enables such people] to distance themselves, materially and emotionally, from the stresses and troubles that afflict the neighbourhood in which they live ... 'Thick' disorder, by contrast, describes a situation where the 'problem of youth' acquires a heightened material and metaphorical force by being embedded in a web of local ties and affiliations. (*ibid.*: 171)

Richard Sparks (pers. comm.) has recently summed up the wisdom emerging from the numerous studies of the spectacular career made by the alarms about 'rising violence' and concerns with crime and punishment in the popular responses to the acutely felt, yet poorly understood, insecurity of existence: 'An apparent rise in vigilante activity is the citizen counterpart of the increase in official punitiveness, striking at those suspected offenders who are at hand as an expression of impotence in the face of crime and insecurity'. Let me add that while governments jump eagerly at the opportunity of killing two birds with one stone (channelling popular anxiety away from uncertainty and insecurity, its true sources which the politicians can do little to block or dam, and being seen by the electorate, at long last, as 'taking a tough stance' and doing 'something real'), the growing sensitivity to crime and the vigilante activity that follows draws yet more energy from the suspicion that the defence of safety, like most other aspects of life, has been all but ignored by the powers that be and has become a 'communal affair' that can be only tackled as a 'do-it-yourselves' job.

The century likely to go down in history as one of violence perpetrated by nation-states on their subjects has come to its close. Another violent century, this time a century of violence exacerbated by the disablement of nation-states as agencies of collective solutions and the progressive individualisation of human condition and fate, is likely to succeed it.

What is crime? Who are the criminals?

The terms deployed by the authors of the United Nations survey (1993) of the crime trends documented in three successive five-year reports covering the period from 1970 to 1985 show them to be aware that what they analysed were not the 'levels of crime' but the levels of crime reporting and crime recording; and they assumed (and made the assumption explicit) that 'crime committed' and 'crime reported' (let alone 'crime recorded') are not the same things. Cautiously, they did not try to estimate the levels of 'actual crime' and confined themselves to the suggestion that there was a general tendency to report crimes to the police, and that the willingness to report them grows 'as countries attain higher levels of socio-economic development'. More contentiously, they suggest this correlation has something to do with more telephones and more goods insured, though it would be equally convincing, and perhaps more telling, to unpack the notion of 'socioe-conomic development' as a name for the relentless tearing apart of the web of social bonds, the web once able to sustain on its own the models of social justice and just deserts, and the shattering of daily-life and habitualised routines together with the local/communal means of their control.

Once this sort of 'socioeconomic development' occurs a multi-link chain of actions is put in place that separates acts from being defined as 'criminal', the definition of acts as criminal from reporting crimes to appointed agencies and reporting crimes from recording them by such agencies. To start with, as David Matza observed a long time ago, 'to give oneself laws and to create the possibility of disobeying them come to the same thing' (1969: 14). As ever more coercive acts once endured placidly as 'part of life' tend to be reclassified as violence to human person, possessions or dignity, the number of occasions for crime reporting grows. It takes time, though, and a lot of reclassifying and stereotyping, to render the kinds of conduct newly recast as criminal and a matter for police and the courts to be willingly reported, and once reported to be readily recorded and processed; to become, in David Sudnow's terms 'normal crimes': 'Offences whose normal features are readily attended to are those which are routinely encountered in the courtroom.... Offences are ecologically specified and attended to as normal or not according to the locales within which they are committed' (1965: 255–68). The likelihood of an act being recorded as criminal grows along with the degree to which it fits the image of crimes 'normal' for a given place and given category of its residents – the image the recording officers share with the public. As to the principal actors in the courtroom, they are concerned primarily with moulding and trimming the representation of the act under consideration so that it may better fit the type of deeds they expect to come to the courtroom and to be judged and sentenced. As a whole, the recording–sentencing procedure serves as the mechanism of 'authentication'. It generates the evidence of the crime and criminals being 'real' and 'normal'.

In the latest edition of his now classic challenge to penal policy, Nils Christie asks some vexing questions:

> Are kings the sons of God, or descendants of particularly successful criminals? And the beautiful people, at the top of business or entertainment, are they there due to virtues comparable to their life-styles? Are poor people to be seen as idle drinkers, good-for-nothing, or as victims of social conditions outside of their control? Are inner cities places where those with no aspirations choose to flock together, or are they dumping grounds for those not given an even share of the benefits of modern societies? The fascinating question ... is why the inner cities of the USA are seen as targets for war rather than as targets for drastic social reform.
>
> (Christie 2000: 109)

The point is, though, that the chain of reporting–recording–sentencing and the policing–judiciary system that services that chain, work – and effectively so – to prevent Christie's questions from being asked – and in case they are asked to refute what they imply and so make asking them irrelevant.

Granted, it is not the policing–judiciary system that produces the swelling cohorts of law-breakers (though by all evidence it does little or nothing to reduce their ranks), nor does it generate the ambient fear and prickly sensitivity to crime and violence that poisons the days and nights of the residents of our uncertain world. This does not mean, though, that it passively reflects the extent of either. Even less does it mean it exerts no influence on their public perception and on the intensity of public feelings about the threats to safety, or the public understanding of their causes. It does all these things, and having entered a marriage of reciprocal convenience with the mass media, the principal weaver of life-narratives and storyteller of human condition, it supplies the cognitive frames and patterns with which the matters of criminality, violence and the responsibility they bear for the acutely felt torments of existential insecurity are comprehended.

Crime thrillers, cop and court dramas (many bearing the credibility-boosting label of 'true stories') constitute these days the staple diet of television viewers and cinema goers. While the screens cover the visible world 'out there' – like carpets cover the floors: 'wall to wall' – the endless cops-and-robbers wars fill the screens. In the world 'as seen on TV' violence is indeed, beyond reasonable doubt, rising. It also gets ever more ruthless and frightening. There is seldom a film or a drama series that does not contain its measure of (often gratuitous) violence. And since the shock, the main tool likely to be deployed by ratings pushers, wears off rather quickly through monotonous exposure, producers compete for the viewers' attention by trying to outdo each other in the cruelty, bloodiness and virulence of the deeds on display. To boost the 'shock factor' yet more, depictions of violence move, more often than not, from Walter Benjamin's category of 'sailor' to that of the 'peasant' stories; instead of locating crafty and deceitful villains in far-away places, they tend to cast them in the all-too-familiar environment of daily life – in the family, in the house next door, in the frequently walked street (not that the villains avoid thereby typecasting – the care is taken to feed on and feed back into the popular stereotypes of the carriers of danger). And having repealed the ban on the camera in the courtroom, American television brings the grizzly details of criminal exploits, and the drama of reforging guilt into incarceration and the culprits into convicts, right into the sitting rooms of 'ordinary folks'.

All in all, daily exposure to the violence lurking in every nook and cranny of the *Lebenswelt* reinforces the conviction that far from being a rare and exceptional event, crime is ubiquitously present in every sector of life, waiting for its chance to leap out of hiding. It remains a moot point whether the continuous display of violent acts prompts violence in the viewers, as the ethically inspired critics aver (though thus far without offering definite proof). More likely, perhaps, it breeds 'horror fatigue' and tones down or extinguishes altogether the moral repulsion violence would have aroused in less emotionally inured beings. But its most certain and arguably most portentous effect is that, in the worldview held by growing sections of humankind, crime and violence are no more deviations from the norm, but the norm itself.

And yet the policing–judiciary–penal system together with its media-generated and -distributed representations merely recycle, rechannel and otherwise manipulate the anxieties that are born daily out of the mundane experience of living in the deregulated and individualised, uncertain and insecure settings, in which long-lasting standards, orientation points and models of 'decent life' are all steadily phased out or thrown back into the melting pot.

Recycling is the great discovery of our times and increasingly a major strategy in all branches of industry, including the culture industry. It might have enhanced creative opportunities, yet could not and did not render them limitless. The qualities of the objects earmarked for recycling set the boundary to the set of objects they can be recycled into, and however ingenious the technology of overhaul, the final product cannot but bear the mark of the 'raw material' from which it has been processed. One can always guess the original behind the finished product of recycling. This includes the figures of fear and hatred, which populate the world as construed in the *Weltanschauung* of contemporary men and women. Those figures could and should be understood as impersonated embodiments of the otherwise vague and scattered, but daily and commonly suffered fears and nightmares. Daily anxieties, emanating from the experience of uncertain future and insecure present, are the 'originals' subsequently recycled into panic-arousing threats to safety. The desperate search for ways and means to fight back anxiety and so to release the already unbearable, yet steadily accumulating, tension is the recycling routine of which the figures of fear and hatred are the ultimate products.

Of the wide assortment of such products, three categories seem to tell most about the nature of sufferings endemic to the present-day human condition, since they occupy an ever-wider shelf-space in the warehouse of fears and tend to trigger the most intense bouts of panic.

Prowlers and stalkers are the most conspicuous specimens of the first category. In our thoroughly individualised world, in which the human condition splits into weakly linked individual performances and every man and woman is expected to face the adversities of fate alone and cope with them using private resources, the stalker and prowler elbow out and replace the spectre of the rebellious/revolutionary 'mob' that used to haunt our ancestors: mob, *mobile vulgus*, the crowd on the move, the rioters bent on destroying the orderly world that our ancestors knew, had grown used to and felt at home in, cosy and secure. The two hate-and-fear characters stand for the new sensitivity to dangers created daily by the things out of place or absent from the places in which they should stay; things appearing from nowhere and without notice and disappearing as quickly and as unexpectedly as they came. This includes a catalogue of all sorts of things – corner shops and bank branches, places of work, jobs, bus lines and railway stations, trustworthy service providers, familiar neighbourhoods, faces in the limelight, partners in marriage and so on. Quicksands spread where hard rocks and firm soil were once expected and found. Features of the landscape, like the sand-dunes' pattern, keep changing shape by the day. Learning that one's home is built on sand is a harrowing experience, a recipe for sleepless nights. The new fluidity of the fast liquidising world makes a laughing stock of long-term planners and tragic figures of those fond of long-term commitments (Bauman 2000).

An eerie sense of danger emanates from the new restlessness of things, all the more odious for making the order of things feel vague, shapeless, diffuse and un-pinpointable. Things on the move cannot be slowed down, let alone arrested. One cannot predict when and where the things one knows will go next, just as one cannot anticipate the new ones about to descend, let alone fix the date of their landing. To rub salt into the wound, there seems no more to be a central office or controlling tower that keeps track on all that mind-boggling toing and froing. So there is no address at which to lodge complaints, no street on which to erect barricades and no building to picket or storm. This is, at least, the process dubbed 'globalisation' (that mismatch between already global powers and hopelessly limited, local capacity of the means that should hold them in check) reflected in the ways the experience of human individuals is lived through and narrated. For the individuals we all are, the absence of controlling towers and binding timetables means the necessity to navigate-through-life using one's own skills and a few shop-supplied gadgets, but without clear itinerary and with but a dim idea of the journey's destination.

To good swimmers, liquidity of the world is an asset. It is an abomination and a portent of disaster for the poor ones. Individuals untied to place, who can travel light and move fast, win all the competitions that matter and count. Their gain is others' defeat, and so the sight of their exploits cannot but offer a painful reminder of one's own indolence. One could not flex one's own muscles to an effect as spectacular as those easy riders obviously had achieved. One may admire and cheer their skills when their exploits are broadcast, securely enclosed in the frame of the television screen and so prevented from spilling over on the viewers' condition. When seen at close quarters, though, and met in combat, they arouse envy, resentment and fear.

We could say that, were there no prowlers and stalkers, they would have to be invented. Public enemies tend to be cut to the measure of the public whose enemies they are proclaimed to be, and to the 'number one' enemies that rule applies more than to any other. Figures of stalkers and prowlers are made to the measure of the incipient, inchoate, yet endemic and ambient, fears haunting the contemporary public. What makes them uniquely fit to absorb and condense our fears is their exquisite freedom to move, to appear and disappear at will and to enter places we thought to be protected against trespass. But they are also individuals like all of us, pursuing their individual trajectories, acting individually, suffering individually and struggling each on his or her own. Like us, they do not join forces, act in unison, form fighting battalions – nor do they aim, individually, against anybody but us, individuals. Prowling and stalking is, as it could only be expected in our individualised society, a one-to-one combat, a score to be settled between us, the individuals. In the figures of prowler and stalker our lonely condition meets its faithful reflection.

Prowlers and stalkers are close relatives of embodied fears that deserve to be allocated to another category, since they can be understood best as incarnations of the more general concerns with the safety of the body, its extensions and its environment. As Antoine Garapon and Denis Salas have pointed out, for contemporary men and women 'delinquency has become a risk like any other' (1997: 10–11): their responses to genuine or putative criminality (more precisely, the way they construe criminality) are part and parcel of their concerns with the risks that fill to the brim the individualised existence. Accordingly, the emergent juridical order is no more founded in communally shared values, but in collated concerns with individual safety. *Tabagisme* (the French concept embracing nicotine addiction and the dangers supposed to reside in the proximity of nicotine addicts), speeding and sexual offences are according to Garapon and Salas the crimes most intensely resented and called for to be punished most severely. This triad of most feared risks seems to be thrown together at random. The three risks seem to have little in common. However, appearances are misleading, since all three most horrifying and resented offences converge on the same object: the human body.

Fears related to the dangers threatening health and fitness of the body are not of course a novelty of our 'liquid modernity' era. These fears have risen, however, to the heights and acquired emotional depth hardly ever seen before. They have settled firmly in the centre of concerns, worries and obsessions of contemporary men and women. We may surmise why this could, or even should, have happened. In the world of moving targets, shifting orientation points and twisted and fluctuating itineraries, the individual's lifespan – once bewailed as miserably brief and fragile when measured by the longevity of commonly accepted standards, values and of the collectivities of belonging – has become (while remaining as short of permanence and as transient as before) an entity with the life-expectation longer than any other part of the *Lebenswelt*. The living body seems to be now the only thread on which the otherwise scattered and disparate episodes into which life in the fluid world has been sliced can be strung together. The mental and emotional energy once expended on the care for immortality or eternal causes now converges on the body, a solitary rock amidst quicksands. Everything that counts will come to its end with the demise of the body – but the odds are that most of the things that count will precede the bodily being on its way to nothingness – and oblivion.

No wonder that the body becomes the focus of most acute concern and a fount of endless anxiety. What makes the anxiety unavoidable and the concern imperative is the fact that the traffic between the body and the rest of the world where so many dangers lie in ambush cannot be avoided; not just because of life being inevitably a process of incessant metabolism, but because we all, the wards and alumni of consumer society, are brought up and trained to live as collectors of sensations and ever more pleasurable sensations – and such sensations can only be gleaned at the interface between the body and the world outside. Risks, therefore, cannot be avoided and withdrawal from the world into hermitry or asceticism is not an option.

On the body's interface with the world 'out there' the sought-after pleasures happen, but also the most awesome dangers lie in ambush. The body orifices and the skin that covers (simultaneously shelters and exposes) the body become therefore battle zones: sites of a war that can never be conclusively won and hence can never stop. The interface is a sublime territory, perhaps the prototype of all sublimity. Whatever occurs in that zone is an object of cognitive ambiguity and behavioural ambivalence, and so inevitably of terrible tension and fearful anxiety. It simultaneously inspires awe and arouses horror.

It is the apprehension, caginess and vigilance focusing on the body–world interface that crystallise in the image of the 'crimes against safety and integrity of the body'. Garapon and Salas (*ibid.*) named three such crimes, making the headlines most often at the time their research was conducted. But the trouble with these, and all successive effigies on which the tensions which are impossible to unload are hoped to be unloaded, is precisely the ultimate unloadability of tensions. Burning any amount of effigies can bring at best only a temporary and short-lived respite, since the 'interface problems' stay as unnerving as before and go on generating new sources of anxiety. The panoply of interchangeable effigies needs to be wide, and new additions are permanently in demand. The range of usual and potential suspects is continually scanned. Attention cannot remain focused for long. The 'hatred fatigue' prompted by the evident idleness of efforts to placate anxiety sets in quickly and other star villains in the galaxy of body threats need to be brought into focus.

The galaxy brought forth by the 'big bang' of body-related fears is potentially infinite – since, except for the parts of the universe which have no visible connection to the body and thus do not matter (though one can never rest assured that such connection will not be discovered when the harm has been already done, as in the case of mad-cow disease or asbestos insulation), all the rest of the world is anything but neutral or straightforwardly good or evil. Genetically modified food, toxic waste-dumping, travellers' camps, passive smoking, gas-emissions causing holes in ozone layers, or a nearby asylum-seekers' or AIDS-victims' shelter, are all in line to be drawn into the spotlight as possible condensations of the threats to bodily safety, and so to demand the rooting out and exemplary punishment of culprits. Few, however, may equal in their panic-arousing capacity the potential of sexual and food-related offences because of the indissoluble association of eating and sexual intercourse with foreign substances 'going inside' the body. Such offences are feared to reach the parts which few, if any, other agents can reach. What makes food and sex into a territory uniquely suitable for the focusing of body-related fears is that unlike chemical-factory emissions or other drivers' speeding they evoke incurably ambivalent emotions. Pleasures are intertwined here with dangers: desire blends with repulsion. Fission is badly needed. One needs to separate the 'nice' from the 'nasty' for either of them to be enjoyed or steered clear of with no regret and no second thoughts. The creation of food and sex offenders is an act of such purification, guided by the hope that once the evil part of an ambiguous condition is pinpointed, unmasked and pilloried, the vexing ambivalence will go away.

This hope is bound to be dashed, though, and so instead of purifying pleasures of life, the nerve-stretching sensitivity to all things edible and sexual pollutes them permanently with uncertainty and apprehension. The line separating the 'right' from 'wrong' is uniquely difficult to draw in an undisputed fashion, and so doubts continue to haunt and hardly anything one does and sees the others around to be doing seems truly innocuous and innocent. Under the circumstances, a villain who could be blamed unambiguously and whose blame would commend wide consent is a God-sent gift for all those whose tensions need venting. There are few villains who can match the paedophile's capacity of relieving the anxiety and self-doubts suffered by all who cannot but fear sex, which they cannot but practise. Standing night-long vigils around a paedophile's home, and better still breaking windows, forcing the doors and pushing a paedophile into suicide, is a redeeming act of exorcising inner demons of ambivalence.

Another category of crime images and criminal figures generated by the anxiety-arousing life-experience is, like the two categories discussed so far, difficult to separate neatly from the rest. Like them, it relates to diffuse and not clearly defined apprehensions, as a rule scattered, elusive and ineffable. Moulding figures of fear and hatred, visualising their ill intention and odious deeds, is an important part of the ongoing effort to render the illegible legible: to give name to anxiety, spot its causes and design the strategies of effective resistance. Since all categories grow from the same ambient experience of generalised insecurity of no visible internal structure, their boundaries are blurred: their semantic fields, at least in part, overlap. Their separation, always an artifice of classifying efforts, tends to exaggerate the differences at the expense of affinities.

With these qualifications in mind, we may consider as the third category of crimes and criminals the widely differing characters and the variety of imputed behavioural patterns that have come in recent years to be habitually packed together in the concept of the 'underclass', coined in the USA but making a truly spectacular career in the rest of the affluent world. The tremendous capacity of the 'underclass' conceptual container is well portrayed by Herbert Gans:

This behavioural definition denominates poor people who drop out of school, do not work, and, if they are young women, have babies without benefit of marriage and go on welfare. The behavioural underclass also includes the homeless, beggars, and panhandlers, poor addicts to alcohol and drugs, and street criminals. Because the term is flexible poor people who live in 'the projects', illegal immigrants, and teenage gang members are often also assigned to the underclass. Indeed, the very flexibility of the behavioural definition is what lends itself to the term becoming a label that can be used to stigmatise poor people, whatever their actual behaviour.

(1995: 2)

What, if anything, sufficiently unites such a variegated collection of misfits and outcasts to justify hurling them all together into one category of beings, arousing the same emotions and calling for the same remedial/ punitive measures? Lawrence Mead (1992), one of the most consistent and influential detractors of the new cancerous growth poisoning the social body, offers a clue, though fails to spell out the conclusions. First, it is not so much the features the 'underclassers' share that prompt the rest of the Americans to favour similar treatment of them all. It is rather the other way round; what unites the starkly divergent types into one 'class outside classes' is the abhorrence the 'normal Americans' feel to the way all such types behave. Secondly, what makes the normal Americans intensely dislike all varieties of the 'underclassers', however different in all other respects they may be, to take a united stand, demand strong measures to be taken against them all and wish them to be chased out of the street and out of sight, is the original sin of which all the 'underclassers' are guilty in the same measure: the sin of offending all the values the 'normal majority' holds sacred and cherishes, while arrogantly claiming the right to partake of the joys of consumer society other people believe they have earned and deserved by sticking to the values the 'underclassers' manifestly ignore.

To put it bluntly, into the manifest sins of the 'underclass' the gnawing suspicions of fault, laggardness or inaptitude of their detractors – the 'normal majority' – are drained. Values of the consumer society may be universally cherished, but following them faithfully is not an easy matter. The life of a consumer is full of choices made under conditions of uncertainty, often a prospectless uncertainty. The need to choose is harrowing, but no less vexing are doubts following each choice made and the fear of coming to regret it. Putting paid to the risks of choosing is therefore always a seductive option, more tormenting yet for being suppressed because of its blatant opposition to the 'values most cherished'. Besides, once the world has been cast as a container of appetising choices, and successful life as the art of picking the most savoury among them, the ends seem forever to run ahead of the means and with no hope of ever reaching 'full satisfaction' and rest can be seriously entertained. Travelling hopefully may be better than arrival. But travelling without hope of arrival is not a prospect likely to be enjoyed. Life for a consumer may be rich in happy moments. But happiness seems to stay stubbornly beyond the horizon and out of grasp.

Life for a consumer is therefore vulnerable, full of tension and given to qualms and misgivings. In the long run, it may be no less exhausting than it is exciting. Every consumer breeds his or her inner demons fed by the apparently incurable ambivalence of joys and anxieties. The repulsive vision of the 'underclass' as incarnation of the failure to rise to the standards that life in a marketplace of infinite opportunities demands to be met, helps considerably to exorcise those demons.

In the individualised society of ours, the socially constructed condition seldom comes fully into view and even less frequently does it happen to be vented and thoroughly discussed. Good fortune may be a social product, but it is the individual victims of misfortune who bear responsibility for the absence of luck; and it is by their own bootstraps they are expected to pull themselves, singly, out of shared trouble. That they have not pulled themselves out of trouble is all the evidence needed to prove they did not try earnestly and diligently enough. The snag, though, is that far from all 'individuals *de jure*' have enough resources at their disposal to settle securely in the position of 'individuals *de facto*': the kind of people who are not only allowed and nagged to make their choices, but capable of making them. Between being pronounced 'individuals *de jure*' and becoming 'individuals *de facto*' a gap yawns. Yet, once again, it is the individuals inhibited by that gap who are called to bridge it using their own wits and muscles.

Samuel Butler must have prophetically anticipated the coming of this kind of society when he made an Erewhon judge inform the defendant brought before him: 'You may say it is your misfortune to be criminal: I answer that it is your crime to be unfortunate' (1998: 116). In Erewhon, as in the society that was to become ours almost a century later, it was

an axiom of morality that luck is the only fit object of human veneration. How far a man has any right to be more lucky and hence more venerable than his neighbours, is a point that always has been, and always will be, settled proximately by a kind of higgling and haggling of the market, and ultimately by brute force: but however this may be, it stands to reason that no man should be allowed to be unlucky to more than a very moderate extent (*ibid.*: 109).

The message that falling on hard times is the victim's crime takes some mind-twisting to embrace. It hardly strikes the hearer as self-evident. To make it credible, words must be made into flesh, and criminalising bad luck through the collective guilt of the 'underclasses' is the means to achieve just that. Indeed, the 'underclass' is guilty of not acquiring what all the rest of us desire, and if lack of success is a punishable crime, we the rest ought to try harder and harder yet to stave off the eventuality of failure. The echoes of whip-cracking aimed at the underclass spines reverberate in the sitting rooms of all affluent consumers. They help the occupants to come to their senses in the moments of self-doubt or shaken resolve.

The poor and miserable are the archetypes of flawed consumers. Flawed, or at least imperfect, inadequate consumers we all one time or another feel ourselves to be. Worse still, it is not clear how to disperse our suspicion of inadequacy. The line dividing the right performance from a flawed one is vexingly thin, often blurred, and it seldom stays in the same place for long. It may help us to cope with doubts if the borderline is clearly signposted and closely guarded by the organs of law and order. To criminalise the flaws in practised consumer patterns means to take a step in that direction. Criminalisation of the underclass obliquely proclaims absolution of all the others. No more ambivalence. At long last, it will be crystal clear what is what and who is who; and whoever is armed with a pair of eyes will no more have the right to seek excuse in ignorance.

What do we do with the criminals?

Puzzled by the rapid spread of crime-related 'urban fears', Sharon Zukin noted in 1995 that the rank-and-file American voters as well as their opinion-making elites had a choice. They

> could have faced the choice of approving government policies to eliminate poverty, manage ethnic competition, and integrate everyone into common public institutions. Instead, they chose to buy protection fuelling the growth of the private security industry.... 'Getting tough' on crime by building more prisons and imposing the death penalty are all too common answers to the politics of fear. (*ibid.* 38–9)

In moving crime and crime fighting to the centre of public concerns (at the expense of and to the detriment of all other worries that could possibly evolve into public issues), individuals and their governments co-operate, with a consensus difficult to find in other spheres of social life; each adding urgency and fuel to the moves made by the other. Individuals (those who can afford it, visiting the haute-couture-security shops; those who cannot, making do with mass-production replicas of the latest fashions of the rich) are busy 'buying security' in the form of 'state of the art' alarms, spying cameras and portable defence gadgets, or buying entry into 'gated communities': the hopefully secure niches fenced out and barricaded from the feared wilderness of the ordinary city space. By so doing, they make the safety-threatening nature of the city space into a fact. Compared to the tranquillity of fortified communities or the safety inside an armoured car, ordinary streets look off-puttingly 'mean' and all districts 'rough'; leaving the no-entry 'safety zone' and walking a street unarmed becomes a hazard only the bold and the adventurous would risk. As to the governments, given the impressive size of political capital that can be creamed off from the voters' safety worries, politicians do their best to outdo each other in demonstrating their steely resolve and lack of scruples in fighting the plague of violent law-breaking. To be filmed in front of a newly commissioned high-tech contraption for swift execution is *de rigeur* for a state governor dreaming of federal presidency, while quoting the (rising) size of the prison population and the (growing) numbers of authorised executions is what all spin-doctors worth their salt would recommend to include in electoral speeches. 'Being tough on crime' is the expedient to which politicians resort with particular zeal, and for a twofold reason. First, when fighting crime, politicians of all levels can be seen as doing something tangible, 'real' and easily understandable to the prospective voters while, secondly, none of them can do anything remotely as tangible and real about any other source of their voters' insecurity.

For long the most popular recent public figure in New York (and a favourite of the Senate race until his dramatic retirement from politics), mayor Rudolph Giuliani, and the head of the New York police force William Bratton, earned enormous applause from New Yorkers for authoring and executing the 'zero tolerance' policy: a war of attrition declared on 'squeegee pests', street prostitutes and beggars, rough sleepers and all the rest of the cityscape sores. No one ventured to suppose they indeed abolished poverty and miserable living, but they did manage to remove the conscience-disturbing sight of both banes from the eyes of 'decent people', and the rate of recorded crime, particularly the violent crime, above all the street violent crime, went indeed down for the first time in many years.

This startling effect has been achieved by sharply increasing the size of the police force on the beat, the capacity of prisons and the numbers of convicts. According to the figures collated by Loïc Wacquant (1999: 19–21, 139), in five years to 1999 the police budget in New York went up by 40% to reach $2.6 billion (four times more than the summary resources of all metropolitan hospitals) and the police force rose by 12,000 to reach 46,000 officers. At the same time, the expenditure on social services fell by 30% and the number of social workers shrank by 8,000 to 13,400. Evidently, problems previously considered (and handled) as *social* were re-classified as problems of *law and order*. Poverty in New York has been *criminalised and displaying poverty in public became a crime.*

New York was not an exceptional case, though. All over USA similar policies have been set in motion. In California, the richest of American states, the penitentiary administration budget rose from $200 million in 1975 to $4.3 billion, leaving behind the total budget of Californian universities, while the number of prison guards went up from 6,000 to 40,000 thousand and 2,700 new full-time parole officers have been put in service. Funds of social assistance, on the other hand, shrank by 42%. The executors of such policies claimed credit for the statistically recorded fall in the number of crimes. Though, as professor Richard Rosenfeld, a member of the US National Consortium of Violence Research, calculated, to prevent one statistically plausible homicide a net increase of the prison population by 670 inmates a year is needed (see *Guardian*, 22 February 2000).

It is all too easy (and so common) to interpret the quoted figures as records of the duel between crime and penitentiary policies: the volume of crime-triggering changes in policies and the effectiveness of the chosen policies modifying the extent of criminality: easy, but misleading. Crime and crime policies are separate entities only in official statistics, once they have been artificially cut out from the totality of social conditions: from the dense web of social processes they affect and by which they cannot but be continuously affected. Wacquant (1999) notes the strikingly close connection between, on one hand, fluctuations in criminality figures and shifts in penitentiary policies and, on the other hand, the degree of the labour-market deregulation (steady jobs and fixed career-tracks becoming by and large things of the past) and the scale of income differentials in the rapidly polarising society (if ten years ago an enterprise manager earned 42 times more than a blue-collar worker, he earns now 419 times more: 95% of the surplus income of $1,100 billion generated in the USA in the last 20 years has been appropriated by 5% of the richest Americans). It so happens that in our 'liquid modern' individualised, consumer society the wilting of labour-market regulation and the spectacular expansion of income differentials do not prompt social dissent and rebellion, but criminal acts. And so they do not conjure the spectre of 'reds under beds' but of 'squeegee pests', beggars and muggers as the 'public enemies number one'.

Wacquant (ibid. 89) concludes that 'the policy of the criminalisation of poverty is an indispensable complement of the imposition of precarious and underpaid employment as the citizen's obligation, coupled with making social welfare programmes more restrictive and punitive'. The 'welfare to work' policy may remove poverty from the statistics of unemployment, only to transfer it to the statistics of crime. Once this happens, the need to build new prisons and to multiply their inmates becomes almost a foregone conclusion. For a sociologist, it should come as no surprise that between 1979 and 1990 the running budget of American penitentiaries had grown by 325%, while the sums assigned to the building of new prisons rose by 612%. Penitentiaries have become the third biggest employer in the USA. Some analysts calculate that the current penal policy removes at least two percentage points from the number of unemployed. Just as the purpose of the fast-fading welfare institution is less and less 'keeping the powder dry' – assuring that the 'reserve army of labour' is ready to return to active service – the purpose of prison confinement is no more the 'rehabilitation' of the offenders and their 'return to society', but instead 'isolation of the categories perceived as dangerous and neutralisation of their most disruptive members' (*ibid.*: 78).

All this said, it still needs to be remembered that criminal statistics, the essential source of information about the current state and tendency of criminality, do not record 'raw facts'. There are hardly any 'facts of the matter' that can be considered as 'raw'. They are all processed by human choices: by the 'definitions of the situation', classifying decisions and the practices that follow.

In the new edition of his book *Crime Control as Industry*, Nils Christie points out that:

a basic tenet of social control is that those who own very much and those who own nothing are the two extremes that are the most difficult to govern. Those who own too much have power also and are able to resist control: those with little have nothing to lose and little to fear. (2000: 68)

Let me observe that in our 'liquid modern', individualised, increasingly polarised consumer society we have decided (whether by design or by

71

default) to let those who own very much not bother with resisting control since we have agreed to control them little or not at all. As to those who own little, our decision is to leave them, as before, with nothing to lose, but to give them something to be afraid of. The gradual, yet seemingly inexorable, shift from welfare state to penal state is the summary product of all those decisions. And so are the officially recorded shifts in crime and punishment.

The overall result is, as Jock Young suggests, the emergent *exclusive society* or, rather, a society that has enlisted social exclusion as the principal method of social control aimed at the 'flawed consumers' of the consumer society, and of the integration of the rest:

> The outgroup becomes a scapegoat for the troubles of the wider society: they are underclass, who live in idleness and crime ... They are the social impurities of the late modern world ... But unlike the reformers from the late nineteenth century, up until the 1960s the goal is not to physically eliminate their areas and integrate their members into the body politic; it is to hold at bay and exclude.
>
> (1999: 20)

And prisons are the dumping ground for 'social impurities'; for that part of social waste that is not meant to be recycled or whose recycling into raw resource of the penal industry is taken to be the sole useful and rational form of recycling. Prison statistics may be read as the record of the volume of social waste and indication of the changing technology of waste disposal.

Prisons are the most resolute and radical (short of capital punishment) of many forms of social exclusion. In technical terms, they serve the purpose, through reducing to a minimum or cutting altogether the communication between the main body of society and the excluded categories, and keeping social waste far enough from 'where the action is', to stave off all contamination. But it may be guessed that the secret of the astonishing seductiveness and popularity of the 'imprisonment solution' to social problems lies primarily in the important symbolic role performed by prisons at the time when the emergent values of the 'liquid modern' society take roots.

In this kind of society the degree of mobility – the ability to change places, roles and identities at will, quickly and painlessly – becomes the major, perhaps the paramount, stratifying factor elbowing out all or most orthodox factors of social inequality. To be unattached, unconstrained by place, ex-territorial, free to embrace any opportunity that comes one's way, is becoming nowadays the most coveted value, indeed a 'meta-value', the key to all other life-enhancing values. Accordingly, immobilisation – the state of being tied to the place, irrevocably defined and barred from moving – turns into the most salient symptom of ultimate deprivation and incapacitation and so also into the harshest form of punishment and pain infliction of which the 'liquid modern' mind can conceive. Nothing conveys the reassuring message that 'crime has been duly punished' as convincingly as the stories of thick walls, heavily armed guards and electronic surveillance. The certainty of staying put is seen, and made to be seen, as the ultimate, the most disastrous of disasters that may befall the denizen of the 'liquid modern' society. By comparison, the discomforts and inconveniences of uncertain, insecure and risk-fraught life on the move seem but minor irritants one can live with happily, perhaps even ever after.

References

Bauman, Z. (2000) *Liquid Modernity*. Cambridge: Polity Press.

Beck, U. (1992) *Risk Society: Towards a New Modernity*. London: Sage.

Butler, S. (1998) *Erewhon*, Amherst, NY: Prometheus Books.

Christie, N. (2000) *Crime Control as Industry: Towards Gulag Western Style* (3rd edn). London: Routledge.

Gans, H.J. (1995) *The War Against the Poor: The Underclass and Antipoverty in America*. New York: Basic Books.

Garapon, A. and Salas, D. (eds) (1997) *La Justice et le mal*, Paris: Éditions Odile Jacob.

Girling, E., Loader, I. and Sparks, R. (2000) *Crime and Social Change in Middle England: Questions of Order in an English Town*. London: Routledge.

Matza, D. (1969) *Becoming Deviant*. Englewood Cliffs, NJ: Prentice Hall.

Mead, L.M. (1992) *The New Politics of Poverty: The Nonworking Poor in America*. New York: Basic Books.

Rorty, R. (1988) *Achieving Our Country*. Cambridge, MA: Harvard University Press.

Sudnow, D. (1965) Normal crimes: sociological features of the penal code in a Public defender office. *Social Problems*, 3: 255–68.

United Nations (1993) *Crime Trends and Criminal Justice Operation at the Regional and Interregional Levels*. Rome: United Nations Publication.

Wacquant, L. (1999) *Les Prisons de la misère*. Paris: Éditions Liber, Raison d'Agir.

Young, J. (1999) *The Exclusive Society: Social Exclusion, Crime and Difference in Late Modernity*. London: Sage.

Zukin, S. (1995) *The Culture of Cities*. Oxford: Blackwell.

Part 2
The governance of crime and insecurity across Europe

Chapter 3

Fighting organised crime: The European Union and internal security

G. Wyn Rees and Mark Webber

The changing nature of security in Europe

'Security' has many different connotations. Taken here to be a concept central to both the practice and study of international relations, its meaning has traditionally been associated with threats of a largely military nature; military threats, that is, directed against the state and against which the state has been obliged to respond with strong countermeasures such as armed defence, espionage, subversion and so on (Booth and Wheeler 1992: 4). In the post-1945 period this was a view of security that ran parallel to the reality and practices of the Cold War. Although a contest with a strong ideological flavour and one, moreover, which pitted two quite different systems of social organisation one against the other, the Cold War's most pressing material component was that of the nuclear arms race – and this, in turn, effectively narrowed the security agenda to military matters (Buzan 1997: 6).

This is not to say that other ways of looking at security were entirely absent. Even such a stalwart of the traditional agenda as Henry Kissinger was moved to argue in the mid-1970s that for the USA and the West more generally issues of energy, the environment and population were of increasing relevance (Salmon 1992: 1–2).

With somewhat more conviction, international opinion-forming bodies such as the Palme Commission reported in the early 1980s that a state-centric and military focus was damaging to broader economic and social concerns. 'Alternative' defence thinking and forms of protest at a renewed militarisation of the Cold War (in the shape of new nuclear deployments in Europe by NATO and Warsaw Pact states) also gained ground at this time. In the academic world, meanwhile, the beginnings of an intellectual reconsideration of security was in motion that sought to validate a broader notion of threat both in terms of its subject (i.e. non-military sources) and its object (i.e. individuals and international society rather than just states) (Tickner 1995: 181–2).

These incipient conceptual shifts were not, however, initially reflected in the practice of security in Europe's international relations. Only with the winding down of the Cold War in the latter half of the 1980s was there a marked move away from strictly military preoccupations amongst national governments. The Soviet leader Mikhail Gorbachev can be rightly regarded as at the forefront of this process. However self-serving his 'new political thinking' may have been, there is no doubt it amounted to a revolutionary departure in Soviet foreign policy in its emphasis on political rather than military routes to security. The concessions this generated on the part of Moscow helped inaugurate a substantial process of demilitarisation in Europe. This removed the threat of great-power war on the continent (a trend compounded by the dissolution of the Warsaw Pact and Soviet state itself in 1991) and thus fundamentally altered the salience of the military issue among political elites in Europe, both East and West. That said, there were, of course, considerable variations of national position. Debate was joined on issues revolving around the most appropriate institutional configuration of European security, the long-term future of Cold War alliances such as NATO, the relevance of nuclear weapons (particularly sensitive in the UK) and the emergence of subregional (as opposed to continent-wide) conflicts (Hyde-Price 1992).

The last of these issues came increasingly to frame the policy debate. Those conflicts that emerged, consequent upon the end of the Cold War in the former Yugoslavia and parts of the former USSR, seemed to some to vindicate an essentially traditional approach to security premised upon issues of war and peace, life and death. These conflicts were, however, quite unlike the ideological-cum-military rivalry of the Cold War, having their roots in what were essentially domestic (as opposed to externally driven) conditions of economic collapse, ethnic mobilisation and post-communist political fragmentation. As such, there was a widespread recognition that the nature of security threat had fundamentally altered.[1]

How significant this shift has been is apparent if one considers NATO, an organisation once considered the very acme of traditional security thinking. Meeting in Rome in November 1991, the alliance heads of state and government issued a *New Strategic Concept*, a document intended to reflect new 'security challenges and risks'. This did not make a full break with the notion of armed military threats and to this extent it retained deterrence and defence as a core NATO mission. The strategic concept did, however, point to a revised policy agenda through its references to the 'multifaceted' nature of risks and the need of the alliance to pursue dialogue and co-operation in order to manage a security environment that has 'political, economic, social, [and] environmental elements' as well as those relating to the 'defence dimension' (NATO 1991). The subsequent evolution of NATO documentation tended to reflect this new frame of reference. Meeting in Washington in April 1999, NATO leaders issued a communiqué outlining NATO's rationale as *An Alliance for the 21st Century*. This referred to partnership (with non-members) and crisis management as well as deterrence and defence as amongst the alliance's 'fundamental security tasks'. The updated strategic concept, meanwhile, listed a number of fairly orthodox threats (nuclear proliferation, the spillover of local conflicts and the possibility of a large-scale conventional military threat in the 'longer term') but in a much more explicit fashion than its predecessor noted the potential problems posed by so-called 'soft security' issues (NATO 1999a, 1999b). Consonant with these changes the militaries of NATO member states have been both reconfigured and downsized and have embraced new missions of peace-keeping and conflict prevention.

This broader understanding of security has also been played out elsewhere. The shift away from a notion of security premised on conventional military threats and instruments has brought to greater attention bodies once seen as marginal or irrelevant to the traditional security agenda of the Cold War. Alongside NATO, these bodies suggest the nascent development of 'security governance' in Europe. In this regard, the following are relevant:

• The EU has taken significant steps towards the development of a Common Foreign and Security Policy (CFSP). Reflecting a broadened agenda, the EU's Brussels European Council in October 1993 defined the security goals of the organisation as 'reducing risks and uncertainties which might endanger the territorial integrity and political independence of the Union and its member states, their democratic character, their economic stability and the stability of neighbouring regions'(cited in Carr 1996: 382). Further, the Western European Union (WEU) under a 1991 declaration expressed the aim of becoming 'the defence component of the European Union' (cited in Hill and Smith 2000: 202) and the European Councils in Cologne in June 1999 and Helsinki in December 1999 formalised the Common European Security and Defence Policy (CESDP) in order to undertake conflict prevention and management tasks. The EU has also aspired towards a role in post-conflict efforts in the former Yugoslavia (the Balkan Stability Pact) and, more generally, it has been crucial in determining the shape of a political and economic order in Europe. This order, in turn, has security implications in that it has helped to all but eliminate inter-state rivalry among EU member states and has created incentives for peaceable behaviour among aspirant members (Laffan *et al.* 1999: 45–50).

- The Organisation for Security and Co-operation in Europe (OSCE) is, on paper, the organisation par excellence for promoting broad security in Europe. It has established a niche in the areas of conflict prevention and management and post-conflict stabilisation, as well as providing a forum since 1994 for discussions on the elaboration of a 'Common and Comprehensive Security Model' and a 'Document-Charter of European Security' (adopted in 1999), and for the implementation of a variety of Europe-wide Confidence and Security Building Measures (CSBMs). The OSCE also represents a normative basis for European order through the articulation of a variety of principles of interstate behaviour and, increasingly, of behaviour within states. The organisation lacks any real powers of enforcement in these regards and its initiatives often reflect the necessities of bland consensus amongst its large membership. However, its influence should not be underestimated (Serbia/Montenegro was suspended from OSCE membership in 1992 and OSCE channels have been used to criticise human rights violations in Chechnya, Kosovo and elsewhere).

- The Council of Europe, a body with a clear west European flavour during the Cold War, has reorientated its political purposes towards the political integration of former communist states. In so doing, it has elaborated the notion of 'democratic security' as a political route to regional stability (Tarschys 1997).

- Subregional initiatives have also flourished. Some of these claim quite explicit alliance-type security functions (the parties to the Collective Security Treaty of the Russian-dominated Commonwealth of Independent States (CIS)) or involve other aspects of military co-operation such as peace-keeping, training and joint exercises (the 'GUUAM' group). A number, however, have undertaken contacts in 'non-traditional' security areas relating to international crime, terrorism, environmental concerns and so on (e.g. the Black Sea Economic Co-operation grouping) (Bremmer and Bailes 1998).

The conceptual and organisational changes in security in Europe's international relations do not necessarily mean that the states and peoples of the continent have enjoyed a greater margin of safety in the post-Cold War period. Indeed, the very fact of a broadened notion of security implies not an amelioration of the condition of insecurity but only an alteration in the source of the threat. Thus, while all who reside in Europe may have been freed (for now) from the existential danger of nuclear conflagration, this danger has for many in the former communist part of Europe been replaced by a series of much more intense and urgent threats to survival and well-being such as ethnic cleansing, political breakdown and economic impoverishment (Wæver *et al.* 1993). Certain more traditional interstate rivalries have also survived: for much of the 1990s Serbia posed a threat to Bosnia's fragile sovereignty; the same has also been true of Russia's position with regard to the Baltic states; and of similar historical pedigree, Greece and Turkey have continued to regard one another with suspicion despite their common membership of NATO. Even in the security (or 'non-war') community of Europe's western half threats abound (Wæver 1998). These are as much about changed perceptions as they are about objective reality.[2] The relative comfort provided by a decades-long absence of interstate war, the successful quarantining of separatist violence (as in Northern Ireland and the Basque country) from external linkages and, more recently, the removal of the adversarial relationship with Soviet communism have meant the projection of anxieties about external developments to political, economic, environmental and social objects rather than straightforwardly military ones. In many instances, these fears play well with a domestic political agenda. Hence, the claim made – among the political right in the UK particularly (Redwood 1997) – that European integration constitutes a 'threat' to the nation-state.

These examples suggest that security and insecurity in Europe are differentiated in so far as the range, intensity and urgency of threats vary considerably. That said, the end of the Cold War has meant an increased interdependence of security such that developments in one part of the continent now invariably have repercussions much further afield. While the boundary that once demarcated the eastern and western halves of Europe has not disappeared, its new manifestation as a legal-political and socioeconomic frontier is much more porous. Security problems in Europe's eastern half can consequently transmute and travel across this border. To take an obvious example, political instability and civil war in the former Yugoslavia have both pulled in other parts of Europe (military intervention and peace-keeping by NATO with the active support of a number of non-NATO Balkan states) as well as pushing outwards security-relevant challenges such as raised levels of migration and refugees. This is, of course, an extreme case, but the connectedness of security in post-Cold War Europe has, in fact, been manifest in other more prosaic, discrete but none the less pervasive ways. Of no small consequence in this regard is the issue of transnational organised crime (TOC).

Crime and the new security agenda in Europe

Just as with the concept of security, discussion of TOC is replete with ambiguities of meaning. There is some dispute over exactly how the phenomenon should be defined: for example, the number of persons that need to be involved in a criminal activity and for what length of time. Similarly, there are differences of view over whether a hierarchical structure needs to be present, whether violence has to be employed and whether the motive is merely to secure profit or to seek power (Politi 1997: 5).

As for the activities that constitute transnational crime, this has also been an area for contestation. The traditional focus of concern has been upon categories of illegal goods such as the trafficking of narcotics and the stealing and smuggling of military weapons. More recently, attention has been focused on the laundering of large amounts of money and the trafficking in human beings. Analysts such as Petrus van Duyne (1996a: 54–5), meanwhile, have argued in favour of an approach that would also include legitimate goods and services that are procured illegally. This would have the effect of including a much wider range of economic activity.

Some debate also exists over the causes and extent of TOC. Discussion of the former is now extensive and a considerable body of opinion sees the heightened risk of TOC as a phenomenon primarily of the last two decades. There are both European and global dimensions to this. In the European context transnational crime has been an outgrowth of two separate developments. The first concerns the demise of communism and its domestic and geopolitical/geoeconomic consequences. Crime was not, of course, invented by the process of post-communist transition; this condition has, however, encouraged the growth and spread of criminal activity. Certain forms of crime were, in fact, much in evidence throughout the communist period. The deficiences of planned economies in the USSR and East-Central Europe (ECE) had resulted in the establishment of black-market activity aimed at freeing up the production and supply of goods and services otherwise in shortage. A good deal of this was tolerated by the authorities. However, the strong surveillance and policing functions of communist states inhibited the organisational development of crime and hampered also the diversification of criminal activities. The presence of strong borders, meanwhile, prevented individuals and groups in communist states from being involved in those activities, such as money-laundering, which relied on transnational connections (Shelley 1999: 20–2).

The overthrow of the pro-Moscow regimes left in its wake a region characterised by political and societal transition and economic decline. The new governments were encouraged by the West to undertake a process of rapid market-led reform, the privatisation of state-controlled enterprises and the convertibility of their currencies. Yet this opened up new opportunities for exploitation by criminals and by the former communist elites, who alone had the ability to access large amounts of capital. The broader social effects of economic liberalisation resulted in large impoverished sections of the population being willing to engage in criminal activities or vulnerable to criminal coercion and inducement. The ability of post-communist states to counter these various activities, meanwhile, has been blunted by both the disruptive effects of restructuring systems of criminal justice and the inadequate resourcing of law enforcement at a time of economic stringency (Shelley 1995: 484).

Of course, there have been variations in this pattern of development. Russia and the Ukraine seem to be cases of particular note given the profundity of post-communist transformation and the criminal consequences that have ensued (Galeotti 1999). Organised crime gangs from Russia, Chechnya and Georgia have been particularly prominent and have been able to spread their activities beyond their host states and to form alliances with crime groups located in the West. The Balkan region is also worth highlighting. Here the transition from communism has been attended by civil war, as in the former Yugoslavia, or a near total collapse of civic order, such as in Albania. These situations of state lawlessness have empowered organised crime groups: Kosovars and Albanians have, since the early 1990s, been active in the transhipment of illicit drugs into Europe via the notorious 'Balkan route', and have organised the smuggling of small arms and illegal migrants (into Italy in particular) (Cilluffo and Salmoiraghi 1999).

The Balkan example illustrates well the second development in the European context of TOC, namely, the opening up of borders. This has occurred in two senses. First, the dismantling of the militarised frontiers that formerly separated the communist states from western Europe; and, secondly, the establishment by the mid-1990s of open borders among EU member states consequent upon the provisions of the Single European Act 1986. It was widely recognised that the Single European Act would increase the vulnerability of western European states to crime due to the complexity of its regulatory regime and the plethora of police forces that were expected to co-operate with one another. Drug trafficking was already known to be on the increase and freedom of movement across the territory of the EU offered criminal groups the potential to conduct their illegal activities on a transnational basis. Although the member states sought to impose an impermeable border between EU and non-EU states, to counterbalance the abolition of internal border controls, this has in no way acted as a fully effective barrier to the collusion and movement of criminal networks or to the trafficking of drugs or economic migrants (Bruinsma 1999: 7–17).

A final area of contention is over the extent of the TOC problem in Europe. Certainly, there is a considerable amount of data that seemingly confirms the rise of a major threat. Interpol figures, for instance, suggest that by the end of the 1990s approximately 1,000 Russian crime groups were operating internationally (Gilligan 1999). Kersten (1999: 71), the head of the German Federal Criminal Police, has suggested similarly that 830 organised criminal gangs were operating in Germany. These gangs were responsible for some 45,000 crimes within the country and 75% of this number involved a transnational link. As for migration, estimates of 'clandestine immigrants' entering the EU had reached a figure of between 3.5 and 5.5. million by 1995 (Benyon 1996: 356). A good deal of this is deemed to be criminally organised (Kusovac 2000) and the German newspaper *Die Welt* claimed in June 1998 that criminal cartels working in Russia, Belarus and elsewhere in the former USSR were earning collectively the equivalent of $5 billion from the proceeds of human trafficking, utilising routes through the Balkans, the Baltic states and thence to western Europe and North America (cited in Bort 2000: 13).

Estimates of the extent of transnational crime are not, however, without their problems (see Goodey this volume). They are often based on data that are collected from a variety of national sources, many of which classify crimes in different ways. Such estimates also often rely upon extrapolations from known crimes to arrive at unreliable statistics of the extent of undetected criminal activity (Hebenton and Thomas 1995: 154–6; Gill and Edwards 1999: 17). Further, the interpretation of data is not just a technical matter but also a political issue. Without doubt, there has been a political awakening to the issue of TOC during the last decade. In 1994, for instance, the first UN World Ministerial Conference on Organised Crime took place in Naples. This meeting issued a 'Political Declaration and Global Action Plan' that was informed by the premise that certain transnational crimes – terrorism, money-laundering, drug trafficking and corruption – posed 'a threat to the international security and stability of states' (cited in Gregory 1998: 134). Longer-standing UN forums also began to devote more attention to these issues. The UN Congress on Crime and the Treatment of Offenders, meeting at its ninth session in Cairo in 1995, adopted a headline resolution that referred to the threat to 'the internal security and stability of sovereign states' posed by TOC.[3] At its tenth session in Vienna in April 2000, similarly, it issued a 'Declaration on Crime and Justice: Meeting the Challenges of the Twenty-first Century' that sought to highlight the 'impact on our societies of the commission of serious crimes of a global nature' and the consequent need for international co-operation (UN Congress on Crime and the Treatment of Offenders 2000).

In addition to recognising the unreliability of statistics on TOC, it is also worth noting the forces that can conspire to exaggerate its significance. Two influences are worthy of mention – processes of 'politicisation' and 'securitisation'. The first refers to a tendency towards the manipulation of crime issues for political ends. It has been argued, for instance, that the prominence given to the agenda of TOC reflects, in part, the instrumental demands (the desire for greater resources and facilities) of national law enforcement agencies and, in part, the more overtly political desire of some national governments and European organisations to promote the political integration of the continent (Benyon 1996: 370–1). This type of move, moreover, can serve other political ends. A greater attention to the external sources of crime may be seen to absolve national agencies of part of the responsibility for tackling its more localised manifestations. One illustration of this is the attention given to the international sources of the supply of drugs rather than to the domestic socioeconomic conditions that generate demand (Hobbs 1998: 139–40).

As for securitisation, this has a rather specific meaning, at least in the academic field. For Barry Buzan and others (1998: 23–6), securitisation is the process by which something is presented as a threat and by which extraordinary measures are permitted in response. The manner in which the security agenda of post-Cold War Europe has altered suggests a securitising search for external enemies to replace the ideological and military threats of Soviet communism (den Boer 1997: 492). It would be too crude to suggest that this process of threat creation has been an explicit, cogent and well articulated political enterprise. Rather, it is part of an unfolding, sometimes contested, narrative search. This is a narrative that is broader than security alone; it reflects also the politics of identity in Europe. In western Europe, the end of communism upset the traditional distinctions between Europe's western and eastern halves – and if identity is premised on juxtaposition ('self' versus 'other') then this alteration has had disorientating effects (Hyde-Price 2000). In this light, emphasising the threat of TOC plays the function previously served by emphasising the menace posed by communism. In western Europe at least it is the 'other' against which identity ('self') can be framed.

Transnational organised crime and the EU

Organisations such as NATO and the WEU have sought to respond to the broadened security agenda in Europe. They have faced post-conflict situations where they have been required to conduct peace-keeping and societal reconstruction efforts that have brought them into contact with the problems posed by organised crime. For example, the WEU orchestrated a police effort in the Bosnian city of Mostar and subsequently undertook a police support operation in Albania from 1996. For its part, NATO has conducted large-scale peace-keeping operations such as the Implementation Forces (IFOR) and Stabilisation Forces (SFOR) in Bosnia. During the Kosovo conflict, NATO came into contact with the Albanian Mafia, which were estimated to be smuggling around 10,000 refugees per month into western Europe (Cilluffo and Salmoiraghi 1999: 22).

Neither NATO nor the WEU, however, have been capable of reinventing themselves fully since the end of the Cold War. Their member governments have regarded their core military functions to be too important to dilute amidst an increasingly unstable and turbulent continent. As a result, apart from acknowledging the existence of a broader security agenda, neither organisation has been in a position to establish a new model of European security governance in relation to TOC. Whilst NATO has paid lip-service to the need to embrace a security agenda that goes beyond military security issues, its structure has rendered it an inappropriate forum in which to deal with soft security. In its 1999 strategic concept, the alliance declared its 'security interests can be affected by other risks of a wider nature, including acts of terrorism, sabotage and organised crime' (NATO 1999a:D9) – but, in practice, NATO has concentrated upon its traditional security functions.

Other organisations, such as the Council of Europe, have also been incapable of undertaking such a role, albeit for different reasons. The Council of Europe has, through specialist working groups and ministerial fora, dedicated considerable attention to the problem of TOC, particularly in relation to the problems of democratic consolidation in ECE states. In the final declaration of its second summit meeting in Strasbourg in October 1997, the Council of Europe (1997) referred to 'the concern of citizens about the new dimension of threats to their security' including the threats of 'terrorism...corruption, organised crime and drug trafficking throughout Europe'. Nevertheless, the Council of Europe has lacked an operational capability to act against organised crime. In addition, the diverse membership of the Council of Europe has resulted in a cautious attitude being shown by its leading western states. It has focused its energies on establishing European-wide norms and values, particularly over the issue of adherence to the rule of law.

Only one organisation, the EU, has been organisationally placed to shift attention from the 'macro security' concerns of the Cold War to the myriad 'micro-security' challenges posed by a range of lesser, more diffuse threats (Grabbe 2000: 320). This has been due to its unique array of strengths. First, the EU has enjoyed a sense of legitimacy in the sphere of non-traditional security, derived from its history as a 'civilian power'. Unlike NATO or the WEU, it was never an organisation that was configured around military security functions. When the Cold War ended, the Union did not have fundamentally to adapt its core functions in order to assume this new role. Secondly, the fact that the EU has always been founded upon a clear legal base has made it well suited to combating transnational threats to the European legal order. Thirdly, the very complexity of the EU, with its system of multi-level governance, has enabled it to respond flexibly to new types of challenges. It was evident from an early stage that the problems of TOC could not be overcome simply by one European organisation arrogating to itself responsibility for this issue; considerations of national sovereignty and the problems of legitimacy would have made such a solution politically unacceptable. The EU offers opportunities for functional development yet retains important intergovernmental processes of decision-making. It has, therefore, been well placed to respond to the challenges of TOC while at the same time enabling its member states scope for bargaining over the powers and responsibilities necessary to delegate to the union for this purpose.

The rationale for the EU to assume a competence in the field of combating transnational crime has long been established. All the governments of the EU have recognised the growing threat from TOC on the continent, even if there have been differences of opinion over the scale of the problem. UK Prime Minister Tony Blair, speaking in 1998, declared that '[o]rganised crime is a global threat...such crimes pose a threat not only to our own citizens and communities...[they] can undermine the democratic and economic basis of [whole] societies' (cited in Zijlstra 1998: para. 2). Similarly, amongst those states seeking accession to the EU, there has been a recognition of the risks posed by organised crime groups. The Polish President Aleksander Kwasniewski (1996) argued in a speech to the UN General Assembly in 1996 that crime confronts the entire 'international community' and poses a threat to the 'material and institutional foundations' of '[all] our societies'.

Such risks have also been appreciated by EU citizens. Crime has ranked amongst the major concerns of European populations, according to opinion polls (69% of respondents named drugs and crime as their foremost concerns in a poll in 1996) (Eurobarometer 45, 1996, cited in European Commission 1997: 4), and the EU's willingness to address the problem is perceived to increase its relevance in the eyes of the public.

In order to combat crime, the case for co-operation has been indisputable. The sharing of intelligence information about criminal groups operating across the territories of the member states and the ability of police forces to work together have become vitally necessary to apprehend criminals. Yet the need to co-operate has not ended there. Securing actual prosecutions, when criminal activity may have been perpetrated across several legal jurisdictions, has demanded the admissibility of evidence between national judicial systems as well as the willingness of courts to respect judicial decisions from neighbouring states. It was widely acknowledged that organised crime was operating fluidly across national frontiers and that law enforcement activities had to learn to do the same if they were to keep pace with the problem.

In spite of widespread recognition by EU members of the need for co-operation against TOC, there have been many complex obstacles to overcome. The most salient has been the historical importance attached to internal security as a core area of national sovereignty. Some member states, particularly those with an inherent scepticism of the integration process, have been reluctant to relinquish national control over internal security matters. These states have feared that the integration dynamic could be advanced through this policy area and consequently have opposed the transfer of more wide-ranging powers to the institutions of the union. Thus in the 1993 (Maastricht) Treaty on European Union, Pillar III on 'Justice and Home Affairs' (JHA) was created but it was made strictly intergovernmental in nature (see Lodge this volume). The subsequent Treaty of Amsterdam (1997) witnessed a 'communitarisation' of some areas of JHA activity, namely, in asylum, immigration and external border control policies, which were moved to the European Community Pillar (Pillar I), under a new Title IV. Issues relating to police and judicial co-operation were not communitarised and were retained under the Third Pillar, new Title VI.

A secondary problem has been the varied historical experience of organised crime amongst the EU member states. Italy, for instance, considers itself a special case owing to the long-running battle between its law enforcement agencies and the Mafia. Further, the threat from TOC impacts unevenly across the continent. Some regions, such as those contiguous to southeastern Europe and the Balkans (Austria, Germany, Greece and Italy) feel particularly vulnerable – after all, this part of Europe is the dominant route for the trafficking of drugs and also for the smuggling of illegal aliens into the territory of the EU.

This diversity has helped to condition the responses of the member states towards TOC. It has also contributed to difficulties of measurement and definition (thus reflecting the more general difficulties in these areas already noted above). That said, determining the extent of the crime problem has, to some extent, been resolved within the EU by the production of annual assessments by the European Police Office, drawn from the inputs of national governments. The problem of agreeing upon a definition of organised crime has proven more difficult to resolve. The EU's Ad Hoc Group on Organised Crime did arrive at a working definition in 1993, but a report by the Multidisciplinary Committee on Organised Crime at the end of 1999 noted that of the eleven criteria agreed upon by the member states as characteristics of organised crime activity, four were problematic and subject to differences of interpretation (Council of the European Union 1999).

The EU model of internal security

The EU's model of internal security has arisen in response to perceptions of an increasing threat to the Union from organised crime. The EU has recognised its vulnerability as a region in which there is free movement of goods, services, money and people within the boundaries of the single market. Organised crime exploits this situation and involves itself in the creation of illicit markets as well as the penetration of legitimate ones. The inherent flexibility of crime structures, moreover, has made it difficult for law enforcement agencies to take counteractive measures.

The EU's internal security strategy comprises two strands. The first has been the creation of a hard external border for the union, built around the Schengen provisions. In the 1980s, the internal borders between member states were dismantled in favour of a common external frontier in which a rigorous system of checks was imposed on those seeking entry. This system facilitated greater co-operation between the Schengen participants on countering drug trafficking and various forms of crime. The threat that was perceived to emanate from organised crime in neighbouring states increased the desire to make this common Union frontier difficult to breach. The Amsterdam Treaty incorporated the Schengen *acquis* into the union. The special Tampere European Council, organised under the Finnish Presidency (15–16 October 1999), announced that the union needed to provide for 'the consistent control of external borders to stop illegal immigration and to combat those who organise it and commit related international crimes' (European Council 1999a: para. 3). The effect of these initiatives has been dramatically to expand the competence of the EU in matters relating to border controls. It has also led to common visa arrangements and the importation of a range of enforcement measures into the EU.

The Schengen system itself reflects a perception that immigration from the south and east of Europe poses a significant threat to the internal stability of the EU and that the movement of peoples has been increasingly subject to criminal organisation. In fact, the EU has pursued a staged policy by which immigration has, in essence, become 'criminalised' (see Albrecht this volume). This has occurred even though much migration is both legitimate (asylum seeking and permitted forms of work-based migration) and beneficial (through transfers of skilled and other labour) to the host state (Grabbe 2000: 322–3), and despite the fact that immigrants into the EU are often as much the victims of crime as its perpetrators. True, some illegal migrants are involved in criminal activity once they arrive in their target state – albeit at probably much lower levels than is often feared in the public imagination (Bort 2000: 9–16). Equally, however, large numbers may be fleeing crimes committed against them in their home state, such as in the case of refugees from Kosovo, or have been coerced into an unwanted lifestyle (for instance, women from the former communist countries working in pornography and prostitution in EU states).

In this light, the EU has been forced to balance considerations of internal security with the need to safeguard human rights, particularly in relation to those people it might be excluding from its territory. This reflects, in part, criticisms that the EU has attempted to create a 'Fortress

Europe' to keep at bay what the organisation construes to be malign external influences. Numerous civil liberties and refugee support groups have criticised the EU for concentrating on measures to discourage immigration into the EU and for cutting down the number of successful asylum applications (Amnesty International 2000). The EU, for its part, has claimed its emphasis on fighting crime and countering illegal immigration does not prejudice the rights of genuine asylum seekers and the ability of families of third-country nationals to emigrate into the EU. This has proven to be a difficult circle to square. EU co-operation in the area of internal security has tended to result in the ratcheting up of measures among the countries to reflect the standards of the most robust exponent. For example, the ratification in 1997 of the Dublin convention on asylum and immigration has stiffened the system of extradition for some EU states. Similarly, the introduction of a common visa system under the Schengen arrangements has ended a privileged relationship that existed hitherto between Latin American and Iberian states (Bort 2000: 3).

The second strand of the EU's strategy on internal security has been co-operation amongst the member states in countering crime that occurs on the territory of the union itself. The EU has recognised that organised crime is more than just an external threat: rather, it is a phenomenon that has long existed within the territories of union members. A Council report in March 2000 accepted that, although crime from outside the EU was growing, 'it is the groups that originate and operate throughout Europe, composed predominantly of EU nationals and residents, that appear to pose the significantly greater threat' (Council of the European Union 2000: 6). This view has resulted in co-operation between national police forces and mutual assistance between countries in matters of civil and criminal law. The Treaty of Amsterdam declared the aim of creating an 'area of freedom, security and justice', thereby acknowledging that the issues of freedom of movement and a secure domestic environment were intertwined. The European Council at Tampere stated there must be '[a] balanced development of union-wide measures against crime...while protecting the freedom and legal rights of individuals and economic operators' (European Council 1999a: para. 40). The right to freedom of movement and the well-being of citizens within the member states had to be safeguarded from threats such as transnational crime.

The EU's model of internal security has not emerged according to a specific blueprint advanced by the Commission or a particular member state. Rather, it has developed incrementally and in an ad hoc fashion, as the need to co-operate over specific problems has been recognised.

Nevertheless, what is presently emerging is a European security regime that will represent a model for the entire continent. This is partly because there exists no organisation in Europe that is capable of constructing an alternative to that of the EU. It is also because the inherent power and influence of the EU act as a platform for its initiatives towards the rest of the continent.

For their part, many of the applicant states have become worried by the ambitious JHA hurdles they are expected to jump before being granted entry to the Union. The ECE countries are effectively being presented with an EU internal security model they must swallow in its entirety – no meaningful input into this model, to reflect their particular concerns, is being proffered. In addition, the aspirant states are aware this area of the EU *acquis communautaire* is dynamic and growing all the time. This raises the problem of entry criteria becoming increasingly demanding and those countries currently involved in accession negotiations have to be aware that the legal provisions under JHA are a constantly expanding domain.

The implications for accession states will be considerable. Accepting the JHA and Schengen *acquis* will require of them wide-ranging changes. It will involve alterations to their domestic legislation, the modification of administrative and judicial structures, the training of personnel in the police and customs services and the purchase of new equipment. All this will be very expensive for countries that are comparatively poor and, as a result, they have looked to EU governments for financial assistance. They have also been expected to prepare for membership of the Europol Convention and have been encouraged to appoint liaison officers with the organisation. In order to ensure the ECE states comply with the EU regime, a Pre-Accession Pact on matters relating to organised crime was established by the Union in the spring of 1998. The pact linked the accession states with the EU's own action plan on organised crime, and was intended to ensure these states had achieved significant steps in implementing the EU *acquis* prior to membership. In June 1998 a Collective Evaluation Group was enacted by the Commission to monitor progress.

In addition to the applicant states, the Union has also reached out to geographically peripheral non-members. Norway and Iceland have accepted key elements of the Schengen regime in order to preserve the special relationships in internal security affairs they have enjoyed with their EU neighbours. Governments in these two states have been determined to maintain the passport-free status between Nordic states, embodied in the 1957 Nordic Passport Union, in spite of the EU membership of Sweden, Finland and Denmark. Thus, as a result of the Treaty of Amsterdam, they were forced to enact key elements of the Schengen provisions (Monar 2000a: 135) – and they did so without having any substantive input into the shaping of these measures. The EU has been able to export its internal security regime without having to compromise.

Things have been somewhat more problematic with regard to Russia and the Ukraine, both of whom the EU has tried to draw into virtuous patterns of co-operation. Of particular significance here have been efforts to improve Russian border controls to combat drug trafficking and procedures to limit the extent of money-laundering through the Russian banking sector. Through such activities, EU ideas and practices have been disseminated throughout the wider Europe.

The development of EU mechanisms to fight TOC

As noted above, the Treaty of Amsterdam marked the occasion on which the EU began to develop a range of mechanisms with which to fight TOC. Yet there remained problems as some topics straddled the boundary between Pillar I and Pillar III. For example, whilst issues related to EC budget fraud were placed within the competence of the Community, the tools for combating fraud, such as extradition, remain within old Title VI, under Pillar III (Monar 2000b: 147–48). Other issues have witnessed the intrusion of intergovernmental features into communitarised areas of activity. This was a price it was regarded as necessary to pay. For instance, qualified majority voting was not extended to asylum and immigration matters and the principle of unanimity was preserved. This can be changed after five years but only if all member states agree. Furthermore, the Commission was granted for a five-year period, only a non-exclusive right of initiative, along with the member states, and limitations were also placed on the role of the European Court of Justice. The European Parliament, meanwhile, was allowed only to be consulted on these new measures for the five-year period and co-decision would only be extended after that time if the member states agree unanimously.

There have thus been political impediments to EU-wide co-operation. However, as with much else in the EU, a functionalist logic of co-operation has often compensated for political laxity. Police co-operation is a good example. One of the principal mechanisms for improving the EU's capacity to prevent, analyse and investigate organised crime has been the development of the European Police Office (Europol) in The Hague. The concept of Europol grew out of its forerunner, the European Drugs Unit, which was created to share intelligence information in the fight against continental drug trafficking. The EU has never been able to agree upon the precise objectives for the organisation; whether it will remain a body that facilitates information sharing amongst its members and lends assistance to actual investigations, or whether it is to be the kernel of a European federal police bureau of a type that Chancellor Helmut Kohl of Germany foresaw in 1991. Its current modest size renders any grand ambitions for the organisation little more than a pipe dream, although Europol has been growing over the last few years at a prodigious rate.

The Europol Convention did not enter into force until October 1998 and only in the summer of the following year did the organisation become operationally effective. The momentum that has built up behind Europol in a short period of time has been impressive. It demonstrates a recognition, among EU members, of the need for a body to co-ordinate the distribution of information on criminal matters across the continent. Although the majority of inquiries to Europol still relate to drugs – in 1999 some 58% were drug related (Europol 1999) – its remit has been expanded to include action against currency forgery, child pornography and measures to protect vulnerable professions (European Council 1998). Europol was also given responsibility for targeting traffickers in human beings and the Tampere European Council increased the priority of this objective (European Council 1999a: para. 23). A particular emphasis was placed on curbing the rising trend of victims from ECEs and on dismantling the criminal networks involved. Thus, for example, between January and September 1998, over 650 criminals involved in the trade in human beings were arrested at the Czech and Slovak frontiers alone (Bort 2000: 7).

Europol will require some time to gain experience and for member states to become confident of sharing national information with the organisation. But there are already indications that Europol, along with its attendant national contact points, will grow into the hub of an intelligence system for the EU covering crime, drug trafficking and illegal immigration. From this foundation it becomes possible to see how a common continent-wide system for monitoring internal security is emerging. Two additional developments support this viewpoint. First, it has been agreed that Europol will have access to the database of the Schengen Information System (SIS, to be renamed the European Information System) and to the Eurodac database of fingerprints from asylum seekers seeking to enter the EU (den Boer 1997: 493). Access to the approximately 14 million records of the SIS and to Eurodac will accord Europol insight into both criminal and immigration matters. Secondly, in the Treaty of Amsterdam, Europol was given powers to conduct investigations and to support investigations carried out by joint teams between member states. This has begun the process by which the organisation will gain an operational capability.

It has been widely acknowledged amongst member states that co-operation between their police forces should not outstrip the capacity of their judicial structures to work together. This is an issue that relates not only to an ability to conduct prosecutions but also to the way in which investigations are pursued. There have been differences of view amongst member states over how best to promote judicial co-operation. On the one hand, all can agree on the need to ratify and implement accords on such topics as mutual legal assistance, expediting extradition and combating financial fraud through the Financial Action Task Force agreements. On the other hand, however, states have disagreed over the optimum means for pursuing future co-operation and they have held contradictory visions about the objectives to be realised.

The most ambitious vision has been to create a 'European Judicial Space'. Such a vision might involve the laws of member states being harmonised through a common criminal code and the development of a prosecuting authority for the whole of the continent. Prior to the Tampere Summit, France was in the vanguard of those states desirous of harmonising laws on TOC. But there was opposition from countries, such as the UK, who felt the so-called *Corpus Juris* project would be too complex and protracted. The British government advocated instead an approach by which governments would recognise the validity of each others' laws. This has been seen as an alternative approach and at Tampere it was agreed that '[e]nhanced mutual recognition of judicial decisions and judgements ...' would become 'the cornerstone of judicial co-operation in both civil and criminal matters' (European Council 1999a: para. 33).

Rather, then, than moving towards a European Judicial Space, the EU has pursued forms of sectoral and institutional co-operation. A priority in this regard has been co-operation against drug trafficking. In addition to well-known problems such as the importation of heroin from the 'golden triangle' of South East Asia and cocaine from South America, the EU has noted the growing danger posed by synthetic drugs. Such drugs are produced within the territory of the member states or originate in nearby external suppliers such as Poland (van Duyne 1996b). Overall, the EU has been compelled by a twofold concern. First, that the consumption of drugs within EU states has been growing[4] and secondly, that the problem is likely to be exacerbated when new ECE countries, with poorly policed borders, are admitted to the EU. The Union has pursued a strategy based upon four-year action plans, with a focus on demand and supply reduction, international co-operation, information sharing and curbs on the sale by member states of the chemical precursors employed in the production of illegal drugs (European Commission 1997: 6). The most recent action plan, the third, was endorsed at the Helsinki European Council and was launched in 2000.

As for institutional co-operation, this includes not only Europol but also initiatives such as the establishment of the European Judicial Network, following a joint action adopted in June 1998. This has been a modest initiative that has sought to enhance practical contacts between the existing judiciaries of the EU states. It has created points of contact so that judicial authorities know with whom they can liaise when an investigation takes on a transnational dimension. Furthermore, some member states have exchanged personnel who will reside within their ministries of justice and thereby facilitate close co-operation when prosecutions cut across national boundaries.

Another initiative worthy of mention is 'Eurojust', championed by the French and Belgian governments. Eurojust seeks to co-ordinate national prosecuting authorities and has a particular focus on TOC. This reflects the experience of abandoned prosecutions following problems derived from case complexity and multiple jurisdictions and legal systems. Eurojust will comprise a team of 15 prosecutors and magistrates to act as co-ordinators between different national investigating teams in particularly complex cases. Such people will be expert in their own national laws and will co-operate with other European authorities on multiple jurisdiction prosecutions. Real political commitment has been forthcoming in realising this project and an interim unit has been in operation in Brussels since the spring of 2001. At the time of writing it remains to be determined where the permanent offices of Eurojust will reside, but there has been a provisional agreement to base it in the Hague, alongside Europol. Through Eurojust attention has been devoted towards the creation of complementary national judicial networks rather than a single European system. Such national networks will be responsible for determining the acceptability of evidence, deciding where a prosecution is to occur and ensuring the protection of the rights of the accused.

The third pillar mechanisms for fighting TOC have come a long way since the signing of the Treaty on European Union. Jorge Monar (2000b:

143) has described the JHA provisions of the Maastricht Treaty as the 'Cinderella' of the EU as the instruments that were created, such as joint actions and common positions, were initially insufficient for the task. Since the entry into force of the treaty, the EU has made strenuous efforts to enhance the means and agencies at its disposal to counter the threat posed by TOC. No one could claim that the end of the road has been reached but, undeniably, significant progress has been achieved.

Conclusion

Amidst a security environment that has been transformed by the end of the Cold War, the EU has proved to be the only organisation with the legitimacy and the range of competencies to respond to a broadened array of security demands (Kröning 2000). The OSCE and, to some extent, NATO have both aspired to the elaboration and implementation of a comprehensive model of security but these have been hamstrung by conceptual, political or resource limitations. The EU's more holistic approach to security is one that has involved its elevation to the position of provider of order within what Laffan *et al* (1999:6) have referred to as 'a still unsettled Europe'. The development of this EU-led order brings in its wake, however, a central paradox. The language of the organisation has since the end of the Cold War been that of inclusion and this has also been true of many of its practices (Smith 1996: 20–3). The clear intention to enlarge along with policies of association (with ECE aspirants) and partnership (with former Soviet states such as Russia and the Ukraine) clearly reflect this. However, these practices result in an unavoidable exclusion. Enlargement, for instance, has developed as a differentiated process and it is clear there are favoured candidates among the states of ECE.

When the EU's first enlargement into post-communist Europe finally occurs (probably sometime around 2005) this exclusion will be further entrenched and will bring with it an obvious implication in the field of security and TOC. The implementation of Schengen provisions among the aspirant states has already created a 'lace curtain' between the 'pre-ins' and adjacent states (evident controversially, for instance, in a reinforcement of the Polish–Ukrainian and the Greek–Bulgarian borders). (*The Economist* 2000: 54; Hearst 2000: 16). As enlargement proceeds, the border between the EU and its former communist neighbours will increasingly take on the character of a crime frontier as the states with little chance of, or desire for, entry to the Union (Albania, Yugoslavia,

Ukraine and Russia) are at one and the same time also those states deemed to be among the main sources of its external destabilisation. There is no easy way of blurring this border. However, a major challenge for the EU will be that of meeting its own internal preoccupations – not least, the consolidation of the security space among its own member states – while at the same time recognising that the wider European setting in which this occurs is not something that is simply a source of threat or instability. A threat mentality, as we have noted, is present in the EU and the retreat into a 'fortress impulse' is possible under the Schengen regime and other forms of EU co-operation on crime (Batt 1999: 7). If this is to become a dominant trend then the comprehensive model of security offered by the EU would clearly be compromised. It would be relevant to its member states and those with a realistic possibility of membership, but of increasing irrelevance to the rest of Europe. The alternative is the extension and continuation of co-operation across the border – a trend also in evidence and one that is ultimately compatible with any realisation of the EU's vision of peace, prosperity and stability on the continent (European Council 1999b).

Notes

1. A similar shift in conceptual thinking was also in evidence in academic work. See in particular Buzan *et al* (1998).
2. We follow here the well-known distinction drawn by Arnold Wolfers (1962: 150) between security in an objective and subjective sense. The latter refers to fears or perceptions of threat that may exaggerate or misconstrue the true situation.
3. This resolution then lists *inter alia* terrorism, drug and arms trafficking, the smuggling of migrants and minors, currency forgery, motor vehicle theft, corruption, money-laundering and computer and telecommunications-related crime as indicative of the transnational criminal threat. See UN Congress on Crime and the Treatment of Offenders (1995).
4. The EU receives reports on the drug problem in western Europe from its European Monitoring Centre for Drugs and Addiction in Lisbon.

References

Amnesty International (2000) *A Common Asylum System for the EU: The International Regime for the Protection of Refugees at Stake?* London: Amnesty International.
Batt, J. (1999) *Final Report of the Reflection Group on the Long-Term Implications of EU Enlargement: The Nature of the New Border.* The Robert Schuman Centre for Advanced Studies/European University Institute and the Forward Studies Unit/ European Commission.

Benyon, J. (1996) The politics of police co-operation in the European Union. *International Journal of the Sociology of Law*, 24(4): 353–80.

Booth, K. and Wheeler, N. (1992) Contending philosophies about security in Europe. In C. McInnes (ed.) *Security and Strategy in the New Europe*. London and New York: Routledge.

Bort, E. (2000) *Illegal Migration and Cross-Border Crime: Challenges at the Eastern Frontier of the European Union. Working Paper* RSC 2000/9. Florence: European University Institute.

Bremmer, I. and Bailes, A. (1998) Sub-regionalism in the newly-independent states. *International Affairs*, 74(1): 131–48.

Bruinsma, G. J.N. (1999) Insecure future of Europe? In G.J.N. Bruinsma and C.D. van der Vijver (eds) *Public Safety in Europe*. Enschede, The Netherlands: International Police Institute, Twente.

Buzan, B. (1997) Rethinking Security after the Cold War. *Co-operation and Conflict*, 32(1): 5–28.

Buzan, B., Wæver, O. and de Wilde, J. (1998) *Security. A New Framework for Analysis*. Boulder, CO, and London: Lynne Rienner.

Carr, F. (1996) The new security politics in Europe. *International Journal of the Sociology of Law*, 24(4): 381–98.

Cilluffo, F. and Salmoiraghi, G. (1999) And the winner is . . . the Albanian Mafia. *The Washington Quarterly*, 22(4): 21–5.

Council of Europe (1997) *Second Summit of the Heads of State and Government of the Council of Europe (Strasbourg, 10–11 October 1997). Final Declaration.* http://www.coe.fr/cm/sessions/97summit2/x3.htm

Council of the European Union (1999) *Interpretation of the Eleven Criteria of Organised Crime*. Brussels: Council of the European Union.

Council of the European Union (2000) *The Prevention and Control of Organised Crime: A European Union Strategy for the Beginning of the Millennium*. Brussels: Council of the European Union.

den Boer, M. (1997) Wearing the inside out: European police co-operation between internal and external security. *European Foreign Affairs Review*, 2(4): 491–508.

The Economist (2000) A Bulgarian way into the EU. 9 December: 54.

European Commission (1997) *The European Union in Action against Drugs*, Luxembourg: Office for Official Publications.

European Council (1998) *Progress Report to the European Council on the Combating of Organised Crime*. Brussels 26 November.

European Council (1999a) *Presidency Conclusions*. Tampere European Council, 15–16 October.

European Council (1999b) *Presidency Conclusions*. Helsinki European Council, 10–11 December, Annex I: 'Millennium declaration'.

Europol (1999) *Annual Report.*, The Hague: Europol.

Galeotti, M. (1999) Crime, corruption and the law. In M. Bowker and C. Ross (eds) *Russia after the Cold War*. Harlow: Pearson Education.

Gill, P. and Edwards, A. (1999) Coming to terms with 'transnational organised crime'. Paper presented at the ESRC seminar series, 'Policy Responses to Transnational Organised Crime', University of Leicester, September.

Gilligan, J. (1999) The role of Interpol in the fight against transnational organised crime. Paper presented to the UK ESRC seminar series, 'Policy Responses to

Transnational Organised Crime', University of Leicester, September.

Grabbe, H. (2000) The sharp edges of Europe: extending Schengen eastwards. *International Affairs* 76(3): 519–36.

Gregory, F. (1998) The case for: there is a global crime problem. *International Journal of Risk, Security and Crime Prevention*, 3(2): 133–7.

Hearst, D. (2000) Lace curtain spoils Poland's view of EU membership. *Guardian*, 29 November: 16.

Hebenton, B. and Thomas, T. (1995) *Policing Europe: Co-operation, Conflict and Control.* New York: St Martin's Press.

Hill, C. and Smith, K.E. (eds) (2000) *European Foreign Policy: Key Documents.* London: Routledge.

Hobbs, D. (1998) The case against: there is not a global crime problem. *International Journal of Risk, Security and Crime Prevention*, 3(2): 139–46.

Hyde-Price, A. (1992) Future security systems for Europe. In C. McInnes (ed.) *Security and Strategy in the New Europe.* London and New York: Routledge.

Hyde-Price, A. (2000) Reflections on security and identity in Europe. In L. Aggestam and A. Hyde-Price (eds) *Security and Identity in Europe. Exploring the New Agenda.* Basingstoke: Macmillan.

Kersten, K.U. (1999) Keynote address: the challenge of organised crime. In J.L. Albini (ed.) *Organised Crime: The National Security Dimension.* Garmisch-Partenkirchen: George C. Marshall European Centre for Security Studies.

Kröning, V. (2000) *Stabilising and Securing Europe: the EU's Contribution.* Draft Report of the North Atlantic Assembly, Civilian Affairs Committee, October. http://www.nato-pa.int/publications/comrep/2000/at-234-e.html

Kusovac, Z. (2000) People trafficking: Europe's new problem. *Jane's Intelligence Review* September: 53–5.

Kwasniewski, A. (1996) *Speech to the UN General Assembly.* http://www.un.int/poland/mission/org_crime/org_crime.htm

Laffan, B., O'Donnell, R. and Smith, M. (1999) *Europe's Experimental Union. Rethinking Integration.* London: Routledge.

Monar, J. (2000a) Justice and home affairs. *Journal of Common Market Studies: Annual Review*, 38: 125–42.

Monar, J. (2000b) An 'area of freedom, justice and security'? Progress and deficits in justice and home affairs. In P. Lynch, N. Neuwahl and W. Rees (eds) *Reforming the European Union: From Maastricht to Amsterdam.* Harlow: Longman.

NATO (1991) *The Alliance's New Strategic Concept (November 1991).* http://www.nato.int/docu/comm/c911107a.htm

NATO (1999a) An alliance for the 21st century. *NATO Review* 47 (2): D2–D7.

NATO (1999b) The alliance's strategic concept. *NATO Review* 47 (2): D7–D13.

Politi, A. (1997) European security: the new transnational risks. *Chaillot Paper* 29.

Redwood, J. (1997) *Our Currency, Our Country.* London: Penguin Books.

Salmon, T.C. (1992) The nature of international security. In R. Carey and T.C. Salmon (eds) *International Security in the Modern World.* New York: St Martin's Press.

Shelley, L. (1995) Transnational organised crime: an imminent threat to the nation state? *Journal of International Affairs*, 48(2): 463–89.

Shelley, L. (1999) Crime of the former socialist states: implications for western Europe. In G.J.N. Bruinsma and C.D. van der Vijver (eds) *Public Safety in Europe.*

Enschede, The Netherlands: International Police Institute, Twente.

Smith, M. (1996) The European Union and a changing Europe: establishing the boundaries of order. *Journal of Common Market Studies*, 34(1): 5–28.

Tarschys, D. (1997) The Council of Europe: strengthening European security by civilian means. *NATO Review*, 45(1): 4–9.

Tickner, J.A. (1995) Re-visioning security. In K. Booth and S. Smith (eds) *International Relations Theory Today*. Cambridge: Polity Press.

UN Congress on Crime and the Treatment of Offenders (1995) *Report of the Ninth United Nations Congress on the Prevention of Crime and the Treatment of Offenders* (UN document A/CONF.169/16, 12 May). http://www.uncjin.org/Documents/9rep2e.pdf

UN Congress on Crime and the Treatment of Offenders (2000) *Declaration on Crime and Justice: Meeting the Challenges of the Twenty-first Century*, at http://www.uncjin.org/Documents/congr10/4r3e.pdf

van Duyne, P. (1996a) *Organized Crime in Europe*. New York: Nova Science Publishers.

van Duyne, P. (1996b) The phantom threat of organised crime. *Crime, Law and Social Change*, 24: 341–77.

Wæver, O. (1998) Insecurity, security and asecurity in the west European non-war Community. In E. Adler and M. Barnett (eds) *Security Communities*. Cambridge: Cambridge University Press.

Wæver, O., Buzan, B., Kelstrup, M. and Lemaite, P. (1993) *Identity, Migration and the New Security Agenda in Europe*. London: Pinter Publishers.

Wolfers, A. (1962) *Discord and Collaboration: Essays on International Politics*. Baltimore, MD: Johns Hopkins University Press.

Zijlstra, K. (1998) *Transnational organised crime – an escalating threat to the global market*. Report of the North Atlantic Assembly, Economic Committee. http://www.nato-pa.int/publications/comrep/1998/at278ec-e.html

Chapter 4

Freedom, security and justice: Pillar III and protecting the 'internal *acquis*'

Juliet Lodge

Introduction

The idea that the EU should develop policies and operational capabilities to combat international organised crime remains contentious. This is because when the European Community (the EU's forerunner) was created in 1957, the emphasis was on the creation of a common market. Economics were paramount. Security and defence were seen as the proper reserve of sovereign national governments and NATO. Until the mid-1980s, this view persisted and came to be seen as the 'security taboo'. The decision to realise a Single European Market by the end of 1992, however, meant the security taboo had to be reassessed. Creating the single market required the removal of all internal barriers – physical, fiscal and technical – to trade by making a reality of the 'four freedoms', that is, the freedoms of movement of persons, services, goods and capital. This was to be complemented by a tightening and reinforcement of the so-called 'external frontier' – that is, the geographical perimeter around the territory of the EU.

All this was plausible in theory. In practice, it raised, and continues to raise, some highly sensitive and politically delicate issues. Moreover, it demands a reassessment of the EU's sense of itself. It has become far more than a trading bloc. But many of its internal procedures are in their infancy when seen from the perspective of combating crime. This makes effective action to confront, prevent and apprehend organised criminals very difficult. Action is inhibited also by the lack of a common criminal code and continuing political uneasiness about the very idea of the EU becoming involved in crime-busting outside the arena of agricultural fraud where, via the commission's small anti-fraud squad, it has operated quietly with varying degrees of success for decades. The development of a genuine operational capability to enhance bilateral and multilateral police co-operation has to be explained and derives from a different imperative from that concerning measures to combat agricultural fraud. It is propelled by two factors: the first, historical and almost accidental; the second, political and connected to contemporary geopolitical and economic imperatives – EU enlargement to central and eastern European countries. Understanding the second requires a brief survey of how EU co-operation among the justice and home affairs (interior) ministries of the member governments came about.

Background and institutional developments

Transnational crime came onto the agenda of the then European Community of nine member states in the middle of the 1970s. The persistence of indigenous terrorism in some states coupled with the spread of international terrorism and international terrorist activity against EC member state targets led ministers to convene outside the normal EC meetings (but with a membership base determined by the fact of being a member of the EC) to discuss how terrorism and political extremism might be combated. Their subsequent meetings and organisation were called 'Trevi' meetings; a term that is variously explained in terms of the name of the Rome fountain where they had their photograph taken (Trevi) and in terms of the French acronym for terrorism, radicalism, extremism and international violence.

Initial meetings were ad hoc and infrequent. The first occurred in December 1975. It helped to confirm the desirability of co-operation among the member states to combat terrorism at a time when they were unable to agree on a common definition of terrorism let alone a common definition of crime. Some states clung to the idea that terrorist acts were essentially political in nature and therefore should not be prosecuted as a crime, whereas others insisted that terrorism constituted a criminal act that should be prosecuted as such. Eventually, this concern combined with anxiety over the difficulties in effectively implementing and using the Council of Europe's Convention on the Suppression of Terrorism (ECST). This convention was based on the principle of 'extradite or try'. It was subsequently endorsed by the EC's growing number of member states and it, and other Council of Europe conventions, inspired the orientation of EC policy in areas now associated with EU efforts to combat internationally organised crime.

It must be remembered that combating terrorism and international crime was among the first issues to be considered by EC government home affairs and justice ministers and that the scope of their work has been informed by these early concerns. Equally important is the fact that the European Parliament not only from the mid-1970s onwards called for action to combat international terrorism but also that its members (MEPs) sought openness from ministers as to progress in these matters and repeatedly suggested co-operation (and mutual assistance agreements) with third countries, the UN and other appropriate international bodies. In 1977, MEPs pressed member governments to sign and ratify the ECST.[1] They also called for the creation of a permanent conference of justice and home affairs ministers; the harmonisation of legal and administrative provisions on internal security; the harmonisation of arms legislation and identity card and registration matters (an issue that remains problematic to this day, partly because some states do not require their citizens or those within their boundaries to have identity cards); extension of mutual legal assistance among the EC member states; the establishment of an integrated system of investigation within the EC;[2] EC accession to the Convention for the Protection of Human Rights and Fundamental Freedoms;[3] and the creation of a European judicial area (Lodge 1981).

Progress on all these matters was slow, sensitive and tortuous. Why? There was divergence between civil law and common law states and governments were anxious to avoid increasing supranational legal competence to criminal law and internal security issues. The EC lacked the legal jurisdiction to deal with such matters and had only relatively recently embarked on the politically delicate process of trying to 'concert' co-operation on foreign policy issues in an intergovernmental, parallel arrangement to the EC known as European political co-operation (EPC). This institutional parallelism remained and found expression in the so-called three pillars of the Maastricht, Amsterdam and Nice Treaties: Pillar I (on supranational matters subject to binding legislation passed by supranational institutions); Pillar II on external security (the partially) intergovernmental successor to EPC; and Pillar III on justice and home affairs (the intergovernmental pillar now dedicated to the realisation of an EU of 'freedom, security and justice').

Trevi

The Trevi group consisted of officials, intelligence officers, and police and government officials. Its work was secret and strictly intergovernmental. This in itself led to problems of overlap with other intergovernmental groups convened under the Council of Europe. It eventually divided into three working groups dealing with problems of law enforcement and security arising out of the free movement of people: police liaison on terrorism; issues of public order (principally football hooliganism at away matches); sharing of fingerprint data (the forerunner of the current Eurodac system); and combating organised crime, including money-laundering and the illegal trade in stolen antiques. Counter-terrorism remained a high priority through the 1980s. In 1987 progress on the exchange of information and improvement of intelligence and police co-operation led to consideration being given to extending co-operation and information-sharing among immigration and passport control services; measures to prevent the abuse of the right of asylum (given Germany's liberal regime); and the setting up of a high-level ad hoc working group of immigration policy advisers and EC commission officials. In May 1987, ten member states signed the Council of Europe's Convention on the Transfer of Sentenced Persons and they considered modernising and simplifying extradition procedures and using the Dublin Agreement as a framework for close judicial co-operation in combating terrorism (Lodge 1988).

The Rhodes European Council of 1988 set up a group of national co-ordinators to examine the elimination of border controls. On 8 December 1988 a fourth Trevi group was set up to look at the implications of the single market programme and measures needed to compensate for any loss of security. In 1990, this group advocated co-operation between police and security services to implement the single market. Its deliberations not only interfaced with those of custom officers (who subsequently formed their own groups and liaised with Trevi, the so-called MAG 92 group) but also with the work of a group of EC member states who were impatient to see a swifter realisation of single market goals and who were prepared to confront the delicate issue of giving the commission more power in the highly sensitive political area of internal security and defining the concept of EU citizenship (Ward 1997).

These states came to be known as the Schengen group. Their work ran parallel to that of the commission but their decisions were drafted with a view to future incorporation into EC/EU law. The Commissioner for the Internal Market was involved in their work: freedom of movement of persons (one of the four freedoms of movement under the 1992 single market programme) implied not only freedom of movement for legitimate purposes of work. While it would be disingenuous to suggest that criminals primarily crossed borders at official border-crossing points, it would be equally disingenuous to think that organised criminals would not take advantage of the removal of internal borders and any weaknesses on the newly defined external border. The latter was notoriously weak at its southern Italian tip and along the eastern flank where West Germany's borders met those of the then East Germany. Reunification, if anything, exacerbated things and quickly pushed illegal movement of persons, asylum, refugees, visa and immigration (see O'Keeffe 1995) onto, and then progressively higher up, the EC's agenda. In the mean time, a special working group had been set up under Trevi (the Ad Hoc Working Group on Europol). Its report was adopted by the Trevi ministers in December 1991 on establishing Europol in stages: first by creating a European Drugs Intelligence and Monitoring Unit (the later EDU), and then by creating Europol. Ministers agreed in June 1992 that a draft convention to facilitate this should provide the appropriate legal basis for Europol: it did not come into effect, however, until late 1998.

From Trevi and Schengen to Maastricht and Amsterdam

The continuing sensitivity surrounding the idea of the commission being involved in initiating policies on internal security matters – which struck at the heart of national sovereignty – meant that governments were loathe to take decisions to expand, in effect, the power of the commission. Accordingly, they opted for a suboptimal approach to ease the way for a very gradual increase in co-operation (not supranational integration) in these sectors. Events were to overtake them. This is why the structures for dealing with international organised crime are inadequate. It also explains why there is so much anxiety about changing either the pillar structure of the treaties (which made most of the issues subject to intergovernmental co-operation) or moving certain issues from Pillar III to Pillar I.

The discrepancy arises between them because Pillar I rests on supranational decision-making practices in which the European Parliament acts as a legislative chamber, the European Court of Justice (ECJ) performs its usual roles, and decisions are justiciable and can be referred to the ECJ for adjudication. Pillar III is the antithesis of this. It rests on intergovernmental agreement that allows dissenting member governments either to veto decisions or to opt out of them. Uniform or common policy is then an impossibility but governments retain maximum discretion to act autonomously. The problem for the EU now lies in the fact that the commitment to realising and sustaining internal security rests on acceptance of a raft of shared norms, values, practices and respect for the principle of the 'rule of law'. While this has been taken for granted among the 15 member states, enlargement raises urgent questions. Accordingly, the German Presidency of the European Council, which assumed office in January 1999, openly insisted on examining whether applicants could meet the requirements of what is now known as the 'internal security *acquis*' as a precondition of EU entry. On 6 October 2000, British Prime Minister Tony Blair could argue: 'another revolution is taking place. What the people of Poland begun, the people of Serbia will finish – opening up for the first time in history the prospect of a European continent united in freedom and democracy.' Clearly, the attainment of freedom, security and justice in the EU could be impeded unless the EU addresses a number of highly sensitive matters concerning the definition of democratic accountability, the respect for the principle of the 'rule of law' and the application of an agreed 'internal security *acquis*'. Enlargement of the EU to central and eastern European countries (CEEC) brings with it particular problems. Their nature and scope differ in significant respects from earlier enlargements. While it is usual to note that the EC managed to accommodate newly democratic states like Spain, Portugal and Greece, they posed somewhat different problems in terms of their polities and traditions from those of the CEECs. Arguably, those states could also be more readily accommodated within the EC because the EC's own political structures were less developed. Certainly, the scope of the EC's policies was far narrower.

This chapter, therefore, briefly alludes to some of the particular difficulties and challenges posed by Pillar III of the Maastricht Treaty (TEU) and its revised versions in the Amsterdam Treaty (TEA) and Nice Treaty for the process of enlargement. It argues that unless steps are taken to ring-fence and protect the 'internal security *acquis*' of the EU, then enlargement might become an excuse to postpone the attainment of freedom, security and justice in the expanded EU and vice versa.

From Maastricht to Amsterdam

Pillar III of the Maastricht Treaty of European Union on Justice and Home Affairs (JHA) has been problematic since its inception (Barrett 1997). Cumbersome decision-making procedures and operational structures have inhibited the swift and successful pursuit of JHA goals. In particular, a sense of failure flowed from the requirements of unanimity in decision-making and the tortuous implementation of the various JHA legal instruments: joint actions, joint positions and non-binding acts (recommendations, resolutions and declarations); and conventions whose entry into force depend on national ratification procedures. Nevertheless, somewhat paradoxically, this pillar is one that is assuming increasing importance for the existing member states of the EU, as well as for those embarking on enlargement negotiations with the applicant states from central and eastern Europe. It is one, however, that is not only sensitive and exceptionally difficult but where the EU is going to have to adopt a strong (possibly unpopular) line if it is to ensure that enlargement does not seriously weaken and impede its efforts to combat international crime.

The Amsterdam Treaty and crime

In June 1997, the heads of state and government of the EU's 15 member states agreed, and then signed on 2 October, a new draft treaty on European union. The new treaty title listed a number of areas in which co-operation is required at EU level: terrorism, organised and other crime, trafficking in persons, offences against children, trafficking in illicit drugs, illicit arms trafficking, corruption, fraud, and racism and xenophobia. These are ambitious and fraught because responsibility for them still rests uneasily between Pillar I (subject to the gamut of supranational decision-making arrangements) and Pillar III (which remains intergovernmental and hence subject to domestic political discretion and vagaries likely to lead to slower and discrepant responses). Action to deal with racism and xenophobia, though endorsed by the establishment of a special observatory, remains problematic because it is a cross-pillar issue. Primarily centred in Pillar I (largely relating to social policy and freedom of movement of persons issues), criminal aspects fall under Pillar III. Work proceeds via co-operation among police forces, customs authorities and other competent authorities, and through Europol. Judicial co-operation was promoted and resulted more recently in Eurojust. Greater approximation of rules on criminal matters was foreseen among the member states. Framework decisions were introduced with a view to giving member states a deadline by which they have to achieve a specified result using national means. The emphasis was and remains, even after the Nice Treaty, on intergovernmental co-operation and nationally based action.

The roles of the commission and the European Parliament are, at least until around 2003, limited. The range of international, national and EU organisations involved in attempting to combat international crime already heightens the scope for interagency rivalry, duplication of effort and confusion. Essential as the EU's commitment to combating international crime is, steps need to be taken to avoid Pillar III's good intentions disappearing into the ether or political rhetoric.

This revision of the existing treaties is particularly significant in terms of the internal security of the EU. The Maastricht Treaty first officially endorsed and recognised the existence of co-operation on internal security and police matters among the EU's member states in what was known as Pillar III on Justice and Home Affairs. This mirrored rather than lent direction to existing and growing police co-operation born of operational necessity. A 'Euro-cop' culture was emerging and steps were underway to develop appropriate training bodies, which led to the first steps being taken in June 2001 to create a European Police Academy. This is seen as vital to enhancing information exchange, mutual under-standing and developing common practices and commitment to shared norms and values among police forces in an enlarging EU.

Whereas sporadic and ad hoc co-operation had grown among police and law enforcement agencies over the years – (beginning with the work of the Trevi Group in 1975 designed to improve co-operation to combat terrorism, and its descendants in the internal market programme leading up to 1993), the Maastricht Treaty outlined, as 'matters of common interest', nine areas:

> asylum policy; controls on crossing the external borders; immigra-tion policy in respect of third country nationals; drugs; fraud; judicial co-operation on criminal and civil matters; customs co-operation; police co-operation (notably for combating drug traffick-ing and other forms of serious crime (European Commission 1997: 130) and on a Union-wide system for the exchange of information with a European Police Office (subsequently, Europol). (Flynn 1998: 18–20)

Co-operation was to remain strictly intergovernmental. The European Parliament and the European Court of Justice were excluded from playing any role under it, something that led to charges of it being inherently undemocratic, non-transparent and open to abuse. Indeed, the difficulty of securing public access to Europol documents exercised many, including the ombudsman who, in April 1999, set up an own initiative inquiry and successfully challenged Europol to produce its code on access. Eventually, Europol confirmed it would give access under the code used by the Council of Ministers even though it was a separate body (set up by a council act, the Europol Convention) with a legal personality distinct from that of the council.[4] This issue continues to bedevil discussion about the appropriate role and scope of competences for Europol (see below).

Pillar III has come into its own despite the heavy criticism of it and despite the difficulty of achieving rapid progress on intrinsically sensitive issues central to member states' conception of themselves as autono-mous, sovereign entities responsible for security. The Amsterdam Treaty adopted a bolder approach in line with operational necessity in giving a far broader definition to the EU's objectives in respect of internal security.

The key goal was to 'maintain and develop the Union as an area of freedom, security and justice, in which the free movement of persons is assured in conjunction with the appropriate measures with respect to external border controls, immigration, asylum and the prevention and combating of crime' (preamble to the Amsterdam Treaty). Member states remain responsible for preserving law and order within their boundaries (which to some extent must be seen now as administrative boundaries rather in the way the border between the former Federal Republic of Germany and the German Democratic Republic was conceived). The external border around the whole of the EU's outer border is the common, external frontier at which nascent common controls (imperfectly conceived and implemented as they are) are to be applied. Accordingly, the Treaty of Amsterdam divided the original Pillar III (the JHA) into three main areas:

1. A new title 'Free Movement of Persons, Asylum and Immigration' is eventually to be subject to Pillar I decision rules; that is, it is to fall under the EU's competence. This is entirely logical given its close connection to the Four Freedoms of the Single Market.

2. A revamped Pillar III that provides for police and judicial co-operation in criminal matters.

3. A protocol to incorporate the Schengen Agreement *acquis* into the new treaty.

The new title 'Free Movement of Persons, Asylum and Immigration' is exceedingly difficult. It not only requires a rethink of existing conventions but has been tested by unforeseen developments. Especially problematic are the intended new borders to the east of the current applicant states. Already poorly policed and protected, corruption and operational weaknesses mean the security of the EU's external border is likely to be severely compromised on enlargement. The EU has had to discuss measures to cope with unexpected, sudden influxes of refugees and asylum seekers as well as with asylum bids by individuals from existing liberal democratic regimes who could not lay claim to a safe haven in the EU on the grounds they needed to escape persecution by their national government. This opened the debate about how much freedom of movement an exile should have within the EU; whether non-state persecution could be used to justify an asylum bid; and what general implications might flow from this for stability within the EU.[5]

The EU is most likely to achieve progress on the second priority: promoting police and judicial co-operation in criminal matters. Practical steps have been elaborated to facilitate this. Deciding what actions should be regarded as criminal ones is not as simple as might be supposed, even in respect of action to combat drug trafficking. Europol's position also needs to be specified. Different articles relate to the general matter of police co-operation and Schengen (Art. 30(I) TEU) and to the role of Europol (Art. 30(2)). Since Schengen matters cover both Pillar I and Pillar III issues, parallel legal instruments may be needed in both. For instance, a free movement measure would require both a Pillar I and a police instrument – Pillar III – action (*Minutes of Evidence*, 11). Police co-operation goes beyond operational matters and raises the issue of what kind of an entity the EU is and how it is to make sure the principle of the 'rule of law' is to be respected. We return to this below.

The issue of agreeing to incorporate the Schengen Agreement *acquis* into the Amsterdam Treaty was discussed and approved. The failure to define the JHA *acquis* before agreeing to its incorporation was greeted with consternation in some circles, notably the House of Lords in Britain (House of Lords 1998). In practice, the Schengen *acquis* was to be incorporated by finding a legal base for each Schengen provision in the EC Treaty or the Amsterdam Treaty on European Union. The Schengen Convention is in force in Belgium, Germany, France, Italy, Luxembourg, The Netherlands, Austria, Portugal and Spain, and partially in Greece. It became part of the EU with the Amsterdam Treaty's entry into force regardless of whether or not agreement had been reached in the interim on how to match each Schengen provision to a specific legal base in either or both treaties. This was problematic enough for the UK and Ireland, both of whom decided to remain outside Schengen (with opt-in clauses), but posed acute difficulties for applicant states. Arguably, the EU has an interest in them only gradually becoming full EU members, and then only when they are able fully to shoulder the responsibilities of implementing the JHA *acquis*. Moreover, a very ragged pattern of implementation is likely to occur even among the 15 member states because uniform practices have not been defined. To take but one example, bilateral arrangements between Schengen states (as for example on the issue of transfrontier hot pursuit) arising from the implementation of Article 41 of the Schengen convention would be the result of a measure and would not be adopted under Article 34 of the Amsterdam Treaty itself (*Minutes of Evidence*: 12). Similarly, information-sharing might be prescribed but even where Chunnel crime is concerned, the local Kent police were unable to access the Schengen Information System (SIS) directly. SIS had over 40,000 search terminals by the end of 1998, and remained one of the principal instruments taken to compensate for the abolition of internal border checks in the Schengen area. It also resulted in a marked rise in SIS alerts on identity documents in 1998, which had risen from 5.6 million to 8.7 million compared to 1997 (Council of the European Union 1999). Interestingly, its effectiveness was particularly marked in respect of arrests for the purpose of extradition. Various procedures for enhancing the apprehension of suspected criminals included the Grotius, Sirene and Vision projects (plus Image Transfer Project) to improve the speed and quality for exchanging fingerprint and photographic images inter alia.

In addition, the TEA had a new Title IIIa providing for member states to take measures to establish progressively an 'area of freedom, security and justice' within five years of the entry into force of the treaty (since ratification and implementation depend on the outcome of referendums in Denmark, Ireland and Portugal, this is not likely to occur before 2002). The focus of Title IIIa, however, confirmed the EU's preoccupation with maintaining internal security while realising the internal market through removing internal frontier checks. Consequently, the emphasis is on securing the adoption of common rules and standards on immigration, asylum and visa policy, common definition of refugee status, and common conditions for the issue of residence permits and short-term visas (based on the principle of the negative list) (McGuiness and Barrington 1997: 164): all matters that had been raised over the years in forums considering ways of combating international terrorism; and all of them matters whose resolution had proved tortuous and problematic. The realisation of the single market, the end of the Cold War, German reunification, the clamour by new states for EU membership and the rising wave of transnational crime that could be traced back into the CEECs merely added urgency to efforts to inject a greater degree of commonality into sometimes very diverse, and hence potentially discriminatory, policies pursued by individual member states owing to different domestic contingencies and histories.

Examples of divergence, based on states' different histories and past links and practices, illustrate this and have been countered by groups pressing for uniform rules to be developed by the EU. On 23 April 1998 in Genoa, the European Co-ordination for Foreigners' Right to Family Life, responding to Agenda 2000, unanimously adopted a resolution for an EU immigration policy to meet the needs of society in the twenty-first century (European Commission 1997: 13). In particular, it advocated the elimination of discrimination to enable third-country nationals legally settled in the EU to have an equal right to family life; respect for human rights; and the definition of the rights of the different types of immigrant group. In appealing for an EU-level immigration policy, it affirmed the need for that policy to be democratic and made accountable to the European Parliament (Agence Europe 24 April 1998). Similarly, pressure grew in respect of the range of matters concerning the cross-border activities of individuals and organised crime. The EU, in its Pre-Accession Pact on Organised Crime with the 11 would-be EU states, insisted on the importance of their ratifying promptly the 1995 and 1996 European Conventions on Extradition, and insisted on the applicants taking all necessary measures to enable them to adhere to them at their point of entry to the EU.[6]

Moreover, given the fact that many applicant countries are also transit countries (and, in some cases, countries of origin) for asylum seekers and immigrants from elsewhere, it will be essential to ensure they are in a position properly to police their borders (which become the eastern edge of the EU's common external frontier) and to apply common asylum and immigration rules in the processing of requests on behalf of the rest of the EU. They must also adopt the Geneva Convention and its implementing machinery, the Dublin Convention (on the state responsible for determining asylum applications) and related measures in the EU *acquis* to approximate asylum measures (European Commission 1997: 131). Without additional EU help, increased mutual assistance measures and judicial co-operation, it is unlikely the applicants will be in a position to effect these tasks competently. The roll-on effects for the rest of the EU are substantial and extremely problematic. EU states fear a rise in illegal immigration and crime. As Agenda 2000 recognised: 'The effective integration of the new Member States into EU judicial co-operation may be constrained by the difficulties encountered by some of them to ratify certain international conventions and the inexperience of the judiciary in implementing them' (Agence Europe 24 April 1998).

States differ in how and why they implement EU provisions but there is growing concern in respect of immigration owing to domestic problems and to the scale of immigration. Indeed, in 1999, the EU expelled by air alone some 170,000 illegal immigrants. However, the figures themselves are open to some misinterpretation as they do not distinguish among re-expulsions of people who had entered one EU state and then gone on to another. Nor do they include explusions at EU borders with the CEECs, which partly accounts for Germany being the state that recorded the highest number of expulsions in 1999.[7]

Table 4.1 (see p. 115) reproduces the information submitted by national delegations in response to a Council of the European Union's Migration and Expulsion Working Party (MEX WP) questionnaire. Iceland and Norway also participated in the working group through association agreements concluded under the terms of the Amsterdam Treaty – despite remaining outside the EU. The EU has certainly increased its attempts to reduce divergence. The Dublin Convention's unanimity provision regarding all EU member states to complete ratification before it could come into force is adapted in the TEA to permit implementation on the basis of a decision by a majority of member states. Moreover, the 1997 draft convention allowed the first two member states to ratify it to put it into practice immediately (*Statewatch* July–October 1997: vols. 4–5). In addition, the EU per se began to increase its co-operation with the FBI in trans-Atlantic surveillance of telecommunications introduced into the draft convention on mutual assistance in criminal matters (in Articles 6–9), even though an explicit treaty basis for the interception of telecommunications is absent. Clearly, the operational needs of combating international crime in the Internet, sophisticated telecommunications age have outstripped the understanding and the awareness of the political institutions set up years ago to guard against the abuse of power and to uphold individual rights and liberty (see Wall this volume). The tension between the two has to be reconciled, and progress here is slow. Indeed, the 'negative press' decelerated EU–FBI developments somewhat but eventually the Convention on Mutual Assistance in Criminal Matters (which provides the legal framework for interception in EU member states) was adopted by Justice and Home Affairs Ministers Council on 29 May 2000.

Nice Treaty and further integration

The Nice Treaty amendments do not confront some of the most intractable issues associated with Pillar III. Transparency and democratic accountability issues remain highly contentious. But they do permit the extension of what might loosely be called the Schengen experience: by permitting 'enhanced co-operation' among a core group of states (which is essentially the process by which both Schengen and much of the original Pillar III came into being), integration will inevitably develop in this sphere. This will, moreover, permit qualified majority voting, prevent states vetoing further action, and facilitate 'common action on judicial co-operation in criminal matters'. The member states may, in the event of the commission not submitting a proposal at their request to advance enhanced co-operation in this field, submit an initiative to the council to obtain

Table 4.1: Explusions from the EU (1999)

Country	Number of expulsions	Country of nationality	Country of destination
UK	45,100	No available data exists	No available data exists
Germany	32,233	Turkey, Romania, Ukraine, Bulgaria, Bosnia Herzegovina, Yugoslavia, Poland, etc.	Not given
Austria	20,207	Romania, Yugoslavia, Poland, Slovakia, Hungary, Republic of China, Macedonia, Czech Republic, Iraq, Moldavia, etc.	All deported to country of origin
Netherlands	12,204	Morocco, Poland, Romania, Bosnia-Herzegovina, Czech Republic, Turkey, Ecuador, Ethiopia, Ghana, Suriname, Colombia, former USSR, etc.	Not given
Italy	12,036	Albania, Algeria, Ghana, Morocco, Moldavia, Nigeria, Tunisia, Romania, Ukraine, etc.	Not given
Denmark	9,276	Slovakia, Iraq, Iran, Pakistan, Russia, Armenia, Turkey, Georgia, Croatia, Poland, India, Sri Lanka, Slovenia, etc.	Not given
France	8,300	Romania, Algeria, Morocco, Tunisia, Turkey, Poland, etc.	In EU countries: I, D, E, NL, P, UK, B, A, GR, DK, IRL, S. In third countries: Romania, Morocco, Algeria, Tunisia, Turkey, Poland, Mali, Senegal, etc.
Sweden	6,735	Poland, Bosnia, Yugoslavia, Bangladesh, Russia, etc.	Not given
Belgium	6,487	Senegal, Guinea, Cameroon, Nigeria, China, Poland, Romania, Bulgaria, Albania, Ecuador, etc.	Not given
Finland	5,426	Estonia, Morocco, Iraq, Belgium	Not given
Spain	5,020	Morocco, Colombia, Algeria, Romania, Brazil, Ecuador, Ukraine, Poland, Russia, Venezuela, etc.	Not given
Greece	2,880	Romania, Bulgaria, Ukraine, Moldavia, Pakistan, Georgia, Poland, etc.	All deported to country of origin
Portugal	529	Ukraine, Moldavia, Brazil, Romania, Morocco, Nigeria, Russia, Angola, Guinea Bissau, Guinea Conakry, Pakistan, China, etc.	All deported to country of origin
Norway	440	Poland, Lithuania, Russia, etc.	Not given
Luxembourg	30	Bulgaria, Tunisia, Albania, Morocco, China, Ecuador, Bosnia, Brazil, Cameroon, Colombia, Mexico, Nigeria, Romania, Slovenia, Ukraine, etc.	All deported to country of origin In EU countries: F. In third countries: Romania, Nigeria, Moldavia.
Ireland	6	Romania, Russia, Nigeria, Moldavia, etc.	–
Iceland	none	–	–
Total	**166,909**	–	

Source: Statewatch

authorisation. At least eight member states must support this, and the council must consult the European Parliament (which has no decision-making power here) and act by qualified majority. A recalcitrant state may refer the matter to the European Council, but a decision will then revert to this practice. The participating states bear the costs for such action unless the Council unanimously decides otherwise after consulting the European Parliament. (Again, the European Parliament's power is undermined: consultation means very little unless MEPs can develop it effectively.) While common action is not the same as uniform legislation or procedures, its objective is convergence and its method geared to permitting different procedures to attain a common goal. Interestingly, too, the idea that the EU was not an organisation that dealt with criminal matters has disappeared. Accordingly, Article 31 of the Nice Treaty now reads:

1. Common action on judicial cooperation in criminal matters shall include (i.e. following its ratification by all 15 member states over the next few years): a) facilitating and accelerating cooperation between competent ministries and judicial or equivalent authorities of the Member States, including, where appropriate, cooperation through Eurojust, in relation to proceedings and the enforcement of decision; b) facilitating extradition between Member States; c) ensuring compatibility in rules applicable in the Member States, as may be necessary to improve such cooperation; d) preventing conflicts of jurisdiction between Member States; e) progressively adopting measures establishing common rules relating to the constituent elements of criminal acts and to penalties in the fields of organised crime, terrorism and illicit drug trafficking.

2. The Council shall encourage cooperation through Eurojust by: a) enabling Eurojust to facilitate proper coordination between Member States' national prosecuting authorities; b) promoting support by Eurojust for criminal investigations in cases of serious cross-border crime, particularly in the case of organised crime, taking account, in particular, of analyses carried out by Europol; c) facilitating close cooperation between Eurojust and the European Judicial Network (set up by Joint Action 98/428/JHA adopted by the Council on 29 June 1998 OJ L191.7.7.1998, p. 4), particularly, in order to facilitate the execution of letters rogatory and the implementation of extradition requests.

In a declaration (number 17) adopted by the Nice Intergovernmental

Conference and appended to the Nice Treaty, it was stated that Article 229a does not prejudge the choice of judicial framework to be set up to deal with disputes relating to the application of Acts adopted on the basis of the Treaty establishing the European Community that create communitiy industrial property rights. This again gives an important signal to the potential expansion of legal co-operation and integration in future. The Nice Treaty overall significantly improved the position of the European Court of Justice and the other courts.

The problems of enlargement

EU enlargement imposes a range of demands on both the existing member states and EU institutions as well as the applicant states. Much has been said about the need for economic and political liberalisation in the applicants states (CEECs). Ways of easing their accession have been examined. Transition periods, pre-accession agreements and special measures have been discussed to assist transition to the western style of government and social market economic systems. The problems of acceding to the EU without simultaneous accession to NATO and the Western European Union (WEU) have also been scrutinised. The matter of how these states might accommodate the requirements of Pillar III and the internal security *acquis* (and all the assumptions about the nature of modern polities it implies) has received less attention.

Adjusting to the EU's internal security acquis

How are the applicants to adjust to and accommodate the internal security *acquis*? Fine words and the adoption and signature of international conventions are important in establishing the psychological milieu in which words must turn into practice. But what of implementation? What problems confront the applicants and the EU's negotiators preparing for enlargement?

Political culture

The absence in the applicant states of political systems and cultures based on universal respect for the 'rule of law' and tolerance of dissent means that corruption is rife, often throughout all tiers of society. Endemic corruption inhibits the development of public trust in just law enforcement. Crime and criminal activity are growing in these states. The police and law enforcement agencies are sometimes inefficient, unable to cope effectively and sometimes compliant and corrupt (see, for example, Anderson and den Boer 1994; Dorn *et al* 1996). Even the best of them require reform.

Law enforcement

Overall, the legacy of a lack of respect for civil liberty and freedom of expression has had a corrosive effect on the public's perception of the integrity, reliability and lawfulness of law-enforcement agencies. This poses acute problems for those in the EU anxious to promote co-operation to combat international crime: intelligence, for example, cannot be shared in confidence.

Combating international crime

Effective action to combat international crime depends on the security of intelligence information to be shared, effective liaison and police co-operation. None of this can be taken for granted. It is unevenly achieved within the existing EU. So what does this mean for the enlargement negotiations?

Pre-accession: a time of opportunity?

The EU enlargement negotiations offer by far the most potent opportunity for the EU to set out and insist on steps that must be taken in the domain of Pillar III as a condition of EU accession. Pre-accession requirements should be elaborated and their *implementation* made an essential precondition of entry. The existing member states might participate with appropriate arrangements with the Commission in screening the JHA *acquis* with the candidate countries. Clearly, appropriate decision-making procedures are essential if coherence is to be maintained both within the scope of the JHA and with the wider enlargement negotiations.

The EU might accept as positive signs of good faith, for example, agreement to *adopt* conventions, practices and protocols. However, entry should proceed only following their implementation to an appropriate standard, which must be judged by relevant EU authorities. An opportunity to test this came at the end of 1998: the CEECs and Cyprus have already expressed their intention to adopt and implement effectively the 1959 European Convention on Mutual Assistance in Criminal Matters as well as a range of international conventions listed in the EU's action plan on organised crime. Some of these have been ratified but not uniformly so. Legislation to enact and enforce these must be put into place now.

The Action Plan on Organised Crime

In June 1997, the Amsterdam European Council adopted an Action Plan on Organised Crime. The Vienna European Council of December 1998 approved the subsequent progress report on its implementation. The action plan provided for the establishment of the Multi-Disciplinary Group (MDG) on Organised Crime. It meets once a month to advance the 30 recommendations contained in the action plan. It comprises operational law-enforcement officers, prosecutors and senior-level policy-makers. It acts as an important forum for evolving policy and addressing practical issues associated with police co-operation in the implementation of the recommendations. It is normal for meetings in its margins to be held with representatives from international organisations as well as other countries.

After a seemingly slow start, progress in judicial co-operation took off in 1998: the Europol convention finally entered into force; joint action on money-laundering was agreed in September and formally adopted in December; the European Judicial Network was launched and the first assessment made of member states' application and implementation of international undertakings in the fight against organised crime. Following agreement by the Justice and Home Affairs Council on 3 December 1998, the Council adopted an action plan establishing an area of freedom, security and justice. It deals with measures needed to facilitate the best implementation of the provisions of the Treaty of Amsterdam regarding the establishment of the area of freedom, security and justice.

The Pre-Accession Pact on Organised Crime

On 29 May 1998 the EU's JHA ministers, acting in their capacity as members of the Council, in full association with the commission and the JHA ministers of the applicant countries (CEECs and Cyprus), adopted a Pre-Accession Pact on Organised Crime. This emphasised their common commitment to democracy, human rights and the 'rule of law' and their awareness of how organised crime 'constitutes a serious threat to these values because it penetrates, contaminates and corrupts the structure of governments, legitimate commercial and financial business and society at all levels' (Pre-Accession Pact).

The pact outlines, in a set of principles, the signatories' determination to co-operate fully in the following:

1.   Fighting all kinds of organised crime and other forms of serious crime.

2. Adopting and implementing effectively existing conventions on crime-related matters.

3. Developing and effectively operating central law enforcement and judicial bodies responsible for the fight against organised crime (including central national bodies responsible for co-ordinating the fight against organised crime; central national contact points for the exchange of information; national multidisciplinary teams; and the European Judicial Network, as outlined in the previously agreed Action Plan on Organised Crime); facilitating rapid and efficient international law enforcement co-operation and judicial co-operation relating to the fight against organised crime, and national co-ordination of the fight against organised crime; and co-ordinating criminal investigations through the establishment of multidisciplinary integrated teams to discuss common strategies and actions, assisted by Europol as appropriate.

4. Rapid and efficient information exchange for purposes of investigations, mutual legal assistance and in the field of operative and investigative support.

5. Mutual exchange of law enforcement intelligence, while safeguarding the protection of data relating to individuals.

6. Mutual practical support for investigations and operations, including training and equipment assistance and joint investigative activities, supported by Europol; facilitating transboundary law enforcement and judicial co-operation, especially by rapid processing of the relevant applications and logistical support; and the mutual exchange of law enforcement officers and judicial authorities for traineeships within the framework of investigations relating to the countries concerned.

7. Bi-lateral and multi-lateral joint law enforcement projects, especially in fields posing serious transboundary problems.

8. Using Europol as a channel for information, analytical expertise and operational support 'also, over time, to the CEEC's and Cyprus' (using EU funds for support and preliminary contacts with the Europol Drugs Unit and the posting of liaison officers to the Hague).

9. Promoting speedy and effective judicial actions through the adoption of good practice.

10. Early ratification of the EU's extradition conventions of 1995 and 1996 to prevent offenders from benefiting from differences in the

various legal systems using the extradite or try principle (*aut dedere, aut judicare*) established in the Council of Europe's conventions.

11. Stimulating training and using established modules such as those of the Association of Police Colleges.

12. Developing a comprehensive policy against corruption through regular consultative meetings with the relevant bodies of the Council and the Commission.

13. Combating money-laundering through setting up, where none yet exist, at national-level financial intelligence units according to the definition of the EGMONT group.

14. Co-operation between liaison officers and liaison magistrates.

15. Follow-up evaluation of the pact, in particular as regards standards for law enforcement, co-operation and judicial co-operation, using the Multidisciplinary Group on Organised Crime; ad hoc teams on how the applicants are taking up the *acquis judicaire* and looking at policy and institutional changes 'affecting judicial authorities and law enforcement agencies'; Troika missions for detailed talks in capital cities; reports from the applicants; occasional collective briefings; seminars; consultations with international forums; briefing by the presidency on developments within the K4 committee; joint meetings of JHA councils; general sharing of information by each presidency; and organised meetings within the framework of the multidisciplinary group.

Implementation of the acquis judiciaire

The implementation of the *acquis judiciaire* remains extraordinarily problematic both for reasons internal to the candidate countries and for reasons associated with the origins of the JHA itself. It was only after a good deal of argument that the member states themselves agreed that immigration and asylum issues, in which the candidates have acute interests, should be transferred from the arrangements of Pillar III under Maastricht to Pillar I under the Amsterdam Treaty and made subject to the European Court of Justice. The 'communitisation' of these issues should help to promote effectiveness and uniformity and gradual steps are built in to smooth the way for the progressive establishment of free movement of persons after a five-year period and once a degree of trust has evolved among the states. Even so, the UK and Ireland were not part of the Schengen *acquis*. Article 2 of their first protocol allows British and

Irish border controls to be retained. Neither participated in the common policies for asylum, refugees and immigration. Although a provision allowed them to opt into debates about measures within three months of the Commission proposing one, the Council could decide to exclude them. Operational considerations, however, impelled a rethink not least because the UK signed up to 22 Schengen instruments and UK police wanted to maximise cross-border collaboration.

Denmark has an anomalous position in that it is politically but not legally part of the Schengen *acquis*. Technically a member of Schengen, it did not accept Schengen's incorporation into the EU. Accordingly, Denmark did not participate in decisions affecting the area of freedom, security and justice, apart from former Pillar I competences on visas (designation of countries to which visas apply and the format of a common visa) but it retained its Schengen obligations on third pillar co-operation on criminal matters (Duff 1997: 31). What is obvious is that the operational requirements of effectively combating organised international crime will impel greater co-operation, co-ordination and ultimately harmonisation and then, possibly, uniformity. The provisions of the new Title VI (Amsterdam Treaty) on police and judicial co-operation in criminal matters underlined this. They also make it imperative to ensure acceding states are brought into the *acquis judiciaire* from the point of their accession. Any derogations from the obligations will be unhelpful all round. Moreover, the rudimentary democratic political cultures and legal traditions of the acceding states make observance of good practice essential. The temptation to seek derogations modelled on or inspired by those of some existing member states must be resisted. The common good will be better served by seeking common solutions to common problems. This in turn places a premium on information exchange and co-operation in identifying, in the first instance, priority action areas.

The role of effective targeting

It would be disingenuous to suggest that all areas are equally important or equally problematic. There is evidence that criminal activity, for example, in respect of drugs trafficking is burgeoning. That is to be tackled in conjunction with measures on border controls and immigration. However, progress on drugs is somewhat less controversial than on immigration. At the beginning of September 1998, the Austrian Presidency of the EU presented a document on future immigration policy which suggested the EU distance itself from the 1951 Geneva Convention on Refugees and argued that the acquisition of refugee status should be understood not as an individual subjective right but as a political offer on the part of the host country (Agence Europe, 2 September 1998: 5; the convention behoves states to admit people with refugee status). Requests for asylum should, it was argued, be treated more flexibly and that a new EU proposal should make this feasible in the form of a convention to complement, annul or amend the Geneva Convention.

It is significant that the Commission, at the initiative of Commission President Santer, held a debate on 22 April 1998 in Brussels on the effort to combat the drug problem. This was convened in advance of the special session of the United Nations General Assembly in New York from 8 to 10 June. It also anticipated the preparation of the EU's Second Action Plan to cover 2000–2005 on which the UK Presidency was already working. The Commission does not envisage the harmonisation of national legislation or any legislative measures, beyond a communication. Its purpose is to set out guidelines that take into account the expanded competence the EU has in this regard following the adoption of the Amsterdam Treaty (Agence Europe 23 April 1998).

Action to combat this is a major preoccupation of the EU law-enforcement agencies for good reason. Not only did Europol have its origins in key respects in the European Drugs Monitoring Unit (EMDU) but a cursory glance at Europol/EMDU data on requests for information showed in 1996 that over 70% were drugs related. Money-laundering and immigration had then only elicited around 8% respectively. Both, however, are areas where crime again is growing exponentially, where concentrations exist in the CEECs, and where effective co-operation is crucial. Cross-border surveillance among Schengen states has grown (with Germany and the Netherlands undertaking the highest proportion of such ventures); and joint policing to combat illegal immigration, immigrant smuggling and drug smuggling (Spain/Portugal and France/Italy) has increased. Border areas also see joint police patrols (Germany with France and the Netherlands) and joint exercises (Germany with Austria and France), including cross-border digital radio inter-operability systems (such as the Tetra three-country project for the Belgian–German–Dutch borders) and some cross-border pursuits. Effective targeting by area would not be enough by itself. While common problems exist, their intensity and the extent to which effective action has been taken to counteract them vary among the applicant states.

However, action was not confined to these areas. By 2001, terrorism and combating cyber-crime had assumed a higher priority. The first European conference on terrorism was held in February 2001 in Madrid with heads of police from all member states, 87 from other countries and

EU Commission members. It was presided over by the head of Europol, Jürgen Storbeck. Europol was described as the main institution in the struggle against terrorism. This was no glib remark for concern has rapidly grown over what terrorism means in different countries: for some, political dissidence equates to terrorism; in others, the more generally accepted definition common to most EU states is the norm. However, the conference indicates proactive strategies on the part of the police. Attention has turned to start up the so-called 'Euro-order' (of search and capture relating to a state that apprehends a fugitive criminal, making him or her available to the country's authorities where he or she allegedly committed the most serious crime in order to side-step difficulties over extradition procedures. At the end of the conference, the police force heads signed the 'Madrid document', known as Europol's guide to combating terrorism. This permitted data collection of a more extensive nature 'beyond what is necessary' and thereby implying intrusion into and limitation of laws on the right to privacy; economic incentives for suppliers of information about terorists (subject to approval by the Executive Committee of Europol); mutual recognition of anti-terrorist legislation among Europol's members; swift and effective implementation of interrogation committees; simplification of extradi-tion; and a feasibility study on creating the Euro-order (something of particular interest to Spain, which has successfully sought bilateral arrangements with member states on this, and which was instrumental in creating the European judicial area in recognising sentences, in promoting judicial co-operation at the Lisbon European Council in March 2000, and in advancing the idea of a European civilian police force of peace missions). Events of 11 September 2001 expedited action.

While operational considerations inevitably lead to creater co-opera-tion, public concerns over the scope of Europol's activities and the apparent inadequacies of parliamentary controls, democratic account-ability and effective openness and transparency have grown. Confidence has been undermined, too, by corruption allegations against Europol officials working on computer and data issues at the very time EU proposals for wholesale data retention for law enforcement purposes and the surveillance of telecommunications have been tabled. The Council of Europe's May 2001 draft convention on cybercrime, for example, has been amended to permit longer storage of computer data and retention of telecommunication data for at least 12 months. While not confined to the EU, its content was heavily influenced both by EU states and by the USA (following EU–FBI co-operation) and informed, too, by G8 which the EU is to join.

This is controversial because EC directives – which are binding – on data protection and privacy require the deletion of telecommunications data. Directives are notoriously difficult to amend (and would be subject to proper parliamentary scrutiny and co-decision). An alternative instrument, the convention – which is not binding – evades the democratic accountability issue without providing compensatory controls. Moreover, it is proposed that users would lose their anonymity (the so-called attack on cybercafé cultures), and that law-enforcement and security services have access to retained and archived data. Currently, time limits on data storage range between three months (The Netherlands) and not less than 12 months (Belgium). Not all countries have time limits but most are rapidly introducing them, thereby providing the operational case for EU co-operation towards 'harmonisation' not on time limits as such but on the principle of storing data and abolishing the anonymity of users.

Uniformity versus diversity in an enlarging EU

What is of increasing importance to an enlarging EU are the principles governing policy areas to be integrated. Different measures may be needed according to region. Geopolitical location poses additional problems for some applicant states. Border demarcation as well as border controls need to be addressed. For example, the physical demarcation of the border between Latvia and Belarus still needs to be completed; Lithuania has demarcation problems; and Poland needs to improve its border control with Belarus and the Ukraine.

Improving the management of border control, preparations to accommodate the requirements of the Schengen Convention and completing alignment to international conventions are issues common to all applicant states. Since it is likely some states will be better equipped to undertake these tasks, it follows that uniform progress is unlikely. Differential arrangements will be essential therefore if a given group of states, which are diverse in terms of their acceptance of the internal security *acquis*, are to accede to the EU simultaneously.

This applies not merely to the clutch of would-be members, including Romania, Slovakia, Bulgaria, Lithuania, Latvia, etc., but also to the group of whom greater progress might reasonably be expected: Poland, Hungary, the Czech Republic, Estonia, Slovenia and Malta and Cyprus. The freedom, security and justice (FSJ)-related problems in these countries are extensive and vary from one to another. The enlargement negotiations, therefore, will have to include the elaboration of transitional measures which, in turn, will mean discriminating against some states.

The value of transitional measures

Transitional measures are useful both to the EU and to applicant states. They allow a gradual adaptation to EU norms and requirements. They may avert the need for large-scale derogations and exceptions to the *acquis*. They feature prominently in domestic arenas: the common agricultural policy, financial measures, etc. Indeed, the Czech Republic's Finance Minister Pilip indicated in April 1998 that his government would probably have to seek derogations for agriculture, the restructuring of certain industries, environmental protection and regional policy. Derogations can, of course, be time limited or flexible.

However, transitional measures for internal security must differ fundamentally from those in other areas, for two reasons. First, no reciprocal adjustment by the EU can be expected. The EU cannot downgrade its standards on action to combat crime merely to condone or accommodate less effective and less democratic or more corrupt practices common to applicants. The internal security *acquis* has to be non-negotiable. Secondly, applicants must set up appropriate administrative, political and judicial machinery enabling them to implement the internal security *acquis* democratically, accountably, responsibly and effectively. This will take time.

The potential political embarrassment of having transitional measures might be avoided if programmes can be devised to help the process of adaptation in the applicant states. These would give an important signal whose psychological impact would be significant. This is why the pre-accession pact is so crucial, even if binding legislation is absent so far.

Compatibility of transitional measures with 'freedom, security and justice'

Effectiveness

It is clear that the operational consequences for law-enforcement and related authorities of having to cope with differential regimes within the expanded borders of the EU would be serious. They would no doubt seriously undermine the attainment of specified goals unless the example of the original Schengen group were to be applied more rigorously. That means the core EU states must be allowed to proceed as planned and that they must be given the right to determine when and whether new states be allowed to become part of the core. This would interfere with the development of a single policy to combat crime but it would ensure that any steps in that area were likely to be successful and be shielded from internal sabotage.

If this view is accepted, it follows that transitional measures must be carefully evaluated and graduated. Objections to long transitional measures are unhelpful. The only way of avoiding long transitional measures would be, first, to except the applicants, individually or en bloc, from the internal security *acquis* in part or in whole or, secondly, to delay enlargement for at least ten years.

The second option is not acceptable politically. The first would have several consequences. It would: (1) create a potential hierarchy among the applicants; (2) increase the prospect of inefficiency among existing EU operations unless the EU internal security *acquis* were 'ring-fenced' like a quasi-Schengen; (3) allow the 15 member states to continue developing Pillar III with a view to enhancing its capacity to attain its goals; and (4) leave the door open for initiatives to be taken among the applicant states – as a group – to develop their own regionally based security *acquis* to expedite co-operation among themselves to standards approximating those of the EU.

Aspiration versus reality

The existing EU members have not always found co-operation easy in areas covered by Pillar III. Co-operation needs to be improved among interior ministers and police forces, for example, over immigration and asylum matters. Acrimonious exchanges have occurred among the 15 member states over the EU's adoption, as provided for by the Amsterdam treaty, of the Schengen *acquis*.

This resulted from disagreement over the size of any secretariat needed to service the new Schengen unit; jealousy over the filling – by competitive examinations or not – of high-level posts, currently dominated by one national group; and tactical manoeuvring by states. Further problems of co-ordination and duplication complicated the picture even before the UK Presidency argued in favour of an 'environmental interpol' to deal with illegal trade in hazardous waste, chemicals and noxious or banned substances, some of which arguably should be dealt with under the Euratom treaty (due to lapse or be incorporated into a new, possibly single simplified treaty at the next intergovernmental conference (IGC) in 2004). In short, the EU needs to address internal matters and render its existing mechanisms effective as a precondition of success and as a precondition of expansion to new members.

Operational effectiveness

Opening very imperfect procedures to participation by possibly corrupt agencies would compound the EU's security problems and undermine rudimentary efforts to combat them. Operational effectiveness has to be assured. This means that, as part of the pre-accession agreements, applicant states must be persuaded to overcome internal disagreements over turf wars: foreign ministers and justice ministers may wish to assess and monitor their state's implementation of Pillar III obligations but existing EU agencies and member states are less than sanguine this will be done either objectively or sufficiently assiduously to underpin Pillar III's operational effectiveness.

Delicate negotiations are, therefore, inevitable. Objectivity can only be assured by a third party. At a minimum, it would seem the Commission must be given this task with backup from appropriate agencies. Similarly, the commission must be entrusted with assessing the extent to which applicant states' national programmes for the adoption of the community *acquis* converge with the short and medium-term priorities set out in the accession partnership agreements with the EU. There must be a high degree of convergence between the two and an objective assessment must be made to ascertain this. Following on from the experience of the operational phase of screening the community *acquis* in two groups (the applicants – the '5 + 1' Group – with whom trade negotiations have begun and the other five CEEC applicants), it would seem logical to apply this practice to the internal security *acquis*. The EU's criteria for judging applicants' readiness to take on the full responsibilities of EU membership must be rigorous and their implementation carefully assessed. The FSJ ministers are willing to make the necessary expertise and advice available where inadequacies are identified. However, this does not mean the EU has another 'pot of gold' into which applicants can dip. It does mean the EU, itself, is clearer about what it means by the FSJ *acquis*. In May 1998, the ministers agreed to a new joint action setting up a mechanism for collectively evaluating progress on the internal *acquis*. Under this, a group of experts from the member states assessed applicants' progress in implementing the internal *acquis*. Their conclusions informed both subsequent recommendations and the wider enlargement process. Equally importantly, the Council in May 1998 agreed guidelines on the principle of the 'rule of law' applicants must observe: the Copenhagen criteria stipulated that democratic and accountable institutions are a necessary precondition of EU membership. The 'rule of law' guidelines help to explain what is necessary to meet this precondition. It then fell to the Austrian Presidency in the summer of

1998 to take forward discussions with the applicants on the practical application of the internal *acquis* prior to their formal accession to the EU. This area remains exceptionally fraught, not least owing to Austria's political profile and semi-exclusion from the EU.

The German Schengen Presidency prioritised the approximation of CEEC applicants and Cyprus with the internal *acquis*. In particular, the Schengen convention will be part of the *acquis* by the time of the next wave of enlargement. Accordingly, the applicants have to put in place effective judicial and police agencies, an appropriate legal framework and effective border controls. The Schengen Executive Committee has joint meetings with applicants, informs them of its deliberations in general and has organised a conference for the customs authorities of the applicants and Schengen countries. Other states work with the Schengen group: Norway and Iceland have a co-operation agreement with them. The ten Schengen states moved forward, harmonising visa policies by suppressing the 'grey list' and introducing a single visa format for foreigners from states from whom visas are required. The aim was to ensure all these projects would be speedily implemented when the Amsterdam treaty came into effect (Agence Europe, 3–4 August 1998: 4). A great deal of effort is being made to put legal and institutional mechanisms into place to improve the operational effectiveness of action under Pillar III.

The operational requirements of successfully pursuing action to combat international crime mean that openness before and during that process is impossible. That is accepted within the EU. It has to be accepted by the applicants. Accountability and openness will continue to be demanded by the European Parliament and civil liberty groups. But they are coming to accept that such openness has to be qualified. They seek assurance that civil liberties and the requirements of democratic accountability will not be abused. They may be brought into a process to impart such norms to the applicants and develop with them consultative and scrutiny procedures that might later become part of Pillar III's institutional and decision-making setup. Clearly, much remains to be discussed and accomplished.

Beyond the EU

The EU needs to develop a multi-pronged strategy to acclimatise the applicant states to the norms and expectations of democratic practice and culture. It might more consciously use other regional and international bodies and agencies to promote dialogue and awareness and, ultimately, to ensure the internalisation of in effect western democratic values and norms by the applicant states. Democratic principles, practices, symbols, ideas and values have to be transferred (Weiler 1995).

While the only organisation capable of devising and implementing binding legislation in these sensitive areas remains the EU, it must not be forgotten the EU itself builds on the work and conventions adopted within the Council of Europe. There is a case for improving co-operation between the two bodies. Indeed, the Parliamentary Assembly of the Council of Europe argued on 21 April 1998 that the EU should comply with Council of Europe conventions whenever possible. In particular, it sought its compliance with the European Convention on Human Rights which a majority of EU member governments had opposed at the IGC favouring instead of EU adherence to that convention its adoption by those member states that had yet to do so. The assembly also felt it would be appropriate for the Council of Europe to take part in the European conference for EU applicant states given the role it believes it plays in preparing them politically and legally for EU membership (Agence Europe 22 April 1998).

There is also a sense in which the Council of Europe might be able to promote the kind of ongoing dialogue among all the would-be future members of the EU that would lead them into bilateral and multilateral, possibly regional dialogues and agreements as a preparation among themselves for taking on the internal security *acquis* at a later date.

The Pre-accession Pact on Organised Crime was, after all, not binding. Taking the form of a political declaration, it remains an expression of intent. Steps will have to be taken to transform its key provisions into the kind of operational arrangements that will genuinely contribute to efforts to combat crime. The commitment to developing and implementing common projects to fight organised crime is significant only if it does lead to a swift identification by the EU of the areas in which the delivery of EU technical and/or financial assistance (and better use of Phare/Media programmes and the special Pillar II programmes – Oisin, Grotius, Stop and Falcone) would help the CEEC candidates and Cyprus prepare to accept the internal security *acquis* and the expected role that Europol will play in future in providing information, analytical expertise and operational support for the EU. The '5 + 1' are supposed to have acceded to the Europol convention by the time of their accession to the EU.

The Pre-Accession Pact on Organised Crime does break some of the taboos. Special mention is made of the need to combat corruption through the joint development of a comprehensive policy to combat corruption in all its guises. Regular consultations are to be arranged between the 26 states and the Council and Ccommission. In addition, regular meetings, organised by the EU presidency, will be convened to develop and review a common strategy to combat crime in clearly targeted areas. Perhaps the greatest immediate importance lies, first, in the public recognition it affords to the need to take action to combat crime and to address problems relating to the internal political and judicial practices of the applicant states. The former cannot be effective unless the latter is addressed as a matter of urgency. Secondly, importance lies in the opportunity its provisions give to the applicant states to participate directly in the continuing evolution of EU policy and the development of the internal security *acquis*.

The Pre-Accession Pact on Organised Crime was a logical development. As Agenda 2000 recognised (European Commission 1997), applicant states would have to participate progressively in community programmes and machinery for applying the *acquis*. Greater assistance for the approximation of laws, information exchange and the opening up of community programmes to the CEECs was envisaged. Participation does not pose a problem of principle: legal procedures to facilitate it have been put in place across the wide range of areas enlargement implies. The problem remains making participation effective for all programmes. Associating CEECs with EU developments exposes them to administrative and policy-making practice and should assist them in transposing the *acquis* sector by sector. The Pre-Accession Pact on Organised Crime should assist in maintaining and facilitating the adoption of the internal security *acquis*. It may also heighten appreciation of the myriad difficulties requiring attention in related areas, which fall under the category of civil crime but are not graced with that label as yet. These would include the problems of enforcing competition laws with the 'ghost system' of criminal law, fraud (an area the Spanish Presidency stressed in 1995)[8] and the ad hoc arrangements following on from the removal of internal frontiers among the applicant states themselves. In short, if good practice among existing states (such as in the Nordic Union) can be extended to others, it must not be assumed they will work as well without many of the basic rules underpinning them being properly applied and entrenched among the new states.

In addition, it must be clearly recognised from the outset that the EU's ability to have much impact in the broad area of criminal law, even though restricted to specific targets, remains extremely limited. Accordingly, the commission has had to rely on 'soft' instruments to sensitise the public and elites to the dimensions of a problem and continues to have difficulty even convincing the member governments that EU-level action is either desirable or feasible. The difficulties of then trying to develop a legislative measure, for example, to combat trafficking in the new synthetic psychotropic drugs is hampered by diametrically opposed viewpoints as to whether the drugs problem (broadly conceived) should be tackled primarily through measures to combat social exclusion and to reintegrate addicts and traffickers into society or through punitive measures to apprehend and punish traffickers. EU divisions over this issue alone inhibit more effective EU action to combat drug flows from third countries, including the states of the former USSR and the CEECs as well as those in South America and the Caribbean where the EU already has programmes in place to encourage peasant farmers/drug producers to find alternative forms of sustainable economic development. It is striking that as the pre-accession discussions have advanced, the concept of Soviet-sponsored narco-terrorism[9] is mentioned less, but concern over the activities of Mafia-type organised criminal outfits has grown.

Not surprisingly, current EU action focuses on awareness and confidence-building measures within the member states themselves (like the long-haul inflight film to counter child prostitution introduced in September 1998 and the luggage leaflets introduced in France and the Benelux later that summer). Such campaigns are likely to be extended to prepare the way for legislative measures such as directives with binding effect over the medium term. Meanwhile, the operational requirements of effective apprehension of those suspected of engaging in cross-border crime rest on the further development of Europol, bilateral police and customs co-operation and clear political signals to legitimise their work.

Notes

1 European Parliament Working Documents 513/76, 327/77 rev: PE 50.776.
2 *Annual Report to Parliament on Political Co-operation* presented on 24 October 1979 by the chairman of the Conference of Foreign Ministers of the member states meeting in political co-operation.
3 *EC Bulletin* Supple. 2/79. Memorandum adopted by the Commission on 4 April 1979.
4 Ombudsman decision closing the own initiative inquiry 01/1/99 1JH stipulates that ART41 TEU endorses the applicability of Art. 195 EC to provisions relating to areas under Title VI TEU (police and judicial co-operation in criminal matters). See *Statewatch* July 2000.
5 The particular case involved a US national seeking asylum in Sweden to escape harassment following his campaign for the local police in Connecticut to be overseen by a civilian board. See press report in the *Guardian* 26 August 1998: 12.
6 Pre-Accession Pact on Organised Crime with the Applicant Countries of Central

and Eastern Europe and Cyprus, May 1998.

7   See *Statewatch* bulletins of 1999, which stated that, according to a report by the Council of the European Union's Migration and Expulsion Working Party (MEX WP), 166,909 people were deported by plane from the member states and Norway during 1999. The UK, with over 45,000 expulsions, accounts for some 27% of the total. Under the Dublin Convention (on determining the state responsible for examining an asylum application), EU cross-border asylum seekers who have crossed another EU state to make an application are returned to that state. This can cause 'chain deportations' as people are deported from one EU country to another, and then expelled after their asylum application is rejected – 'refugees in orbit' within Schengen (each state claiming a migrant entered the Schengen area from another member state). *Statewatch* also noted that CIREFI, the EU's Centre for Information, Discussion and Exchange on the Crossing of Frontiers and Immigration, collects more detailed statistics on the extent and nature of expulsions from the EU, but these are still produced through systems of national reporting. In any case, this information is deemed potentially beneficial to 'illegal immigration networks' and withheld from the public on the grounds of public security.

8   European Council of the Union, Priorities for the Spanish Presidency of the Council of the European Union, SN3021/95.

9   This concept is often castigated as devoid of meaning or as being open to any interpretation whatsoever. It has been used as shorthand to suggest that the earnings of the narcotics/drug-trafficking trade and cartels have been used by terrorist bodies (see Miller and Damask 1996).

References

Anderson, M. and den Boer, M. (1994) *Policing across National Boundaries*. London: Pinter Publishers.

Barrett, G. (ed.) (1997) *Justice Co-operation in the European Union*. Dublin: Institute of European Affairs.

Council of the European Union (1999) *1998 Annual Report on the Implementation of the Schengen Convention*. Brussels: Council of Europe.

Dorn, N., Jepsen, J. and Savona, E. (1996) *European Drug Policies and Enforcement*. London: Macmillan.

Duff, A. (1997) *The Treaty of Amsterdam*. London: Sweet & Maxwell.

European Commission (1997) *Agenda 2000: For a Stronger and Wider Europe. Bulletin of the European Union*, Supple. 5/97 Brussels: European Commission.

Flynn, V. (1998) The Treaty of Amsterdam and the implications on free movement of persons and internal security. *Intersec*, 8 January: 18–20.

House of Lords, Select Committee on the European Communities (1998) *Incorporating the Schengen Acquis into the European Union, 31st Report, Session 1997–98*, London: HMSO.

Lodge, J. (1981) The European Community and terrorism: establishing the principle of 'extradite or try'. In J. Lodge (ed.) *Terrorism: A Challenge to the State*. Oxford: Martin Robertson.

Lodge, J. (ed.) (1988) *The Threat of Terrorism*. Brighton: Wheatsheaf.

McGuiness, D. and Barrington, E. (1997) Immigration, visa and border controls in the European Union. In G. Barrett (ed.) *Justice Co-operation in the European Union*. Dublin: Institute of European Affairs.

Miller, A.H. and Damask, N.A. (1996) The dual myths of 'narco-terrorism': how myths drive policy. *Journal of Terrorism and Political Violence*, 8: 114–31.

O'Keeffe, D. (1995) 'The Emergence of a European immigration policy. *European Law Review*, 20: 20–36.

Ward, I. (1997) Law and the other Europeans. *Journal of Common Market Studies*, 35: 79–96.

Weiler, J. (1995) Idéaux et construction européenne. In M. Telo (ed.) *Démocratie et construction européenne*. Bruxelles: Editions de l'Université de Bruxelles.

Chapter 5

Whose insecurity? Organised crime, its victims and the EU

Jo Goodey

Introducing imperfect minorities and protected zones

> There are imaginary geographies which place imperfect minorities in marginalised locations: in a social *elsewhere*. These locations consist of protected zones which ensure the reproduction of those who inhabit them, who are separated from the majorities living outside. (Ruggiero 2000: 1, emphasis in original)

Vincenzo Ruggiero's book, *Crime and Markets: Essays in Anti-Criminology* (2000), opens with an evocation of historical and present-day imagery of the social 'other'. This imagery, most perfectly illustrated in David Sibley's book *Geographies of Exclusion* (1995), has drawn most consistently on representations of filth and degradation, or 'social misery', which are assigned to the world's most marginalised groups and are reflected in images of their criminality.

To this end, this chapter draws on Ruggiero's opening statement and, taking the EU as its political and geographical reference, sets out to illustrate how Ruggiero's 'imaginary geographies' are also realities of exclusion and criminalisation for those 'imperfect minorities' whose origins lie outside the gated walls that have come to be known as 'Fortress Europe' or, more accurately, 'Fortress EU'. These 'imperfect minorities' have conveniently come to embody the EU's political and populist concerns about security with respect to crime committed by marginalised 'others' as 'outsiders'. While Ruggiero's work critiques the 'sociology of misery', for a broader discussion of criminal experience and causality, this chapter returns to this theme in its attempt to highlight the neglect, in criminology's ready reference to the criminality of organised crime as committed by 'imperfect minorities', of victimisation as experienced by those 'imperfect minorities' at the hands of organised crime.

In posing the question 'whose insecurity?' I intend to examine two central themes in relation to the above: first, the EU's perceived threats to its security that are seen to lie with the criminality of certain non-EU citizens as 'outsiders'; and secondly, the insecurity and threats to personal safety for marginalised non-EU citizens who are vulnerable to victimisation and abuses in the EU. The chapter focuses on organised crime as the mainstay of EU concerns regarding the criminal threat to EU security posed by the 'other', and the case of victims of human trafficking as the 'flipside' of this security threat. The chapter begins with a series of overlapping concerns that explore the globalising security threat that is seen to lie with transnational organised crime as it specifically relates to EU policy and experience with regard to criminalising labels, perpetrators and actual victims.

EU insecurity: overlapping concerns

Internal security and external threats

Immigration and asylum control have become ever more closely wedded to questions of crime control in the EU (Schmid 1996). Individual states, and those that are working towards accession to the EU, cannot develop immigration and asylum policies without reference to measures that address threats to internal EU security, in the form of crime, from external sources. The EU, in protecting its own interests and in its attempt to present a unified whole, is particularly good at highlighting the potential threat posed by particular 'outsiders', in the form of crime, to the union's security. Crime provides a real and emotive target for EU concerns and crime committed by non-EU citizens is a particularly good subject with which to unify the various states that make up the EU.

The *recent* path to policy-makers' concerns about crime (with external origins and threats to 'security' in the context of the EU) can be traced to a series of socio-political developments in the last decade of the twentieth century. The subsequent merging of migration and security issues, around crime, has been in response to these developments. The reasons behind this enhanced 'crime–security' threat have been well rehearsed (Ruggiero *et al.* 1998; Goodey 2000, Rees and Webber this volume) and, at this point in the chapter, need only be listed as follows:

- The collapse of communist regimes in the former eastern bloc and subsequent economic instability and criminality.

- Civil war and the refugee crisis in the former Yugoslavia leading to mass displacements of people and enhanced cultures of lawlessness.

- The EU's opening of its internal borders facilitating the movement of goods and people by Europe's legitimate and illegitimate economies.

- The EU's increasing policing of its external borders which has, inadvertently, enhanced the role played by criminals, at some financial and human cost, in evading these controls.

These broad developments merge under the heading of globalisation, as an economic force alongside advances in information and transportation technologies, which has been co-opted by the illegitimate economies of crime and, of more recent concern, the forces of transnational organised crime (TOC) which are variously presented as the latest threat, both real and perceived, to world security.[1] The EU has enthusiastically adopted concerns about the negative forces of globalisation, particularly in the form of TOC, in its reaction to recent developments in neighbouring states. Links between long-established demonisation of the 'other', in the form of the criminal threat posed to the EU by undesirable 'outsiders', and increasing pressures for migration into the EU from outside, have allowed for an easy marriage between crime concerns and migration concerns as focused on certain non-EU citizens. As Turnbill comments: 'Since the early 1990s the member states of the EU have attempted to create a unique institutional architecture to address internal security challenges. The fusing of immigration and crime issues into an "internal security continuum" has become a defining element in both institution building and substantive policy responses' (1997: 189). The 'security continuum' in the EU is a result of the self-fulfilling perpetuation of internal EU co-operation, through enhanced security measures in the form of policing, against perceived external threats to the union. Reference by transnational policing and criminal intelligence organisations to externalised criminal problems does appear as something of a self-fulfilling response to these organisations' need for legitimisation since the collapse of the Cold War. In addition, measurement of TOC activities, from drug smuggling through to human trafficking, continues to be an elusive and highly inaccurate enterprise which, none the less, is routinely undertaken by security and intergovern-mental agencies in their attempts to quantify the extent of the problem while, at the same time, justifying their own existence and providing the fodder for politicians' speeches which are liberally sprinkled with references to the 'war' on TOC.

Through these processes of legitimisation, grounded in oft-repeated references to the negative effects of globalisation as a theoretical concept and 'real' events, the EU has enhanced its defensive-aggressive efforts at policing its borders and those who enter the EU in the name, purportedly, of protecting its own citizens from the criminal 'other'. Here, a citizenship hierarchy is centrally embedded in the EU's response to this apparent 'migration–crime–security' continuum. At the top are EU citizens of individual member states who are afforded full rights of residence and freedom of movement within the EU under the auspices of the Maastricht Treaty. There then follows a non-citizenship hierarchy that privileges the rich from, primarily, developed countries, and underprivileges the poor from developing countries with respect to their access to the EU. The EU returns to the age-old distinction between the 'deserving' and 'undeserving' poor in its response to demands for entry into the EU by disadvantaged outsiders.

While refugees have traditionally come under the 'deserving' poor category, and states have been obliged to respond to refugee crises under the 1951 convention,[2] the status of 'refugee', and the accommodating response demanded of this status, has gradually been eroded to reflect the strains placed on receiving countries by increasing numbers of immigrants, both refugees and non-refugees, in recent years. The emergence of temporary protection (TP) in the 1990s as a response to the refugee crisis resulting from civil war in the former Yugoslavia, notably Kosovo, can be seen as a practical and politically viable solution for EU member states faced with the dilemma of having to accommodate hundreds of thousands of refugees. As its name suggests, TP is based on the short-term accommodation of refugees on the basis they will be repatriated to their home countries in due course (Fitzpatrick 2000). Unlike giving someone refugee status under the terms of the 1951 convention, TP circumnavigates a state's long-term obligations to refugees which include the right to residence and employment opportunities. However, TP is more than a practical response to the problems faced by individual states in trying to accommodate the world's growing numbers of refugees but, more pointedly, reflects concerns that asylum applications, in the effort to gain privileged refugee status, are hiding people's attempts to enter developed countries for economic betterment under the guise of claiming asylum. Here the question of 'deserving' and 'undeserving' poor, or 'legitimate' or 'illegitimate' immigrant, merges in the 'migration–crime–security' problem.

The idea that poor non-EU citizens are attempting to enter the EU through illegitimate means, as asylum applicants, helps support enhanced policing responses to prevent their entry. The bogus asylum applicant, if he or she gains entry to the EU through either legitimate or illegitimate means, is illegal by his or her very status. In turn, genuine asylum applicants, under the restrictive terms of the 1951 convention, are increasingly held under suspicion because of the association now made between 'asylum seeker' and 'economic scrounger'. While the desire for economic betterment, in relation to the world's poor and not the world's rich, is not, as yet, regarded as a valid reason to allow unrestricted entry to the EU, the union, in enforcing highly restrictive entry policies, is equally to blame in creating the demand for illegal entry to the EU that criminals are willing to exploit. As Rory Carroll insightfully commented in a British national newspaper, in the aftermath of the Dover tragedy which saw the death of 58 Chinese, in a lorry container, who tried to smuggle themselves into Britain: 'By closing virtually all legal methods of entry, Europe has ensured that outsiders have no choice but to try the trafficker. He sets a price based on demand, cost and risk. Europe's strategy is to make that cost and risk as high as possible' (2000: 8). One might add here, with respect to the inadequate penalties against trafficking that currently hold sway across the EU, that the risk is made highest for the trafficked person and not the trafficker.

The emergence of a 'migration–crime–security' continuum is reflected in the gradual merging of policing and immigration policies in the EU. Turnbill (1997) identifies the 1986 Single European Act as a forerunner of later policy developments that saw the fusion of crime and immigration concerns in the EU. The Act, in committing the European Community to free movement of goods and persons through the opening up of the community's internal borders, also demanded compensatory measures in the form of enhanced policing for the community's external borders and the development of a unified immigration policy. This play-off between increasingly relaxed internal border/market controls, and the correspond-ing need to police the movement of goods, capital and people at the EU's external borders, has been repeatedly reflected in a number of policy developments in the EU – for example, the Schengen Convention (1990) and the Maastricht Treaty (1991). The three separate pillars of Maastricht – 1) the European Commmunity; 2) a common foreign and security policy; and 3) justice and home affairs co-operation – were, from the very outset, overlapping in their concerns about immigration, security and crime (for a detailed account, see Lodge this volume).

However, exactly how illegal immigration became a 'crime-security' issue for member states and, in turn, for the EU, is somewhat more complex to answer than the dichotomous positioning of 'internal freedoms' and 'external threats' suggests. The globalising influence of TOC, in the context of post-Cold War Europe, would appear to offer a ready explanation as to 'why' the EU is responding to externalised threats as something more than poor immigrants' desire for economic betterment or an intermittent refugee crisis at the EU's borders. The convenient explanation that enhanced security against undesirable and illegitimate outsiders is justified in the EU as a response to the threats posed by TOC is, however, somewhat lacking as a wholesale argument given the reality that internal criminal markets, led by EU citizens, are, and have always been, the mainstay of criminal problems in the EU.

Migrant criminality and domestic criminal markets

It is interesting to note that the all-encompassing external threat to the EU, as attributed to TOC, is rarely compared with the equal threat to EU security and individual safety that lies with 'home-grown' sources. 'Facts' about the extent and nature of crime committed by different nationalities are not only difficult to gauge accurately, based as they tend to be on official statistics, but are also particularly difficult to compare between member states of the union given their different criminal justice jurisdictions (Goodey 2000). While the subjects of 'migration' and 'crime' are usually treated as separate disciplines in academic circles, politicians and policy-makers do not hesitate to connect one with the other and to act accordingly. Academic studies examining the interconnectedness of immigration and crime are there to be found (Marshall 1997; Tonry 1997; Ruggiero *et al* 1998), and begin with the Chicago School of Urban Sociology, but politicians have more readily embraced questions of migration and crime that academics, for reasons of competing interests between disciplines and the more altruistic concerns of the ethics of undertaking research which might be used for racist ends, have been extremely wary of. And, in the political debates about immigration and threats to EU security, the abuses of marginalised migrant groups, by indigenous and external sources, are also readily overlooked. As criminological comparativists such as Melossi (1994) and Nelken (1997) have commented, cultural responses to crime by 'outsiders' tell us a great deal about a culture's own internalised problems, more so than the extent and nature of any external threat – the EU being a case in point.

In critiquing Donald Cressey's foundational work on organised crime, Joseph Albini comments: 'There is a serious historical weakness in Cressey's approach – that of isolating and limiting his historical analysis of organised crime to the period in American history when the Italian and Sicilian immigrants came to America. One has to ask, Was there no organised crime before this period?' (1997: 22) In the same vein, looking at the EU, one has to ask – can organised crime, from the 1990s, be attributed to the rise of the Russian and Albanian mafia; and, was there no organised crime in individual member states of the EU before the end of the Cold War? Looking to Italy, with respect to the first question, obviously not. The Italian mafia, both in Italy and the USA, has a long and much romanticised history. Similarly, the East End of London had, and has (Hobbs 1998), a 'healthy' culture of organised crime. However, with these two examples, the problematic construction of organised crime around nationality, and ethnicity, emerges for consideration.

While the criminality of recently settled migrant groups is repeatedly found to be relatively low and petty when compared to the amount and nature of crime committed by the 'domestic' population of a country, this pattern tends to change with respect to crime committed by the sons and grandsons of original migrants (Albrecht 1997). Immigrants' offending, with respect to conventional crime, comes to reflect levels displayed by equally disadvantaged and socially excluded populations of young males who are citizens of a particular state. The alarm caused by immigrants' criminality in the EU is often out of proportion when compared with the 'home-grown' crimes committed by a country's citizens – be these young disaffected males or city brokers. However, foreigners' involvement in organised criminal activities, as evidenced by Europol situation reports on organised crime in the EU, can be very high. This would appear to support the argument that foreigners, or non-EU citizens in the case of the EU, present a real threat to the union's security.

What closer examination of the Europol figures for individual member states reveals,[3] as with closer examination of prison statistics for foreign nationals in any member state,[4] is that significant numbers of suspects and incarcerated non-nationals in the EU are, in fact, other EU citizens. The 'outsider' threat to EU security, so often assigned to criminal non-EU citizens, is also an 'insider' threat. It would appear that concerns about 'migrants and crime' typically draw on people's base fears and misunderstandings about difference and social competition in relation to racist stereotyping and the undesirability of accommodating large numbers of 'the poor' who don't belong to the privileged group – in this case, EU citizens. With stereotyping, partly based on facts, the details of who actually commits which type of crime and, more importantly, 'why', are lost in the convenience of targeting EU 'outsiders' as a generic crime problem.

Whether comparisons are usefully drawn between the type of petty offending, in the realm of conventional crime, carried out by second and third-generation immigrants, as 'outsiders', and the types of criminal activities undertaken by members of TOC networks, as 'outsiders', is questionable. The point to be made, though, is that the 'migration–crime–security' continuum, as noted above, does not stop short with members of TOC networks but is evoked, at times, with respect to all immigrants who can be portrayed as less than desirable outsiders. Also, when considering the type of activities TOC is involved in, the reality of these enterprises is not, at its lowest levels of operation (from an individual dealing drugs in the street or driving a lorry bringing trafficked people into the EU), any different from the activities of conventional crime. What characterises crime as 'organised' and 'transnational', and here the UN's definitions of TOC are not always helpful,[5] is the existence of criminal networks that draw together cells of criminal activity at the national and transnational level (McIllwain 1999). This can be seen as a response to the globalising demand of crime 'markets' which have blurred earlier distinctions between origin and destination countries with respect to the demand, supply and consumption of certain criminal activities. Coupled with this is the inability of individual states, or political/market entities like the EU, to effectively control their domestic population's demand for and supply of the goods and services offered through TOC networks – be this, for example, the production and consumption of synthetic drugs or the supply and use of prostitutes originating from overseas. Here the local becomes merged with the global and TOC cannot be solely attributed to 'outsiders' or criminals who are not part of the domestic scene.

The local realities of (organised) crime have been most successfully illustrated by Dick Hobbs (1998) in his work on criminal networks in London's East End and the northeast of England. Hobbs emphasises the fact that crime is always local in its impact. In other words, real crime impacts on real people in particular localities. On the other hand, the globalising threat presented by TOC is, perhaps, most usefully employed as a theoretical and political tool for understanding crime whose markets now go beyond the local. TOC could not effectively exist in any state without establishing contacts with local customers who provide the demand for certain services and local criminals who distribute, and supply, the goods. As the Council of Europe's European Committee on Crime Problems,[6] set up in the wake of the dramatic changes in Europe at the beginning of the 1990s, notes: 'foreigners do not operate in an isolated "foreigner market" but rather engage in many kinds of systematic and symbiotic contacts with domestic crime markets' (1999: 45). However, these obvious connections between 'domestic-led' and 'foreign-led' crime markets are generally overlooked by EU politicians, unlike the more rounded insights offered by the Council of Europe, who prefer to enlist the latest discourses on organised crime, and the criminal threat posed by undesirable outsiders, in their efforts to keep immigration at a minimum.

In turn, TOC can more easily flourish with the assistance of corrupt officials in any country – be these border guards, immigration officers or police officers. To state the obvious, low detection of TOC activities does not necessarily equate with low levels of TOC activity in a country. As more cases of trafficked people or drugs shipments come to light, so we might view this as the blanket increase in these activities, or as an indication of law-enforcement officials' 'efficiency' in detecting the efforts of TOC. But with the extent of TOC activities notoriously difficult to gauge, and with respect to politicians' demands that criminal justice agencies take threats from 'outside', in the form of TOC, more seriously, so any apparent increase or decrease in TOC activities must be viewed with caution. Similarly, when considering how internal corruption aids and abets the problem and problematisation of TOC, so we need to acknowledge how the 'grey' economy, as influenced by globalising criminal enterprises, merges the so-called legitimate and illegitimate economies of a country (Ruggiero *et al.* 1998). Off-shore financial havens, such as the Isle of Man, alongside the big banking centres of London and Frankfurt, exist to furnish the needs of the legitimate and the 'grey' economies. Once again, distinctions between morally upright 'insiders' being corrupted by criminal 'outsiders' are difficult to present as a dichotomous reality given what is known about activities such as money-laundering and international banking.

National security and human problems

In the political debates about illegal immigration, bogus asylum claims and threats to EU security, the abuses of marginalised migrant groups, by domestic and external sources, are generally overlooked. Instead, reports usually draw on the security threat posed to the EU by illegal immigration in the form of smuggling and human trafficking. As an *Oxford Analytica* (30 August 2000) item on the Balkans reported:

> Since the Kosovo crisis there has been an increase in the activities of South-East European organised crime networks, particularly those concerned with illegal immigration and the trafficking of humans. This represents a serious security risk to the EU member states and could, in the longer term, jeopardise South-East European countries' efforts to join the Union.

This extract exemplifies how transnational organised crime, as a national security threat, is compounded with human smuggling and trafficking as a human security *problem*. The human security problem, caused by TOC as a national security threat, should not forget the human rights issues that lie at the heart of smuggling and trafficking cases. As Beare comments: 'To label "illegal immigration" as a generic form of national security threat would be an equivalent of blaming the victims *and* will prove to be futile' (1997: 39).

Typically, illegal immigration is regarded by law-enforcement bodies, first, as an issue of national security rather than one of human security; as Kelly and Regan state in their comprehensive report on the extent of and responses to trafficking in women in the UK: 'For governments, the individual interests of victims of crime are located in a context where the integrity of borders and immigration are sensitive political issues' (2000: 4). National security responses are aroused, in more stringent calls for tighter military style policing, in response to the security threat that is seen to lie with unwanted immigration which has become part of the 'migration–crime–security' continuum. The dilemma with this kind of response is that the causes of illegal immigration and, in particular, abject cases of human smuggling and trafficking, are negated in the effort to deal with the immediate 'problem' rather than effect a long-term cure.

Although illegal immigrants do present member states of the union with a human security problem, they do not tend to present a national security threat. Rather, it is members of organised crime networks, who smuggle and traffic people into the union, that present the real security threat for member states. While many members of organised crime networks operating in the EU are 'foreigners', who are non-EU citizens, and there is evidence to suggest that some people who were smuggled into the EU do, in turn, become involved in crime (often as a result of debt bondage incurred as a result of their smuggling/trafficking – see Schmid 1996), this should not confuse the criminal security threat posed by some non-EU citizens with the human security problem raised by the majority of underprivileged outsiders wanting access to the EU. In turn, organised crime networks present the greatest immediate threat to personal security for people who are either smuggled or trafficked into the union; yet the actions of these TOC groups, and in turn their 'victims', are presented, primarily, as a threat to EU citizens' security.

It is interesting to note how the response to 'immigration', as a blanket response to demands for economic immigration *and* asylum, has evolved in EU member states over the last few decades to reveal the interchangeability of a 'human security problem' with a 'national security threat'. The British government's white paper *Fairer, Faster and Firmer – A Modern Approach to Immigration and Asylum* (July 1998), which formed the backbone of the Immigration and Asylum Act 1999,[7] makes it clear that unwanted asylum seekers are a social and potentially criminal problem. Likewise, traditional emigration countries, such as Italy and Spain, have recently developed more restrictive immigration policies in light of an increase in illegal immigration to their countries, from neighbouring non-EU states, and the EU's demands that their borders be more closely patrolled and guarded against large influxes of people who are perceived as a security threat to the EU as a whole.[8] The beginning of calls for increasingly restrictive immigration policies can largely be attributed to the worldwide economic slump of the 1970s, and corresponding decreases in the demand for immigrant labour from Europe's industrial powerhouses. Here, the shift from encouraging immigrants as welcome employees to unwelcome economic burdens was also abetted by populist references to these groups' potential for criminality. Subsequently, the dramatic changes in eastern Europe, as noted earlier, compounded the EU's need to be seen to protect its own interests, on behalf of its citizens, against unwanted immigration and asylum claims.

Sympathy towards refugees who attempt to enter the EU as asylum applicants, in the context of human security, tends to be rationed in a highly discriminatory fashion. In turn, as was the case with Kosovan Albanians, the criminal 'underbelly' of certain groups can be conjured up to place the national security threat alongside the human security problem. However, the question of 'whose insecurity?' – citizens', immigrants', nation-states' or the EU's? – is nothing new with reference to how refugees and asylum applicants are received in Europe. As the telling biography of Anne Karpf (1997) reveals, when relating her parents' experiences as Jewish holocaust survivors in the Second World War, Europe was not always as sympathetic to the plight of 'worthy' refugees as we may like to believe. Karpf illustrates how many Jewish refugees, in Britain and elsewhere, were made into dangerous outsiders by some citizens who had been socialised to believe, in the context of a war, that all people with strange accents were the potential enemy. Here, echoes of the past reverberate in the present with respect to the limited sympathy that some asylum seekers receive in the EU because of their criminalisation by association. Ideas about 'victimhood', and human security, become lost when rich countries, like the majority of those in the EU, feel threatened by uncontrolled immigration from the world's poorest countries.

The human cost of smuggling and trafficking, in the wake of events such as that at the English port of Dover (referred to earlier), illustrates the human security problem behind smuggling that has its origins in global economic inequalities. There is ample evidence revealing the extent to which people are mistreated at the hands of smugglers and traffickers as they enter and pass through the EU (Morrison 1998). In turn, once people have arrived at their final destination in the EU they can experience dire working conditions and maltreatment (Kelly and Regan 2000). Horrific events do command sympathy, but this is short lived and limited when compared with calls for even stricter immigration controls that tend to follow news that more illegal immigrants or asylum seekers have entered a member state of the EU – either alive or dead.

The EU's desire to control immigration has gone beyond a limited reading of enforcement success, as judged by the number of illegal immigrants stopped at the union's internal and external borders. 'Control' of illegal immigration now encapsulates a broad range of issues concerning the social, economic and criminal impact of illegal immigration for the EU and its citizens. What is absent from the majority of government-led legislation and initiatives in the field of 'migration–crime–security' is the human rights part of this continuum with respect to non-EU citizens. As the Organisation for Security and Co-operation in Europe (OSCE) comments in one of its reports entitled *Trafficking in Human Beings: Implications for the OSCE*:

> ...most States have not integrated human rights concerns or strategies into their laws or policies relating to trafficking. The 'human rights approach' to trafficking defines trafficking first and foremost as a violation of individual human rights, and only secondarily as a violation of state interests...Advocates stress the need to integrate a 'human rights analysis' into anti-trafficking legislation, strategies, and initiatives, which have historically focused solely on controlling illegal immigration, prostitution, and organised crime.' (1999: 24–25)

It may be the case that non-governmental organisations (NGOs) and well meaning intergovernmental organisations are able to engage with the human rights element of trafficking, and other TOC crimes, but governments are slower to consider these issues as part of the 'migration–crime–security' continuum as it impacts on victims of TOC.

Migrants' insecurity: resurrecting forgotten victims in the EU

Significant improvements have been made in recent decades in consideration of victims' rights and standards of service provision across the EU (Wergens 1999; Brienen and Hoegen 2000). Since the mid-1980s the Council of Europe, with its human rights agenda, has been particularly active in highlighting the position of victims in Europe's criminal justice jurisdictions which extend beyond the member states of the EU. The Council's Recommendation (85)11, on the 'Position of the victim in the framework of criminal law and procedure' (Brienen and Hoegen 2000), coming at the same time as the United Nations' 'Declaration of basic principles of justice for victims of crime and abuse of power', was a benchmark document towards European recognition of victims' needs and rights. More recently, in April 2000, the Council of the European Union received an initiative from Portugal with a view to the adoption of a framework decision on the standing of victims in criminal procedure in the EU.[9] This initiative, reflecting the remit of discussions ensuing from the Treaty of Amsterdam (May 1999) and the Tampere Summit (October 1999), reveals the extent to which the European Parliament and the European Commission are moving towards enforceable legislation for victims in the development of an 'area of freedom, security and justice' in the EU.

However, the central onus of both the Treaty of Amsterdam and the Tampere Summit is to combat the latest EU 'folk devils' of TOC and illegal immigration. Justification for ever more stringent external border controls and the policing of the least desirable immigrants (the poor) is made in the name of providing a safe environment for *EU citizens* who are depicted as the potential victims of these threats from outside. What is lacking in the discussion and moves to combat these particular 'folk devils' is a more accurate reminder of 'whom' is victimised by, in particular, organised crime groups operating in the EU, and the relationship between these victims and the EU's criminal justice authorities in the fight against organised crime. In the fusion of 'migration–crime–security', under a continuum of insecurity issues, the EU (under the auspices of the Council of the European Union, the Parliament and the Commission) tends to present a confusing array of responses to immigration, crime and victimisation which, on the one hand, demonises 'outsiders' whilst, on the other hand, seeking to protect them.[10]

Within-country legislation and EU-wide recommendations and binding treaties, which purport to be for *all* victims of crime, have tended to refer, both implicitly and explicitly, to citizens of individual states within the EU or to citizens of other EU member states. At the same time, documentation can also confusingly mention 'foreign' victims without clarifying their citizenship status in the EU. A recent study on *Crime Victims in the European Union* (Wergens 1999), funded by the Grotius Programme of the EU, is illustrative of the limited remit of many studies in consideration of 'foreignness'. Wergens introduces 'available assistance to foreign victims' as the primary aim of the study. However, the focus of the study, although not made explicit, would seem to be victims who originate from other member states of the EU.

Crime Victims in the European Union, which fed into the discussions at Tampere, focuses on the special problems of victims of crime in a member state of the EU *other than their own*, so indicating that 'foreign' victims essentially refers to other EU citizens. The same communication then adds: 'Although the Commission will occasionally refer to victims as "European citizens", this will, where applicable, also include third country nationals who are legally residing in the European Union' (*ibid.*: 3). Here, the crucial wording is 'where applicable' and 'legally residing'. This restrictive wording would appear to contradict the communication's statement that 'The importance of victim support has also been demonstrated in respect of women being trafficked for the purpose of sexual exploitation' (*ibid.*) – as trafficked women are often illegal immigrants. However, recent initiatives by different police forces across the EU have indicated that certain member states are willing to assist some of the most marginalised and vulnerable immigrants in the EU – such as trafficked women – who fall foul of organised crime groups.

An acid test of the advances made for victims of crime in the EU can, surely, be gained through an insight into how favourably the EU's most disadvantaged victims are treated. Likewise, one is able to see how 'serious' the EU is about convicting people for involvement in organised crime activities, such as trafficking in human beings, through an assessment of any legislation, procedures and services that facilitate the protection and, perhaps, testimonies of these vulnerable victims.

Trafficking women into the EU for the purpose of sexual exploitation

Definition and extent of the problem

'Trafficking' has been variously defined by a number of international agencies in the EU. For example, the European Commission defines it as:

> the transport of women from third countries into the European Union (including perhaps subsequent movements between Member States) for the purpose of sexual exploitation ... Trafficking for

the purpose of sexual exploitation covers women who have suffered intimidation and/or violence through the trafficking. Initial consent may not be relevant, as some enter the trafficking chain knowing they will work as prostitutes, but who are then deprived of their basic human rights, in conditions which are akin to slavery.[11]

In turn, 'trafficking' and 'smuggling' tend to be confusingly employed to refer to the illicit movement of people into the EU. The UN provides the latest comprehensive international definitions of 'trafficking in persons' and 'smuggling' as separate items under the Protocols on trafficking[12] and smuggling[13] which supplement the UN's Convention against Transnational Organised Crime. While definitions are open to debate and disagreement, there is overwhelming consensus at the beginning of the twenty-first century that trafficking in women (and children), for purposes of sexual exploitation, is a real and extensive problem on a global scale. However, the 'true' extent of the problem is somewhat difficult to gauge given its covert operation and the unwillingness and inability of its victims to come forward to denounce their abusers.

In the EU, the International Organisation for Migration (IOM) is a respected NGO that has provided the most quoted estimate on the number of women trafficked into the EU, the figure being 500,000 for the year 1995 (IOM 1995). Alongside NGO 'guesstimates' on the extent of trafficking into the EU, one can turn to a few police sources for officially recorded data on the phenomenon that represent the tip of the iceberg when attempting to provide an approximation of the problem.

The German Bundeskriminalamt (BKA or Federal Criminal Police Office) produces annual situation reports on trafficking in human beings that are based exclusively on information gathered from German police sources. In 1999, the BKA recorded 801 victims of trafficking, only two of whom were male (BKA 1999). Of these 801 victims, the overwhelming majority, 88.9%, were nationals of central and east European countries. The BKA also reports on the nationality of trafficking suspects, the highest percentages for 1999 being German (38.9%) and Turkish (15.3%), with the remainder from central and east European countries. Interestingly, 20% of German nationals who were suspects were not born in Germany. However, this does not detract from the fact that German nationals, as EU citizens, are most closely involved in the trafficking business alongside Turkish nationals who are exhibiting the more serious offending patterns that can be expected of established immigrant groups. However, as the BKA report notes, suspects acting abroad, as part of a trafficking network, were not included in the figures. Therefore, the number of foreign suspects is probably an underestimation.

The BKA's range of suspects and victims from central and east European countries reflects the economic and social factors, discussed earlier, which have exacerbated this region's slippage into crime, and the geographical proximity of the region to Germany. With the exception of German and Turkish suspects, and noting the underestimation of the numbers of suspects operating outside Germany, the BKA figures clearly indicate the extent to which non-EU nationals victimise other non-EU nationals from the same geographical region. Taking the above into account, the official evidence from Germany, which can be read as the basis for a more extensive pattern, points to the fact that German nationals and non-EU nationals are working in tandem to provide a transnational supply of women for the German sex industry.

Turning to evidence from Britain, Kelly and Regan (2000) provide the most comprehensive account of the phenomenon of, and responses to, trafficking in women in the UK. Kelly and Regan's account is based on official police figures for 1998, which they received from 36 of the 43 police forces in England and Wales. The results of their survey reveal that, of the five police forces handling trafficking cases in 1998, the total number of women involved amounted to a mere 71. This figure is in striking contrast to the officially recorded figures from the BKA and might appear to support Beare's (1997: 17) warning that the scale of the smuggling problem (and here one can transplant 'trafficking') is not as great as the political (over-)reaction to this 'national security threat' would have us believe: 'In addition to labour market issues and sovereignty issues, there are linkages between alien smuggling and organised crime. Mixed with "real" issues is the sense that some of the concern may be out of proportion to the actual size of the illegal alien problem.' However, Kelly and Regan's official figures can be reassessed in light of evidence, before 1998, of two large trafficking cases each involving one hundred or more women from Brazil and Thailand (Kelly and Regan 2000: 18). Also, Kelly and Regan draw on evidence alongside the questionnaire returns they received from the police (immigration, health projects dealing with the sex industry, newspaper reports, the Internet, etc.) to calculate, through a highly subjective but logically progressive formula, that the extent of the problem may be two to twenty times greater than their official research findings suggest. This would indicate that the 'true' number of trafficked women, for 1998, is anywhere between 142 and 1,420 in number.

Kelly and Regan's report does not provide any detail on suspect nationalities. Instead, a picture of victims' nationalities is offered with respect to the 18 trafficking cases, involving 71 women, noted for 1998. As stated by Kelly and Regan 'Current information suggests that the most likely countries of origin for women trafficked into the UK are Thailand and Central and Eastern European countries' (*ibid.*: 23). The report goes on to provide a picture of sending countries and trafficking routes into the UK, as based on police and immigration intelligence. The range of countries, spread over several continents, confirms the truly global nature of trafficking in women as it impacts on the UK's sex industry which, according to Kelly and Regan's extrapolation of police data and other sources, is an extensive criminal activity that is grossly under-investigated by the police.

Gendering the security threat

As with so-called 'conventional' crime, TOC – as crime – is predominantly committed by males. TOC can have an impact on men and women but, in the case of trafficking, TOC is a gendered phenomenon with respect to its perpetrators, victims and, one should add, its 'clients'. Trafficking in women is no different from other crimes of violence and oppression committed by men against women. With recognition of the gendered nature of the crime, as outlined in a number of policy documents (Council of Europe 1997; OSCE 1999), we begin to unearth the inequalities – social, economic, sexual – which point to poor women's over-representation as victims of trafficking in the EU.

The feminisation of poverty in central and eastern European countries is the result of increased polarisation between rich and poor, coupled with discriminatory employment practices, which have disproportionately affected women (OSCE 1999). Poverty has encouraged women to seek employment opportunities beyond this region. While some women who are trafficked into the EU are aware of the true nature of the work they will be doing once they reach their destination (BKA 1999), many are deceived by their traffickers and assume they are being recruited to work as waitresses, bar attendants and dancers in affluent western European cities.[14] Even women who know they will be working as prostitutes are not prepared for the level of abuse they are likely to receive en route to their destination, nor are they aware of the 'slavery' like conditions under which they will be held once they start their 'employment'. The level of abuse incurred through trafficking, which negates women's most basic human rights, warrants that the women involved be treated as victims, rather than culpable partners in TOC, by criminal justice and immigration authorities in the EU.

Women, as victims of trafficking, risk being routinely misdiagnosed and inappropriately responded to as 'offenders' and 'undesirable immigrants' on the basis they may have illegally entered an EU country without a legitimate visa and, in the case of certain member states, may be guilty of breaking prostitution laws. However, if the EU were to scrutinise women's visa applications to a greater extent than men's, in an effort to combat trafficking, this would unduly impinge on women's freedom of movement into the EU from poor developing countries. By the same token, women, rather than traffickers, are the easiest targets for the police and immigration authorities to apprehend, deport and, potentially, punish. Recent calls for more consideration to be given to the needs and rights of trafficked women, from the White House down,[15] are not matched, as yet, by effective action on the ground that responds to women, first, as victims and, secondly, as illegal immigrants associated with TOC networks.

A fundamental problem that forestalls adequate responses to trafficked women, as victims, rests with police attitudes towards women as both victims and offenders (Worrall 1990; Lees 1997) and, in particular, women who are prostitutes. Coupled with this are negative police attitudes towards 'undesirable' poor foreigners. The combination of these factors – gender, ethnicity, poverty – does not bode well for women who either want to report to the police, to escape their victimisation, or are found by the police in routine raids on brothels and other establishments where prostitutes work. A recent Council of Europe report on witness protection states:

> The use of witness protection in cases of human trafficking is seen as less effective [than in other cases], at least from a prosecutorial viewpoint. This is due to the fact that the illegal immigrants involved usually only have information on one or two traffickers and therefore their testimony is not sufficient to dismantle the criminal organisation. (1999: 12)

While this statement may be true, and having regard to the EU's recent initiatives that purport to take all victims of crime more seriously, the criteria for victim assistance cannot remain with the extent to which the victim can assist the prosecution. Victim protection should be offered regardless of whether a trafficked woman, as an (illegal) immigrant working as a prostitute, decides to give evidence. The victimisation of some of the most vulnerable people in the EU, such as trafficked women, cannot be overlooked as a gendered human rights phenomenon under the guise of a genderless security threat facing the EU.

Responding to the problem

There is a wealth of recommendations, guidelines and action plans, from the European Commission down to local police force initiatives, which attempt to address the problem of trafficking in women in the EU. At the level of trafficking as a human rights abuse, the Council of Europe has been very active in responding to the need for research and policy guidelines in this area.[16] The European Commission and the European Parliament have also produced extensive input at the level of legislative reform and criminal justice initiatives.[17]

In 1997, the Council of the European Union announced a comprehensive joint action plan in their effort to combat trafficking in women (and children) for sexual exploitation in the EU. Within this over-arching agenda there are a number of parallel joint actions that address trafficking either directly or indirectly through efforts to combat organised crime. Two of the most ambitious programmes in the EU, which attempt to put guidelines into action, are the 'STOP' programme and the 'Daphne' initiative. The STOP programme, initiated by the Justice and Home Affairs Council of the EU, funded research and action initiatives that set out to combat the sexual exploitation of women and children, including trafficking. The programme was aimed at public officials and representatives of NGOs responsible for combating the trade in human beings for purposes of sexual exploitation.[18] The programme was set up in 1996 and ended in 2000. It was complemented by the Daphne initiative which supports NGOs working on programmes and international exchanges that aim to combat violence against women and, therefore, includes projects on trafficking. At the same time as the STOP programme was instigated, the Justice and Home Affairs Council agreed to a joint action to extend the remit of the European Drugs Unit (the precursor to Europol) to include the collection, analysis and exchange of information and intelligence on trafficking.[19]

While all these communications, recommendations and action plans may be laudable, and while trafficking is now a criminal offence in all 15 member states of the EU (Kelly and Regan 2000: 11), this does not guarantee results against trafficking at any substantive level. There is, as the previous paragraphs illustrated, a continuing problem of trafficking in the EU. Turnbill's enthusiastic commentary on EU co-operation in the area of justice and home affairs, suggesting that trafficking in women and children 'appears to be an area where there has been significant success' (1997: 203), contrasts with Kelly and Regan's (2000: 12–13) observation, three years later, that 'it appears there has been much talk but limited action. Certain recommendations recur in the literature with little sense of progress being made'. If 'success' against trafficking in the EU were measured by awareness of the problem and the development of transnational action plans seeking research and co-operation at the criminal justice and NGO level then, to some extent, success is a given. However, should 'success' be measured in terms of the numbers of traffickers prosecuted for the crime of trafficking, then it has been an abysmal failure.

In defence against this harsh critique, one can offer examples of ongoing programmes in a few member states, such as Germany (BKA 1999) and Belgium,[20] which have seen the co-operation of the police and NGOs in the prosecution of traffickers and the rehabilitation of female victims. However, these progressive 'success' stories tend to be localised exceptions, as most police forces lack the adequate resources to deal with the problem of trafficked women. While Mameli (2000) explores the role Europol does and could play against the transnational sex industry, his comments need to be set against the reality of the skeleton staff at Europol who are dedicated to combating trafficking.[21] This chapter does not allow sufficient space to engage in a discussion of how local, national and transnational police/NGO co-operation might be improved to combat and prosecute traffickers. The simple remit of this chapter is to turn attention back towards the plight of trafficked women as the 'forgotten' victims in much of the national and international discussion to date on TOC as a national/EU-wide security threat.

Concluding comments

Transnational organised crime presents the EU with a ready-made 'enemy'. Undesirable immigrants are the EU's social 'other' and the scapegoats, representing TOC, under which the union's internal criminal problems are able to hide. TOC is a criminal problem, but its status has been elevated to that of a 'national security threat' against the union's member states and their citizens. As a 'security threat', the predominant discourse on TOC tends to negate its victimising role beyond that of an abstract threat. The neglect of TOC's most immediate victims, in this case trafficked women, has been offered as a balance to TOC's construction, primarily, as a 'criminal' concern rather than a 'victim' concern. In asking 'whose security?', this chapter has questioned the EU's construction of itself as the primary victim of organised crime. Recognising that TOC impacts most directly on some of the most marginalised and vulnerable people in the EU, this chapter has critiqued the EU's claim to take all victims of crime more seriously as some victims in the EU, the 'least desirable', are not offered the protection and support they obviously need. While significant developments are being made in an effort to assist victims of trafficking, through EU-wide criminal justice initiatives, there is still considerable progress to made in this area as, to date, the focus remains with TOC as a crime problem for the union and its member states.

Notes

1 The Tenth United Nations Congress on the Prevention of Crime and the Treatment of Offenders (Vienna, 10–17 April 2000), where member states debated the UN's latest Convention against Transnational Organised Crime, is illustrative of the high profile TOC currently enjoys on the world stage.
2 The Convention Relating to the Status of Refugees, 28 July 1951, 189 UNTS 150, which entered into force on 22 April 1954.
3 The Europol Drugs Unit *Situation Report on Organised Crime in the European Union, 1996* revealed that only one third of all organised crime suspects in Belgium were Belgium nationals, but the most frequently investigated nationalities, in descending order, were Italian, Dutch, Turkish, French, Moroccan, Russian, Yugoslavian, German and Romanian. On the other hand, Germany's suspects, in descending order, were Turkish, individuals from the former Yugoslavia, Polish, Italian, Vietnamese and Russian.
4 Home Office prison statistics for England and Wales, as of 31 March 1999, reveal that nationals from the Irish Republic represent the highest number of sentenced male foreign nationals in prison. Though these findings cannot be weighted alongside figures that reveal the representation of foreign nationals in prison according to their numbers in the general population, the same data source also shows that 86% of non-criminal prisoners are foreign nationals mostly detained for Immigration Act violations.
5 The definition of 'organised criminal group' (at the time of writing) for the purposes of the UN Convention against Transnational Organised Crime, debated at the Tenth United Nations Congress on the Prevention of Crime and the Treatment of Offenders (10–17 April 2000, Vienna), is '"Organised Criminal Group", shall mean a structured group of three or more persons existing for a period of time and acting in concert with the aim of committing one or more serious crimes or offences established pursuant to this Convention, in order to obtain, directly or indirectly, a financial or other material benefit.' Article 2 of the draft UN Convention against Transnational Organised Crime proposes that an offence is transnational in nature if: 1) it is committed in more than one state; or 2) it is committed in one state but a substantial part of its preparation, planning, direction or control takes place in a different state.
6 See Council of Europe Recommendation (96)8 on crime policy in Europe in a time of change.

7 See: www.homeoffice.gov.uk/ind/asylum/asylum_home.html

8 See *The Financial Times* report (Weekend 8–9 July 2000) on Spain's bill to curb illegal immigration, as a result of increased numbers illegally entering the country, through increased penalties against traffickers and employers of illegal immigrants.

9 Document 10387/00 COPEN 54 *Draft Framework Decision on the Standing of Victims in Criminal Procedure.*

10 Compare the main remit of the Treaty of Amsterdam and the Tampere Summit with initiatives such as the joint action of 24 February 1997, adopted by the Council of the European Union (on the basis of Article K3 of the Treaty on European Union), concerning action to combat trafficking in human beings and sexual exploitation of children.

11 Communication from the Commission to the Council and the European Parliament on Trafficking in Women for the Purpose of Sexual Exploitation, Brussels, 20 November 1996 COM (96) 567 final, p. 4.

12 *UN Draft Protocol to Prevent, Suppress and Punish Trafficking in Persons, Especially Women and Children*, supplementing the UN Convention against Transnational Organised Crime, Article 2 *bis*, (a): '"Trafficking in persons" shall mean the recruitment, transportation, transfer, harbouring or receipt of persons, by means of the threat of use of force or other forms of coercion, of abduction, of fraud, of deception, of the abuse of power or of a position of vulnerability or of the giving or receiving of payments or benefits to achieve the consent of a person having control over another person, for the purpose of exploitation. Exploitation shall include, at a minimum, the exploitation of the prostitution of others or other forms of sexual exploitation, forced labourer services, slavery or practices similar to slavery, servitude or the removal of organs' (A/AC.254/L.250/Add. 1) – as of 10 October 2000.

13 *UN Draft Protocol against the Smuggling of Migrants by Land, Sea and Air*, supplementing the UN Convention against Transnational Organised Crime, Article 2, (a): '"Smuggling of migrants" shall mean the procurement, in order to obtain, directly or indirectly, a financial or other material benefit, of the illegal entry of a person into a State Party of which the person is not a national or a permanent resident' (A/AC.254/L.250/Add. 3) – as of 17 October 2000.

14 *IOM News* June 2000: 'Don't get hooked' – IOM anti-trafficking campaign in Hungary.

15 President William J. Clinton, executive memorandum 11 March 1998 on 'Steps to combat violence against women and trafficking in women and girls', Washington DC, in *Trends in Organised Crime* (1998) Special focus: modern slavery: trafficking in women and children 3(4): 20–1.

16 For example, Council of Europe (1994) *Final Report of the Group of Specialists on Action against Traffic in Women and Forced Prostitution as Violations of Human Rights and Human Dignity.* Strasbourg: CDEG.

17 For example, European Commission (1996) *Communication from the Commission to the Council and the European Parliament on Trafficking in Women for the Purpose of Sexual Exploitation* COM (96) 567, Brussels (20.11.96), European Parliament (1996) *Resolution on Trafficking in Human Beings* OJ C 32 (5.2.1996).

18 STOP programme: joint action 96/7090/JHA; *Official Journal* L.322, 12 December, 1996.
19 Europol Drugs Unit: joint action 96/748/JHA; *Official Journal* L. 342 31 December 1996.
20 Personal communication with Professor Brice De Ruyver at the 10th United Nations Congress on the Prevention of Crime and the Treatment of Offenders, Vienna, 10–17 April 2000.
21 According to Kelly and Regan (2000: 12–13), at the time of writing their report, there were only 1.5 staff dedicated to trafficking in Europol.

References

Albini, J.L. (1997) Donald Cressey's contributions to the study of organized crime: an evaluation. In P.J. Ryan and G.E. Rush (eds) *Understanding Organized Crime in Global Perspective*. London: Sage.
Albrecht, H.J. (1997) Minorities, crime and criminal justice in the Federal Republic of Germany. In I.H. Marshall (ed.) *Minorities, Migrants and Crime*. London: Sage.
Beare, M.E. (1997) Illegal migration: personal tragedies, social problems, or national security threats? *Transnational Organized Crime*, 3(4): 11–41.
BKA (1999) *Trafficking in Human Beings. Situation Report 1999*. Wiesbaden: Bundeskriminalamt.
Brienen, M. and Hoegen, E. (2000) Victims of crime in twenty-two European jurisdictions. PhD thesis, Katholieke Universiteit Brabant, Nijmegen, The Netherlands.
Carroll, R. (2000) In praise of smugglers. *The Guardian* 2 September: 8.
Council of Europe (1997) *Report on Traffic in Women and Forced Prostitution in Council of Europe Member States* (Doc. 7785, rapporteur Mrs Renate Wohlwend).
Council of Europe (1999) *Recommendation R (96)8 on Crime Policy in Europe in a Time of Change*. Strasbourg: Council of Europe Publication.
Fitzpatrick, J. (2000) Temporary protection of refugees: elements of a formalized regime. *American Journal of International Law*, 94(2): 279–306.
Goodey, J. (2000) Non-EU citizens' experiences of offending and victimisation: the case for comparative European research. *The European Journal of Crime, Criminal Law and Criminal Justice*, 8(1): 13–34.
Hobbs, D. (1998) Going down the glocal: the local context of organised crime. *The Howard Journal*, 37(4): 407–22.
IOM (1995) *Trafficking and Prostitution: The Growing Exploitation of Migrant Women from Central and Eastern Europe*. Geneva: IOM.
Karpf, A. (1997) *The War After*. London: Minerva.
Kelly, L. and Regan, L. (2000) *Stopping Traffic: Exploring the Extent of, and Responses to, Trafficking in Women for Sexual Exploitation in the UK. Police Research Series*, paper 125. London: Home Office.
Lees, S. (1997) *Ruling Passions: Sexual Violence, Reputation and the Law*. Buckingham: Open University Press.
Mameli, P.A. (2000) Interpol, Europol and the transnational sex industry. Paper presented at the Tenth International Symposium on Victimology, 6–11 August 2000, Montreal.

Marshall, I.H. (ed.) (1997) *Minorities, Migrants and Crime.* London: Sage.

McIllwain, J.S. (1999) Organized crime: a social network approach. *Crime, Law and Social Change,* 32(4): 301–23.

Melossi, D. (1994) The 'Economy' of illegalities: normal crimes, elites and social control in comparative analysis. In D. Nelken (ed.) *The Futures of Criminology.* London: Sage.

Morrison, J. (1998) *The Cost of Survival: The Trafficking of Refugess to the UK.* London: Refugee Council.

Nelken, D. (1997) Understanding criminal justice comparatively. In M. Maguire, R. Morgan and R. Reiner (eds) *The Oxford Handbook of Criminology* (2nd edn). Oxford: Oxford University Press.

OSCE (1999) *Trafficking in Human Beings: Implications for the OSCE.* Background Paper 1999/3. Warsaw: Organisation for Security and Co-operation in Europe, and Office for Democratic Institutions and Human Rights (ODIHR).

Ruggiero, V. (2000) *Crime and Markets: Essays in Anti-Criminology.* Oxford: Oxford University Press.

Ruggiero, V., South, N. and Taylor, I. (eds) (1998) *The New European Criminology: Crime and Social Order in Europe.* London: Routledge.

Schmid, A.P. (1996) Organized crime and refugees. In A.P. Schmid (ed.) *Whither Refugee? The Refugee Crisis, Problems and Solutions.* Leiden: PIOOM.

Sibley, D. (1995) *Geographies of Exclusion.* London: Routledge.

Tonry, M. (ed.) (1997) *Ethnicity, Crime and Immigration.* Chicago, IL: University of Chicago Press.

Turnbill, P. (1997) The fusion of immigration and crime in the European Union: problems of co-operation and the fight against the trafficking in women. *Transnational Organised Crime,* 3(4): 189–213.

Wergens, A. (1999) *Crime Victims in the European Union: Reflections on Standards and Actions.* Umeå, Sweden: The Crime Victim Compensation and Support Authority.

Worrall, A. (1990) *Offending Women.* London: Routledge.

Chapter 6

Immigration, crime and unsafety

Hans-Jörg Albrecht

Introduction: immigration, feelings of unsafety and violence

In February 2000, in a medium-sized Spanish city named El Ejido, a pogrom erupted, the results of which were widely covered by European newspapers.[1] In this city of some 52,000 inhabitants, the population of foreign nationals (11,000, most of them Moroccans working on the farmlands around El Ejido) became the targets of violence for three full days. Immigrants' shops were vandalised and burnt down, cars were set on fire and some 40 people were injured when hundreds of Spanish citizens hunted down migrants – some of whom fled to remote mountain areas to escape the waves of violence. The police finally intervened after three days of violence and rioting to restore a semblance of order, which remained precarious thereafter. The basic facts as presented in the media were as follows: two weeks before the outbreak of violence, two Spanish farmers had been killed, allegedly by two Moroccan field workers. The outburst of violence was also related to a second incident of murder that followed shortly after the initial killings. A 20-year-old (and obviously psychologically disturbed) Moroccan immigrant stabbed to death a young woman during a robbery attempt in the open street.

The El Ejido incident is significant as this region of Spain has enjoyed very rapid economic development during the last decade or so due to successful farming methods aided by thousands of immigrants working on the fields. This outbreak of violence is different from other pogrom-like events that have occurred in recent years, for example that which erupted in Germany in the early nineties in the New Bundeslaender. In Rostock-Lichtenhagen hundreds of violent German youths tried to burn down the homes of asylum-seekers under the eyes of passive police and of thousands of rather condoning adult spectators (see Althoff 1997: 395). Here large-scale economic and socio-political changes after German reunification led to mass unemployment and related issues of anomie.

Immigrants from Morocco, however, come from a background comprising poor and uneducated field workers and they are over-whelmingly male and young. Furthermore, clandestine migrants also make up a substantial proportion of the immigrant population of El Ejido. Hence, not only did the economy boom but crime rates went up as well, as could be expected from the demographic structure of the immigrant group. The El Ejido incidents were preceded by less spectacular incidents of collective violence against migrants in Spain. During 1999, similar sprees of violence occurred in Melilla, Terrassa and Banyoles.[2] However, it is not only Spain where such pogroms take place. Hate violence directed against immigrants has occurred since the end of the eighties and re-emerges on a regular basis throughout the whole of Europe. Accounts of such pogrom-like events – as well as individual acts of hate motivated violence – are recorded in the annual reports of the European Monitoring Centre on Racism and Xenophobia (EUMC 2000: 17) and are summarised in the country reports of the European Commission against Racism and Intolerance (e.g. ECRI 2001a). The 1999 EUMC report and the ECRI (2001b) report describe hate incidents and pogroms as being widespread and as affecting every European country. Statistical accounts vary considerably. In particular, statements on longitudinal aspects seem almost impossible to make as there do not exist common definitions or approaches as to what should be regarded as established hate violence or racist violence and related acts (over time and across countries). It is only recently that some countries (such as Germany and England and Wales) have started to collect data on hate crimes as part of police crime data collection. Nevertheless, it is the emergence of group violence directed against (visible) minorities that particularly attracts attention and evidently has – though it can also be regarded as a rare event – the power of creating considerable fear and feelings of unsafety not only in minority groups but also in societies at large. European-wide surveys confirm that – measured through attitudes and perceptions – quite substantial parts of autonomous populations see themselves as being racist. From the Eurobarometer opinion poll carried out in 1997 it is estimated that some 33% of the population of EU member states perceive themselves as being 'quite' or 'very' racist (Eurobarometer 47.1 1997).

The availability of, and the need for, folk devils and folk dangers

The possible sources of such hostilities and, ultimately, violence are almost certainly located somewhere in the process of developing into modern and, then, late modern societies (Young 1999). However, it should be acknowledged that preying upon minorities, marginalisation and moves towards total extinction are not phenomena that have emerged all of a sudden and are certainly not restricted to the last decades of the twentieth century. Crime and crime control-related accounts of late modernity sometimes give an (unfounded) impression that late modernity, or the last three decades of the twentieth century (that is, socioeconomic and cultural changes characterising late modernity), have seen the emergence of waves of violence, the opening up of new paths to violence (Young 1999) and the production of instability and crisis to a hitherto unknown extent (Hobsbawm 1994). However, as viewed from the first half of the twentieth century, the second half indeed looks rather peaceful, almost so quiet it is as if the second half of the century came close to being something of a 'golden age' to use an image usually restricted to North America). However, histories of Europe from the Middle Ages through the Enlightenment and beyond demonstrate a search for folk devils and scapegoats, the demonisation of the 'other' and the permanent exclusion of the stranger.

What is in fact different in modern societies is the increased availability of minority groups that can be scapegoated, the easy exchangeability of ideological prey mobility presents and large-scale migration and immigration. These factors have been compounded by a state that has evidently lost substantial parts of its power to regulate and to govern with the aim of solving social and economic crises by way of traditional forms of governance. Moreover, we have seen the emergence of mass media (and markets) that, in a certain sense, are dependent on finding and creating demons and folk devils and constructing pictures that convey messages of threat, tensions and distraction (as well as entertainment). The mass media have developed the power of creating images that are much more influential as they are disseminated much more rapidly. The media are more consumer led and reach more consumers than ever. What has also changed since the Enlightenment are the basic concepts of folk devils and demons; they have been transformed into dangers and risks. Demonisation has been replaced by the concept and the strategy of 'dangerisation'. Political governance, therefore, has become partially dependent on the deviant other and the mobilisation of feelings of safety. Political power, and its establishment, as well as its preservation, are today dependent on carefully selected campaign issues, among which safety (and feelings of unsafety) is paramount (Sack 1999). Safety is one of those political topics that forces all political parties and discussants into a vicious circle of consent and the annihilation of conflict and discourse. Such forced consent allows only for a response of 'more of the same' (that is, more safety and more instruments that promise immediate safety). This can be expected as safety is like no other political issue. It is exploitable and may serve as an instrument to mobilise feelings and, ultimately, votes (Linder 1995). Sack (1999) quotes the former Republican leader of the US Senate, Newt Gingrich, who, when asked how elections can be won, said through 'cutting taxes and the death penalty').

Other changes concern the remedies implemented and made available for controlling ethnic hatred, discrimination, racism and related violence. The concepts of 'hate crimes' and of the legal control of discrimination find support in most European countries. These countries have contributed to the debate on the possibilities of preventing hate violence and discrimination by way of criminal law. They have also made clearly visible signs that group conflicts, racism, etc., will not be tolerated. Firm anti-discrimination policies can also be observed at the European level. The Council of Europe (as well as the EU) have initiated policies devised to create tolerant environments and to reduce intolerance, discrimination, racism and hate violence (see, e.g. the activities of the EUMC and ECRI).

What do these stories of violence and hate tell us? Very simply that violence, fear and angst, hate and perceptions of threats to safety and stability, perceptions of vulnerability, victims and offenders, all exist. They also tell us that there are beliefs about who those people and groups are, and who should be blamed for unsafety, feelings of insecurity and seemingly rising crime rates. These beliefs point to immigration and migration; they point to groups and individuals that seemingly are unsettled, different and are believed to create substantial risks and dangers. These stories, however, do not tell us much about how these elements are inter-related and how political and cultural contexts are involved in triggering collective and individual acts of violence. On the other hand, these stories tell us about local arrangements of social exclusion and the social construction of exclusion. Individual stories that reach the headlines are part of a bigger story that tells us how conceptions of order and norms (as well as policies and social forces) interact in producing targets of fear and, subsequently, hate, as well as excluded social groups – among which today the new immigrants and the old minorities are evidently evenly top ranked.

Bauman (2000; this volume) has elaborated on these issues. He has highlighted those mechanisms that are initiated by the enforcement of criminal norms, namely, a process of self-exclusion (with the result that the norm-breaking individual is made responsible for criminal behaviour as well as for the consequences attached to criminal behaviour – that is, punishment). It is thus not others who enforce exclusion; the message points to an individual who commits crimes and who himself or herself deliberately chooses the way to the margins of society or even out of society.

The waves of hate and hate violence referred to earlier perhaps also reflect what Adam Crawford has called 'defensive exclusivity' (1999: 516). This is an act of collective identity that emerges from the perception of external threats and that breeds not only the feeling the community has to be defended but also generates intolerance and organised violence against those who are made responsible for those threats to the safety and stability of communities. Fear and angst push the search for a suitable and visible target or – as Christie and Bruun (1991) have put it – for 'convenient enemies'. Convenient enemies are those where unanimous consent can be reached as regards their potential to serve as threatening images and of explanations of social problems of the kind that create fears and feelings of unsafety – in particular, feelings of instability and social unrest. Drugs and drug traffickers, organised criminals and corrupt officials, illegal immigrants and sexual predators are all eligible for a top position in this group of convenient enemies. Exclusivity has also been linked to late modernity in so far as market societies are said to produce at one and the same time crime and criminals as well as citizens who are eager to punish those criminals (Young 1999: 6–10). The causes of fear and angst are sometimes seen to be located in those conditions that produce frustration in norm-complying and conformist people who are confronted with the phenomenon that crime and deviance have become even more than 'normal' – in the Durkheimian sense – and who are not equipped with a criminological potential of reflexivity that allows them to make theoretical sense out of the normality of crime and deviance. This argument comes close to that developed by Garland (2000), who suggests that new punitive crime policies based on intolerance, criminal law and the prison are part of a reaction provoked by high crime societies and that are propelled into operation by the loss of political and ideological support the middle classes once offered to those old penal policies that were based upon inclusion and tolerance. Over the last two decades or so, however, it is the precarious group of new immigrants in particular who have, at the same time, attracted hate and produced fear and feelings of unsafety. This defensive exclusivity is based and transported through what might be called a defensive discourse on immigrants and, in particular, on asylum seekers. These groups are described in the media, in parliamentary and political party debates and in criminological discussions as groups that are heavily involved in crime (in particular, in organised crime and drug trafficking as well as in trafficking in humans). Immigration linked to organised drug trafficking or organised crime at large is sometimes referred to as an act of invasion. Descriptions of from where and with what commodities organised crime groups invade country A, B or C remind us of the military-like mapping of armies breaking through defensive lines (Huppertz and Theobald 1998). They are described as threatening the peace of society as, allegedly, they create for themselves the conditions that, in turn, lead to hate violence and pogroms (Althoff 1997: 400).

What have these various groups and individuals in common besides the obvious element of breaking the law and, thus, in a very simple sense, initiating the process of exclusion themselves? The illegal immigrant does not respect immigration procedures and the criminal does not respect criminal norms; the criminal illegal immigrant respects neither. Beyond this, they carry an agenda made up of topics that cannot be disputed (as regards their potential in terms of risks and threats) – topics that are not disputed by politicians or in professional circles, by the media or by the public. These individuals initiate a vicious spiral of rhetoric and talk as mentioned earlier that evidently does not allow for balances but is ultimately headed towards an escalation and a setting-up of selected groups as being responsible for problems and as being the legitimate target of control efforts, punishment and – in the case of immigrants – as targets of physical exclusion.

It is certain groups that evidently carry with them a potential for escalation. They do so from an enforcement view that says the problem has to be eradicated or, in modern language, has to be placed under a regime of zero tolerance, and from a perspective that attracts emotions in terms of feelings of fear and hate. The zero-tolerance model is readily evoked when considering sexual offences, drugs, organised crime and immigration. Immigration, in turn, has always been linked with feelings of xenophobia that, conceptually, involve both fear and aggression or hate and that tell about the potential of such targets to send societies into spirals of escalation.

However, what has to be acknowledged is a more complex relationship between immigration, crime, feelings of unsafety and the responses developed in European societies than usually is assumed. The political system, political parties, non-governmental organisations (NGOs) and other social groups, the criminal justice system and professions dealing with deviance and crime all interact in organising the response and implementing policies. These interactions lead to several layers of correlations but public discourses on immigration and related problems, political debates about these issues, the actual problems themselves (such as crimes committed by immigrants, etc.) and criminal justice, administrative or informal responses to immigrants could also, ultimately, lead to views independent of each other.

Research has underlined these views. Although until now there has been little empirical research devoted to possible links between cultural fears, on the one hand, and fear of crime, on the other (Boers 1993b), some German studies demonstrate that immigration problems are, in fact, less important from the viewpoint of public attitudes and perceptions than are other social problems, such as unemployment, economic crisis, environmental problems and traffic nuisances (Boers 1993a). According to this research, fear of crime and fear of specific types of crime are correlated with concerns for immigration. However, the size of the coefficients is rather small. The strongest coefficient was observed for the relationship between fear of violence and concern for immigration (0.18 – *ibid.*). The size, however, is still not high enough as to assume that such a correlation could be useful in explaining fear or concern of immigration. Rather, it can be assumed that concern for immigration is linked to a fear of rioting, social unrest and instability. The latter view is in fact supported by public opinion research that shows the public associates immigrants and, in particular, asylum seekers with such phenomena as hate, unrest and instability, while crime is rather rarely associated with immigration and asylum (Noelle-Neumann and Köcher 1993: 357).

Crime, feelings of unsafety and immigration

Presumptions about causal links between migration and crime and deviance suggest there exist powerful belief patterns concerning the potential for conflict and instability as a result of immigration and the 'stranger' or the 'other'. Immigration is commonly associated with invasion, and immigrants are often portrayed as 'invaders' (Agozino 2000: 362). Hence they are frequently portrayed as groups against whom defence is not only needed but also legitimate. The issue of 'immigration and crime' is, moreover, extremely sensitive as it can lead to polarisation of views and to political exploitation. Indeed, the potential of immigrants (and especially asylum seekers) to threaten safety and order has become a rallying point for authoritarian voices in society as well as for new right-wing political parties and extremist groups (Walter and Kubink 1993). It has also moved to the centre-stage of mass-media attention (Kubink 1993: 87; Althoff 1997). It has been estimated that drug trafficking and organised crime form the content of approximately 60% of crime issues reported in newspapers (Kubink 1993: 93). This picture has changed somewhat recently as immigrant and ethnic minorities now make it to the newspapers not only as offenders but also as the victims of (hate) crime. This change has been further compounded by a rise in the immigration of demographically and professionally valuable groups who are needed to take on those jobs for which there is a shortage of workers (e.g. in nursing, medicine and information and communication technology). However, the message conveyed to the public has not changed: illegal immigration and uncontrolled (unselected) immigration are causally related to crime and violence, unrest and instability. This message becomes even sharper when well educated and trained, economically important immigrants are compared with those immigrants or immigrant groups visible particularly in the metropolitan areas of Europe, who are predominantly young males and who are characterised as being unemployed and living on social security and in public housing. The liberal discourse on demography and on the needs of the economy and commerce, as well as on victimisation and the protection of human rights, finally vanishes when the focus of attention is on inner-city drug markets, prostitution, other parts of the shadow economy or prisons. Such a view of immigration reduces the European immigration agenda to the following:

1   Putting a total hold on unwanted immigration to Europe, in particular through the imposition for heavy penalties on the smuggling and trafficking of immigrants.

2   Where zero immigration is not possible, the problems (costs) associated with immigration are to be distributed evenly across the EU through the harmonisation of immigration, refugee and asylum laws (and practice).

3   The strengthening of the external borders of the EU.

4   Stepping up of internal controls through the empowerment of the police to engage in immigration controls and through investments

in deportation procedures and facilities.

5   Adopting a two-tier system of administrative and criminal law control for foreign national immigrants, which provides for permanent exclusion from the territory of the EU as a consequence of committing crimes or of living on social security.

In this process, the concept of immigration (and with it the concepts of ethnicity and minority) and the concepts of deviance and crime are separated from their respective theoretical bases. This is particularly true of the links that are commonly believed to exist between drug trafficking, organised crime and immigrants (Gordon 1994). The problems of immigration and illicit drugs are thus confounded each with the other and serve to re-enforce each other. However, creating social problems and establishing causal links in this way is not a phenomenon that was unique to the closing days of the twentieth century. In nineteenth-century North America, for example, the control of opiates is said to have been motivated by the opium-smoking habits of Chinese immigrant workers, and in the UK in the twentieth century, the National Drug Law Enforcement Unit's work was closely connected to the immigration control activities in the Central Drugs and Illegal Immigration Unit (Pearson 1992).

The potential for immigration and crime issues to be exploited politically and socially is also clear in criminology and social science more generally. Critical approaches and 'realist' views present their opposing cases, either stressing that the absence of research on immigration and crime renders the topic exploitable by right-wing politicians or assuming that a fear of immigration and ethnic minorities (as well as hate crimes committed against members of ethnic minorities) are provoked by the reporting of crimes committed by immigrants or members of ethnic minority groups their causes and preventive devices. In fact, the provocation argument seems to have some merits. Longitudinal data available for Germany demonstrate a strong correlation between the number of asylum seekers and the number of hate arsons (Figure 6.1). Figure 6.1 reflects the intensity of the debate on the asylum problem in Germany – particularly in relation to the number of cases of hate arsons. This figure also supports the assumption that the dramatic increase in hate arson is linked to German reunification and not solely to the number of asylum seekers (the number of asylum seekers is not something the general public in Germany is aware of).

Whatever argument is used about the validity or not of such assumptions, the research agenda throughout Europe is clear: analyses

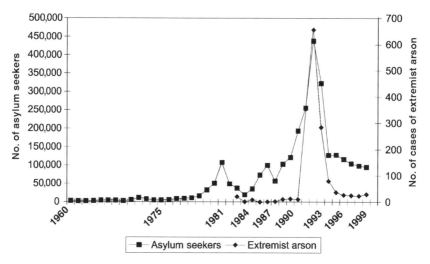

Figure 6.1: The numbers of asylum seekers and cases of extremist arson in Germany

Source: Bundesamt für Verfassungsschutz, Jahresberichte 1982–2000. Berlin: BAV (1983–2001); Bundesamt für Statistik, Statistisches Jahrbuch. Wiesbaden: BfS (1960–2001)

focus on the assumptions that a disproportionate number of crimes involve foreign minorities (see the reports in Tonry 1997), or on the hypothesis that the European criminal justice system is discriminatory (Mansel 1988). When we consider these analyses we often obtain the impression the essential question should be: whose side are we on? This debate is also surely fuelled by an apparent lack of comparative research designs that could provide valid data on the actual contributions of minority and majority members to the overall crime figures and by an apparent lack of adequate research on the discrimination hypothesis (which poses the very same problems in terms of ensuring sound research designs).

Immigration and crime have thus become central issues in debates about safety in EU countries (Tonry 1998: 60) and, as demonstrated by the Schengen treaties, safety is one of the most important concerns regarding EU policies about crime and crime control (Kühne 1991; Bundeskriminalamt 1999). This relationship between safety and immigration has arisen as a result of the process of globalisation, the shrinking of the first labour market and the rapid expansion of shadow economies, as well as a result of mass unemployment. The consequences of this perceived relationship are feelings of unsafety, segregation and the emergence of inner-city ghettos (Wiles 1993), a loss of social solidarity and massive signs of bias, hate and violence. Thus people's attitudes towards immigration and immigrants (and ethnic minorities) are such that immigrants are now seen as contributing to instability and violence (either actively as offenders or passively as violence-provoking victims); or as exploiting host countries and host societies (either through the marketing of illicit goods and services or through living on social security and property crime). This view is re-enforced through other signs of disintegration and conflict as displayed by immigrant groups – particularly their high share of unemployment, which makes immigrants (especially immigrants from non-EU countries) a social group evidently living at the margins of societies. Unemployment rates among non-EU immigrants are at least double those among the majority group (Muus 2001: 45).

However, European societies are rather diverse and, hence, sometimes inconsistent in their responses to immigration. Policies concerning the nationalisation of immigrants vary, as do policies concerning administrative detention and criminal justice responses to (offending) legal and illegal immigrants. While the political discourses in Europe in the last decade have highlighted nationalisation, asylum, refugee policies, employment and immigration policies concerning transnational crime have been accompanied with 'protection talk' that serves to camouflage an underlying and prevailing interest in reducing immigration. Administrative policies have displayed inconsistencies (and with this ambivalent attitudes) about the numbers of illegal immigrants over certain periods of time and, subsequently, about issues of regularisation (whereby an illegal immigrant is formally admitted and receives legal status). So, for example, in Italy, in 1999 the regularisation of illegal immigrants addressed some 250,000 cases, of which 145,000 were accepted and 14,000 were rejected (some 91,000 are still being processed). In Belgium, the authorities received (during January 2000) some 33,443 demands for regularisation. In France, the operation 'Chevènement' generated 140,000 applications for regularisation (*Le Monde*, 12th February 2000: 2; Muus 2001: 37). These figures demonstrate that European societies are still absorbing scores of immigrants, although the instruments used to grant immigrants a safe legal position have evidently changed. Today, the price immigrants must pay for a safe position (in many instances) comprises a prolonged period of uncertainty, illegality and risk of criminalisation.

Ethnicity, immigration and crime: changing frameworks and concepts

During the 1950s and 1960s in western Europe, immigration was almost exclusively the result of active labour recruitment or a consequence of post-colonial relationships. Today (as highlighted earlier) immigration is predominantly triggered by military conflicts, civil wars and the rapid processes of economic and cultural transformation in third world countries (Reyneri *et al.* 1999). Immigration perceived as a social, economic, political and criminal problem gained momentum as a result of the socio-political and economic changes that have affected Eastern Europe, as well as the opening up of the formerly tightly controlled borders between Western and Central European countries.

If we were to summarise our current understanding of the links between immigration and crime and deviance (Tonry 1998: 63–66), we might include the following.

- Some immigrant groups exhibit much higher incidences of participation in crime than the majority groups. However, certain immigrant groups display the same degree of (or even less) involvement in crime as is observed in the majority group.

- First generation immigrants arriving the 1950s and 1960s are much less involved in crime than second or third generation immigrants who arrived in the 1980s and 1990s.

- What most immigrant groups have in common, is their disadvantageous and precarious social and economic position.

- Cultural differences between similarly situated social groups can result in different crime patterns, both in terms of the scale and magnitude of criminal involvement.

- The cultural differences found between different immigrant groups relate to a capacity for community building and for the preservation of cultural and ethnic homogeneity within the immigrant group.

- Such cultural differences are evidently important in explaining the varying degrees of social and economic opportunities (be these legal or illegal) in different ethnic or immigrant communities and social groups.

- Social and economic changes in the last 20 years have, in general, worked to the disadvantage of immigrants. The immigration success stories from nineteenth- and twentieth-century Europe and North America concern immigrant groups that managed to work their way up and to integrate (economically and culturally) into mainstream society.

For example, at the end of the nineteenth century and the beginning of the twentieth century, several waves of Polish labour immigrants settled in the west of Germany (particularly in coal-mining areas) where they dissipated rapidly into mainstream society and had become invisible as a distinct group within half a century.

- The traditional concept of immigration and cultural conflict that was developed to explain the social problems attributed to immigration to North America is not one that fits the European situation: most immigration to Europe emanates from other European countries (including Turkey) or areas neighbouring Europe (e.g. the Maghrebian countries). This, in turn, creates new networks of migration and a pluralism of 'transnational communities'.

- The disappearance of low-skilled work and the transformation of industrial societies into service and information societies dependent on highly skilled staff have contributed to drastic changes within labour markets and, with that, to the basic framework of traditional mechanisms of social integration (which was always based upon labour and employment). Shadow economies and black markets (particularly in metropolitan areas) now offer precarious employment opportunities for newly arriving immigrants.

- Political changes in Europe have contributed considerably to transformations in the legal status of immigrants – through changes to the statutory framework of immigration as well as through enforcement policies. While in the 1960s and 1970s most immigrants entered Europe legally (as labour immigrants or on the basis of family reunion), today the status of new arrivals suggests illegality or the precarious status of 'asylum seeker', 'refugee' or 'tolerated immigrant' subject to strict administrative controls and threatened by a serious risk of criminalisation (as a consequence of not complying with administrative controls).

- With the transformation of labour markets into places requiring highly skilled workers, immigrants have acquired the image of being unemployed and dependent on social security. Crime policies no longer focus solely on crime and victimisation but on the assumed precursors of crime and deviance: family problems, unemployment and lack of education and training.

- Immigrants tend to concentrate in inner-city ghettos: immigration in Europe is largely targeted at metropolitan areas and, within those areas, towards ones that are increasingly plagued by all sorts of social problems.

- There have been important changes in the demographic structure of immigration. Labour migrants of the 1950s and 1960s were predominantly from rural areas while immigrants in the 1980s and 1990s were mostly from metropolitan areas (where the resources for migration are more readily available than in the more disadvantaged areas of developing countries).

- Migration and immigration in the second half of the twentieth century thus led to the fast-developing phenomenon of ethnic and migration networks and, with these to the establishment of transnational communities that represent an alternative to the EU master plan of the free movement of goods and people (Portes 1999: 23–4).

This chapter now turns its attention to the question of the disproportional involvement of immigrants in crime in order to look more closely at what is at the heart of the fear of immigration and of immigration control policies. To do this, data drawn from police sources in the Federal Republic of Germany are used as an example of the picture of immigration and crime that can be drawn from official crime statistics. In Germany, the numbers of criminal suspects who were non-nationals rose continuously until the mid-1980s, a statistic that reflects fairly well the increasing numbers of immigrants to that country in the 1960s to the 1980s. In 1953, when police statistics were published for the first time since the Second World War, the number of foreign suspects was as low as 1.7% (Albrecht 1997). In the mid-1990s this number had risen to approximately 30%. Since then, the number has been declining steadily (by 2000 it was approximately 26%), which reflects the drastic decrease in the number of asylum seekers from 1993 onwards (when the German constitution was amended in respect of the right of asylum). However, this decrease was especially marked in the area of small property crimes (notably shoplifting). This statistic hints at the types of crimes which asylum seekers are most actively involved in. Data from other European countries confirm the significant numbers of foreign nationals considered criminal suspects but there are distinct differences between countries (see Tonry 1997).

Figure 6.2 shows the numbers of foreign nationals suspected of involvement in cases of murder, and it is evident from these data that there are significant differences between various European countries. These differences must be explained by variations in nationalisation policies between countries. For example, Switzerland is known for its rather restrictive policy in this field; in France, on the other hand, substantial numbers of immigrants from Maghreb countries have acquired French nationality. While the numbers of foreign murder

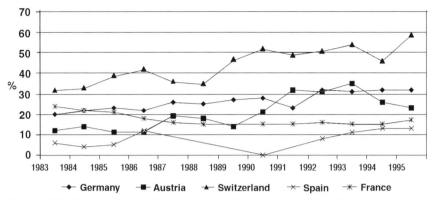

Figure 6.2: The numbers of foreign nationals suspected of involvement in cases of murder.

Source: International Police Organisation, International Crime Statistics (1983–95)

suspects remained rather stable and at a low level in Spain and France between 1983 and 1995, Germany, Austria and Switzerland exhibited significant increases that coincide with the opening up of borders between east and west Europe. It should also be noted that most violent crimes committed by immigrants are intragroup crime.

As German police information systems break down aggregated crime data into specific nationalities, we can observe that offender rates among certain groups of minorities are two to four times the rates found in society at large. Some minorities, on the other hand, demonstrate below-average offender rates (e.g. Spanish, Portuguese and Chinese ethnic groups). What the German data also tell us is that crime rates among labour immigrants were stable during the 1980s and 1990s. Similar patterns can be observed throughout Europe. As regards crime participation rates, data from England and Wales point to vast differences between black and Asian minorities, as do data from North America and other European countries (Tonry 1998). A consideration of the time involved in these statistics also highlights certain trends. These reflect changes in the behaviour patterns of second and third-generation immigrants, as well as changes in migration patterns. While during the 1960s the rates of suspects and the rates of immigrants followed each other closely, this gap widened during the 1970s. At this time there were disproportionate numbers of minority group members amongst recorded crimes, particularly in the 14–17- and 18–20-years-old age ranges. A tentative explanation for this could be that first-generation immigrants (in particular, labour immigrants) did (and still do) experience improvements in living conditions – in terms of better housing, better medical care, etc. – that outweighed existing differences in socioeconomic placement between minority and majority groups. Furthermore, one could argue that some form of selection took place as a result of workforce recruitment schemes, and that the interaction patterns of first-generation immigrants remained largely bound to the ethnic group itself, while contacts with the majority group were mainly confined to the workplace. Second and third generation immigrants, therefore, are more likely to be conscious of deprivation and socioeconomic inequality as well as the conflicting expectations placed upon them by a minority group still bound to traditional values as opposed to those values prevalent in modern societies. Moreover, as the intensity of interactions with the host society increases, so does the risk of conflicts. Research on the social and economic integration of ethnic and immigrant minorities throughout Europe reveals that significant numbers of people have slipped into marginal positions as regards socioeconomic status, income, housing conditions, education and employment. The basic conditions for social and economic integration worsened steadily during the 1980s and 1990s, and two groups in particular were affected by this development:

1. Those generations subsequent to the first labour immigrants who, on average, had a lower class background, were characterised by poor education and poor training, and who were, therefore, particularly exposed to the risk of unemployment – moreover, to the risk of never being able to enter the labour market.

2. New immigrants who arrived in the second half of the 1980s and in the 1990s. These groups immediately adopted marginal positions, falling into social security dependencies, becoming dependent on solidarity networks (as, possibly, provided by resident ethnic minority groups) or entering the shadow economy or black markets.

It is perhaps these solidarity networks and the capacity (as well as potential) of minority groups to build up ethnically homogeneous communities that work towards keeping down the level of participation in crime. These two factors are perhaps, also major obstacles to attempts to penetrate ethnic groups through traditional forms of policing and control strategies. On the other hand, ethnically homogeneous communities may be affected by an indisproportionate amount of hidden victimisation as a consequence of their reduced access to conventional legal resources. What can also be observed among many ethnic minority groups (particularly Asian communities) are high rates of self-employment and close-knit communities. This observation has been made particularly with regard to England and Wales, where it was found that Asians are much more reluctant to make contact with the host society than black people, who are much more 'outgoing' and, therefore, also more likely to experience discrimination and hostile treatment (Smith 1997: 174).

As noted earlier, police crime statistics clearly demonstrate marked changes in the motives for immigration. While in the 1960s–1980s it was immigrants motivated by prospects of employment who dominated the statistics in Germany, by the end of the 1980s and into the 1990s it was the asylum seekers, refugees or illegal immigrants who make up the bulk of foreign offender suspects. While this change in status cannot account for the personal reasons that motivate people to emigrate (with the exception, perhaps of the wars in Bosnia and Kosovo) it does reflect changes in immigration laws and policies. It is evident that the search for employment opportunities and, with that, for a better quality of life, are still the main forces driving people to immigrate to European countries. The target destinations of various ethnic groups across Europe certainly follow the distribution patterns of existing immigrant populations as these settled in Europe in the 1960s and 1970s. These patterns can be partially explained by historical factors (immigration from former colonies, etc.) as well as ease of immigration (language, employment prospects etc.).

Returning to crime statistics from Germany, we can differentiate at least four groups of immigrants each one of which exhibits a distinct pattern of offending. The first group is characterised by offences that relate to immigration fraud or forgery – attempts to enter the country illegally (forgery refers mainly to the use of false documents or passports). In Germany it is essentially immigrants from India, Pakistan, Afghanistan and Sri Lanka who display this offence pattern. Looking beyond nationality and focusing on the motivational factors behind such immigration, a rather homogeneous group emerges: unemployment and poverty are the main driving forces for these immigrants.

The second group is characterised by an extremely high level of property offences. Such offending patterns are prevalent among nationals from the former European socialist countries (Poland, Rumania, Bulgaria, Russia, etc.). The main type of offence committed by this group is small-scale theft. This might be a consequence of the formerly sealed borders of eastern Europe: shoplifting was perhaps something that was done – one might assume – on short-term visits to western European countries.

The third group is made up of nationalities that belong to traditional 'guest-worker' countries. This group comprises a large, stable resident population in Germany (as in other European countries). Within this group (represented in Germany mainly by Turks) more or less 'ordinary' offence patterns can be observed: a large share of property offences and crimes of violence. Immigration offences in this group are rather marginal. This group is marked by socioeconomic marginalisation that confines most of these labour immigrants (as well as their offspring) to the lowest social segment. A trend towards ghettoisation – observable in most European metropolitan areas – reinforces this marginalisation and social exclusion. However, among this group crime involvement may vary considerably, depending on nationality or ethnicity. Social solidarity, ethnic community building and self-employment may be decisive with regard to involvement in crime. However, it might also be that, as stronger social solidarity develops, less crime is reported and, as a consequence, crime investigation becomes more difficult.

The fourth and final group is characterised by its involvement in drug offences. In Germany as well as other European countries the demand for illicit drugs continues to be met by various ethnic and foreign national groups – for example, South Americans in the case of cocaine, and North African, black Africans and Kurdish and Arab groups in the case of heroine and cannabis. International drug networks require the participation of people from all sorts of background, either on the supply side or on the demand side of such illicit markets (see van Doorn 1993). Consequently, as trafficking routes change (in response to police pressures and changed border controls), the various national groups involved in drug trafficking and who are subsequently arrested also change. The black economy of drug smuggling provides some marginalised immigrant groups illicit income and the possibility of upward mobility (Tarrius 1997). For example, it has been estimated that, in the former East Germany, the market for untaxed cigarettes involves as many as 10,000 Vietnamese out of a total of 30,000 living in that part of Germany (Lehmann 1998).

As a consequence of such activities, organised crime has become a major concern for policy-makers all over Europe (Fijnaut et al. 1995). There are two sides to the organised crime debate. One sees organised crime as something that has been imported into Europe; the other sees it as something created by ethnic minority subcultures already established in host countries. Whatever position one assumes, organised crime is still conceived as a threat posed by alien groups (e.g. the Sicilian, Russian or Chinese mafia) who, it is assumed, extend their criminal activities to include western European countries (Krevert and Kohl 1996). Debates concerning American organised crime have had a considerable influence on the concept of organised crime in Europe (Fijnaut 1990). Such debates essentially assume that organised crime ultimately takes the form of crime syndicates and that such syndicates are themselves the result of an 'alien conspiracy' (Potter 1994). Immigrant communities in western Europe are believed to supply a basic logistic support for these syndicates, by providing 'bridge heads' and safe environments for organised criminals.

If we were to summarise the evidence on crime and immigration, we could conclude that immigration is in no way directly related to crime (except for those offences associated with illegal immigration and illegal residence and, perhaps, subsistence crime, which particularly charac-terises asylum seekers excluded from the labour market through immigration and asylum laws). However, immigrants and foreign nationals are undoubtedly involved in various forms of criminal activity amongst which illicit market activities (and crimes related to illicit markets) are certainly the most prominent. Crimes committed by second- or third-generation immigrants reflect precarious economic and social conditions as well as the fact that the immigrants of the 1960s and 1970s (as well as their offspring) have moved into positions once held by (national) underclasses.

Immigration, crime and exclusion policies

The extent to which the European criminal justice system has adopted punitive responses towards new immigrants may be ascertained from an inspection of the data on prison sentences and imprisonment. When one looks at European prison systems, it is clear immigrants continue to represent the most important single category of sentenced and unsentenced prisoners. Figure 6.3 shows that the numbers of foreign nationals in prison in many European countries come close to those reported for some parts of the USA. While the question, of course, is whether these data can be interpreted as indicating punitiveness towards immigrants, they must be treated with caution as reliable data on the number of foreign nationals held in prison do not exist. In any event, the numbers of foreign nationals held in prison will be an underestimation as substantial numbers of immigrants will be excluded from statistics as a result of the fact they have adopted the nationality of the host country (e.g. ethnic Germans who have immigrated from the former USSR or citizens of former colonial territories living, for example, in England, France or The Netherlands). The data, however, do demonstrate quite

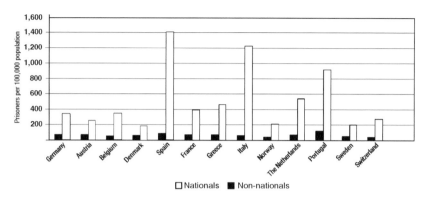

Figure 6.3: Prisoner rates in Europe (1997).

Source: Palidda *et al.* (1998)

clearly that Europe is closer to the USA in the numbers of non-nationals held in prison than is normally assumed.

When we look at the statistics concerning the prison population of Europe, we find that in many countries a large proportion of the immigrant detainees have been incarcerated for crimes relating to drug trafficking and drug offences in general. Almost 50% of foreign nationals detained in Spanish prisons were incarcerated for drug offences (Direccion General de Instituciones Penitenciarias 1999). In Germany in the second half of the 1990s, some 15% of prison sentences of 10–15 years, 24% of prison sentences of between 5 and 10 years and 31% of prison sentences of 2–5 years were imposed as a result of drug offences. In Italy, the doubling of the prisoner rate between 1990 and 1992 can be explained as a result of the tougher responses to illegal immigrants, on the one hand, and to drug offences on the other (Pavarini 1994). We may assume, therefore, that the response to the illicit drug market explains the high rates of imprisonment among certain selected groups of immigrants. However, there is evidently another area of change that accounts for the heavy use of imprisonment among groups for specific immigrant groups. Here, too, the German data are used to discuss and explain these trends.

From the late 1960s onwards in Germany, unconditional and conditional discharges, fines and suspended prison sentences were used to replace prison sentences . Looking at German sentencing practices of the last decades, we can observe several long-term trends. For example, the absolute annual numbers of convicted and sentenced offenders were stable during the 1970s and 1980s (at around 700,000 per year). In the 1990s there were 1,000–1,100 criminal convictions per 100,000 of the population. However, in the mid-1990s the figure for absolute annual convictions rose towards 760,000. While the stability of the conviction and sentencing rates is certainly due to the successful implementation of non-custodial sentences, the increase in the numbers of offenders sentenced during the 1990s can be accounted for by the rapidly growing proportion of foreign offenders. Nevertheless, the overall rate of sentenced offenders amongst the German population has decreased over the last 20 years: whilst there were 1,342 sentenced German offenders per 100,000 of the population in 1975, in 1996 this amounted to 1,076 per 100,000.

As just noted, prisoner rates since the 1960s demonstrate very clearly the apparent success of alternatives to imprisonment (such as day fines and suspended sentences). Prisoner rates dropped from some 100 per 100,000 at the end of the 1960s to approximately 65 at the beginning of the 1970s. In the early 1980s they rose as a result of the increasingly custodial response to drug trafficking (and also, partially as a response to sexual offences). In the mid-1980s the rates decreased once more and, since the start of the 1990s, the rates have shown an unbroken upward trend. These latter trends can be attributed to non-national and immigrant offenders: (new) immigrants and (new) immigrant drug offenders account for the increase in the use of imprisonment in the 1990s. With regard to resident offenders, on the other hand, not much seems to have changed in the last decade or so. This is the case for resident immigrant offenders as it is for German nationals. Imprisonment as a course of action for these groups will most probably continue to decline in use. However, illegal immigrants, asylum seekers and other unsettled groups fall immediately into a regime of pre-trial detention and remand in prisons. These groups are more likely to be given prison sentences because they cannot meet the criteria that apply to alternatives to imprisonment.

Immigrants therefore, fall under a second system of control that consists of administrative mechanisms as made available through immigration or foreign national laws. The basic approach of conventional European immigration and foreign national laws fits well with the construction of the immigration problems as comprising a mix of concerns such as crime, unemployment, poverty, illicit drugs and informal economies. Foreign national laws, in fact, have been enacted with the aim of regulating the risks and dangers associated with foreign nations (or immigrants): basic risks that have been made the grounds for expelling (or excluding) foreign nationals on account of concerns regarding crime, poverty and prostitution.

Illegal immigrants have slipped into the role once occupied by the *Lumpenproletariat* – the 'dangerous classes' of the developing metropolitan areas of the nineteenth century. They have become part of the new 'dangerous classes' of postmodern societies or, as modern sociology would put it, migrant and immigrant populations have become 'manageable risks'. In analysing how manageable these risks are, however, we must take into account that, besides normative questions related to immigration and asylum, there are subsidiary questions that affect the manageability of such risks. Today, there is a black market in illegal immigration that continuously adjusts itself to changes in the legal immigration framework within Europe. Related to this is the informal or shadow economy, which obviously operates very efficiently because of the ongoing and cheap supply of immigrant labour. The more tightly immigration is controlled, the more expensive immigration gets and, consequently, the more illegal immigration will be organised to reduce the costs for those organising such illegal immigration. To this, moreover, normative and moral costs must also be added as tighter controls generally also mean greater risk to life and limb for immigrants (discussions on death rates amongst illegal immigrants and how to respond to these are a good example of how such costs are weighed in current European immigration policies). A basic dilemma presents itself here – one known from other social-problem fields and one that should prevent us from adopting strategies of elimination in responding to these problems: namely, we should be reminded that migrants and immigrants are a very vulnerable group. While as a group they may contribute to the risks inherent in modern societies, as individuals they are most vulnerable and endangered people.

During the last decade Europe has invested heavily in creating and implementing immigration laws and policies (Albrecht and van Kalmthout 2001). Among the common features of such laws and policies are the following:

- A push towards reducing the legal opportunities to immigrate (including laws of asylum).

- A reduction in access to the labour market, to welfare and to other services.

- The widening of criminal laws and increasing penalty for illegal immigration, clandestine labour and organised immigration activities.

- The stepping up of the enforcement of immigration laws by extending the capacity for detention, expulsion and deportation.

- An increase in the capacity for the physical control of subgroups of illegal aliens in terms of secure detention facilities.

- The linking of administrative and criminal law in important new ways.

New laws have been created in the field of immigration and asylum to cover a mix of criminal and regulatory offences. These regulatory offences are aimed at controlling illegal immigration and the trafficking in immigrants and include restrictions on the free movement of asylum seekers who are placed under threat of criminal punishment should they leave those districts they are assigned to. Labour laws have also been tightened up during the last few years. Such developments are part of the move from a rather liberal concept of labour immigration in the 1960s to a conception of migration and immigration as a social problem.

There are two basic approaches to controlling the immigration and migration of foreign nationals:

1   Exclusion at the point of entry (partially also in terms of immediate entry into a detention centre or into an airport detention centre).

2   Exclusion after the individual has entered legally or illegally. Such an expulsion or deportation must be justified in that the individual represents a serious risk of crime or simply that the individual has overstayed a period of legal entry or has failed in asylum proceedings.

The first approach has established a preventative model of control. In Europe this has led to airport detention and to immediate transportation back to the country of origin on the basis of 'safe third country' rules. The second approach represents a mix of preventative and repressive measures. The grounds to withdraw a residency permit reflect the risks immigration policies and foreign national (immigration) laws seek to prevent. Basically, these include having committed criminal offences, having created other dangers or represented other risks (such as involvement in prostitution) and poverty (or becoming dependent on social security).

Thus a combination of administrative and criminal controls on immigration is being established that allows greater flexibility in responding to criminal offences committed by immigrants than does the criminal law alone. Expulsion and deportation are repressive or punitive measures that may be added to (or exchanged for) ordinary criminal penalties. Administrative procedures may replace criminal procedures which makes for administrative convenience but does away with the safeguards emanating from the rule of law.

If we review the statistical information available on the number of immigrants detained prior to deportation, similar trends can be observed

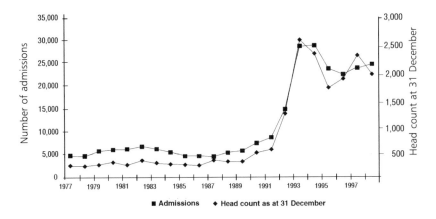

Figure 6.4: The numbers of administrative detentions in Germany (1977–98).

Source: Federal Ministry of Justice, Prison Statistics. Bonn/Berlin (1977–98)

across Europe. What is clear is that administrative detention has become more important during the 1990s. This coincided with the political and economic changes that occurred in eastern Europe as well as the implementation of the Schengen treaties and the emergence of the EU as outlined in the Maastricht Treaty. In the light of these developments it is remarkable that administrative detention accounts for the increasing numbers of immigrants held in custody.

Figure 6.4 shows the numbers of administrative detentions of foreign nationals in Germany. The messages from these statistics are that: 1) there was an enormous extension of detention capacity at the beginning of the 1990s; and 2) the administrative detention of foreign nationals outweighed the criminal detention of foreign nationals (or immigrants), with between 25,000 and 30,000 foreign nationals admitted annually to administrative detention facilities.

A consideration of the relationships between criminal justice and administrative immigration procedures reveals an intertwining of criminal and administrative approaches to the control of immigrant populations:

1   Procedures have been introduced into criminal law that allow for consideration to be given to administrative decisions when deciding to dismiss a case.

2   Sentencing decisions may take into account the possibilities of expulsion.

3   Prison sentences increasingly allow for consideration to be given to deportation in order to cut down the minimum amount of time to be served in prison prior to parole. Parolees might be deported immediately after release from prison.

Conclusion

Changes in European immigration patterns during the last four decades have been accompanied by increases in hate violence and pogrom-like attacks on immigrants. Newly arrived immigrants are particularly at risk and face many dangers, amongst which crime (organised crime and drug trafficking) plays a crucial role. This reflects the changing roles played by new immigrants. In Europe today they occupy from the outset of their entry a precarious status of illegal immigrant, refugee or asylum seeker – all of which carry a high risk of criminalisation. However, the response of criminal justice systems has been a selective one, targeting in particular illicit drug markets and drug offenders. Moreover, newly arrived immigrants do not seem to fall into the same category of offender group as those who are eligible to alternatives to detention and imprisonment (notably those alternatives created during the 1970s). Newly arrived immigrants, therefore, make up a large proportion of the prison population. Finally, administrative responses seem to have become more important than criminal justice responses, as have the links between the criminal justice and immigration systems through which the (physical) exclusion of immigrants is organised in many European countries today.

Notes

1   *Frankfurter Rundschau* 10 February 2000: iii 'Die Maurenjäger von El Ejid'; *Le Monde* 12 February 2000: 2: 'La peur et al colère de Said: "tu sortais, tu étais mort!"'.
2   *Le Monde* 12 February 2000: 2.

References

Agozino, B. (2000) Theorizing otherness, the war on drugs and incarceration. *Theoretical Criminology*, 4: 359–76.
Albrecht, H.-J. (1997) Ethnic minorities, crime and criminal justice in Germany. In M. Tonry (ed.) *Ethnicity, Crime and Immigration. Comparative and Cross-National Perspectives*. Chicago, IL: University of Chicago Press.

Albrecht, H.-J. and van Kalmthout, A. (eds) (2001) *Illegal Immigration and Detention in Europe*. Freiburg: Max Planck Institut.

Althoff, M. (1997) Die Herstellung von rassistischen Bildern in den Medien. Der 'ideale' Asylbewerber. In D. Frehsee *et al.* (eds) *Konstruktion der Wirklichkeit durch Kriminalität und Strafe*. Baden-Baden: Nomos.

Bauman, Z. (2000) Social uses of law and order. In D. Garland and R. Sparks (eds) *Criminology and Social Theory*. Oxford: Oxford University Press.

Boers, K. (1993a) Kriminalitätseinstellungen in den neuen Bundesländern. In K. Boers *et al* (eds) *Sozialer Umbruch und Kriminalität in Deutschland, Mittel- und Osteuropa*. Bonn: Forum Verlag.

Boers, K. (1993b) Kriminalitätsfurcht. *Monatsschrift für Kriminologie und Strafrechtsreform*, 76: 65–82.

Bundeskriminalamt (ed.) (1999) *Moderne Sicherheitsstrategien gegen das Verbrechen*. Wiesbaden: Bundeskriminalamt.

Christie, N. and Bruun, K. (1991) *Der nützliche Feind. Die Drogenpolitik und ihre Nutznießer*. Bielefeld: AJZ-Verlag.

Crawford, A. (1999) Questioning appeals to community within crime prevention and control. *European Journal of Crime Policy and Research*, 7: 509–30.

Direccion General de Instituciones Penitenciarias (1999) *Gabinete Technico, Datos Penitenciarios*. Madrid: Ministry of Justice.

ECRI (2001a) *Annual Report on ECRI's Activities Covering the Period from 1 January to 31 December 2000*. Strasbourg: Council of Europe.

ECRI (2001b) *Second Report on Germany. Adopted on 15 December 2000*. Strasbourg: Council of Europe.

EUMC (2000) *Annual Report 1999*. Vienna: European Union.

Eurobarometer Opinion Poll 47.1 (1997) 'Racism and xenophobia in Europe. First results presented at the closing conference of the European Year against Racism, Luxembourg, 18–19 December.

Fijnaut, C. (1990) Organized crime: the forms it takes, background and methods used to control it in western Europe and the United States. In G. Kaiser and H.-J. Albrecht (eds) *Crime and Criminal Policy in Europe*. Freiburg: Max Planck Institut.

Fijnaut, C., Goethals, J., Peters, T. and Walgrave, L. (eds) (1995) *Changes in Society, Crime and Criminal Justice in Europe. Volume II. International Organised and Corporate Crime*. Antwerpen: Kluwer Law International.

Garland, D. (2000) The culture of high crime societies: some preconditions of recent 'Law and Order' Policies. *British Journal of Criminology*, 40: 347–75.

Gordon, D.R. (1994) Drugs, race, and the 'Dangerous classes': policy politics in American drug prohibition. In L. Böllinger (ed.) *De-Americanizating Drug Policy*. Frankfurt: Peter Lang GmbH Verlag der Europäischen Wissenschaften.

Hobsbawm, E. (1994) *The Age of Extremes*, London: Michael Joseph.

Huppertz, M. and Theobald, V. (eds) (1998) *Kriminalitätsimport*. Berlin: Berlin Verlag A. Spitz.

Krevert, P. and Kohl, A. (1996) *Europa und die innere Sicherheit*. Wiesbaden: Bundeskriminalamt.

Kubink, M. (1993) *Verständnis und Bedeutung von Ausländerkriminalität. Eine Analyse der Konstitution sozialer Probleme*. Pfaffenweiler: Centaurus.

Kühne, H.-H. (1991) *Kriminalitätsbekämpfung durch innereuropäische Grenzkontrollen? Auswirkungen der Schengener Abkommen auf die innere Sicherheit*. Berlin: Duncker & Humblot.

Lehmann, B. (1998) Bekämpfung vietnamesischer Straftätergruppierungen in Berlin. *Der Kriminalist*, 30: 50–8.

Linder, W. (1995) Innere Sicherheit und Unsicherheit als politisches Problem. In Caritas Schweiz (ed.) *Verunsicherung durch schwindende Sicherheit – Strafrechtsreform unter Druck?* Luzern: Caritas.

Mansel, J. (1988) Kriminalisierung von Gastarbeiternachkommen durch Organe der Strafrechtspflege in der Bundesrepublik Deutschland. In G. Kaiser *et al.* (eds) *Kriminologische Forschung in den 80er Jahren. Vol. 35/2.* Freiburg: Max Planck Institut.

Muus, P. (2001) International migration: trends and consequences. *European Journal of Crime Policy and Research*, 9: 31–49.

Noelle-Neumann, E. and Köcher, R. (eds) (1993) *Allensbacher Jahrbuch der Demoskopie 1984–1990* München: Verlag Saur.

Palidda, S., Frangouli, M. and Papantoniou, A. (1998) *Les conduites déviantes et la criminalisation des immigrés.* Milano: Fondazione Cariplo-Ismu.

Pavarini, M. (1994) The new penology and politics in crisis. The Italian case. *British Journal of Criminolgy*, 34: 49–61.

Pearson, G. (1992) Political ideologies and drug policy. Paper presented at the Third European Colloquium on Crime and Public Policy in Europe, Noordwijkerhout, 5–8 July.

Portes, A. (1999) La mondialisation par le bas. L'émergence des comunautés transnationales. *Acte de la Recherche en Sciences Sociales*, 129: 15–25.

Potter, G.W. (1994) *Criminal Organizations. Vice, Racketeering, and Politics in an American City.* Prospect Heights: Waveland.

Reyneri, E., Palidda, S., and Frangouli, M. (1999) *Migrants' Insertion in the Informal Economy, Deviant Behaviour and the Impact on Receiving Societies. The Comparative Reports. Tables of Contents and Abstracts.* Milan.

Sack, F. (1999) Jugendgewalt – Schlüssel zur Pathologie der Gesellschaft? In Programmleitung NFP 40 (ed.) *Gewalttätige Jugend – ein Mythos? Bulletin 4.* Bern: SFN.

Smith, D.J. (1997) Ethnic origins, crime, and criminal justice in England and Wales. In M. Tonry (ed.) *Ethnicity, Crime and Immigration. Comparative and Cross-National Perspectives.* Chicago, IL: University of Chicago Press.

Tarrius, A. (1997) *Fin de siècle incertaine à Perpignan. Drogues, pauvreté, communautés d'étrangers, jeunes sans emplois, et renouveau des civilités dans une ville moyenne Française.* Canet: Édition Trabucaire.

Tonry, M. (ed.) (1997) *Ethnicity, Crime, and Immigration. Comparative and Cross-National Perspectives.* Chicago, IL: University of Chicago Press.

Tonry, M. (1998) A comparative perspective on minority groups, crime, and criminal justice. *European Journal of Crime, Criminal Law and Criminal Justice*, 6: 60–73.

van Doorn, J. (1993) Drug trafficking networks in Europe. *European Journal on Crime Policy and Research*, 1: 96–104.

Walter, M. and Kubink, M. (1993) Ausländerkriminalität – Phänomen oder Phantom der (Kriminal-) Politik? *Monatsschrift für Kriminologie und Strafrechtsreform*, 76: 306–17.

Wiles, P. (1993) Ghettoization in Europe? *European Journal of Crime Policy and Research*, 1: 52–69.

Young, J. (1999) *The Exclusive Society.* London: Sage.

Chapter 7

Insecurity and the policing of cyberspace[1]

David Wall

Introduction

If the Internet is one of the most rewarding inventions of recent years, then the cyberspace it has created is, simultaneously, a most complex and contradictory environment.[2] The 'prosaic set of wires and switches' that was originally designed to connect together the computers of researchers and technicians has rapidly become an emblem of national pride and economic and social vitality (Walker *et al.* 2000: 3). Yet the new business, governmental and social opportunities the Internet generates are also accompanied by new criminal opportunities – cybercrimes – and much of the public debate about the Internet has focused upon the risks and anxieties they generate. Consequently, 'cybercrime' is a term that has widely come to symbolise insecurity in cyberspace. Yet, in itself, the term is fairly meaningless, other than signifying the occurrence of a harmful behaviour that is somehow related to a networked computer (NCIS 1999). More importantly, perhaps, it is largely an invention of the media and has no specific reference point in law. Indeed, many of the so-called cybercrimes are not necessarily crimes in law, they are harms. Yet it is the term 'cybercrime' that has acquired considerable linguistic agency and has become absorbed into the vernacular. Furthermore, cybercrimes have become widely identified as 'something that must be policed'. This chapter, therefore, will consider the insecurities the Internet creates within the new 'social' field (see Manning 2000: 177) of cyberspace. The chapter goes on to explore the ways in which these insecurities can be, and are being, policed.

This chapter is divided into three sections. The first section identifies the challenges that arise for criminologists when trying to make sense of the divergent range of behaviours that are being called cybercrimes. The second maps out what needs to be policed by identifying points of convergence within the framework of a matrix that will assist our understanding of cybercrimes in terms of their levels of impact and types of behaviour. The third section then discusses the policing of the insecurities that cybercrimes represent and the maintenance of order and law on the Internet.

Points of divergence: the problematic nature of cybercrimes

Opinions about the impact of the Internet are by no means cohesive. As we enter the twenty-first century, there is little doubt the Internet is both accelerating the 'disembedding' of time and space (Giddens 1990: 6) and further shaping debates over modernity (see Escobar 1996: 113). Consequently, the Internet is causing us to reformulate the ways in which we understand societal change (Wall 1997: 209), albeit there are a number of different views about the precise nature of this change. On the one hand, there is the view that the Internet has had a significant transformative impact upon society by generating discontinuities with the past. Borrowing from Giddens (1990: 6), it has accelerated the breaking of the traditional bonds that bind society. On the other hand, there is a counter-veiling position that the Internet does not represent a particularly significant rupture with the past and thus its impact is considered to be more muted. So the big question, then, is to what extent the Internet has propagated harmful behaviours or cybercrimes.

Although it is clear there is a fairly high level of agreement within media sources that new cybercrimes exist, few commentators actually agree as to what they are (Wall 2001b: 168). Indeed, public understanding about cybercrimes fluctuates, largely because the Internet is so news-worthy that a single case can shape public opinion and feed public anxiety (Grabosky and Smith 1998). This media-shaped public anxiety frequently demands 'instant' solutions to what are extremely complex situations. Moreover, these anxieties can border on the fictitious yet cannot be ignored, precisely because of the widespread fear of the consequences they generate. The hitherto lack of criminological commentary about cybercrimes suggests that criminologists are clearly frustrated by the absence of familiar tools that generate 'reliable data' – in much the same way as when called to respond to any new type of harmful behaviour about which there has been (usually a media-inspired) public panic. Other contributors to this volume observe that comparative data across Europe are very complex with regard to the crime-related issues they discuss because different definitions are used in different jurisdictions (see, for example, by Albrecht and Goodey this volume). Where cybercrimes differ from many of these issues is the overall pervasiveness of the medium of the Internet and its ability to reach such an expanse of people with relative instantaneity. Let us consider this lack of 'reliable data' about cybercrimes in some further detail.

Statistics

An immediate hindrance to those seeking to study cybercrimes is the lack of any form of officially recorded statistics other than a number of reports and surveys that purport to estimate the extent of cybercrime, particularly with regard to cracking/hacking and commercial crime. However, most of these reports have been produced by commercial organisations that constitute the emerging cybercrime security industry and they tend to lack not only standardised conceptualisations of the 'crimes' but also systematic reporting or recording methodologies. Even if such standardised and systematically obtained statistics were to be readily available, then it is arguable that the following factors would still obscure the visibility of the behaviour and its impacts.

Victims

There is confusion over who the victims of cybercrime are and the manner of their victimisation. Not only can victims vary from individuals to social groups but the harms done to them can also range from the actual to the perceived. In cases such as cyber-stalking or the theft of cyber-cash, victimisation is very much focused upon an individual. However, in other cases, such as cyber-piracy or cyber-spying/terrorism, the impact of victimisation is usually directed towards governmental or corporate bodies. Similarly, the focus of hate crimes tends to be on minority groups. Moreover, as has been found with the reporting of white-collar crimes, it is likely many victims of cybercrimes, be they primary or secondary victims, individuals or organisations, may be unwilling to acknowledge that they have been victimised or, at least, it may take them some time before they realise it. At a personal level, this could arise because of embarrassment, ignorance of what to do or just simply 'putting it down to experience'. Alternatively, where victimisation has been imputed by a third party upon the basis of an ideological, political, moral or commercial assessment of risk, the victim or victim group may simply be unaware they have been victimised or may even believe they have not been victimised, as is the case in some of debates over pornography on the Internet.

For corporate victims, fear of the (negative) commercial impact of adverse publicity greatly reduces their willingness to report their victimisation to the police. Of importance here is the observation that the model of criminal justice the police and other public law enforcement agencies offer to corporate victims is not generally conducive to their business interests (Goodman 1997: 486). For these reasons, corporate victims tend to operate a 'private model' of justice that furthers the corporate, rather than the public, interest. Put simply, corporate victims prefer to sort out their own problems by using their own resources in ways that are more likely to meet their own instrumental ends. Even where prosecutions are forthcoming, corporate bodies tend to favour civil recoveries rather than criminal prosecutions because of the lesser burden of proof and because they feel they can maintain a greater control over the justice process. Alternatively, they might find it easier to claim for losses through insurance, or simply to pass on the costs of victimisation directly to their customers.

Offender profiles

The little factual knowledge that does exist about cyber-offenders from celebrity cases and the cases involving celebrities suggests they tend not to be burly folk devils of the streets. Rather, they are more likely to share a much broader range of social characteristics. The cases of hacking and other Internet-related offences that have been reported in the media suggest hackers and crackers are likely to be young, fairly lonely yet clever individuals, who are more likely of middle-class origin and often without prior criminal records. They possess expert knowledge and are motivated by a variety of financial and non-financial goals. So, for example, we find that the hackers, Pryce and Bevan, who were once described as 'a greater threat to world peace than Adolf Hitler' (Gunner 1998: 5; Power 2000: Chap. 6), were very young – Pryce was still at school (Ungoed-Thomas 1998: 1). Similarly, the much reviled cyber-stalker, Jake Baker, was a young introverted student (Wallace and Mangan 1996; *United States of America* v. *Alkhabaz*, 1997). It is very likely offender profiles vary according to the type of crime. However, the important point to emphasise here is that the Internet enables individuals to commit crimes that would previously have been beyond their means. As such, they can become the law enforcer's worst nightmare: the 'empowered small agent' (see Pease 2001: 22).

Jurisdiction

The trans-jurisdictional capability of the Internet, and therefore of cybercrimes, creates problems for the police in the following three ways. The first problem is that of resource management, because policing strategies are often reduced to decisions that are made at a very local level over the most efficient expenditure of finite resources (Goodman 1997: 486). Such decisions become complicated where different jurisdictions cover the location of the offence committed, the offender, victim and impact of the offence. The second problem is the effective investigation of crimes. Most policing tends to be based upon local and 'routinised' practices that define occupational cultures and working patterns. Thus, investigative difficulties tend to arise when non-routine events occur (Wall 1997: 223; Reiner 2000). In this case, the non-routine events will arise because of the Internet, such as cross-border investigations, or types of behaviour that are not normally regarded as criminal by police officers. The third problem arises from inadequacies in criminal procedures. Complications can surface where the harms fall under civil laws in one jurisdiction and criminal law in another. One example is the theft of trade secrets, which is a criminal offence in the USA but not in the UK. In the UK, only the manner by which the theft takes place can be criminal (see Law Commission 1997).

It must also be noted here, however, that trans-jurisdictionality can also be used by resourceful police officers and prosecutors to their advantage, especially to maximise the potential for gaining a conviction. Forum shopping can be employed to increase the prospect of achieving the most effective investigation and/or prosecution. This was the case in *United States of America* v. *Robert A. Thomas and Carleen Thomas* (1996) where the prosecutors 'forum shopped' to seek a site where they felt a conviction would best be secured. Tennessee, rather than California, was chosen because of the greater likelihood of conviction. In *R* v. *Arnold and R* v. *Fellows* (1996) the investigation was passed on from the US to the UK police because the former believed the latter were more likely to gain a conviction.

Public knowledge

As indicated earlier, an important factor in shaping both public knowledge and also the subsequent debate over cybercrimes is the 'media sensitisation' of Internet-related issues. Many cybercrimes are newsworthy items and the frequently invoked dramatic imagery of the 'Electronic Pearl Harbor' (Smith 1998; Taylor 2001: 69) or the 'Cyber-

Tsunami' (Wall 2001a: 2) by the media serves to perpetuate levels of public anxiety. Such sensitisation, and the resulting anxiety, is gradually manipulating the legal and regulatory responses to harms by moulding public expectations, therefore providing the regulatory bodies with an, often implied, mandate for taking action.[3] Moreover, public anxiety is perpetuated, if not further heightened, by the common failure of journalists, pressure groups and policy-makers (but also some academics) to discern between 'potential' and 'actual' harms. This is facilitated by difficulties of making any systematic calculation of the extent of cybercrimes. Once risk assessments are confused with reality (see Speer 2000: 259), the only perceivable way to combat cybercrime is to use hard law and stringent technological countermeasures. This tends to shift debate towards the needs of the state and corporate interests and away from important principles such as liberty and freedom of expression.

Common definitions of crime

The final consideration is the tension that arises from the power struggle for control over cyberspace, which actively shapes definitions of 'good' and 'bad' behaviour. As the increasing political and commercial potential of the Internet gives rise to a new political economy of information capital, a new set of power relationships is being forged. Consequently, the definitions of acceptable and unacceptable cyber-behaviour are themselves shaped by this ongoing power play or 'intellectual land grab' that is currently taking place for (market) control (see Boyle 1996). Of great concern is the increasing level of intolerance that is now being demonstrated by 'the new powerful', dominant groups that have emerged out of the power struggle towards certain 'risk groups' they perceive as a threat to their interests. A very practical example of this intolerance is reflected in the magnitude of the reaction by the music industry to the peer-to-peer World Wide Web sites (such as Napster and Gnutella) which, until recently, distributed MP3 music files in breach of copyright law (see Carey and Wall 2001: 36).[4] Although such intolerance tends to mould broader definitions of deviance, it would be wrong to assume the construction of deviance is merely one-sided. Definitions of crime and deviance arise, not only from the social activity of elites or powerful groups, but also from understandings of ordinary members of society as well as offenders themselves. As Melossi notes: 'the struggle around the definition of crime and deviance is located within the field of action that is constituted by plural and even conflicting efforts at producing control' (1994: 205).

Points of convergence: the matrix

Having outlined the challenges to our understanding of cybercrimes, this section seeks to establish some points of convergence that will facilitate that understanding. It was established earlier that views about the impact of the Internet range from those who believe it has had a wholly transformative impact upon social behaviour and those who believe it has not, and that existing bodies of knowledge can be applied to these behaviours. I wish to argue that both positions are, in fact, entirely reasonable. The Internet is so encompassing that it is possible for it, simultaneously, to have a transforming impact within one context and not within another. In fact, there are differences to be found not only in terms of the level, but also in the type, of impact. These are set out in Table 7.1.

Table 7.1: The matrix – levels and types of cybercrimes

Crime types				
Impact level	*Trespass*	*Theft/deception*	*Obscenity*	*Violence*
Enhancing existing opportunities for old crime (e.g. through communications)	Phreaking/ cracking/ hacking/	Frauds – pyramid schemes	Trading sexual materials	Stalking
New opportunities for old crime across boundaries (e.g. organisation across boundaries)	Issue-based hactivism	Multiple frauds – trade secret theft	Organised paedophile rings	Hate speech campaigns
New opportunities for new types of crime	Information warfare	Intellectual property theft/ cyber-gambling	Cyber-sex/ cyber-pimping	Organised bomb talk/ drug talk

Different levels of impact upon criminal behaviour

Each of the following levels of impact invokes different policy responses and requires quite different bodies of understanding about cybercrimes. First, the Internet has become an advanced vehicle for communications that sustains existing patterns of harmful activity, such as drug trafficking, but also hate speech, bomb talk, stalking and so on. Newsgroups, for example, circulate information about how to bypass the security devices in mobile telephones or digital television decoders (Mann and Sutton 1998; Wall 2000). The subjects of this level of impact are not new and they are serviced by the criminological literature on white-collar crimes.

Secondly, the Internet has created a transnational environment that provides new opportunities for harmful activities that are currently the subject of existing criminal or civil law. Examples of such activities include trading in sexually explicit materials as well as many types of fraud (see Grabosky and Smith 2001: 30; Levi 2001: 44). Again, this level of impact is not new and is also serviced by the criminological literature on white-collar crimes.

Thirdly, the nature of the virtual environment, particularly with regard to the way it distanciates time and space (Giddens 1990), has engendered entirely new forms of (unbounded) harmful activity, such as the unauthorised appropriation of imagery, software tools, music products, etc. Indeed, at the far extreme of this third category, the trans-jurisdictional, contestable and private nature of some of the harms indicates a scenario where there exists new wine, but currently no bottles at all! At this level the criminological literature is challenged as the activities fall outside the current paradigm(s) of criminology.

Different types of criminal behaviour

Cutting across the above three levels, or depths, of impact lie four broad areas of harmful activity that are currently raising concerns (see Wall 1999, 2001a: 3). They are obscenity, trespass, theft and violence, and each group illustrates a range of behaviour rather than actual offences, reflecting not only bodies of law but also specific courses of public debate.

Cyber-pornography/obscenity is the trading of sexually expressive materials within cyberspace. The cyber-pornography/obscenity debate is very complex because pornography is not necessarily illegal. The test in the UK and other jurisdictions is whether or not the materials are obscene and deprave the viewer, but there are considerable legal and moral differences as to what the criteria are that enable law enforcers to establish obscenity and depravation (see Chatterjee 2001: 78). In Britain, for example, individuals daily consume risqué images through the various facets of the mass media that might be legally obscene in some middle-eastern countries, and yet are deemed perfectly acceptable in more permissive countries.

Cyber-trespass or *hacking/cracking* is unauthorised access across the boundaries of computer systems into spaces where rights of ownership or title have already been established. A distinction is increasingly being made between the principled trespasser ('the hacker') and the unprincipled trespasser ('the cracker') (Taylor 2001: 61). In its least harmful form, cyber-trespass is an intellectual challenge that results in a harmless trespass. At its most harmful form, it is full-blown information warfare between social groups or even nation-states. Somewhere between these positions falls the cyber-vandal, spy and terrorist.

Cyber-deceptions/thefts describe the different types of acquisitive harm that can take place within cyberspace. At one level, there are more traditional patterns of theft, such as the fraudulent use of credit cards and (cyber-)cash. Of particular concern is the increasing potential for raiding online bank accounts. There have already been incidents of this activity.[5] At another level, there are those acts that will cause us to reconsider our understanding of property and therefore the act of theft, such as cyber-piracy: namely, the appropriation of intellectual properties.

Cyber-violence describes the violent impact of the cyber-activities of another upon an individual or social or political grouping. Whilst such activities do not require a direct physical manifestation, the victim nevertheless will *feel* the violence of the act and may bear long-term psychological scars as a consequence. The activities referred to here range from cyber-stalking to hate speech to 'tech-talk' – a term that describes the information that is circulated, typically through news groups, about the technical aspects of cybercrime – e.g. about how to make weapons, break the codes on smart cards, etc. (Wall 1999).

By breaking down the analysis of cybercrimes into a matrix of different levels and types of impact, criminological debates can focus more clearly upon the implications for policing, crime prevention and control. This analysis suggests that the resolution of the above-mentioned behaviours is not simply a matter of engaging specific bodies of criminal law. The issue is rather more complicated, as the harms are defined by a complex combination of normative, political and legal values. Importantly, the categorisation of cybercrimes in terms of this matrix spares criminologists and practitioners the frustration of comparing very different categories of activity (for example, the 'apples' of cyber-violence with, say, the 'Tuesdays' of cyber-theft).

Policing the matrix: maintaining order and law on the Internet

Despite the outward appearance of disasters waiting to happen on a global scale, the anarchy and widespread criminality that were widely predicted by the media and also by the (cyber) security industry have yet to materialise (see Taylor 2001: 69). In fact, cyberspace is remarkably ordered considering the large numbers of individuals who inhabit it and also the breadth of their involvement with it (see Wall 2001b: 171). This level of order may be explained by three important observations.[6]

The first observation is that cyberspace has the potential to be regulated. Greenleaf (1998) and Lessig (1999) take a 'digital realist' stance and argue that the law by itself is not a particularly effective means of regulating behaviour, in this case criminal behaviour expressed through the Internet. However, the law can effectively shape the architecture of the space within which behaviours take place and the norms that govern them, and the law can also shape the markets that create opportunities. Consequently, cyberspace is a regulatable environment, even if it is one that Grabosky and Smith (1998: 233) suggest is, both subject to, and also the product of, a series of regulatory dilemmas.[7] So, although laws do not engender complete compliance, nevertheless they 'cast their shadow' (Manning 1987) over normative behaviour, architectures and markets. It is under this shadow that policing the Internet will take place (Wall 2001b: 171). The types of behaviour, included earlier in the matrix, are each covered by specific bodies of criminal law in nearly all jurisdictions.

The second observation is that, as the matrix shows, although there are clearly new types of crimes that are emerging which require entirely new forms of understanding (such as the thefts of intellectual properties), when cybercrimes do occur they are mostly resolvable because they are fairly common offences. Rather than being the widely anticipated 'big bang' type crimes often feared, they tend to be minor impact multiple frauds that are usually resolved at a corporate level rather than by criminal justice systems. So, the main problem here is not one of substantive law but of applying criminal procedures.

The third observation is that a multi-tiered structure of governance already exists within cyberspace to maintain various types and levels of order (see further Wall 2001b: 171). This model reflects the bifurcation of terrestrial policing. It progresses from maintaining order to the enforcement of law, whilst also seeking to achieve public and private models of justice (see Table 7.2 page 202).[8] The explanation of this multi-tiered structure forms the remainder of this section.

There are currently five main levels at which policing[9] activity is being effected within cyberspace: Internet users; Internet service providers

(ISPs); corporate security departments/organisations; state-funded non-police organisations; and state-funded public police organisations. At each level, the organisations or groups involved will also tend to find an expression in transnational forms (Sheptycki 1998a, 1998b).

Internet users and user groups

The Internet users and user groups form the mainstay of policing the Internet. Within user groups are a number of subgroups that have formed around specific issues in order to police websites that offend them. Largely transnational in terms of their membership and operation, these groups tend to be self-appointed and possess neither a broad public mandate nor a statutory basis. Consequently, they lack any formal mechanisms of accountability for their actions which themselves may be intrusive or even illegal. Nevertheless, they appear to be fairly potent. A number of visible examples of virtual community policing have already occurred (see below). In addition to the various complaint 'hotlines' and the development of software to 'screen out' undesirable communications (Uhlig 1996a), there are a few recorded netizen groups that have attempted to organise Internet users.

Perhaps the most well-known netizen group that actively polices cyberspace is the CyberAngels,[10] a 1,000-plus strong organisation of net users who are also based, as their name indicates, along the Guardian Angel model. Divided into 'Internet Safety Patrols', they operate in the four main areas of the Internet: Internet Relay Chat (IRC), Usenet, World Wide Web (WWW) and the net services provided by the largest USA-based ISP, America Online (AOL). Their function is actively to promote, preserve and protect 'netiquette', which 'is the collection of common rules of polite conduct that govern our use of the Internet'.[11] Their mission statement declares they are dedicated to fighting crime on the Internet 'where there are clear victims and/or at-risk users'. They seek to protect children from online criminal abuse, they give support to online victims and advise them upon how to seek a remedy, and they seek out materials that will cause harm, fear, distress, inconvenience, offence or concern, regardless of whether it is criminal or not. Like most user groups, the CyberAngels claim the right to question what they encounter and argue they have a civil, legal and human right to bring it to the attention of the proper authorities.[12]

Internet user groups, such as the CyberAngels, perform a fairly broad range of policing functions, but other groups of netizens dedicate themselves to specific types of cyber-harm: the most common being the policing of child pornography, for which there is considerable public support and sympathy. For example, Phreakers & Hackers (UK) Against Child Porn (PH(UK)ACP),[13] claim not to be vigilantes, but seek to track down offensive sites and interfere with their operation. A similar group are Ethical Hackers Against Porn (EHAP)[14] who, like PH(UK)ACP, 'want to stop child exploitation' and claim to work in loose co-operation with government and local officials, even though they admit to 'using unconventional means to take down the worst, most unscrupulous criminals known'. It is, of course, impossible to ascertain whether or not these claims are actually fulfilled.

One of the most interesting alliances that currently exists with regard to the issue of child pornography on the Internet are alliances of 'mainstream' (consensual) adult sites who wish to distance themselves from the more illegal aspects of the trade in sexually explicit materials. One visible strategy they employ to legitimise their own activities is to report offending WWW sites to public authorities. One of the larger alliances, Adult Sites Against Child Pornography (ASACP), for example, claims to have over 700 members and to represent over 300 adult websites.[15]

Internet service providers

The Internet service providers (ISPs) have a rather fluid status. This arises from the fact that although they are physically located in a particular jurisdiction, they tend to function in a transnational manner (Walker *et al* 2000: 6). The moral panic surrounding the Internet during the mid-1990s over the perceived threat of widespread pornography (Chandler 1996: 229), and the subsequent threats of legal action (Uhlig 1996b), forced ISPs to consider the possibility of controlling some of the activities that take place on their servers, especially the news discussion groups. In August 1996, the then Science and Technology Minister (in the UK), warned that 'in the absence of self-regulation, the police will inevitably move to act against service providers as well as the originators of illegal material' (Uhlig 1996b). This statement was quickly followed by a letter from the Metropolitan Police Clubs and Vice Unit to ISPs, warning they could be liable for any illegal materials that were found to have been disseminated from their servers.[16] Their response in September 1996 was to promote SafetyNet, a mix of self-ratings, classification, user control and public reporting plus law-enforcement action (Arthur 1996). SafetyNet was jointly endorsed by the Metropolitan Police, Department of Trade and Industry (DTI), Home Office and the associations of the ISPs, such as the Internet Service Providers Association and the London Internet Exchange (Uhlig 1996c). In December 1996, SafetyNet became the Internet Watch Foundation (IWF) (Tendler 1996). Since its initial formation, the standing of the IWF has increased and it has become the quasi-public face of Internet regulation in the UK. One of its functions is to overview the use of the Internet and to bring to the attention of ISPs any illegal materials that are reported to its hotline. Between December 1996 and November 1997 the IWF received 781 reports, mostly by email, which covered 4,324 items (mostly on newsgroups). Action was taken with regard to 248 reports, and the greater majority (85%) related to child pornography, the eradication of which is one of the objectives of the foundation.[17]

The IWF has a mandate from both the ISPs and the UK government, but Akdeniz (1998) argues that the IWF does not command an established body of public support as its Internet-rating system has had very little public discussion.[18] However, it is probably the case that were the IWF openly to canvass public opinion over issues such as fighting child pornography then it is likely public support would be forthcoming. Of further concern is the fact the IWF retains the status of being a private organisation with a very public function and as such lacks the structures of accountability normally associated with organisations that have a formal public function.

Although the legal status of ISPs as publishers is now quite widely acknowledged, their liabilities vary under different bodies of law and have yet to be fully established (see Rowland and Macdonald 1997; Edwards and Wealde 2000; Lloyd 2000). However, cases such as *Godfrey* v. *Demon Internet Ltd* (1999) and *League Against Racism and anti-Semitism and The Union of French Jewish Students* v. *Yahoo Inc. and Yahoo France* (2000) have had a 'chilling' effect upon ISPs. The fear of civil sanctions encourages ISP compliance with many of the regulatory demands that are made of them by the police and other state bodies. Consequently, ISPs tend to tread fairly carefully and be responsive to requests for co-operation. Not only are they very wary of their potential legal liabilities, but they are also fearful of any negative publicity that might arise from their not being seen to act responsibly. Interestingly, the police themselves also appear to be fairly uncertain about their general position with regard to the prosecution of ISPs. Whilst they have continued to warn the ISPs about possible prosecutions since 1996, none of the promised prosecutions has been brought against ISPs in the UK. The general rule of thumb that appears to have been adopted across many jurisdictions is that liability tends to arise when the ISP fails to remove offensive material, whether obscene or defamatory, provided it has been brought to their attention following a complaint (Center for Democracy and Technology 1998: 3; Leong 1998: 25; *Somm* 1998; *Godfrey* v. *Demon Internet Ltd.* 1999).

ISPs tend to organise themselves within specific jurisdictions.

However, there is also a further level of transnational organisation, for example, the Commercial Internet eXchange,[19] the Pan-European Internet Service Providers' Association (EuroISPA)[20] and Internet Service Providers' Consortium (mainly USA).[21] These transnational organisations tend to focus upon technical/practical and commercial issues that are germane to ISPs rather than specifically with the self-policing of ISPs.

Corporate security organisations

Following the widespread mass integration of information and communication technology within most organisational structures from the 1980s onwards, and most notably since the growth of e-commerce during the late 1990s, the security departments of commercial, telecommunications and other related organisations have been strengthened to ensure further the protection of their own interests. As e-commerce grows, it is anticipated that corporate security organisations will become major players in policing the Internet. The difficulty in assessing their impact upon the policing of the Internet, however, is that their overall 'public' visibility is low because their primary function is to police their own 'private' interests. Importantly, they tend to pursue a 'private model' of justice because the public criminal justice system does not offer them the model of criminal justice they want (Wall 2001b: 174). Consequently, their relationship with the (state-funded) public police is often minimal (see later). Yet the public police are organisationally ambivalent about this position because, on the one hand, they resent the loss of important criminal intelligence but, on the other, police managers appear happy not to expend scarce and finite police resources on costly investigations.

State-funded, non-police organisations

The state-funded, non-police organisations are not normally perceived as 'police' nor are they accorded that title. They include bodies such as customs, the postal service, etc. Their role in policing the Internet tends to be either defined by national Internet infrastructure protection policies, or through the enforcement of those protection policies. National infrastructure protection policies vary, and so therefore do the respective organisations under them. Some governments, such as Singapore, China, Korea and Vietnam, have actively sought to control their citizens' use of the Internet, either by forcing users to register with governmental monitoring organisations or by directly controlling Internet traffic coming into their countries through government-controlled ISPs (Caden and Lucas 1996; Center for Democracy and Technology 1996; Standage 1996).

Within the EU, each of the constituent countries has its own Internet infrastructure policies. However, the *Convention on Cybercrime* (European Committee on Crime Problems 2001), for example, seeks to create an EU-wide Internet infrastructure protection policy although each country has its own policy and response. Germany, for example, has set up a regulatory agency, the Internet Content Task Force, and has passed telecommunications laws that require ISPs to provide a back door so security forces can read users' electronic mail if necessary.[22] The Internet Content Task Force also has powers to force German ISPs to block access to materials deemed to be undesirable.

In the USA the National Infrastructure Protection Center (NIPC) has since 1998 articulated the National Infrastructure Protection Plan, which includes the Internet. The NIPC 'brings together representatives from U.S. government agencies, state and local governments, and the private sector in a partnership to protect our nation's critical infrastructures' (NIPC 1998). Within the NIPC many state-funded non-police organisations are also involved in policing the Internet in order to resolve specific problems, for example, the USA Postal Service deals with cross-boundary trading of pornography and the US Securities and Exchange Commission with fraud.

In addition to increasing the policing function of state-funded non-police organisations, the US government has sought, with mixed success, to introduce technological devices to regulate cyberspace in order to 'protect the interests of US industry' (Reno 1996) – devices such as the V-chip technology, which is designed to filter out violence or pornography, and the 'Clipper Chip', an 'escrowed encryption system' that provides the government with codes to unscramble encrypted files (Post 1995; Akdeniz 1996: 235–61). Since the impact of many of these measures also curbs individual freedom of communication, it is therefore not surprising that much of the debate over Internet regulation has revolved around potential conflicts with the First Amendment of the USA Constitution.

Accompanying state-funded non-police organisations are a growing number of hybrid arrangements. The USA is home to the Computer Emergency Response Team (CERT), based at Carnegie Mellon University in Pittsburgh.[23] CERT has subsequently provided a model for similar organisations throughout the world. CERT exists to combat unauthorised access to the Internet, and its programmers log reported break-ins and carry out the initial investigations. Where security breaches are found to be too complicated to deal with in-house, they are farmed out to an unofficial 'brains trust' (Adams 1996) and to the relevant public police organisations where an offence is serious and could lead to prosecution. Unlike the UK's IWF, CERT is based within a public institution. However, it appears to be funded by mainly private sources but, like the IWF, it has a public function.

State-funded, public police organisations

A final group of bodies that contributes to the overall policing of the Internet are the state-funded public police organisations whose formal status allows them to draw upon the (usually) democratic mandate of government. Whilst located within nation-states, they are nevertheless joined by a tier of transnational policing organisations, such as Europol and Interpol, whose membership requires such formal status (see Lodge this volume).

In the UK, the public police are organised locally, but there also exist national police organisations that deal with the collection of intelligence and the investigation of organised crime. Within the local police services, several specialist individuals or groups of police officers respond to Internet-related complaints from the public (Davies 1998). Some police forces have set up their own units, whilst others have entered into strategic alliances with other police forces to provide such services. At a national level, the National Criminal Intelligence Service (NCIS)[25] has become responsible for providing intelligence on serious offences such as child pornography, which cross both force and also international boundaries. Since April 1998, the investigation of such offences came under the auspices of the National Crime Squad (NCS), a role that was previously held by the various regional crime squads. In April 2001, the NCS's National High Tech Crime Unit became operational to protect the UK's critical infrastructure from offences such as paedophilia, Internet fraud and any other offences that emerge at a national level.

The five levels of policing described above each seek to achieve different policing outcomes in terms of models of justice and policing functions (these are summarised in Table 7.2).

Table 7.2: The multi-tiered structure of policing

Level of policing	Primary Policing outcome	Prevailing model of justice
State-funded public police	Law enforcement	Public
State-funded non-police	↑	Public
Corporate security		Private
Internet service providers	↓	Public/private
Internet users/user groups	Order maintenance	Public/private

Policing insecurity on the Internet?

The exploration of the multi-tiered system of policing, described above, clearly demonstrates the public police form only a small part of the overall process of policing the Internet. As in the terrestrial world, 'not all policing lies in the police' (Reiner 2000: xi). This pluralistic system combines elements of both public and private models of policing to maintain order and also to enforce the law. However, whilst this arrangement may form a logical basis for improvements to the policing of the Internet there are a number of disjunctures that need to be addressed.

Different justice outcomes

The private/public divide described earlier is not as simple as is often assumed in discourses over the privatisation of terrestrial policing. Underlying these (terrestrial) discourses is an assumption that the private provision of policing will ultimately pursue the public criminal justice model. This is not the case with the Internet because quite *different justice outcomes* are independently being pursued at each of the levels of policing (see Table 7.2).

The principle of 'competency'

Following on from the above, *the principle of 'competency'* applies to the policing of cyberspace. 'Competency' is where cases are passed on from lower to higher levels if it is felt the lower level is not competent to resolve the issue. So examples of child pornography might be passed on to the public police by a relevant Internet user group. However, like the terrestrial policing system, the principle of 'competency' does not always apply. For example, it is common knowledge that frauds involving credit cards tend to be reported to banks rather than to the public police. On the Internet this problem is writ large as the existing multi-tiered system encompasses a more diverse range of justice outcomes. Consequently, the majority of offences are reported to the specialist organisations to resolve and fewer are reported to the public police.

Structures of accountability

Most policing of the Internet is conducted through a self-policing model. This is based either upon a self-appointed mandate, as in the case of the Internet users and user groups that seek to maintain a sense of order on the Internet, or the corporate security organisations that seek to protect their own interest. Alternatively, this self-policing model can be ascribed, as in the case mentioned earlier of the ISPs, which were literally told to clean up their acts or face legal action. Self-policing works because the participants are motivated by the benefits they accrue from the collective outcomes of their efforts. The downside is that the self-appointed mandate *lacks formal mechanisms of accountability* and there is little recourse to appeal to prevent miscarriages of justice from taking place, especially those of a minor nature. Self-policing is inherently limited in scope and has a fairly low ceiling of efficacy.

One major source of these disjunctures is the changing relationship between the public police and the nation-state. A frequent response to revelations of the existence of new Internet-related crimes (almost regardless of the facts) has been a general call for the public police to intervene. Appropriate responses to these calls have been found to be problematic for a variety of organisational and occupational reasons. This raises questions as to whether or not the public police should integrate the policing of cyberspace within their 'regular' functions (Wall 1997: 223–9). After all, there exists a strong argument to support the view that, since the state-funded public police forces operate within existing (albeit contested) structures of accountability, especially with regard to due process, they are the ideal organisation to police the Internet. In addition, from the nineteenth century onwards, their reputation was forged by their provision of what became an all-purpose emergency service. However, a combination of the following two factors has defined the current level of public police involvement. First, the control of public policing by (planned) managerialism, within a framework of finite police resources, has effectively narrowed police service provision to those functions that are measurable by performance indicators. Secondly, the role of the state is shrinking as more functions and responsibilities shift from central to local government (see Crawford 1997), resulting in police forces having to give greater focus towards achieving local priorities.

These observations also broadly apply to other countries. Goodman (1997: 494), for example, has argued that the combination of social, cultural and political factors has meant cybercrimes are simply not seen as a priority by police departments around the world. This is because greater and greater political emphasis is being placed on issues such as violent crime reduction and community-based policing. Furthermore, Goodman (*ibid*: 479) states that when police forces are challenged over their lack of engagement with computer crime, police managers frequently claim not to have the resources. The situation is not dissimilar at transnational or trans-jurisdictional levels. Generally speaking, nation-states have tended to underplay the impact of trans-jurisdictionality with regard to policing the Internet. Johnston (2000: 110) argues that the focus of the public police has tended to fix upon 'terrestrial crime' related to the relaxation of physical border controls across the emergent EU. This explains the failure to respond to criminal activities that are conducted through non-territorial spheres such as cyberspace.

Conclusion

This chapter has mapped out some of the key issues germane to policing the insecurities that arise because of the Internet. First, in terms of the impact of the Internet, although new technologies do present some new anxieties and complications, there are also many familiar ones already with well trodden paths to resolution. So the problem is not so much about substantive criminal law, rather criminal procedures, occupational imaginations and organisational practices. With only a few exceptions, the crimes that tend to occur are mostly resolvable through existing bodies of law. Walker *et al* observe that:

> the Internet is not lawless, nor does it operate either as a legal utopia nor dystopia. But special problems are created because of the now-familiar features such as disembedding in time and space of actor and action, the amount of traffic and the instantaneity and universality of the traffic. The consequent legal difficulties are often evidential and procedural. The problems are not insuperable, and there is 'no general normative argument that supports the immunisation of cyberspace activities from territorial regulation'. In substance, there is applicable law, though it was rarely designed with the Internet in mind and so there is a 'hotchpotch' rather than a codified set of rules.' (2000: 16)

Secondly, in terms of governance, cyberspace is not only regulatable through laws and directives as the 'digital realist' argument suggests, but it is also fairly well ordered because users tend to bring with them their (terrestrial) social values. Thirdly, there already exists a multi-tiered system of maintaining order on the Internet and also for enforcing laws. This demonstrates that policing the Internet is a much broader activity than the (public) police role can accommodate. This observation also illustrates the state of the relationship between the public and private provision of Internet security, not only in terms of resource allocation but also in terms of the models of justice that are being sought. In this sense, the public police have 'missed the boat' with regard to policing the Internet. To this extent, the future policing/governance of cyberspace will have to draw upon other existing structures.

Events in cyberspace have captured the public imagination and they are extremely newsworthy. The mass media balance stories of Internet success with tales from the dark side. But, as has been argued, there is little reliable data to hand, and therefore little substantive research upon which to base reliable opinions. Thus the public becomes even more reliant upon the media for information. So there has arisen a gap between levels of public understanding and reality. Consequently, a substantial aspect of policing the Internet, as in terrestrial police management, lies in the politics of policing or, more specifically, managing the public appearance of the maintenance of law and order. Organisations whose mandates are to seek the rational control of risk find themselves managing the effect of emotive-laden forms of anxieties.

Notes

1 This chapter builds on the arguments and observations that have been previously rehearsed elsewhere (Wall 1997, 2000, 2000a, 2001b). Please note that, unless stated differently, all WWW addresses were checked on 12 September 2001.
2 The terms Internet and cyberspace are fairly interchangeable. However, where possible, the term 'Internet' is used to describe the series of technologies that have been brought together by the TCP/IP (Transmission Control Protocol/Internet Protocol) protocols, and the term 'cyberspace' is used to describe the space the Internet creates (see Walker *et al.* 2000: 3 f/n 3).
3 See, for example, the history of the Communications Decency Act in the USA (Heins 2001: 100).
4 MP3 (MPEG-1 Audio Layer 3) is an audio compression format that facilitates the process of supplying music on the Internet by improving on old forms of digitalisation in terms of time and memory space (Carey and Wall 2001: 36).
5 For example, some students invited people to register to win a $50,000 prize. The students then used a program they had developed to search for online banking programs. If one was found, the student's program, or 'cookie' as it is called, would automatically mail an invoice for $20. The students collected a total of $640,000 before they were caught (Lorek 1997).
6 This is based upon observations that are informed by the early findings of the author's research on cyberscams that was being conducted for the Home Office at the time this chapter was written and also research for the DTI (Wall 2000).
7 These include: 1) privacy v. accountability; 2) national sovereignty v. globalism; 3) user-friendliness v. security; 4) trust v. efficiency in law enforcement; 5)

security v. creativity; and 6) individual v. state interests.
8 See also the debates over 'high' and 'low' policing in Brodeur (1983) and Sheptycki (2000: 11).
9 The term is being used here in its broadest sense to include a variety of activities aimed at the promotion and maintenance of order and security.
10 http://www.cyberangels.org/
11 http://www.proaxis.com/~safetyed/CYBERANGELS/cyberangels02.html
12 http://www.cyberangels.org/
13 http://freespace.virgin.net/pure.kaos/PH(UK)ACP/index.htm (last accessed September 1999).
14 http://www.ehap.org/mission.htm
15 http://www.asacp.org/
16 See http://www.cyber-rights.org/documents/themet.htm
17 http://www.Internetwatch.org.uk/stats/stats.html (accessed September 1999, before the relaunch of the Internet Watch Foundation). IWF site at http://www.internetwatch.org.uk/
18 For a more detailed discussion of the status of the IWF, see Akdeniz (1998); http://www.cyber-rights.org/watchmen-ii.htm. The IWF was relaunched in 2000.
19 http://www.cix.org/
20 http://www.euroispa.org/
21 http://www.ispc.org/
22 See Teleservices Act 1997.
23 http://www.cert.org/
24 The roles of the various security services are not included here.
25 NCIS and the NCS are respectively defined by the Police Act 1997, Parts I and II.

Cases cited

Godfrey v. *Demon Internet Ltd.* (1999) 4 All E.R. 342.
League Against Racism and anti-Semitism (LICRA) and The Union of French Jewish Students (UEJF) v. *Yahoo Inc. and Yahoo France (2000).* Interim Court Order, 20 November, The County Court of Paris, No. RG: 00/05308.
R v. *Fellows and R* v. *Arnold* (1996) (Court of Appeal, Criminal Division) *The Times,* October 3.
Somm (1998) Somm, Felix Bruno, File No: 8340 Ds 465 JS 173158/95, Local Court (Amtsgericht) Munich.
United States of America v. *Alkhabaz* (1997) U.S. App. LEXIS 9060; see also (1996) 104 F.3d 1492; (1995) 48 F.3d 1220; U.S. App. Lexis 11244.
United States of America v. *Robert A. Thomas and Carleen Thomas* (1996) 74 F.3d 701; 1996 U.S. App. Lexis 1069; 1996 Fed App. 0032P (6th Cir.).

References

Adams, J.A. (1996) Controlling cyberspace: applying the Computer Fraud and

Abuse Act to the Internet. *Santa Clara Computer and High Technology Law Journal*, 12: 403–34.

Akdeniz, Y. (1996) Computer pornography: a comparative study of US and UK obscenity laws and child pornography laws in relation to the Internet. *International Review of Law, Computers and Technology*, 10: 235–61.

Akdeniz, Y. (1998) *Who Watches the Watchmen Part II. Accountability and Effective Self-Regulation in the Information Age.* http://www.cyber-rights.org/watchmen-ii.htm

Arthur, C. (1996) New crack-down on child porn on the Internet. *The Independent* 23 September.

Boyle, J. (1996) *Shamans, Software and Spleens: Law and the Construction of the Information Society.* Cambridge, MA: Harvard University Press.

Brodeur, J.-P. (1983) High policing and low policing: remarks about the policing of political activities. *Social Problems*, 30(5): 507–20.

Caden, M.L. and Lucas, S.E. (1996) Accidents on the information superhighway: on-line liability and regulation. *Richmond Journal of Law and Technology*, 2(1). http://www.richmond.edu/jolt/v2i1/caden_lucas.html

Carey, M. and Wall, D.S. (2001) MP3: more beats to the byte. *International Review of Law, Computers and Technology*, 15(1): 35–58.

Center for Democracy and Technology (1996) *Silencing the New: The Threat to Freedom of Expression On-Line.* gopher://gopher.igc.apc.org:5000/00/int/hrw/expression/7

Center for Democracy and Technology (1998) *Regardless of Frontiers: Protecting the Human Right to Freedom of Expression on the Global Internet.* Washington, DC: Global Internet Liberty Campaign.

Chandler, A. (1996) The changing definition and image of hackers in popular discourse. *International Journal of the Sociology of Law*, 24: 229–51.

Chatterjee, B. (2001) Last of the rainmacs? Thinking about pornography in cyberspace. In D.S. Wall (ed.) *Crime and the Internet*. London: Routledge.

Crawford, A. (1997) *The Local Governance of Crime.* Oxford: Clarendon Press.

Davies, D.J. (1998) Criminal law and the Internet: the investigator's perspective. *Criminal Law Review*, 48–60.

Edwards, L. and Wealde, C. (eds) (2000) *Law and the Internet: E-Commerce.* Oxford: Hart Publishing.

Escobar, A. (1996) Welcome to cyberia: notes on the anthropology of cyberculture. In Z. Saradar and J.R. Ravetz (eds) *Cyberfutures: Culture and Politics on the Information Superhighway.* London: Pluto Press.

European Committee on Crime Problems (2001) *Draft Convention on Cyber-crime*, ETS, no 85. Brussels: Council of Europe.

Giddens, A. (1990) *The Consequences of Modernity.* Cambridge: Polity Press.

Goodman, M. (1997) Why the police don't care about computer crime. *Harvard Journal of Law and Technology*, 10: 645–94.

Grabosky, P. and Smith, R. (1998) *Crime in the Digital Age: Controlling Communications and Cyberspace Illegalities.* New Brunswick, NJ: Transaction Publishers.

Grabosky, P. and Smith, R. (2001) Telecommunication fraud in the digital age: the converging of technologies. In D.S. Wall (ed.) *Crime and the Internet*. London: Routledge.

Greenleaf, G. (1998) An endnote on regulating cyberspace: architecture vs law? *University of New South Wales Law Journal*, 21(2). http://www.austlii.edu.au/au/other/unswlj/thematic/1998/vol21no2/greenleaf.html

Gunner, E. (1998) Rogue hacker turned legit code-cracker. *Computer Weekly* 7 May: 5.

Heins, M. (2001) Criminalising online speech to 'protect' the young: what are the benefits and costs? In D.S. Wall (ed.) *Crime and the Internet*. London: Routledge.

Johnston, L. (2000) *Policing in Britain*. London: Longman.

Law Commission (1997) *Legislating the Criminal Code: Misuse of Trade Secrets* (Consultation Paper 150) London: Law Commission. http://www.lawcom.gov.uk/library/lccp150/summary.htm

Leong, G. (1998) Computer Child Pornography – the liability of distributors? *Criminal Law Review*, 19–28.

Lessig, L. (1999) The law of the horse: what cyberlaw might teach. *Harvard Law Review*, 113: 501–46.

Levi, M. (2001) 'Between the risk and the reality falls the shadow': evidence and urban legends in computer fraud. In D.S. Wall (ed.) *Crime and the Internet*. London: Routledge.

Lloyd, I.J. (2000) *Information Technology Law*. London: Butterworths.

Lorek, L.A. (1997) Outwitting cybercrime. *Sun-Sentinel (South Florida)* 14 September: 1.

Mann, D. and Sutton, M. (1998) >>Netcrime: more change in the organisation of thieving. *British Journal of Criminology*, 38: 210–29.

Manning, P.K. (1987) Ironies of compliance. In C.D. Shearing and P.C. Stenning (eds) *Private Policing*. London: Sage.

Manning, P.K. (2000) Policing new social spaces. In J. Sheptycki (ed.) *Issues in Transnational Policing*. London: Routledge.

Melossi, D. (1994) Normal crimes, élites and social control. In D. Nelken (ed.) *The Futures of Criminology*. London: Sage.

NCIS (1999) *Project Trawler: Crime on the Information Highways*. London: NCIS.

NIPC (1998) 'Mission Statement', National Infrastructure Protection Center. http://www.nipc.gov/about/about.htm

Pease, K. (2001) Crime futures: the challenge of crime in the information age. In D.S. Wall (ed.) *Crime and the Internet*. London: Routledge.

Post, D. (1995) Encryption vs. the alligator clip: the Feds worry that encoded messages are immune to wiretaps. *New Jersey Law Journal* 23 January.

Power, R. (2000) *Tangled Web: Tales of Digital Crime from the Shadows of Cyberspace*. www.usatoday.com/life/cyber/tech/review/crh625.htm

Reiner, R. (2000) *The Politics of the Police* (3rd edn). Oxford: Oxford University Press.

Reno, J. (1996) Law enforcement in cyberspace. Address given to the Commonwealth Club of California, San Francisco Hilton Hotel, 14 June.

Rowland, D. and Macdonald, E. (1997) *Information Technology Law*. London: Cavendish.

Sheptycki, J. (1998a) Reflections on the transnationalisation of policing: the case of the RCMP and serial killers, *International Journal of the Sociology of Law*, 26: 17–34.

Sheptycki, J. (1998b) Policing, postmodernism and transnationalism. *British Journal of Criminology*, 38: 485–503.

Sheptycki, J. (2000) Introduction. In J.E. Sheptycki (ed.) *Issues in Transnational Policing*. London: Routledge.

Smith, G. (1998) Electronic Pearl Harbor? Not likely. *Issues in Science and Technology*, Fall. Available at: http://www.nap.edu/issues/15.1/smith.htm

Speer, D. (2000) Redefining borders: the challenges of cybercrime. *Crime, Law and*

Social Change, 34(3): 259–73.

Standage, T. (1996) Web access in a tangle as censors have their say. *Electronic Telegraph*, 475 (10 September).

Taylor, P. (2001) Hacktivism: in search of lost ethics? In D.S. Wall (ed.) *Crime and the Internet*. London: Routledge.

Tendler, S. (1996) Public to help police curb Internet porn. *The Times* 2 December.

Uhlig, R. (1996a) Hunt is on for Internet dealer in child porn. *Electronic Telegraph* 518 (23 October).

Uhlig, R. (1996b) 'Safety Net' on Internet will catch child porn. *Electronic Telegraph* 488 (23 September).

Uhlig, R. (1996c) Minister's warning over Internet porn. *Electronic Telegraph* 16 August.

Ungoed-Thomas, J. (1998) The schoolboy spy. *The Sunday Times* 29 March 29 5: 1–2.

Walker, C.P., Wall, D.S. and Akdeniz, Y. (2000) The Internet, law and society. In Y. Akdeniz, C. P. Walker and D. S. Wall (eds) *The Internet, Law and Society*. London: Longman.

Wall, D.S. (1997) Policing the virtual community: the Internet, cyber-crimes and the policing of cyberspace. In P. Francis, P. Davies and V. Jupp (eds) *Policing Futures*. London: Macmillan.

Wall, D.S. (1999) Cybercrimes: New wine, no bottles?. In P. Davies *et al* (eds) *Invisible Crimes: Their Victims and their Regulation*. London: Macmillan.

Wall, D.S. (2000) The theft of electronic services: telecommunications and teleservices, published as an annex to *Turning the Corner*. London: Office of Science and Technology.

Wall, D.S. (2001a) Cybercrimes and the Internet. In D.S. Wall (ed.) *Crime and the Internet*. London: Routledge.

Wall, D.S. (2001b) Maintaining order and law on the Internet. In D.S. Wall (ed.) *Crime and the Internet*. London: Routledge.

Wallace, J. and Mangan, M. (1996) *Sex, Laws and Cyberspace*. New York: Henry Holt.

Part 3
The local governance of crime and insecurity

Chapter 8

Towards a new governance of crime and insecurity in France

Sebastian Roché

There have been major shifts in realms of insecurity and crime during the last 25 years in France and, while these changes have taken place in France, many of these are, as such, not specifically French: numerous of these features can also be found in England, Germany and other European countries. Insecurity has become more than a subject in itself. Rather, it has become a new way of looking at society. 'Security' and 'insecurity' are terms commonly used by the public, the press, academics and the political elite. Since 1975, the political history of insecurity has been the history of the modernisation of the frame of reference for understanding this issue. This modernisation process has been particularly painful for French left-wing parties but was, undoubtedly, of prime importance in allowing them to remain in power after the election of François Mitterand as President in 1981.

In this chapter I want to stress how the various components of the crime problem are undergoing change. In debates about these problems in France, reference is commonly made not to crime (the French word 'crime' means serious offences like rape or homicide) but rather to insecurity. These two words are clearly polysemic but, in this chapter, they refer to theft and aggression, fear of these and related public policies.

To understand fully recent innovations in the field of insecurity, it is necessary to analyse the cognitive categories that have arisen in the discourses of the national and local political elite. The vocabulary and the introduction of a renewed lexicon are part of the general understanding that influences the elaboration of public actions. However, attention must also be given to the organisation and implementation of public policies themselves and, notably, to the relations between those organisations involved in crime reduction (or those appearing to do so).

Political frame of reference: security and the end of class struggle

As always, semantic evolution creates mutations, and I want to pay particular attention to such changes here. Gradually, the issue of crime as an element of the *question sociale* has given way to the issue of 'insecurity'. In 1888, Henri Joly published a book entitled *La France criminelle*. Like the sociologists Gabriel Tarde or Emile Durkheim, Joly interpreted crime in the light of the construction of the 'bourgeois society', which was based on private property and representative democracy. The major social issue was the integration of peasants and workers into society. The title of the book by Eugen Weber (*Peasants into Frenchmen*), combined with that of Louis Chevalier (*Working Class, Dangerous Class*) are certainly summaries of the main tensions within society at that time. During the Third Republic (1870), the working class was seen as a potential threat to the newly established order, and theft was not only a property offence but also a menace to the foundations of the bourgeois order. Theft, therefore, was more heavily punished than personal violence (Martinage 1989). At the same time, a central issue was political participation: the right of an 'uneducated' working class to the vote (who did not 'know how' to vote) and mass protests in cities (cf. the psychology of the crowd of Gabriel Tarde) worried the French élite as well as sociologists. As a collective actor, the working class was born alongside its urban presence: its trade unions and political parties.

This issue is very different today (or over the last three decades at least). I would argue that western countries have experienced a 'democratisation of security', but also that this democratisation took place within an age of economic prosperity and then one of turmoil. I am referring to a 'democratisation of security' in the sense of rising expectations from all sectors of society, including the lower classes, and in the sense of government acknowledgement of the legitimacy of these expectations. I see democratisation of security as a continuing process – one that has not actually been achieved. Today, the police are no longer seen as a means for the ruling élite to protect its prerogatives and privileges. Security has come to be perceived as a social service amongst other services (health, transportation and so on). The police have improved their public image since 1981, specifically among young adults (aged 18–35 years), including those with left-wing preferences (Schweisguth 2000: 173). During the last quarter of the twentieth century, the dominant paradigm changed. It became no longer possible to subsume the issue of crime and deviance under that of class struggle. Left-wing European parties had to wrestle increasingly with this new context of social perceptions (among the electorate), which was antagonistic to their own ideological orientations.

Let me now sketch out the entry of the issue of insecurity into the political system in order to explain how and why this came about. From 1950 to 1975 (a period of prosperity) insecurity did not emerge as a political problem either during elections or in public policies. Economic progress seemed to open the horizon for a new middle-class-based society, a society with diminishing injustices offering social welfare, education and social security benefits for all. Also, the important national issues were related to the end of the colonial age in Indo-China and Algeria, or the the end of the Cold War with Soviet bloc countries. It is therefore not long ago that politicians were not worried about safety in the streets. In 1968, the Ministry of the Interior, Raymond Marcellin, when questioned about security, talked of the 'defence of the Republic'. Threats to political order and to the stability of the political institutions were on the agenda, but there was not much political room for insecurity as it is defined today — although recorded crime statistics were on the increase and opinion polls (taken from the 1960s onwards) displayed a rise in attitudes in favour of punitiveness that went unnoticed for a long time (Roché 1993).

The new middle-class society that emerged with prosperity was under heavy fire: the 'consumption society' and 'spectacle society' are symptomatic of book titles that speak volumes. The French left, not in power at a national level until 1981, was very busy criticising the securitarian right-wing parties and governments in office. The police were depicted as a tool of class struggle: a tool for the bourgeoisie to tighten its grip on the proletariat (Gleizal 1974).[1] At the same time, state bureaucrats (social workers as well as police officers) were seen as a threat to individual freedom and rights. The Foucaldian perspective was very popular among intellectuals in France, which depicted the state as a coherent entity moving towards subtle but efficient control of the population.

When economic crisis occurred with the first oil shock in 1973, it resulted (in France at least) in long-term mass unemployment. The modernist right-wing government of President d'Estaing was confronted with a rise in domestic issues, including crime. In 1975 there were signs of change within political discourse. The then Minister of the Interior, Michel Poniatowski, stated:

> I wish that the Ministry of the Interior were named Ministry of Security of Frenchmen, because this is its real name. It ensures security and order, for everyone's freedom, but freedom is not specifically political. It is also about being able to go out at night after 8 pm, in large cities.

A new era had begun. More than 20 years later, the Socialist Minister of the Interior, J.P. Chevènement, articulated a similar discourse. In 1977, Alain Peyrefitte published his report *Responses to Violence* which is acknowledged to be the first comprehensive political approach to the problem of insecurity. He became the Minister of Justice in 1977, holding this office until 1981. His diagnosis stressed the rise of fear of crime and the necessity for taking this into account at a political level, the need for more co-ordination among public organisations and a local approach to the problem. This was to be heavily criticised by his political opponents. However, his ideas were to prove to be very close to the subsequent propositions of such influential socialists as Gilbert Bonnemaison when in power a few years later.

The French Socialist Party had a hard time recognising there was a rise in crime against person and property. Whilst it was in opposition (before 1981), it depicted insecurity as a 'war machine' to win elections, as a means to legitimise the 'police state' and to make people forget about the economic crisis (Coing and Meunier 1980). The view held was that crime was not a real threat, and the fear of crime was a matter of the imagination (Ackerman *et al.* 1983). After 1981, things slowly started to change. The traditional downplaying of crime that occurred in line with changes in values could no longer be regarded as appropriate. The electoral fortresses of the socialists (the workers and employees living in modest or deprived areas of large cities) were in trouble when it came to crime and delinquency: the socialists were losing votes. The mayors of large cities – that is, at a local level – were the first to raise the question of crime and delinquency. However, the political analysis did not evolve rapidly at a national level. Insecurity remained to be seen as an ideology and not as an opinion wave related to daily disorders that made life unlivable. But, in 1982, the socialist Gilbert Bonnemaison, MP and mayor (this was to be very important as a trigger to a pragmatic approach), initiated a defining work within the Socialist Party. He articulated the first public policy related to insecurity in his report to the Prime Minister entitled *Facing Crime: Prevention, Repression, Solidarity*.[2] The title itself reflects a significant shift: it sought a compromise between the old and the new vision of insecurity (i.e. with repression as a central component). So deep was the change that, today, the prevention–repression dualism is constantly referred to in official interagency contracts (to which I return later).

In summary, one could say that the situation today is the result of a series of mutations. The conclusion of this ideological voyage was the National Conference of Villepinte, named 'Des villes sûres pour des citoyens libres' (for the proceedings, see Ministère de l'Intérieur 1997). It was held in the autumn of 1997 and every major socialist minister could be heard to endorse the view that prevention and repression are both useful. J.P. Chevènement stated that 'security is a concept belonging to the left' and the promotion of security is a leftist public policy as 'the most deprived social layers suffer from insecurity' (*Le Monde* 28 October 1997).[3] Insecurity is now depicted as a social injustice. This metaphor allows for the integration of the issue into a renewed socialist frame of reference with a persistent emphasis on equality.

Since Villepinte it has become a prevailing policy assumption that the police contribute to democracy, to the security of the deprived sections of the population. The police are no longer perceived as a tool of domination serving the objective interests of the capitalists. Social inclusion through work is seen today as quintessential and it can no longer be indicted as 'exploitation through work'. No class struggle is spoken of. Even the word 'class' is no longer mentioned. The changes in the political parties' language echo modifications in the feeling of belonging to a social class that is diminishing in France, especially among workers and employees: only 22% of workers identify with the 'working class' (Michelat and Simon 1996). A new line is drawn between the 'insiders' and the 'outsiders'. The social control theories of the 1970s are outdated. Even the theoreticians, such as the Foucaldian Jacques Donzelot who vehemently criticised the extension of the state apparatus ('the continuum from social workers to police'), now favour 'more state' when it comes to the prevention of crime (Donzelot and Estèbe 1999).

A vocabulary for depicting the problem

The commonly used vocabulary for depicting the problem of insecurity has changed substantially. What was said to be a crime-centred problem is now analysed using non-penal-based concepts (we will see later the consequences of this for the practical organisation of anti-crime 'responses'). The new lexicon of insecurity (as a problem) consists mainly of the following expressions: 'feelings of insecurity' (the French equivalent for 'fear of crime'), 'incivilities' (or disorders, but the word 'disorder' is not in common use, if at all), 'urban violence' and the *banlieues* (the outskirts of large metropolitan conglomerations as well as deprived neighbourhoods within metropolitan areas made up of housing estates).

Although contested by the major actors within the judicial system for reasons of heterogeneity, all these concepts have progressively pervaded public discourse and become targets for public policies. I tend to relate this new lexicon that arose with the end of class struggle as a paradigm for understanding society. In a post-industrial (postmodern) age, sociologists seem to make use of 'weak definitions' when debating insecurity, in the sense they no longer refer to a theoretical framework or to the necessity of 'epistemological rupture' with 'common sense'. Examples include notions such as 'young people (*les jeunes*) or *la rage, la 'galère'* (the modern experience of a mix of welfare and exclusion) (see Dubet 1987)) and the *banlieues*. These are very descriptive words that originate in the spoken language and vernacular of these urban areas. Are French sociologists and criminologists less able than before? I don't believe so, but this paradigm shift has direct consequences: intellectuals, be they politicians or sociologists, cannot use the old lexicon to portray the new reality as it no longer fits. They do not have a theory to offer. As a consequence, they are merely reflecting and taking for granted the common langage.

In France, the notion of 'incivility' emerged in public debate around 1995–96, clearly some considerable time after the publication of Wilson and Kelling's famous 'Broken windows' thesis (1982). Although some sociologists had used this notion before 1995, the press and the political élite had not picked it up. Alain Juppé, Jacques Chirac's right-wing Prime Minister, in his first address to the Parliament in May 1995 (when setting out the general guidelines for the government), set 'incivilities' as a key target for the police. Lionel Jospin, at the national conference of Villepinte in October 1997, also emphasised the need for action against 'incivilities'. The last minister to use the term was probably the Minister of Justice. One can find reference to the term 'incivilities' in the circular of 15 June 1998 on penal policy towards juvenile delinquency and in a speech given by the Justice Minister herself when Elisabeth Guigou stressed the link between 'school drop-out rates, incivilities and delinquency' at the Assises Nationales de la Police de Proximité, in March 2000.[4] The notion of incivility constituted one of the ways in which the left could address issues of insecurity on the basis their supporters were concentrated in the most deprived areas of large cities.

Today, the notion of 'urban violence' is used very widely in France both in the media and in the sphere of politics. However, the notion is not a very precise one. It suggests merely that some acts are violent and that these are located within cities. Given that France is 80% an urban country this does not reveal much. What is more important, however, is that, within the Ministry of the Interior, the notion of 'urban violence' does not rely upon any legal categories that are generally used for portraying the crime situation. Urban violence is a notion that is targeted at anti-institutional acts: the throwing of stones at buses, fire trucks and police cars; small or large riots; setting buildings on fire; drug trafficking; joy riding; and so on. For example, the Renseignements Généraux – the Central Directorate of General Information that acts as the internal intelligence agency – built a scale for measuring urban violence (Bui-Trong 1993). However, any acknowledgment of a collective dimension to these acts is very uncommon in the Ministry of the Interior's approach.

Debates about 'feelings of insecurity', as a political notion, date back to the mid-1970s. Alain Peyrefitte, the right-wing Minister of Justice in 1977–81, made the term the 'central thread' in his influential report *Réponses à la violence* (1977). The manner in which this heralded a subjectivisation process – whereby crime became reducable to personal accounts and feelings – is deserving of attention. As of then it became clear that politicians should see the problem through the eyes of the public, not only through depersonalised, agreggate crime statistics. Gilbert Bonnemaison, the socialist initiator of the prevention programme of 1982, adopted much the same language. 'Feelings of insecurity' had been frequently labelled 'irrational' or as 'overestimated' in the 1970s and early 1980s. However, once the political parties (both left and right) had endorsed the notion, this concern for any disjuncture between subjective perception and objective data became less and less relevant. From 1997 onwards, the government even made concerns over 'feelings of insecurity' a condition of its assessment for an interagency approach. Before an interagency contract could be signed between the central state administration and the local public administrations, feelings of insecurity had to be monitored and assessed along with the level of crime and published in a local crime and security audit (*un Diagnostic local de sécurité* – DLS).

Between 1976 and 1984, opinion polls (with comparable questions) suggested an increase in 'feelings of insecurity' for those respondents in housing estates. The percentage of those saying they felt insecure 'frequently' or 'sometimes' rose from 36% to 60% (an increase of 24%) for residents of housing estates as opposed to a change from 39% to 48% (an increase of over 8%) in private residencies. In 1976, the highest levels of fear were recorded in relation to residents of houses; by 1984 this had changed and the highest levels were to be found in housing estates (Roché 1994). This is a measure of the rise of the problem of the *banlieues* which politicians could no longer ignore. In 1996, Insee (the National Institute of Statistics and Economic Studies) published the results of an opinion poll that made a distinction between the *banlieues* and other parts of cities. Figure 8.1 shows that, in 1995, the greatest feelings of safety were found outside of *banlieues*. The *banlieues* constitute the central axis of

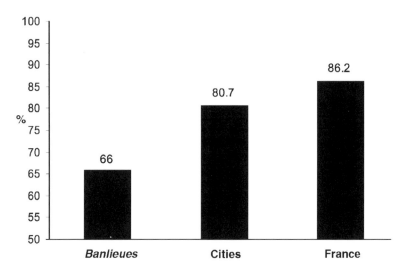

Figure 8. 1: Feelings of safety according to the type of neighbourhood (1995).

Note: *Banlieues* refer here to urban zones that were eligible for special initiatives or urban regeneration (known as 'priority neighbourhoods') from the national government. Cities are all those urban areas including the priority neighbourhoods or *banlieues*.

Source: Choffel (1996: 132)

political cleavages. As the descendants of recent immigrants have no distinct legal status in France, they cannot publicly be the object of public policies (be this positive discrimination or repression). Therefore the *banlieues* are the natural cradle for ethnic tensions. It is impossible to ignore immigration as a key issue in the *banlieues* with a youth population with foreign origins often over 40% and sometimes closer to 90% when focusing on a subneighbourhood level. These figures are drawn from sociological surveys, not from official government statistics (see Tribalat 2000, for example). It becomes more and more complex to address the issue of 'ethnic minorities' (which is not a recognised French expression) without allowing for the idea that there could be a Frenchman with 'origins'. But this is contradictory to the notion of French citizenship as this is supposed to be the negation of all differences and a symbol of the fusion of all people in one. There is clearly an ethnic dimension to insecurity, but there cannot be any formal expression of this: no trade union or political party is ethnically based, no non-profit or voluntary organisation has an ethnic-community-related name.

The various polls clearly present the *banlieues* as places where residents are fearful for their security. Therefore the picture is not that of a bourgeoisie frightened by the working class, but of a large proportion of workers and employees living in housing estates fearful for themselves. Moreover, the critical issue concerns the behaviour of the middle classes, not the upper class. The problem of insecurity is presented as one of *mixité sociale* – social blending (i.e. the contemporary melting pot and the lack of social segregation). The question is: will the middle classes remain in these *banlieues*? Or will they try to flee as soon as they have the opportunity to do so?

It is not only the sociological approach that suggests the percentage of fear is higher in the *banlieues*. It must be stressed that the political issue of insecurity also concerns fears among the less privileged (and not among the élite) and how this should be tackled.

In sum, the lexicon of insecurity demonstrates change. The focus is now on the social dimension of insecurity more than on delinquency as the result of a strictly penal approach. However, it is not my intention to imply that the police are not presented by the government as a key element in the reduction of crime. Despite the fact that the police and the judiciary resisted the introduction and use of some of these notions (feelings of insecurity, incivilities, etc), nevertheless, within the police and judiciary, it has not been possible to ignore the importance of terms based on public perceptions and on the limits to a legal approach and definition of security. This has had consequences for the emergence of a new paradigm for organising interagency co-operation and the relations between agencies.

Governance and crime

At present it is increasingly unclear if anybody in particular governs in the field of crime. A new deal in crime prevention and repression is underway. A new governance of crime is surfacing. But it is not yet fully established. Nevertheless, I believe it is still possible to shed light on a number of tensions that organise the new governance. There are three main tensions: first, between central and local government; secondly, between public and private organisations; and, thirdly, between the professionals and the community.

Tensions between central and local government

The need for a local response to crime was clearly expressed in the mid-1970s. Alain Peyrefitte, in his report referred to earlier, proposed that national bureaucracies at a local level should be in charge of the crime problem. Of course this stemmed from the need to decompartmentalise the various national bureaucracies operating at a local – i.e. subgovernmental – level. This model has established itself across Europe under the name of a partnership (and even 'interpartnership') or multi-agency approach.

Alain Peyrefitte emphasised the departmental level (as opposed to the regional level or the metropolitan one).[5] The departments, in his view, should be the appropriate level for the co-ordination of the police and social services. He proposed the creation of new agencies: the 'departmental centres for violence prevention'. For electoral reasons this was never implemented. Valery Giscard d'Estaing lost the presidential election in 1981 and in his place the socialist François Mitterand was elected.

The need for decentralisation was shared by the parties on both the politcal left and right. Therefore the decentralising legislation Giscard d'Estaing was unable to implement was, nevertheless, subsequently passed by the socialist Parliament in 1982. Legal powers and responsibilities were to a great extent transferred to a local level, mainly to the department concerned with social services, but not policing. In the field of crime prevention, on the basis of the Bonnemaison report (1982), the local level was identified with a communal level.[6] Local mayors were given the leadership role with regard to the new agencies: the Conseils Communaux de Prévention de la Délinquance (CCPD). Of course in large part this arose in response to the early involvement of the mayors in connection with concerns about the rise of insecurity.

If it was clear to the politicians a new deal was necessary, the functions that could be fulfilled by the partners were not that clear. This was especially the case in relation to crime reduction and not only crime prevention. This is reflected in the various contracts for prevention negotiated between governments and the municipalities.

Gilbert Bonnemaison introduced the idea of the CCPD. Within this scheme of prevention at a local level, the mayor was to be the key element. Although Bonnemaison pleaded for a linkage between the apparatuses of prevention and repression, the two subsequently became dissociated. Although the mayor was the head of the CCPD, the CCPD could not incorporate the chief of the police force. In fact in France the police force is a national administration. Hence a paradox: a locally elected politician (namely the mayor) within the French system is not supposed to be able to instruct a (nationally accountable) chief of police (*commissaire*) or a public prosecutor (*procureur de la république*). It was no surprise, then, that the police and the judicial system were absent from the CCPD. Moreover, the CCPD were heavily criticised for their formalism (one large meeting a year) and for their lack of efficiency. For example the CCPD conducted very little or no decision-making or policy steering. This was only a place for funding projects that could be construed under a crime prevention label. However, it should be noted that no evaluation was conducted with regard either to outputs or outcomes. Local observation, however, showed that, frequently, cities with a CCPD did not have any permanent position with regard to how to engage with or co-ordinate the various social services (Berlioz and Dubouchet 1997 les CCPD, état de Lieux – unpublished paper). This is rather telling, given that the CCPD's main task was to promote co-ordination.

The CCPD were never abolished (some are still in existence today although official figures are unavailable). However, a number of new agencies have been created. After the election of a socialist majority to Parliament in 1997, the government of Lionel Jospin and the Minister of the Interior, J.P. Chevènement, launched the new 'local security contracts' – *contrats locaux de securité* (CLS). The guidelines for the CCPD and the CLS are very similar: both revolve around the dual notions of partnership and *proximité*.[7] However, with the introduction of the CLS, the focus and terminology changed. There was no longer any mention of prevention or repression. Rather, in their place the emphasis was upon 'security'. This can be explained by the fact that the initiative for the CLS lies in the hands of the government and of the national police, not the local mayor. Despite the fact that it was not possible, after the decentralising reforms of the 1980s and the experience of the CCPD, to prevent the presence and involvement of mayors in matters regarding security, nevertheless the CLS clearly constitute a means for bringing the (central) state back into the equation.

Today, the resultant tension is particularly perceptible with regard to policing matters. Even if prevention, to a certain extent, could be seen to be a matter for local government, policing is seen by central government as its monopoly. The police must be financed and provided by (central) state agents working at a local level, not by municipal agents (however, as we will see in the next section this monopoly is no longer claimed *vis-à-vis* the private sector). At the same time, the mayor is actually a police authority (*officier de police judiciaire* on the basis of legislation dating back to 1884) and has a right to constitute a municipal police force. These municipal forces had been nationalised under the Vichy Regime in 1941. The police unions and the Vichy government had both agreed to nationalisation for corporatist and practical reasons. It was easier to instruct a national police than many independent police forces in municipalities.

For the last 20 years the municipal police forces have experienced a rapid growth. There were twice as many municipal police officers in 2000 as there were in 1980. But with a total of 15,000 officers they are still significantly outnumbered by the national police (136,000 in 1998) and the *gendarmerie* (97,000).[8] The sheer existence of a local police force in 9 out of 10 municipalities (where there are 10,000 inhabitants or more) changes the relations between the local mayor and central government. Moreover, it signals to the population a firm commitment to ensure security. This is true although the police are a small force. For example, only 25 municipalities have more than 50 officers. A large police force is more likely to be found in municipalities with more than 10,000 and fewer than 100,000 inhabitants (Simula 1999: 50).

Legislation on the relations between the national and municipal police forces has been long awaited. No Parliament had been able to enact such legislation. It was only in 1999 that the socialist government passed a new law. The legislation also contributes to the re-engagement of the (central) state by extending the powers given to central government to monitor (through the *préfet*[9]) the municipal police force and their possession of guns (Froment 1999). At the same time, however, there were small changes that augured what was to follow: increased powers for mayors in relation to the police. In fact, the legislation allows the municipal officers to verify the identification of any person.[10] From a judicial perspective, historically this power lay only with the national police force as it was assimilated into the apparatus of repression. The new legislation encourages greater monitoring by the (central) state (through the *préfet*), but provides for more autonomy from the (national) state police.

During the last 30 years, every prime minister has stated how much he has been committed to a national police force and opposed to an expanded municipal police.[11] It has only been as a result of the current political 'cohabitation' (with a right-wing president and a socialist government) that we have the possibility of a president holding on to a different position from that of the government, as Jacques Chirac did in 2000. In so doing he reflected the demand of important mayors across the country, which had been politically significant as mayors are often also elected members of Parliament under the French system. More and more mayors have voiced their support for the municipalisation of the national police (at least that part of the national police known as the public security police). Recently, Alain Marsaud, a right-wing (RPR) member of Parliament, called for a 'police under the authority of the mayor' in the daily newspaper *Le Figaro* (15 May 2000). He wanted the mayor to be *the* decision-making authority when it comes to local policing. Why? The answer would seem to be that he understands better than the bureaucrats in Paris the reality of crime. Whilst this is clearly a partisan issue, a way of attacking a socialist government that does not have a brilliant record on crime reduction, this debate is also about the decentralisation process and its extension into further aspects of governance.

Public and private organisations

Besides the national–local tension we find a second tension between the public and private sectors. These two are increasingly intertwined. In France, the underlying issue is the end of the monopoly of violence. The government's capacity to ensure security (and to ensure that citizens perceive they are trying hard to do so) is increasingly problematic and exacerbated at the same time as the government tries to impose limitations on the rise of new actors entering the field of security.

I would suggest there is no longer a belief among today's rulers in a public monopoly of violence, but that, at the moment, they cannot fully acknowledge this publicly. This is partly the case because a large part of the social demand for safety is targeted at the public sector, and also partly because of the remaining ideological options of the French left: they have repeatedly opposed privatisation reforms before actually going on to enact them in power and, hence, their ideological preferences (against privatisation) have been transferred to issues of policing. I also maintain that the defence of a public vision of security is largely bound up with the defence of civil servants and their labour organisations. To put this more directly, the minister of the Interior is also the Minister responsible for the employment of police officers. The identity of the public sector is threatened by both neo-liberalism and the construction of the EU. Therefore the police trade unions have tended to underline the specificity of their 'public' features. At the same time, however, the changes to the police have become so important and the demands for security have grown at such a pace that government ministers can no longer opt for the status quo. Within such a system of constraints the only way to act is to change things without actually saying you are doing so to ensure nobody is losing face.

A few years ago, in response to muggings in the public transport system, the Minister of the Interior was able to assert that an increase in the number of public police officers would solve the problem. On 28 October 1976 Michel Poniatowski, the Minister of the Interior, in responding to MPs, promised to maintain a large number of police officers in the metro system. He declared there would be 'a veritable permanent national police force inside the metro' and went on to add there would also be 'plain-clothed policemen' in night trains. Today, the need for more police on the streets or in buses is still asserted, but no minister is willing to pledge there will actually be more officers or that the police by itself could solve the problem. The emphasis is on partnerships, which implies a need to revisit the concept of the monopoly of legitimate violence. In the meantime, the authority responsible for the metro in Paris (RATP) has created a police force of its own that, today, is one of the largest in the country. This is not an isolated example as, together, all public transport authorities constitute the biggest employers of security officers. The left-wing workers' unions representatives, traditionally opposed to any private police, have completely changed their views and now demand 'a private security system to compensate for the failures of the state' within the system of public transportation (Larriere Cardoso 1999: 36).

The dominant idea now concerns the sharing of former government regalian responsibilities and, incidentally, also the costs of security. It is becoming less and less possible to refer to state penal policy as a sufficient means to an end. This is true within official public discourse as within pieces of legislation. During the mid-1990s, a code for good practice (*code d'éthique*) was established that every police officer should carry and follow. This code states that the police contribute to security but do not ensure security on their own. In January 1995, a very important piece of legislation was enacted: the LOPS (*Loi d'orientation et de programmation de la sécurité*). At the time Charles Pasqua was Minister of the Interior and, consequently, the legislation is often referred to as the 'Pasqua Law'. This law states that central government co-ordinates security, which consti-tutes a different and less central status accorded to the state. The legislation for the first time also places an emphasis on environmental design. It makes it compulsory to have an analysis of the impact on crime of any large construction and for housing estate managers to employ a proportionate number of 'guardians' or 'wardens' calculated on the basis of the number of apartments. Moreover, the legislation specifically acknowledges that security firms contribute to security in the country alongside the public police forces (see Appendix 1 of the Act). This Act of Parliament has a very different spirit compared to the first Act of 1983 that introduced restrictions on private policing and penal sanctions in cases of violations (Ocqueteau 1999: 418). Ocqueteau (*ibid.*) also notes that in 1997 three new decrees encouraged highly 'at risk' professionals (including the banking sector, jewellers, pharmacists, shopkeepers, the owners and users of private car-parking, lots etc.) to use the market in security to protect themselves. In 2000, after lethal attacks on security trucks, the state was asked by the trade unions representing the workers concerned to impose new legislation, which encouraged the use of situational prevention to reduce risks when transfering funds from banks to security trucks. This is typical of a new schema whereby the state increasingly tries to entrust security to the private sector and, at the same time, some organisations demand more state action, if not through more police officers then at least through the introduction of more legislative constraints.

The number of private security officers has rocketed in France since the early 1980s, especially after the first law of 1983 was passed. There were 10,212 officers in 1981; by 1995 this figure had risen to 78,786 (Simula 1999: 74), and by 2000 it was estimated there could be more than 100,000 private security officers. The figure has multiplied tenfold or more in 20 years. In a few years France has experienced a dramatic change: from a situation of a quasi-monopoly in the hands of the central police to a context involving multiple organisations. Private security guards were perceived by French MPs and top civil servants as a *mal necessaire* – something that could not be avoided. However, progressively, they have become 'partners'. The fact that 18% of them were formerly members of the state police or the army (ibid.: 89) has probably assisted in this change of view. Of course they are considered a junior partner by the national force, but this is actually a very convenient status for the managers of security firms as it has given them considerable leeway to grow and sell their services.

Moreover, expertise in conducting security assessments increasingly tends to be located within the private sector. A consultancy market has been created by the new pieces of legislation (circular of 1998 regarding the public partnership schemes), notably the requirement before signing local security contracts (CLS) to conduct an evaluation of crime (its geographic distribution and trends) and the fear of crime (these audits are termed DLS).[12] However, the municipal authorities did not have the expertise to conduct these audits within their own services. Moreover, they were unable to access such expertise from the national administration. While an institute funded by the Ministry of the Interior (Institut des Hautes Études sur la Sécurité Intérieure – IHESI) provided help to a number of them, the municipal authorities had to pay for this. Moreover, given the small size of the IHESI team (a handful of police captains), they were unable to cover all the demands across France at the same time. Hence the mayors had to buy the expertise on the market. This directly gave birth to two large consulting firms that, together, performed two-thirds of the total number of audits, as well as a number of less important consulting groups.

The public and the professionals

There is a constant rhetoric in favour of the participation of the public, either in relation to regeneration programmes or localised policing. From 1971 onwards the organisation Social Life and Habitation (Habitat et Vie Sociale – HVS) has argued for citizen or user involvement in public policies, be it in decision-making or evaluating programmes. In relation to policing, one can find the first such circular in 1973 (Monjardet 1997). This asserted that the police should be out on the streets (as opposed to in the office) and in contact with the general population. The judicial system adopted a similar discourse in the 1990s with the creation of the *Justice de Proximité*, which refers to the provision of greater local legal information and promotion of mediation and conciliation within the judicial system (Wyvekens 1997; Crawford 2000). The very same discourse has been held by every major public actor during the last 30 years, albeit with no significant visible change in public policies.

One after the other, officials in charge of various public policies at a governmental level (not critical sociologists), when taking office, depict the same panorama. With regard to HVS, one can read that citizen involvement and resident participation have been awkwardly prepared and not implemented (Figeat 1982). Years after HVS, commentators have noted that public participation has been a ritual invocation (Lévy 1988; Delarue 1991). When examining public expenditures, it is clear that money tends to be devoted to capital projects – notably the maintenance of buildings – rather than to projects focused around investments in people, either through social relations or social participation (Geindre 1993).

When we come to public participation in policing, things are even more complicated. Participation in France means the population is under a duty to report an incident of victimisation to the police. Any form of other participation is prohibited for it could be seen as an interference with the regalian powers of the state. The spectre of the militia looms large on the horizon of the French Republic. Initiatives as benign as Neighbourhood Watch do not exist in France. Public participation in policing amounts to (what I have referred to elsewhere as) 'passive participation' (Roché 1998). This refers more to a relatively recent French political culture (reflected in the republican model) than to a historical tradition. For in France, citizen participation in the militia in cities was commonplace until the nineteenth century. Any information given to the police, even by law-abiding citizens, is seen as *délation*. The English words for *délation* (to denounce or to inform) do not quite give the full spirit of the French expression. As an example, today there is no television or radio programme dedicated to helping provide information to the police. The statement by Kelling and Coles (1996: 9) referring, in an Anglo-American context, to 'the citizens as police and police as citizens' is almost meaningless in France. To understand this we need to remind ourselves of the Vichy Regime and of the enduring collective memory of collaboration.

Together with colleagues I had a chance to study the street-level bureaucrats' reaction to the participation of the public on the outskirts of Paris (Roché *et al.* 1998). Although every social worker or police captain referred to participation as a requirement for democracy, in practice there seem to be three obstacles. First, police managers believe or say the public is not sufficiently knowledgeable (they are lay people rather than skilled professionals). Secondly, they say it is not legitimate for the public to engage in participation in policing. And, finally, they argue the public could endanger themselves if they try to get involved.

As a consequence, it seems there is no room for citizen participation. Rather, the trend is in the opposite direction towards more professionalisation in the field of crime reduction. On the one hand, we have more municipal police forces and more private security officers and, on the other, we have more 'mediation agents' (see Faget 1997) on mediation in France and Macé (1997) with regard to public transportation). In France, 'mediation agents' do not actually act as mediators.[13] Rather, they can ensure the surveillance of a parking lot, help pupils to cross the road, help people find their directions in a train station and so on. With the job of 'mediation agent' subsidised by the (central) state (up to 80% of the salary), since 1997 local municipalities all over the country have hired, for a five-year period, a total of 220,000 mediation agents (known in France as *emplois jeunes*).

Concluding remarks

In France one could argue that everything has changed during the last 30 years. The political problem of crime has been disentangled from issues of the class struggle, the lexicon used to present the problem is different and the role attributed to the police is now new.

From the perspective of the frame of reference that produces a cognitive map of the role of the various organisations dealing with crime, it appears the government has lost its centrality. We have now multi-actor (private firms, local municipal authorities and national services at a local level) and multi-level (local and national) governance. Government ministers have broadened the spectrum of police work to include incivilities and disorder and, simultaneously, have produced an official discourse that locates the national police as only one of the many services contributing to security, thus reducing its impact on crime.

With the rise of the ideology of partnerships, central government is in an unprecedented position. At one instance it tries to confirm the key role of the state as a principal organ of society and, at the same time, it has to recognise the reduction of its ambitions when it comes to its capacity to maintain the monopoly of legitimate violence. As the state has lost control over the rise of private policing (in terms of numbers of firms and employees), it seems to have focused on claiming the monopoly *vis-à-vis* the local municipal authorities (here the police have grown but remain weakly manned). I suggest it constitutes something of a paradox to see a conflict between national and local public sectors. The usual line drawn by theoreticians of public policies – be they economists or political scientists – is between the private and the public sector. If it can be asserted that the importance of the state is declining, it must be understood in relative terms. Today there are not actually fewer taxes, fewer civil servants or fewer police officers but, rather, there has been a higher increase in private expenditure devoted to crime reduction or loss compensation (insurance) than there has been from the public purse. In addition, any government initiative now has to be thought of, and implemented, in relation to local government.

The missing actor in the new governance of crime is the citizen. If, as I have suggested, the fear of crime among the population has become a major concern for central and local governments (as well as a major generator of business for the private security industry, for whom the public represent potential clients), there is a completely different story with regard to actual citizen participation. Successive governments have not been able to implement public participation schemes in the field of social crime prevention. I would add they have actually tried to keep citizens away from anything that could resemble police work. The preference was given either to private security firms (as providers of services to shopping malls, housing estates, public transport, etc.) or to new subsidised jobs in the field of 'mediation'. Before the socialist government came to power in 1981, it promised to 'change life'. Soon thereafter the left-wing magistrates' representative organisation (Syndicat de la Magistrature) declared the judicial system should be rendered accountable to its citizens, and the member of Parliament, J.M. Belorgey, in his report (1991, first published in 1981) on policing, said that policing had to become more democratic. Today, citizens are not at the forefront of responses to crime. A managerial style has emerged. *Proximité* in the hands of professionals, but no citizen participation, is the implicit watch-word. But, in the mean time, the opposition parties have become the ruling élite and this might well hold the underlying explanation.

Notes

1 It must be remembered that work itself is seen as alienation by some Marxist thinkers.
2 'Repression' in this context refers to the repressive arm of the state – namely, the formal criminal justice institutions and processes and punitive sanctions.
3 It is interesing to note that reference is made here to 'social layers' rather than 'social classes'.
4 This was at the time of the official launch of the new policing organisation known as *la police de proximité* (note that any reference to community is inappropriate, for community could be of ethnic origins).
5 In France, 'departments' exist as an administrative level below regions and above local metropolitan authorities.
6 For a discussion, in English, of the French crime prevention reforms as contrasted with English developments, see Crawford (2001).
7 *Proximité* is the word used in France to indicate a desire that the public authorities and the police work more closely together and respond to the needs of people living in particular neighbourhoods. As the term 'community' is not recognised in French public discourse, there is no direct equivalent of 'community policing'.
8 The *gendarmerie* is a police force belonging to the Ministry of Defence. Its jurisdiction mainly comprises rural areas (as opposed to the national police working in the cities). However, as a result of increasing urbanisation, some rural settings have become included in large cities.
9 The *préfet* is the chief representative of national government operating at a local level.
10 Froment (1999) provides a good account of the details of the changes. The police force has to be agreed to by the chief of the judicial system (*procureur*) and the chief of the state administration (*préfet*) at a local level.
11 For the most recent example, see Lionel Jospin at the conference on '*La Police de proximité*', Paris, March 2000.
12 As already noted, the CLS are contracts signed between the local authorities and State representatives at a local level.
13 'Mediation agents' act in a similar capacity to 'neighbourhood wardens' in England and Wales (see Jacobson and Saville 1999).

References

Ackermann, W., Dulong, R. and Jeudy, H.P. (1983) *Imaginaires de l'insécurité.* Paris: Librairie des Méridiens.

Belorgey, J.M. (1991) *La Police au rapport.* Paris: Presses Universitaires de Nancy.

Bonnemaison, G. (1982) *Face à la délinquance: prévention, répression, solidarité.* Paris: La Documentation Française.

Bui-Trong, L. (1993) L'insécurité des quartiers sensibles: une échelle d'évaluation'. *Les Cahiers de la Sécurité Intérieure*, 14: 235–47.

Chevalier, L. (1978) *Classes laborieuses et classes dangereuses.* Paris: Hachette.

Choffel, P. (1996) Les conditions de vie dans les quartiers prioritaires de la politique de la ville. In D. Pumain and F. Godard (eds) *Données urbaines.* Paris. Anthropos.

Coing, H. and Meunier, C. (1980) *Insécurité urbaine: une arme pour le pouvoir?* Paris: Anthropos.

Crawford, A. (1997) *The Local Governance of Crime: Appeals to Community and Partnerships.* Oxford: Clarendon Press.

Crawford, A. (2000) Justice de proximité – the growth of 'houses of justice' and victim/offender mediation in France: a very unFrench legal response? *Social and Legal Studies*, 9(1): 29–53.

Crawford, A. (2001) The growth of crime prevention in France as contrasted with the English experience: some thoughts on the politics of insecurity. In G. Hughes, E. McLaughlin and J. Muncie (eds) *Crime Prevention and Community Safety: New Directions.* London: Sage.

Delarue, J.M. (1991) *La Relégation.* Paris: La Documentation Française.

Donzelot, J. and Estèbe, P. (1999) Réévaluer la politique de la ville. In R. Balme, A. Faure and A. Mabileau (eds) *Les Nouvelles politiques locales.* Paris: Presses de Sciences Politique.

Dubet, F. (1987) *La Galère.* Paris: Seuil.

Faget, J. (1997) *La Médiation.* Paris: Erès.

Figeat, D. (1982) Bilan des opérations habitat et vie sociale. *Correspondance Municipale*, 231.

Froment, J.-C. (1999) Le maire et la sécurité. *Revue Française d'Administration Publique*, 91: 455–70.

Geindre, F. (1993) *Villes, démocratie, solidarité: le pari d'une politique. Préparation du XIe plan, commissariat général au plan.* Paris: La Documentation Française et le Moniteur.

Gleizal, J.J. (1974) *La Police nationale.* Grenoble: PUG.

Jacobson, J. and Saville, E. (1999) *Neighbourhood Warden Schemes: An Overview. Crime Reduction Research Series 2.* London: Home Office.

Joly, H. (1888) *La France criminelle.* Paris: Alcan.

Kelling, G. and Coles, C.M. (1996) *Fixing Broken Windows: Restoring Order and Reducing Crime in our Communities.* New York: Free Press.

Larriere Cardoso, D. (1999) Vaincre la violence dans les transports urbains. *La Revue de la CFDT*, 19: 34–8.

Lévy, F. (1988) *Bilan des contrats de plan DSQ.* Paris: La Documentation Française.

Macé E. (1997) Les contours de la médiation à propos d'un dispositif de la RATP. *Revue Française des Affaires Sociales*, 2: 18–27.

Martinage, R. (1989) *Punir le crime.* Paris: L'Espace Juridique.

Michelat, G. and Simon, M. (1996) Changements de société et changements d'opinion. In S.o.f.r.e.s. (ed.) *L'État de l'opinion 1996*. Paris: Seuil.

Ministère de l'Intérieur (1997) *Des Villes sûres pour des citoyens libres* (24-25 octobre). Paris: Éditions SIRP-Ministère de l'Intérieur.

Monjardet, D. (1997) *Ce que fait la police*. Paris: La Découverte.

Ocqueteau, F. (1999) Le secteur de la sécurité privée: structuration économico-politique. *Revue Française d'Administration Publique*, 91: 413–20.

Peyrefitte, A. (1977) *Réponses à la violence*. Paris: Presses Pocket.

Roché, S. (1993) *Le sentiment d'insécurité*. Paris: PUF.

Roché, S. (1994) *Insécurité et libertés*. Paris: Seuil.

Roché, S. (1998) *Sociologie politique de l'insécurité*. Paris: PUF.

Roché, S., Four, P.A., Poisblaud, K., Blattier, C., Courtaud, P. and Grasset, Y. (1998) *L'Ordre social et la loi ou le problème des incivilités*. Grenoble: CERAT.

Schweisguth, É. (2000) Liberté, autorité et civisme, trente ans après mai 1968. In P. Bréchon (ed.) *Les Valeurs des français*. Paris: Armand Colin.

Simula, P. (1999) *La Dynamique des emplois dans la sécurité*. Paris: IHESI.

Tribalat, M. (2000) *Dreux: voyage au coeur du malaise Français*. Paris: Syros.

Weber, E. (1984) *La Fin des terroirs*. Paris: Fayard.

Wilson, J.Q. and Kelling, G. (1982) Broken windows. *The Atlantic Monthly*. March: 29–38.

Wyvekens, A. (1997) *L'Insertion locale de la justice pénale. Aux origines de la justice de proximité*. Paris: L'Harmattan.

233

Chapter 9

Commercial risk, political violence and policing the City of London

Clive Walker and Martina McGuinness

Introduction

Commercial risks, insecurities and crimes come in all shapes and sizes. However, the types addressed in this chapter – namely, terrorism and political violence – should be viewed as at the pinnacle of such risks and insecurities, for this chapter considers crime – or even high treason – against the political economy. In precise terms, it is intended to study the IRA's bombs in the City of London in 1992 and 1993 (plus the London Docklands and Manchester bombings in 1996) mainly in terms of the legislative attempts to shore up confidence of the City of London reinsurance market.[1] Alongside those responses are policing reactions – both public and private. By adopting this focus, it is intended to elucidate several themes of this book. These include aspects of risk that have become novel or heightened in late modern society, as well as the manner in which a blur of public and private actors responds to these heightened insecurities. The nature of the risk and response also connects with the themes of the interplay of transnational and local – how the nature of financial markets produces global opportunity and risk but how these can become concentrated within a very small locality, such as the 'Square Mile' of London. Unlike some of the other chapters in this volume, it also documents a very palpable risk and an equally tangible set of reactions.

There may be two observations about crime against the political economy at this level that can underline several of these themes. The first is that this type of crime clearly mixes forms of traditional harm associated with the criminal law – loss of property and injury to life and limb – with motivations that are not typically criminal but are highly politicised. In addition, the destruction and destabilisation are not to be taken too personally by the victims – the attack is symbolic, and the real impact is to be on the state, again differing from the normal criminal who would rather the crime were never noticed rather than that it should provoke an official response. This observation about the nature of the crime should lead to a state response that is equally mixed in its aspects and, as indicated, often is mixed not only in terms of the deployment of criminal justice agencies but also in terms of the reformulation of economic and political policies. This shows the essentially organic nature of the processes of the 'risk society' – 'an epoch in which the dark sides of progress increasingly come to dominate social debate' (Beck 1995: 2). To refer to the notion of a risk society is to attempt to articulate the significant change in social relations that is currently underway and the accompanying dawning of a new era. The old era was that of the industrial age, predicated upon the organisation and distribution of capital, as well as settled class culture and consciousness, gender and family roles, whilst the new age of the risk society is predicated upon the creation and distribution of risk, hazard and danger. New risks result in novel understandings of risk and danger – for example, 'reflexive criminology' (Nelken 1994) and 'actuarial justice' (Feeley and Simon 1994). They also require new responses; as Beck (Beck 1992: 98) states: 'risks presume industrial, that is, techno-economic decisions and considerations of utility.'

The second observation is that this type of crime can also tell us as much about our political economy as about the manifold nature of threat to it, since it can open up the social matrix surrounding the environment in which it occurs (Jasanoff 1994: 2). Accordingly, the appropriate targets selected for this type of crime must be politically as well as economically important. Another characteristic important for this type of crime is globalisation, in this case of commercial enterprises and the economies in which they operate.

This chapter proceeds by describing the IRA bombings as case studies, with an attempt to explain why commercial targets were selected during this time and what strategies were involved. The most direct response of the UK government connected with the issue of insurance, which was at once both a local and global issue. The complex legislative response will be detailed, followed by a commentary on how the strategy fitted with wider political and social considerations, how it worked in practice and how further strategies, both political and policing, affected the outcome. There is also some consideration of the extent to which the individual, whether human or corporate, can demand a state response to insecurity, especially through the invocation of a claim to right.

The case studies: background

By far the most important source of terrorism in the British Isles has been, and continues to be, Irish nationalism (Walker 1992; Bishop and Mallie 1994; Poole 1997). Rather than rehearse the full details of the current campaign that has existed in Ireland since 1969 and in Britain since 1973, this commentary will be confined to IRA strategy as it has been practised in Britain in the 1990s. The issues to be answered comprise: why were commercial targets selected during this time, and what did the strategy involve?

As for why commercial targets were selected, the objective of the attacks differed markedly from the many previous attacks within London. Rather than front-line targets (such as from political life or the security apparatus), the attempt was made to disrupt and diminish the commercial and corporate life of the City of London. This location is functionally and legally in the private, rather than public, sphere. Nevertheless, unsustainable damage to the City would result in general public concern and pressure on the government from the corporate and financial lobbies. This disruption and consequent concern and pressure could not be achieved by bomb damage itself. However, by offering a credible threat of potential attack, it might prove possible to achieve indirect disruption through the undermining of the confidence of investors, especially foreign investors, and through raising the costs for office-based operations, including insurance costs.

In terms of explaining the emphasis on these British economic targets, the main interpretation must be one of opportunism in the light of the growing importance of these economic targets within the post-Fordist state. The Fordist state is identifiable by the established presence and preponderance of mass production of manufactured goods (Taylor 1911). Other identifiable features of Fordism are its stable mode of economic growth, which is built upon a demand cycle reliant on this mass-production labour process and accompanying economies of scale. Large hierarchical organisations, which are subject to central controls, dominate and exemplify the social mode of economic regulation. Economic crisis in the 1970s led to a discrediting of Fordism in many western industrialised states and encouraged a more decentralised, knowledge-based and technology-based form of production taking pride of place in the economies, reshaped under the administrations of leaders such as Ronald Reagan and Margaret Thatcher. The markets associated with the financial exchanges in the City of London became prime candidates for growth in the post-Fordist world, which means that, in terms of symbolism and attendant publicity, they have become appropriate targets for terrorism

(Kelly 1993; Rogers 1996: 24). The City of London is one of the world's three major international financial centres, Tokyo and New York being the others. London differs from its two major competitors in that it is primarily an international centre. Financial services are a major UK industry, which accounts for approximately one-fifth of the gross domestic product. In an interview with Martin Dillon (1996: 271) a senior member of the IRA explicitly stated the IRA's thinking: 'It's really about getting their attention. London is one of the major cities in Europe and when we make it unstable that's when the talking begins.' It would be an overstatement to imply that the IRA's strategy was entirely focused or coherent from the outset (Mallie and McKittrick 1996: 148). Nevertheless, with hindsight, three distinct strands can be identified.

The first strand concerned bomb attacks on City of London targets. The two most notable were, first, in 1992, the day after the general election, the bombing at St Mary Axe, in which three died and 100 were injured (Kelly 1993). Approximately 14 buildings suffered significant structural damage with the worst-hit buildings being the Baltic Exchange and the Chamber of Shipping at an estimated cost of £350 million in damage. On the 24 April 1993 there was another large explosion in the City, at Bishopsgate, when a large bomb on a tipper truck killed a photographer, injured 94 persons and also resulted in damage initially estimated by the Association of British Insurers (ABI) at more than £300 million, mainly to prestigious commercial City buildings (City of London Police 1994a: 32). The end of the first cease-fire in February 1996 was marked by a return to the emphasis on the financial and business sector with a 500 lb bomb at Canary Wharf that killed two and slightly injured up to 100 persons.

The second strand, also with economic implications, involved disruption of the transport system in London and elsewhere, which again gathered pace and ferocity as time went on. It included attacks on the rail system, especially the London underground, and road transport also came under fire, most notably with a large bomb at Staples Corner in April 1992.

The third strand related to the targeting of other economically strategic locations both inside and outside London. These included targets relating to the tourist industry (such as, in March 1994, three mortar attacks on Heathrow Airport). Later, there was a car bomb at the Arndale Shopping Centre in Manchester in June 1996. A large part of the city centre had to be closed for months, and damage was later assessed at £250 million, with uninsured losses at £175 million.

The state response

The bombing in 1992 produced a response from the government, concentrated around the Reinsurance (Acts of Terrorism) Act 1993 (Gloyn 1993; Bice 1994).

Prelude to the 1993 Act

Reinsurance is the mechanism for spreading the risk of insurance. It is in essence the insuring of insurers who cannot perfectly calculate in advance the necessary premiums to cover all claims. Miscalculations might arise through false values being placed on assets or costs or through a false calculation of the probability of claims over a period of time or the value of claims. In a reinsurance contract the insured is an insurance company or underwriter and is referred to as the 'reinsured', or the 'ceding company', and the insurer, a specialist insurance company or underwriter, is referred to as the 'reinsurer'. In plain terms, the reinsurer absorbs the impact of particularly hard blows to insurers and, by providing this service, a whole range of people and organisations are protected. In particular, the reinsurance contract enables the insurer to spread any premium increases consequential on significant insured losses over a period of time, and possibly a range of insureds.

It was the bomb at St Mary Axe that precipitated crisis in the reinsurance market. The level of loss to the insurance and reinsurance sector was unprecedented for this type of policy cover. The first signs of trouble came in a statement in October 1992 by one of the world's largest reinsurers, Munich Re, to the effect it would prefer to exclude terrorism from its reinsurance treaties. It was not just the possibility of large losses that was the problem but the difficulty of calculating those future losses when they would be effected by a purposive third party (the IRA) whose actions were intentionally reflexive with the viability of the insurance market and whose capacity for destruction seemed enormous. Thus, the premium to cover such a risk would have to be so high as to be wholly unattractive in the market-place. By November 1992, it was clear reinsurance renewals would not provide cover for terrorism. The issuance of a model terrorism exclusion wording by the ABI to its members on 12 November confirmed that, effective from 1 January 1993, cover was no longer available to businesses (Souter 1992).

Immediately, pressure mounted on the government to take action, as the consequences of the absence of cover began to be contemplated. On the 21 December 1992, Michael Heseltine, Secretary of State for Trade and Industry, announced that the government had decided in principle to act as insurer of last resort. It was the government's intention its involvement would be for a finite period of time (that is, so long as exigencies required it) and should result in no additional burden to the taxpayer. The vehicle for government intervention was to be a new reinsurance company, Pool Re, which limited cover to that related to buildings, contents, computers, engineering and business interruption sections of commercial insurance policies. Cover was to be bought back in return for an additional premium that would then be paid into a mutual pool managed and staffed by insurance industry personnel on behalf of over 200 insurance companies and almost 100 Lloyd's of London syndicates; the government agreed to meet 90% of any subsequent claims not covered by the pool – insurance companies would meet the remaining 10%. It became clear later cover would also be available for blocks of flats, often owned by commercial holding companies, whose total sum insured was in excess of £2.5 million. Once the scheme had been agreed, the ABI advised members to limit cover, unless the special premium was paid. The scheme was back-dated to 1 January 1993.

The details of the 1993 legislation

The legislation consists of just three brief sections. The passage of the Bill provided little opportunity for detailed scrutiny, and no debate was ever held on the Pool Re agreements (especially the retrocession agreement entered into by the Secretary of State for Trade and Industry and Pool Reinsurance Company, by which the Secretary of State undertakes to indemnify Pool Re in respect of Pool Re's 'ultimate net loss' in excess of its retention). The arrangements under the Act were ratified by the Treasury and approved by Parliament on 30 July 1993, as were the credit facility and guarantee. The following points should be noted from the 1993 Act itself.

Financing of reinsurance liabilities

Section 1 outlines the reinsurance powers of the Secretary of State:

1. – (1) There shall be paid out of money provided by Parliament such sums as may be necessary to enable the Secretary of State to meet his obligations under –

(a) any agreement of reinsurance which, with the consent of the Treasury, is entered into (whether before or after the passing of this Act) pursuant to arrangements to which this Act applies...

The vehicle for the transaction of the arrangement, Pool Re, is nowhere mentioned in the Act. But it is clear that if moneys are to be made available from the Consolidated Fund, this means it is primarily the individual taxpayer who is providing the security for any financial liabilities incurred by the Secretary of State.

Extent of reinsurance cover

Section 2 outlines the reinsurance arrangements to which the Act applies:

2. – (1) This Act applies to arrangements under which the Secretary of State, with the consent of the Treasury, undertakes to any extent the liability of reinsuring risks against –

(a) loss or damage to property in Great Britain resulting from or consequential upon acts of terrorism: and

(b) any loss which is consequential on loss or damage falling within paragraph (a) above; and to the extent that the arrangements relate to events occurring before as well as after an agreement of reinsurance comes into being, the reference in section 1(1) above to the obligations of the Secretary of State shall be construed accordingly.

(2) In this section 'acts of terrorism' means acts of persons acting on behalf of, or in connection with, any organisation which carries out activities directed towards the overthrowing or influencing, by force or violence, of Her Majesty's government in the United Kingdom or any other government de jure or de facto.

(3) In subsection (2) above 'organisation' includes any association or combination of persons.

'Damage to property'

It is first made clear that the reinsurance agreements the Secretary of State shall enter into are those pertaining to property damage alone; injury to persons is already dealt with by other state compensation schemes. Unfortunately, the Act does not closely define 'damage' or 'property'. As far as 'property' is concerned, it becomes evident from the agreements actually entered into under Section 1 that it is commercial buildings which are the core concern. One result is that two possible forms of damage which might not be covered are losses to vehicles and losses to utilities, equipment (street furniture, water pipes, telephone wires and the like). On the other hand, care was taken to specify that cover is provided not only for 'damage' as a result of acts of terrorism but also for consequential loss.

'Act of terrorism'

The definition of an 'act of terrorism' under the Act differs from that in what was then Section 20 of the Prevention of Terrorism (Temporary Provisions) Act 1989 (PTA) (now added to, and replaced, by Section 1 of the Terrorism Act 2000). It seems this has arisen because the legislative draftsmen were told to have regard to the model terrorism exclusion clause issued in November 1992 by the ABI.

The 1993 Act is much narrower than the PTA which makes no attempt to delimit the possible perpetrators. Adding the qualifier of the perpetrator having a connection with an organisation eliminates any acts that might be carried out by individuals with eccentric or singular purposes. An organisation includes 'any association or combination of persons' for the purposes of the legislation. This leaves a number of questions. Is there a minimum number of members for a group to constitute an organisation, and must the organisation be known previously by the authorities? What of anarchist groups for which chaos and disorganisation are the goal and, theoretically, the *modus operandi*? Would a collection of anarchists, such as have from time to time attempted to 'stop the City', constitute an organisation?

In at least one other important respect the 1993 Act definition of 'act of terrorism' might be narrower than that contained in the PTA. The latter contains a reference to the terrorising of persons – the use of violence for putting the public or any section of the public in fear. One can argue that as the Reinsurance Act concerns itself solely with damage to commercial property, reference to the public is redundant – hence its exclusion and the sole focus on the terrorising of governments. It is also stated explicitly that an organisation's activities do not have to be directed at the government of the UK only – a precursor to the extended definition in the Terrorism Act 2000.

Jurisdiction

Finally, the geographical bounds of the reinsurance scheme are specified by Section 3(2). The coverage extends to the whole of the UK but with the exception of Northern Ireland, where other, more generous arrangements were already in place in the shape of the Criminal Damage

(Compensation) (Northern Ireland) Order 1977 (SI no. 1247) (Greer and Mitchell 1982).

Performance of Pool Re after establishment

1994 cease-fire

By the end of 1994, after the IRA cease-fire on 31 August, premiums pooled into the fund reportedly stood at £410 million. In November 1994, Pool Re, satisfied that the mutual's loss experience was sufficiently low, offered a potential discount of 40% on policyholders' premiums at renewal time. This system was retained the following year. By this time Pool Re was feeling sufficiently confident to raise the loss threshold to £75 million. The continuation of the cease-fire also led the company to reduce rates so that in 1996 the premiums charged were 20% lower than those set in 1993. Both these savings would be lost, however, in the event the £75 million limit was crossed (the trigger point at which the year's 20% discount on rates and 40% premium reduction were to be revoked). The bomb at London Docklands in 1996 did eventually result in losses of £105 million. It is also very notable that most of the 1996 insured losses were with Pool Re, suggesting commercial reinsurers had not entered the market significantly up to that time.

Docklands

There was a major material difference between the South Quay bomb and previous London attacks. This lay in the social extent of the damage. As well as the impact upon commercial property (around £107 million), there was extensive loss sustained by non-commercial property. More than 10,000 residents lived within half a mile of the explosion, and approximately 650 homes, located mostly on the Barkantine estate and belonging to Tower Hamlets Council, sustained structural damage. The bill facing Tower Hamlets council was high. Tower Hamlets complained it was faced with £70 million worth of repair works, but it had been provided with a government grant of just £6 million to carry out demolition work. Later it was agreed to increase the Department of the Environment funds to £30 million to cover the additional costs of demolition and refurbishment.

Manchester

On 15 June 1996 the IRA detonated a bomb in a shopping centre in the centre of Manchester, containing an estimated one to one and a half tons of fertiliser explosives. Damage and loss were enormous, though as always difficult to quantify at the time. The owners, P & O (who sold on to Prudential in late 1997) were insured with Pool Re and, speaking at the end of September 1996, Leslie Lucas, the chief executive of Pool Re, estimated the bill to Pool Re would be in the region of £400 million (it was later put at £285 million). Manchester City Council calculated that the council could be left to find £3 million to cover loss due to damage and lost income.

On visiting Manchester on 3 July 1996, Michael Heseltine, the Deputy Prime Minister, announced a number of measures aimed at alleviating the repercussions of the explosion. First, there was to be a £20 million injection from the UK's allocation of European Structural Funds, a reallocation of funds originally earmarked for other parts of the UK. There was also to be a further £1 million to come from the current European programme to prepare a master plan for the future redevelopment of the city centre. From UK government coffers would come an immediate contribution of £150,000 to support an international urban design competition, and substantial aid by mid-1997 was reckoned at £43 million. Manchester City Council has also made attempts to obtain additional government financial assistance under the 'Bellwin rules', now set out under Section 155 of the Local Government and Housing Act 1989.

At least in Manchester's case, the city was wealthy enough to provide some self-help. After the bombing, the 'Lord Mayor of Manchester's Emergency Fund' was set up as a non-charitable fund to assist the self-employed and small businesses that would not normally fall within the permitted benefactors of a registered charity.

For both Tower Hamlets and Manchester Councils the gap in funds lay primarily in the costs to the council of cleaning up after the bomb, together with the anticipated hike in insurance premiums anticipated as a result of the bomb. Zurich Mutual estimated that councils had paid a premium of up to £10 million and their renewal bills could face increases of £6 million. In the end a fund of just £2.5 million was made available to both Manchester and Tower Hamlets in January 1997 to cover extra policing costs and consequential loss.

Summary

These challenges in 1996 for the 1993 Act showed up some of its limitations. Pool Re is essentially facilitative. It ensures that insurance against terrorism damage is always available, but the costs are increased (discounts returned only in late 1997) and many property owners may decide against coverage. In addition, the private insurance path inevitably brings delay. But where the loss is to an important public space such as a shopping centre, neither problem can be allowed to determine entirely the response. As a result, the Department of Trade and Industry (DTI) effectively side-stepped its own reinsurance scheme by its direct grants to redevelop Manchester.

Assessment from the perspective of the state

Pool Re and the nature of the state

In order to comprehend how Pool Re operates and its appropriateness, one must look beyond the structure of the company *per se* and examine its political and economic environment. This environment may contain two significant shaping features that have coalesced around the evolution of the Pool Re arrangements. The first is an understanding of the nature of risk in high modernity. The second is the evolution of the (de)regulatory state.

Risk in society

According to Beck, risk is pan-endemic (1995: 2). The pandemic nature of risk poses severe problems for the nation-state and requires it to seek global rather than national solutions, and to respond by reflexive strategies of management and dispersal rather than solution and termination – especially through the compilation and dispersal of knowledge. Applying these perspectives to the issue of political violence and commercial victims, a number of features emerge that can be seen to shape the state's reactions.

One is the transition from government to governance (Hirst and Thompson 1995, 1999). In the risk society, alternative forms of governance include corporate or local governance, or governance predicated on participatory pressure/interest groups. This theme of transference of power and influence is echoed in discourses about the 'hollowing out' of the state (Jessop 1994; Rhodes 1997). This 'hollowing out' of the state and the accompanying 'glocalisation' (whereby national power is ceded both through globalisation and devolution or localisation) carry important implications for any examination of large and mass risk. These processes are antithetical to the powerful bureaucratic 'nanny' state of the Keynsian/Fordist paradigm. So, in the crisis of 1992 onwards, the reinsurance system did involve the exercise of old-fashioned state sovereignty in the form of an Act of Parliament. But through that there was spun a web of public/private relationships, building on well established policy networks. These were especially pronounced in the City of London, where the City of London Corporation is itself a cipher for private rather than public interests.

A second feature is the emergence, or at least recognition, of new forms of risk that reflect progress and knowledge (Beck 1992: 97). This is demonstrated by the physical vulnerability of the City. Its success makes it an attractive target to terrorists. Before the 1990s, targets of terrorists were direct symbols of government. It was unforeseen that the concentration of business and finance in the Square Mile would mean a terrorist explosion would result in an amount of damage dispropor-tionate to the size of the bomb. Insurers, reinsurers, business, government and property owners became aware of the potential for loss arising from large risk. Knowledge brought both security and insecurity. Insurers and reinsurers decided the distribution of risk was too heavily weighted against them and consequently eliminated the risk to themselves by withdrawing cover for property arising out of terrorist incidents. This impacted on business and property owners by creating added insecurity for them. As ever, the risk was not eliminated, only transferred (Luhmann 1993: 165). But fragmentation in society cuts both ways. Just as targets are in a sense proliferating and becoming less covered by the protective arms of the state, so each in turn may become less vital to state and society since network arrangements provide flexibility and alter-natives to any encountered disruptions (Castells 1996: 468). One of the psychological and practical solutions on offer to the risk of the IRA bombs is an increase in private security. In this way, it has been found that the bombings of the IRA have not only increased fear but also the receptivity to private security measures to counter them (Beck and Willis 1993).

Thirdly, globalisation goes hand in hand with the process of modernisation. The pandemic, global nature of hazard results in globalised multilateral international agreements and arrangements in order to combat risk (Giddens 1994). Risks in the developing risk society do not recognise frontiers, and therefore global responses and strategies are necessary. Whilst globalisation involves the transfer of power upwards, that is to supranational structures such as the EU, there is a corresponding transfer of power downwards to locally based structures in the form of increased localisation founded on flexible specialisation and efficient adaptability (Hay 1995). In the 1992–93 crisis, the UK government recognised the potential of globalisation and the possible relocation of financial institutions. But it also was keen to draw upon the local City of London Corporation and City of London Police to provide the vehicles for the state side of the strategies.

A fourth factor is the key role of new technologies as the dynamics of change echo Beck's hypothesis of progress through knowledge. For example, the City of London could never have achieved its predominant position as an international financial centre without the revolution in telecommunications. The development of technology also creates more risk and a quantitative shift in risk. Equally, technology was then deployed to manage the risks thus created.

The (de)regulatory state

Post-1979, the keystone for facilitating good government in the risk society lay in a programme to lessen the government's intervention in every facet of public, and much private, life. The increase in complexity and multiplicity of risk and hazard is at odds with an extensive and interventionist welfare state, which purports to absolve individuals of the need to plan for risk and to resolve for them the threat of risk. The organic nature of risk makes for a rapidly changing world that requires flexibility and speed of response – this is difficult to achieve within the highly structured framework of the welfare state. The keystone for facilitating the first two aims lay in a programme to lessen the government's responsibilities. Though these policies were never to achieve a monolithic coherence (Jessop 1992: 192), they were applied with particular zeal to financial markets. To this end, the 1980s saw a series of legislation aimed at liberalising and deregulating markets, especially financial services (Brearly and Ireland 1995). They culminated in the 'big bang' in October 1986 that, in real terms, meant the overnight internationalisation of the Stock Exchange through the entry of foreign multinationals (Gower 1988).

Viewed in this history, the choice of the structures adopted in the Reinsurance Act 1993 seems largely appropriate as being politically and economically consistent with the general thrust of government policy. A scheme that incorporated models and personnel from the private sector on the part of the insurance industry and continued personal responsibility and risk management on the part of the insureds fitted well with government demands for both the encouragement of free enterprise and also the assumption of individual risk rather than welfarism. Of course, one can at the same time point to contradictions and anomalies. Ultimately, there was state support for business insurance, and there was also state involvement in the administration of the scheme. But in intention at least, the idea was to limit state intervention so far as practicable whether in terms of operational matters, subvention or the very life of the arrangements. And the state intervention was arguably narrower than alternative schemes within the insurance market, such as a special levy on all insurance contracts, both business and personal, so as to create a fund for the payment of terrorist damage. That design would have involved substantial direct state intervention with costs in terms of administration and the creation of the temptation for terrorists to confront the state. And it would also be unattractive politically, since the effect would be to subsidise the international finance and corporate sectors. It has been suggested this alternative or addition has in fact been adopted. So, as well as extra premiums under the Pool Re scheme that came into being under the 1993 Act, the government also announced in the budget in November 1993 it would raise funds by a special levy on all household and motor vehicle policies in Britain and that it expected to raise £750 million and to add £18 per year to an annual household insurance bill on average. The subsequent Finance Act 1994 (Section 48) duly introduced the Insurance Premium Tax as a levy on insurance premiums (Macleod and Milnes 1996). Whether the Insurance Premium Tax really is a lasting testament to the power of IRA bombs to impact on the taxation system may be debatable. Certainly, the tax still exists and its rate has actually increased, but the Chancellor of the Exchequer who first announced it in 1993, Kenneth Clarke, made no explicit link with the terrorist campaign (Clarke 1993). Instead, the new tax was presented, along with a new air passenger duty, as a way of broadening the indirect tax base.

By contrast, the grander and more supportive scheme of direct compensation for terrorist property damage in Northern Ireland would not have suited the Conservative government's post-Fordist discourse, especially in the flagship sectors of financial services in general and the City of London in particular. Though some argued the Northern Ireland system should have been extended to Britain, it was not an attractive option, for two reasons. First, the potential liability assumed by the government under such a mechanism would be enormous by any standards. Even in a relatively small business market such as Northern Ireland, losses incurred by the government still managed to reach £616.7 million in the period 1968 to 1991/92. Secondly, this solution would have been ideologically very unpopular. The cost of direct compensation in Britain would be a noticeable additional burden on taxation that would be politically dangerous both as a signal to the terrorists and also in terms of the official policy of Ulsterisation. Although the government was nominally insurer of last resort under the 1993 Act, it was its aspiration that the reinsurance arrangement established should be self-funding.

Equally, the alternative of doing nothing was unappealing. Should businesses be left without insurance cover for terrorism because of the withdrawal of reinsurance, financial ruin was a real possibility in view of the magnitude of potential loss from damage and dislocation in the event of a bombing. Those businesses that could survive financially would still be severely economically disadvantaged. Those who could attempt to budget for such an eventuality would do so at the cost of the effective loss of working capital and a consequential loss of flexibility and effectiveness in the market. Facing this scenario and assessing the level of risk, how many City organisations would choose to relocate? For the wider ramifications upon the insurance industry, the government was concerned about the effect upon companies' solvency margins. Aside from financial considerations, an insurance collapse would have attacked the very notion of the legitimacy and sovereignty of the state and subjected the British government to embarrassment on an international level, not to mention handing the IRA another propaganda coup.

Looking at a broader perspective, one can see the establishment of Pool Re as, if not the ideal government response to the threat of large risk, then equally not the worst. It was one part of a three-pronged strategy in response to the threat, the other two being the peace process (involving secret talks with the IRA) (Mallie and McKittrick 1996), plus a national security policy. Arguably these decisive actions by the British government demonstrate that talk of a hollowed-out nation-state is premature. Only an active and sovereign state could have taken on the holistic role the British government assumed.

The efficiency and effectiveness of Pool Re

Assessment

As for efficiency, Pool Re has operated at modest cost to government. There are no doubt process costs associated with its administration, though an indirect system of reinsurance avoids the creation of a large state infrastructure. In this way, the 1993 Act can rely on the workforce of assessors, clerks and so on within commercial insurance companies. But, at the bottom line, there has to date been no notified recourse to government funds by Pool Re.

Looking at effectiveness, it has already been noted there was overall success in the sense there was no foreign exodus from the City. There were real concerns that the IRA activity could have had this impact. For example, in April 1993, the London-based Japanese Chamber of Commerce and Industry was reported as writing to the Home Secretary expressing concerns about the dangers of further attacks, and that Japanese companies would look for safer alternatives in Europe if security were not improved (Mullin and Kane 1993). But the measures taken, both security and insurance related, did seem to steady nerves and thereby achieved the fundamental objectives of insurance of increasing business stability through reducing investment risk and the uncertainty of financial exposure and more fundamentally averting the political anxiety about uninsurable chaos. Insurance cover in respect of terrorist damage remained available, though at a price not all could afford. In addition, insurance companies have managed to maintain liquidity and no collapses have resulted from terrorist damage. Even in 1993, there were profits for leading insurance companies.

At the same time this achievement is undermined by other forms of state subvention, especially the Department of Environment grants to Manchester, or even (allegedly) the Insurance Premium Tax. In addition, there remain inherent problems with the 1993 Act scheme, namely, that it concentrates risk within Britain (especially as the government is the ultimate recessionnaire), and it concentrates risk within commercial property insurers who act as insurers and then as members of Pool Re, effectively as reinsurers of themselves.

Another important aspect of effectiveness, the aim of time-limited intervention by the DTI, has not been secured. It was hoped the private market in reinsurance for terrorist attack would gradually reassert itself as confidence returned. The events in 1996 strongly suggest this has not happened and that some redesign might be necessary if this aim is to be taken seriously. The picture of the failure of the private sector to re-enter the market is largely, but not entirely, true. From 1994 there had been a small and selective reinsurance market available, and some of the losses at Manchester were borne by reinsurers other than Pool Re. This grew later in 1996 and afterwards, encouraged by rigidity in Pool Re's terms and the prospects of peace, firms such as Hiscox became active in the market, though they still do not offer unlimited coverage.

Taking the circumstances of risk as a whole, considerations of effectiveness might also have suggested some increase in the discounts given to properties wherever they might demonstrate increased security precautions. This condition (which might have to be set out in statute in order to achieve competitive equality in an international market) would not only have the effect of reducing risk, but it would also encourage insurers to take a more proactive role in risk amelioration by rewarding individual responsibility in regard to approved building strengthening or security measures. This link to the assumption of responsibility for security would build on experience in regard to mainstream crime, where it has been recognised that insurance can 'constitute a powerful means by which financial incentives or disincentives can be offered for the adoption of crime prevention measures' (Litton 1990: 1). It would also avoid the shifting of risk back to the public sector by undue reliance upon police prevention.

In response to these ideas, Pool Re and the DTI produced guidance on security practice in 1994, showing an awareness of the importance of this issue. However, there is little evidence to suggest this concern has been backed up in hard terms through the application of discounts for good practice or through warranties and conditions. Of course the encouragement of target-hardening in this way then brings up the vexed question of the displacement of large risk. Unlike a storm or earthquake, large risk in the guise of terrorist attack is responsive to change in the environment, whether political, security or economic. It seems a tenable inference that security measures applied in one part of the country – such as increased security in the City of London – encouraged reactions elsewhere: namely, Heathrow, Docklands and Manchester.

Provisos

Any achievements of Pool Re must be firmly situated within the contexts – economic, political and otherwise – which have developed since 1993. There are three worthy of mention.

The first is the circumstance of the IRA cease-fires. The first lasted from 1994 to 1996. The second was announced in July 1997. As well as the current cease-fire, the period interim to the two cease-fires experienced a period of relative quiescence on the part of the IRA both in Britain and Northern Ireland. The impact as far as the 1993 Act is concerned is that it has not been tested to anything approaching destruction. Though Docklands and Manchester did offer a severe test, like St Mary Axe and Bishopsgate, they have been followed by a lull that has allowed for the spreading of payments rather than a constant stream of massive losses.

The second point is that the policy initiative was received in especially propitious circumstances. One was that the economy was generally on the upturn during the period so that the ability to pay higher insurance premiums was also on the increase. Another was that the policy was largely applied within the singular circumstances of the City of London. This community (whose economic guise is more or less coterminous with its political and policing guises – all share the same territory and cross-membership) is able to take quick, decisive and concerted action in a way more diversified polities cannot. This feature, which persists despite the global tendencies of the financial markets, was particularly important in terms of resisting the pressures towards relocation and of presenting a common front against the outside threat. More practically, it allowed the mobilisation of mutual assistance and the rapid conclusion of decisions about policing and urban design at the time of crisis caused by the bombings without the usual problems of consultation, dissent and exclusion. The commodification of security came naturally to this community.

The policing response is the third circumstance to be mentioned. This response to the more physical aspects of the bombing campaign is worthy of a further study in itself and cannot be more than outlined here, but its importance is great. The features of the response reflect the likely approaches predicted by Ericson and Haggerty (1997: 1–5) – the management of criminal risk through surveillance, information gathering, communication and brokering both by the police themselves and powerful non-police power-holders – which, in the case of the City of London, include the Corporation of London and the financial institutions.

The policing story might begin in 1992, when the major IRA economic pattern of attacks became evident and there were already in place two special codes of powers in the Prevention of Terrorism (Temporary Provisions) Act 1989 (applicable throughout the UK) and the Northern Ireland (Emergency Provisions) Act 1991 (applicable only in Northern Ireland). Both have now been replaced by the Terrorism Act 2000, though most of the relevant provisions remain unaltered. These Acts already contained several powers of arrest, detention for questioning and stop and search that were directly applicable to attempts to attack the political economy (Hogan and Walker 1989; Walker 1992). Nevertheless, they were significantly augmented after 1993 in two stages.

The first stage came with a number of additions to the Prevention of Terrorism Act brought about by the Criminal Justice and Public Order Act 1994. The changes were expressly designed to deal with vehicle bombs and smaller devices carried by individuals. The first amendment was made by Section 62 of the 1994 Act, which inserts a new stop and search power in Section 13A into the Prevention of Terrorism Act (now in the Terrorism Act 2000 Section 44). Next, Section 63 of the 1994 Act inserts a new offence of possession of materials intended for terrorist purposes as Section 16A of the PTA (now in the Terrorism Act 2000 Section 57). In addition, the offence, also in Section 63, of unlawful collection of information is inserted as Section 16B (now in the Terrorism Act 2000 Section 58), which is a more general version of Section 33 of the EPA (now in the Terrorism Act 2000 Section 103).

Further measures were invoked by the Prevention of Terrorism (Additional Powers) Act 1996, a response to reviews following Docklands and to future fears (Jason-Lloyd 1996; Reid 1996, 1997). First, there were new stop and search powers in Section 13B (now in the Terrorism Act 2000 Section 44). Section 2 of the Prevention of Terrorism (Additional Powers) Act 1996 augments Schedule 7 of the Prevention of Terrorism (Temporary Provisions) Act 1989 in relation to searches of non-residential premises. A new paragraph s. 2A enables the police to apply for a magistrates' warrant to search a list of non-residential premises, and not just specified premises (now in the Terrorism Act 2000 Schedule 5 paragraph 2). Targets of this new power include lock-up garages or lorry parks. Schedule 5 of the 1989 Act (dealing with port controls) is amended by Section 3 of the new Act – which inserts a paragraph 4A – a power to search unaccompanied baggage and goods (now in the Terrorism Act 2000 Schedule 7 paragraph 9). Sections 4 and 5 of the 1996 Act give the police a power to impose a police cordon (Section 4, inserting Section 16C and Schedule 6A into the PTA) (now in the Terrorism Act 2000 Section 33) and a power to impose parking prohibitions and restrictions and to remove vehicles (Section 5, inserting Section 16D) (now in the Terrorism Act 2000 Section 48).

A *sine qua non* to extra security efforts was additional personnel, and this augmentation was authorised after the large bomb in 1992, when extra City of London Police officers were appointed (City of London Police 1993: 4). However, it was only after the Bishopsgate explosion in April 1993 that sustained and drastic action was taken in the City to implement tight security on the ground. The single most important and overt security measure undertaken as a result was the implementation of an area subject to traffic restrictions and surveillance in July 1993 – widely known as the 'ring of steel'. Further money was voted upon by the City of London Corporation in November 1994 to allow CCTV of exit routes.

Alongside these official initiatives, it must be recognised that policing in the late modern era is a mixture of public and private forms (Ericson and Haggerty 1997; Jones and Newburn 1998). In this way, the security of individuals becomes a multi-tiered activity, partly a state responsibility, but equally privatised or marketised, with the privatised sphere of risk assumption a matter very much for enterprise rather than regulation. After the first major bombing in 1992, the ideas of private responsibility for security and the creation of 'defensible space' (Newman 1972; Poyner 1983) were heavily promoted both by the City of London Police and the City of London Corporation, as well as by the Home Office. This encouragement was made in promising circumstances. The business community was more easily able than most to absorb the extra costs of security, and initiative and proactivity were of course key to the very culture of the City. In addition, the topography of the City was suited to this kind of strategy; its relatively dense streets and buildings facilitated the scrutiny of outsiders, just as it had made the same area particularly vulnerable to bomb blast. In terms of the implementation of this wide agenda, the most prominent effects have been contingency planning (Kelly 1993: 93) and CCTV (City of London Police 1994b). The lessons from the City of London were applied in Docklands, and electronic surveillance is gradually being extended to all main roads and sensitive sites in London. Following the Manchester bombing in 1996, there was not the same emphasis on private security as in the City of London, given that control of movements is much more difficult to achieve in a city shopping centre rather than its financial quarter.

It is reasonable to suppose that heightened security resulted in the elimination of the City as a soft target for terrorist attack, and CCTV footage has also been used to detect terrorism, such as David Copeland, found guilty of racist bombings in February 2000. But one consequence is displacement or deflection to equally alluring targets within the striking distance, such as Heathrow or Docklands. In this sense, one can hark back to Beck's hypothesis of the inescapable pandemic nature of risk, but with a caveat. Resources can be used to buy out of risk manifestation in certain circumstances, at the expense of others.

One is left with the feeling the City of London has been treated with as much favouritism in regard to security matters as it has been with insurance matters. The encouragement of private security can be taken to excess, with privileged occupants, especially those with the cohesion and lack of social diversity as in the City of London, able to close off areas of what was formerly communal space to 'strangers'. The result is a fragmentation of society that is disturbing in its implications for risk distribution and social cohesion. Another impact is that special powers are extended and become embedded in the law on a permanent basis. As Beck (1992: 79) argued, in the risk society 'the state of emergency threatens to become the normal state', and there are signs the Terrorism Act 2000 does indeed embed and extend state coercive powers (Walker 2000).

Assessment from the perspective of the individual: protection and fairness

The concepts of post-Fordism and risk society may not exhaust the rationales for the catalogue of state reactions to political violence. One competing discourse, normative rather than descriptive, which ought to be considered is the language of rights and duties, which in the post-

Fordist risk society can impart vital side-constraints both to official and unofficial action. There may be two levels at which such claims might be made. First, one might talk in terms of direct state responsibility to protect life, liberty and property from violent attack. Secondly, there might be a consequential state duty to pay for damage or injury resulting from defaults in the stronger duty to provide protection.

Rights to physical protection

The state's recognition and protection of rights to life, liberty and property involve its most fundamental duty, indeed perhaps its only legitimate duty (Wilkinson 1986: 300–1). It is interesting to note that reminders from the insurance community of these types of duties were indeed in evidence during the crisis created by the IRA's City of London bombs in 1992–93 (Kielmas 1993). Do these normative considerations translate into laws? The answer would seem to be that protection by the state is a legitimate demand in domestic law under the broad reach of the Royal Prerogative (*Calvin* 1609; *Mutasa* 1980). And one might reach similar conclusions in regard to international law. The focus here might first be turned towards the interpretation of the right to life under Article 2 of the European Convention on Human Rights and Fundamental Freedoms of 1950. The state must put in place laws, security personnel and security tactics such as can secure a reasonable amount of protection for all citizens (*McCann* 1995). This duty has now been reinforced by the Human Rights Act 1998.

Rights to compensation for the failure of personal protection

The picture here is likewise favourable to the citizen (Greer 1996: Chaps. 15 and 16). No general legal right to claim against the state for damage or injury has been accorded in Britain, but a scheme to compensate individuals for bodily injury arising from crimes of violence began as an extra-statutory concession in 1964 and has since been placed on a statutory basis. At the same time, there continues to be legal resistance to the application of compulsion to the state, and so one must again picture rights to compensation as policy based rather than principled. Perhaps the leading case where the right to compensation was tested was *Hill* v. *Chief Constable of West Yorkshire* (1989). The House of Lords concluded on grounds of public policy that it would be undesirable to impose civil liability on the police, preferring to allow them to use their professional judgement in the use of resources and the direction of policies unworried by the threat of potentially endless civil actions by concerned or disgruntled citizens. The European Court of Human Rights in the case of *Osman* (1998) later cast considerable doubt on any absolute exclusion of liability on grounds of public policy and required on grounds of due process the possibility of a claim to be considered case by case.

The rights of corporate personalities

Aside from the variable force of the substantive arguments for rights to state compensation and protection, there may be added difficulty in asserting these claims on behalf of commercial victims. There may be three distinctions between commercial or corporate bodies and natural persons in these respects. One is that bodily injury is more acute for the individual – the loss of quality of life caused by a serious injury is much more pervasive than the denting of the balance sheet of a company. Secondly, there is less of a sense of social solidarity in the case of a fate suffered by a non-natural person. In this way, one might doubt whether the concerns for democracy and dignity that underlie the conferment of human rights on natural persons (Clapham 1993: 143) can apply with the same force of meaning to corporate personalities. Thirdly, the financial costs to the state are more modest and manageable for individual personal injury and so become a more acceptable burden in the risk society.

The issue of the recognition of corporate bodies as rights-holders might be considered further in the context of Article 1 of Protocol 1 of the European Convention (Sermet 1992). It is here clear that the reference to a legal person as well as natural persons is meant to recognise that corporate bodies can have claims in respect of this right. This right also expressly includes 'peaceful enjoyment', which suggests it is a right to be protected against acts of violence against private property. This is indeed a right as against the state and its agencies – the state will be liable for its interferences that affect the economic value of property. However, we are dealing in this work with interferences not by the state but by paramilitary groups – wholly independent third parties. How far can the state be held responsible for failing to prevent their attacks on property rights? It has been argued the state has a duty at least to provide a legislative framework discouraging and providing remedies for third-party interferences (Clapham 1993: Chap. 4).

Another potentially relevant code of international law is the European Convention on the Compensation of Victims of Violent Crimes of 1983 (ETS 116, 1983; Cm. 1427, 1991) (Katsoris 1990–91; Greer 1996: Part I). Though designed to encourage compensation for the victims of crime across all states adhering to the Council of Europe, it is clear this convention will not avail corporate entities seeking compensation for property damage. The problem in this case is not so much one of personality, for the convention refers to 'persons', 'nationals' or 'applicants'. Rather, the limit arises through the type of loss, which is limited to serious bodily injury, impairment of health or death arising from crimes of violence (Article 2) and not property damage.

Conclusions on the perspective of the individual

The results can be seen as making sense in terms of the development of post-Fordism and risk society. The nation-state cannot tolerate unaccountable expansions of responsibilities for security, and so it is the private sector, either commercially or individually, that becomes the increasingly important bearer of risk. In this way, there is a postmodern twist to the duties of public protection of the state, in that the recent era of terrorist bombings has also encouraged parallel private duties of protection, with a consequent melding between public and private responsibility for security. This responsibility not only takes the form of the *de facto* assumption of responsibility for one's own security (such as by the purchase of security hardware) but also includes the recognition of private duties of care to other individuals.

Final reflections

If one is seeking a theme that cuts across the issues raised in this chapter and harmonises the different strands, it must be themes of late modernity and the responses to risk. These are reflected in the targets of political violence. The point of attack becomes a global and private concentration of economic power. At the same time, the private commercial victim is a vital part of the public political economy and also exercises wide powers of self-regulation which are not only used in the financial sector but are also very influential in the deployment of both public police officers and private security guards.

These strands are equally reflected in the central response of the 1993 Act. It recognises risk is to be managed rather than soothed away by the Keynsian welfare state. Moreover, management is a task for both public and private sectors of society. The broad conclusion must be that the state's role has changed over time and that it has moved, to use new public management symbolism, from 'rowing to steering' (Osborne and Gaebler 1992). This can be seen most clearly in the Reinsurance Act 1993. State intervention and leadership are essential to constitute the scheme. But, the scheme having been constituted, the state then attempts to retire from the spotlight and hopes its shadowy backstage presence will instil in the leading actors, commercial insurers and reinsurers, sufficient confidence to play their parts. So it is the role of the state to express sympathy and to encourage individual choice and responsibility in dealing with risk (Lewis 1996), but these tasks are achieved through many tiers of agency, both governmental and non-governmental. It follows that calls to create forms of normative or even legal rights to compensation and protection for victims are likely to be met with considerable resistance in the risk society. The state can no doubt live with a duty to promote, as in the words of the preamble to the European Convention on the Compensation of Victims of Violent Crime, 'equity and social solidarity'. But its relationship with individual potential claimants is likely to become more rather than less distant, both for pragmatic and ideological reasons. Though there may be some benefits in terms of the encouragement of personal responsibility, it is also clear social solidarity can be damaged through reliance on market choice. The reality, as illustrated by the cases of Docklands and Manchester, is that the market rarely works perfectly and that a public price must be paid for public benefits.

It may equally be possible to discern within the state's security responses the same late modern features and influences. This is illustrated by a familiar fragmentation of governance, including the mixing of public and private arrangements and an emphasis upon surveillance. After all, as Ericson and Haggerty contend: 'Risk society is fuelled by surveillance' (1997: 450).

As a final correction, there may be an ideological pull from the duties of protection that constrain the insouciance of the deregulatory state. However, as has been shown, these are diminished in the case of commercial victims, whose claims to protection or even recognition are fragile. So, even for the large multinational corporation just as for the seven-stone weakling, it's a risky world out there – more so because of their target-worthiness but less so because of their ability to dissipate the risk.

Note

1   This research was funded by a grant from the Airey Neave Trust. The authors thank Anthony Kennedy, Insurance Division, DTI, for supplying source documentation.

Cases cited

Calvin's case (1609) *77 English Reports 377.*

Hill v. *Chief Constable of West Yorkshire* (1989) *Appeal Cases* 53.
McCann, Savage and Farrell v. *United Kingdom* (1995) Application no. 18984/91, Series A, Volume 324 (1995) *The Times* 9 October (1996) 21 *European Human Rights Reports* 97.
Mutasa v. *Attorney General* (1980) *Queen's Bench Reports* 114.
Osman v. *United Kingdom* (1998) Application no. 23452/94, Reports 1998-VIII. (1998) *The Times* 5 November.

References

Beck, A. and Willis, A. (1993) *The Terrorist Threat to Safe Shopping*. Leicester: University of Leicester.
Beck, U. (1992) *Risk Society*. London: Sage.
Beck, U. (1995) *Ecological Enlightenment*. Atlantic Highlands, NJ: Humanities Press.
Bennett, H.N. (1996) *The Law of Marine Insurance*. Oxford: Oxford University Press.
Bice, W.B. (1994) British government reinsurance and acts of terrorism. *University of Pennsylvania Journal of International Business Law*, 15: 441–68.
Bishop, P. and Mallie, E. (1994) *The Provisional IRA*. London: Corgi.
Brealey, R. and Ireland, J. (1995) *The Competitive Position of London's Financial Services: Final Report*. London: City Research Project.
Castells, M. (1996) *The Rise of the Network Society. Volume 1*. London: Blackwell.
City of London Police (1993) *Annual Report for 1992*. London: City of London Police.
City of London Police (1994a) *Annual Report for 1993*. London: City of London Police.
City of London Police (1994b) *'CameraWatch' Closed Circuit Television Scheme*. London: City of London Police.
Clapham, A. (1993) *Human Rights in the Private Sphere*. Oxford: Clarendon Press.
Clarke, K. (1993) *House of Commons Debates*, Volume 233, column 932, 30 November 1993. London: Hansard.
Dillon, M. (1996) *25 Years of Terror: The IRA's War against the British*. London: Bantam.
Ericson, R.V. and Haggerty, K.D. (1997) *Policing the Risk Society*. Oxford: Clarendon Press.
Feeley, M. and Simon, J. (1994) Actuarial justice: the emerging new criminal law. In D. Nelken (ed.) *The Futures of Criminology*. London: Sage.
Giddens, A. (1994) Living in a post-traditional society. In U. Beck, A. Giddens and S. Lash (eds) *Reflexive Modernisation*. Cambridge: Polity Press.
Gloyn, W.J. (1993) Insurance against terrorism. *Law Society's Gazette*, 90(22): 20, 23.
Gower, L.C.B. (1988) 'Big bang' and city regulation. *Modern Law Review*, 51: 1–22.
Greer, D.S. (ed.) (1996) *Compensating Crime Victims*. Freiburg: Edition Iuscrim.
Greer, D.S. and Mitchell, V.A. (1982) *Compensation for Criminal Damage*. Belfast: SLS Legal Publications.
Hay, C. (1995) Re-stating the problem of regulation and re-regulating the local state. *Economy and Society*, 24(3): 387–407.
Hirst, P. and Thompson, G. (1995) Globalization and the future of the nation state. *Economy and Society*, 24(3): 408–22.
Hirst, P. and Thompson, G. (1999) *Globalisation in Question* (2nd edn) Cambridge: Polity Press.
Hogan, G. and Walker, C.P. (1989) *Political Violence and the Law in Ireland*.

Manchester: Manchester University Press.

Jasanoff, S. (1994) *Learning from Disaster.* Philadelphia, PA: University of Pennsylvania Press.

Jason-Lloyd, L. (1996) The Prevention of Terrrorism (Additional Powers) Act 1996 – a commentary. *Justice of the Peace,* 160: 503–6.

Jessop. B. (1992) Flexibilization and state strategies: coal and the City. In M. Dunford and L. Kafkalas (eds) *Cities and Regions in the New Europe: The Global–Local Interplay and Spatial Development Strategies.* London: Belhaven Press.

Jessop, B. (1994) Post-Fordism and the state. In A. Amin (ed.) *Post-Fordism. A Reader.* London: Blackwell.

Jones, T. and Newburn, T. (1998) *Private Security and Public Policing.* Oxford: Clarendon Press.

Katsoris, C.N. (1990–91) The European Convention on the Compensation of Victims of Violent Crime. *Fordham International Law Review,* 14: 186–215.

Kelly, O. (1993) The IRA threat to the City of London. *Policing* 9: 88–98.

Kielmas, M. (1993) Minimizing terrorism losses. *Business Insurance* 27(29): 17, 19.

Lewis, N. (1996) *Choice and Legal Order.* London: Sweet & Maxwell.

Litton, R. (1990) *Crime and Crime Prevention for Insurance Practice.* Aldershot: Avebury.

Luhmann, N. (1993) *Risk: A Sociological Theory.* Berlin: Walter de Gruyter.

Macleod, J. and Milnes, P. (1996) Insurance premium tax. *British Tax Review,* 155–67.

Mallie, E. and McKittrick, D. (1996) *The Fight for Peace.* London: Heinemann.

Mullin, J. and Kane, F. (1993) The scared mile. *Guardian, 3 August.*

Nelken, D. (1994) Reflexive criminology? In D. Nelken (ed.) *The Futures of Criminology.* London: Sage.

Newman, O. (1972) *Defensible Space.* New York: Macmillan.

Osborne, D. and Gaebler, T. (1992) *Re-inventing Government.* Reading, MA: Addison-Wesley.

Poole, M.A. (1997) Political violence – the overspill from Northern Ireland. In A. O'Day (ed.) *Political Violence in Northern Ireland.* Westport: Praeger.

Poyner, B. (1983) *Design against Crime: Beyond Defensible Space.* London: Butterworths.

Reid, K. (1996) Prevention of Terrorism (Additional Powers) Act 1996. *Web Journal of Current Legal Issues,* 4. http://webjcli.ncl.ac.uk/1996/issue4/reid4.html

Reid, K. (1997) Businesses and the Prevention of Terrorism (Additional Powers) Act 1996. *Journal of Financial Crime,* 4(3): 245–50.

Rhodes, R.A.W. (1997) *Understanding Governance.* Buckingham: Open University Press.

Rogers, P. (1996) *Economic Targeting and Provisional IRA Strategy. Studies in Political Violence,* 96.1. Bradford: University of Bradford.

Sermet, L. (1992) *The European Convention on Human Rights and Property Rights. Human Rights Files* 11. Strasbourg: Council of Europe.

Souter, G. (1992) London reinsurers expect restrictions due to catastrophes. *Business Insurance,* 26(43): 10–12.

Taylor, F.W. (1911) *Principles of Scientific Management.* New York: Harper & Bros.

Walker, C.P. (1992) *The Prevention of Terrorism in British Law.* (2nd edn). Manchester: Manchester University Press.

Walker, C.P. (2000) Briefing on the Terrorism Act 2000. *Terrorism and Political Violence,* 12(2): 1–36.

Wilkinson, P. (1986) *Terrorism and the Liberal State* (2nd edn). London: Macmillan.

Chapter 10

The introduction of CCTV into a custody suite: some reflections on risk, surveillance and policing

Tim Newburn

Introduction

Allegedly, we live in 'new times'. Post-Fordist means of production and the emergence of new technologies, particularly communications technologies, have led to a profound restructuring of the late modern world. There has been a significant shift towards the privatisation of public space, as well as radical changes to the organisation of urban environments and to the sources of identity formation. According to Giddens (1990), the disembedding of social activity from localised contexts, and the changing of sources of trust from localised systems to abstract systems, have resulted in a heightening of what he terms 'ontological insecurity'. Correlatively, security has become 'commodified' (Jones and Newburn 1998) and new technologies of surveillance, particularly CCTV, have become increasingly prominent as the means of governing particular (especially public) spaces. Such technologies have enabled the emergence of a form of 'digital rule' (Jones 2000), where 'at-a-distance monitoring' becomes a key element in electronic crime control. Criminologists have been much taken by these new technologies. Hitherto, however, their gaze has rested primarily on the impact of such technologies on public space, and has been characterised by a somewhat dystopian view of such developments. In this chapter, I wish to depart from this trend, first by focusing by the use of CCTV in a different form of space and, secondly, by adopting what I consider to be (philosophically) a more critical approach whilst resisting some of the easier normative judgements about such technologies.

This chapter arises out of the early stages of an evaluation of an experimental project that is taking place in the police station in Kilburn, North London.[1] The project involves the introduction of closed circuit television cameras (CCTV) into all the cells in the custody suite at the station. These cells are to be subject to continuous 24-hour CCTV surveillance by custody officers and gaolers working in the custody suite. This is an unprecedented use of CCTV in a police station in England and Wales; previously, CCTV has been confined, at most, to one or two cells within a custody suite for particularly 'vulnerable' prisoners. I begin by briefly considering the history and explicit purpose of the experiment and then go on to consider what appear to be some of the emerging issues. I conclude with some reflections on how this project fits within existing criminological discourses around risk, surveillance and policing.

Background

The criminal justice system has always given some official body the power to inquire into offences and to question suspects. Originally these powers were conferred on juries, with the police taking over the role of investigating offences in the first half of the nineteenth century. For as long as the police have had powers of detention for the purposes of questioning there have been concerns about the treatment and welfare of people in custody in police stations. From 1912 until the early 1980s, police powers were governed by 'Judges' Rules', a non-statutory statement of principles and practice that set out what the police could do when 'they were endeavouring to discover the author of a crime' (Judge 1986: 176). There were, however, important gaps in the rules and their legal status was unclear. As a result of this and concern about apparent miscarriages of justice, and a Royal Commission on Criminal Procedure which reported in 1981, the Police and Criminal Evidence Act 1984 (PACE) was passed.

PACE both increased police powers and introduced a new system of safeguards. It created a new type of police officer – the 'custody officer' – on whom responsibility rests for the protection of the rights of suspects and who is independent of the investigation of the crime. PACE, and its associated codes of practice, set out how suspects are to be treated. The custody officer has to pay special regard to the needs of 'vulnerable prisoners', such as the mentally handicapped and mentally disordered, to juveniles in general and to those for whom English is not a first language (Brown 1997).

The lead-up to the introduction of CCTV in Kilburn

PACE was the subject of vociferous criticism at the time of its passage, and critics continue to scrutinise its limitations. There is considerable criminological debate over whether or not the changes it introduced represented a 'sea change' in the treatment of detained suspects (Dixon 1991; Sanders 1997). Despite this ongoing debate, PACE is widely accepted by commentators as representing a significant step forward in relation to the rights of people detained in police stations. Indeed, safeguards for suspects contained in the Act go considerably beyond what is available in many other European countries (Morgan 1996). None the less, in some communities suspicions about the treatment of suspects in police stations remain high and, despite the protections in place, incidents of injury, (self-)harm and, occasionally, death still occur.

In recent years the Police Complaints Authority (PCA) has investigated the deaths of suspects in custody in Cambridge, Cheltenham, Colchester, Crawley, Gwent, Hull, Leeds, Plumstead, Rawtenstall, Smethwick and Swansea. In 1997–98, 56 people died in police custody in England and Wales (PCA 1998) and a further 65 died in 1998–99 (PCA 1999). This led the PCA to call for improved training of custody staff, improved cell design to reduce suicide risks and the extension of CCTV to cover 'observation cells' (for 'at risk' suspects). A relatively recent PCA conference, 'Deaths in Police Custody: Reducing the Risks', highlighted three major areas of concern: suicide and self-harm; drug and alcohol misuse; and restraint methods. The report went on to note that 'deaths in custody associated with some form of restraint generate considerable public concern, particularly when the deceased is from an ethnic minority' (ibid.). Again, the PCA called for expansion of CCTV in custody suites to include observation cells for particularly vulnerable detainees. The potential importance of CCTV has more recently been reaffirmed by the PCA, which noted that within the last year 11 forces have installed CCTV cameras inside cells for the first time and a further 14 have plans to do so or have plans under consideration (ibid.).

The Metropolitan Police is one of those forces that has started to utilise CCTV within major custody suites. Force policy restricts cameras to the charging areas and cell passages only. Within the last four years two men, Marlon Downes and Godwin Abbaffi, have died whilst in custody in police stations in the London Borough of Brent. These deaths, about which there is considerable dispute as to the causes (Newburn and

Hayman 2001), have fuelled the perception locally that the police continue to mistreat certain types of detainee. As the local police commander noted: 'three years ago there was a death of a person in custody. After all the inquiries had taken place and the inquest held, it was clear the police had one view of what happened and the family another' (*Evening Standard* 14 March 2000). His perception that community confidence had been severely and possibly lastingly dented led him to propose a radical experiment with CCTV in the custody suite.

The Kilburn experiment

Kilburn, unlike any other station in England and Wales, now has CCTV cameras in every cell in the custody suite. There are now quite a number of police stations that have one, or perhaps two, cells identified as those where the most 'vulnerable' prisoners will be kept. In some cases these cells are now subject to CCTV monitoring. What makes the Kilburn experiment unique is the extent of CCTV coverage. The experiment has a number of general features. First, it has CCTV cameras in the reception/booking areas and custody suite corridors. These monitor all activities in these areas. Secondly, there is now a camera in every cell in the custody suite – 17 cells in all. There are no cells without cameras. Thirdly, there is complete cell coverage. All parts of every cell are filmed by the cameras. There are no blind spots and there is no pixillation of the pictures. Thus the toilet area of each cell is completely visible to the camera and is filmed at all times. At the time the experiment was first being planned there was considerable discussion of the putative filming of the toilet area of the cells and some concern it was overly intrusive. In the event the decision not to pixillate the pictures was taken. Finally, there are monitors displaying coverage from all 17 cells on the custody sergeant's desk. The cameras have sound capability but, as yet, this has not been activated. There are two monitors, one displaying continuous coverage from all cells, and one that can be programmed just to focus on one cell at a time. The monitors are placed on the custody sergeant's desk and cannot ordinarily, therefore, be seen by the casual observer. Tapes are kept for retrospective viewing if appropriate and necessary.

Some issues arising in the Kilburn experiment

In the next section of this chapter I want to focus on four issues that are thrown up by the Kilburn experiment and its evaluation. These are:

- the objectives of the experiment;
- balancing 'privacy' and 'protection';
- 'privacy' – the prison cell as hybrid space; and
- the question of impact.

Objectives

Much of the extant literature focuses on the use of CCTV in public space (a point to which I return later in the chapter). The objective(s) of CCTV in public space is generally straightforward. Its aim is either to deter those who might break the law from doing so and/or to provide filmed evidence that will allow arrests to be made and charges to be brought. It might be argued that CCTV cameras are also intended to make people feel safer, though this is less often advanced as a motive for introducing CCTV schemes.

Crudely speaking, the Kilburn CCTV experiment has four primary objectives. First, clearly one of the central objectives in installing cameras is to increase the level of surveillance of people detained in custody and, as a consequence, to reduce the likelihood that harm, however inflicted, may befall them. That is, the aim is that the existence of cameras will alert police officers in the custody suite to risks they might not necessarily otherwise observe. Linked to this aim, though less often or so explicitly made, is the assumption CCTV will impact on the behaviour of police officers and reduce the likelihood they may harm suspects. The second aim, and one of the longer-term objectives of the CCTV project, is to improve levels of confidence among the local residents in the treatment of suspects in the police station. Historically in Brent there has been deep mistrust of police treatment of suspects in police custody. Thirdly, should anything befall a suspect whilst under the care and protection of the police, the hope is CCTV can be used to provide evidence of 'what really happened' to the person(s) concerned. Finally, it is hoped the installation of cameras will reassure staff that police managers will provide them with the protection they require in order to work effectively within the custody suite, and to guard them against malicious complaints from suspects.

Two issues are worth highlighting here. The first concerns priorities rather than simply objectives. Thus, one question that arises is which of the objectives will receive greatest priority? Will some objectives gain primacy? The launch of the scheme provides one small example of the privileging of particular objectives. The issues highlighted in publicising the initiative have been deaths in custody (through natural causes or as a result of suicide) and complaints against the police. Interestingly, though perhaps not surprisingly, guarding against the mistreatment of suspects in custody has not been mentioned when the experiment has been publicised. The headline in the *Evening Standard* on the day of the launch of the experiment (14 February 2000) summed up the way in which it was presented publicly: 'Cameras to cut cell deaths and protect police.' This message was promulgated both by the senior officers in charge of the experiment and by the Home Office minister who attended the launch.

The second issue that arises is the emergence of new, perhaps unanticipated, objectives. Will it be the case that the experiment generates new aims as it develops? One unanticipated outcome of the introduction of cameras, and this happened early on in the life of the experiment, was the use of cameras to collect evidence of criminal offences committed by suspects whilst locked in their cells. In this regard it is interesting to note that one suspect has already been charged with criminal damage against his cell (writing graffiti on the cell's wall) as a result of video evidence.

Privacy versus protection

It is clear the potential protection afforded to detainees through the introduction of CCTV is only available at a cost in terms of privacy, not only to themselves but also to police officers. There has been very real concern at Scotland Yard that the installation of cameras in all cells will, at some point, give rise to a legal challenge for a breach of human rights. The implications of the incorporation of the European Convention on Human Rights into domestic law for covert surveillance have been quite widely discussed (see, for example, Uglow 1999). Such consideration has, for understandable reasons, generally focused on the use of covert techniques for the collection of intelligence and evidence. The example of CCTV in the cells raises similar issues but in a context where the use of surveillance is overt. The primary concern with the Kilburn experiment is that it will give rise to challenges under Article 8 (the respect for the right to a private life). As yet no such challenge has been made and, moreover, it is not clear that such an action would succeed for, as Uglow notes, 'it is clear that the right to privacy is not absolute' (*ibid.*: 294) – as is always the case, rights have always to be negotiated and set against others. The protection of liberties and freedoms always has a price-tag.

Privacy – the custody suite as 'hybrid space'

Given that rights have always to be negotiated and set against others, in assessing the particular situation under consideration at Kilburn we must be careful how we understand 'privacy' and its limits. The early indications from the research suggest those incarcerated in police custody often take a rather different view of privacy from those of us who live in a non-custodial setting. They give a sense that, in the face of potential or actual physical threat from those responsible for their custody, they are willing to accept compromises to their privacy. The following suspect illustrates neatly the willingness to compromise certain 'rights' in order to increase the likelihood others will not be infringed: 'As long as the cameras are around we are protected from anyone and everyone... Privacy is important but I would sacrifice that in the cell for the protection of one's safety' (Detainee 02/07/99). It is easy to assume suspects will necessarily object to being constantly 'watched'. For some, however, not only were the protections a sufficient justification for the presence of the cameras, but they viewed the activities they undertook in the cell as being merely mundane and consequently of little concern: '[CCTV] would prevent police harassment in the cell. It would make me feel much safer. It wouldn't affect my behaviour here because my behaviour here is not deviant. All I'm doing in here is eating, sleeping, pissing and shitting – everyone has to do those things' (Detainee 07/05/99). Moreover, as the following two respondents indicate, the experience of prison was often an important mediating factor. Far from resenting the intrusion of the cameras, suspects with experience of imprisonment had radically different expectations about privacy; they had, it appeared, long been used to such 'observation':

> Privacy? That's not so important. Once you've been in prison, you realise toilets don't have to be private, though that's not very nice. If it stops police kicking someone about, then going to the toilet doesn't matter so much (Detainee 30/06/99).

> Everyone watches you shit and shower in prison, so why does it matter here? (Detainee 24/06/99).

Under such circumstances it would be somewhat ironic if an innovation designed to protect suspects from physical harm (a 'right' they hold dearer than most) were to be undermined because of concerns about the invasion of privacy (a 'right' that is already compromised and that many suspects would willingly compromise further). Although the police cell is, in some respects, a space characterised by a degree of privacy, in our view this is often exaggerated. In reality, cameras or not, the police cell is closely monitored by police officers and others – largely without the consent of the detainee. It is, therefore, best regarded as 'hybrid space': a place in which there is far from free public access but where privacy is also very restricted.

The question of impact

The final issue concerns what the likely impacts of the CCTV experiment will be. At the most straightforward level this means to what extent will its objectives be met? Will the levels of harm befalling prisoners in custody be reduced? Will local community confidence in the treatment of suspects in custody increase? Finally, will the number of (malicious) complaints against police officers – and indeed injuries suffered by police officers – reduce? These general questions conceal a variety of other issues:

- What will the mechanism be that brings about these particular consequences? Will it be deterrence, anticipatory compliance or whatever?

- Will the presence of cameras undermine what in other circumstances would be called 'natural surveillance'?

- Will the presence of cameras impact upon officers' compliance with PACE?

- What will be the implications of CCTV for the cultural and social relations in and around the spaces surveyed?

- Will this particular 'security commodity', as others have argued (Spitzer 1987; Loader 1997), increase feelings of security or will it simply serve to remind those occupying the custody suite of their insecurities?

Risk, surveillance and policing

The bulk of contemporary writing on CCTV focuses on public space. There is, by contrast, relatively little focus on private space, the only exception being work focusing on shopping centres – anyway generally better thought of as 'hybrid space' (see Jones and Newburn 1998). The social circumstances of the 'custody suite' are obviously somewhat removed from what generally pertains in 'public space'. None the less, the issues raised by the use and experience of CCTV in the custody suite are in some respects similar to those arising from the use of electronic surveillance elsewhere. However, they are also some potentially instructive points of departure. My first argument, therefore, is that in attempting to understand the uses and consequences of CCTV, it should not be assumed the study of its application in public space is sufficient.

Numerous social theorists have focused on the set of structural and cultural changes associated with the transition to 'late modernity'. In relation to criminal justice much attention has been paid to the notion of 'risk' and to what is taken to be the increasing domination of actuarial forms of discourse and practice in crime control (e.g. Feeley and Simon 1992). This, it is argued, has affected policing as it has affected the entire panoply of crime control agencies. Though there are differing approaches within social science to understanding 'risk', for our purposes here the key features of risk-based practices may be summarised as:

- an increasing preoccupation by government with aggregate populations rather than individuals;
- a shift away from disciplinary techniques towards actuarial practices;
- an increasing centrality of information collection and analysis (particularly about those 'at risk' or likely 'to cause risk'); and
- a shift towards anticipatory activities, particularly surveillance and proactive intervention.

Clearly such changes have potentially far-reaching consequences for policing (see Ericson and Haggerty 1997). My focus here, however, is rather narrower. As Johnston argues 'CCTV is the exemplar of actuarial technology since, under it, aggregate populations as well as particular offending groups, constitute the community of risk' (2000: 62). Here I want to focus on the use of such electronic surveillance and, more particularly, on the possible implications and consequences of 'watching' people held in police custody. I want to begin with a general point about the treatment of surveillance within criminology.

Against dystopianism

There is an inclination towards dystopianism within contemporary criminological literature on surveillance. There is a tendency to talk of the 'maximum security society' (Marx 1988; Norris and Armstrong 1999), 'big brother' (Davies 1998) and of a further 'thinning and strengthening of the mesh' and 'widening of the size and reach of the net' of social control (Cohen 1985). To take such a position is to adopt a particular normative stance in relation to the 'new surveillance'. Within this stance, the possibility that such techniques may have positive consequences is (at best) minimised. That such surveillance might be a part of what might normatively be considered to be the 'good society' is rendered impossible.

By contrast, David Lyon (1994) quite rightly argues that surveillance shows more than one face. He says the prominent paradox is 'that surveillance simultaneously represents both a means of social control and a means of ensuring that citizens' rights are respected' (ibid.: 219). This is the position that, I would like to argue, clearly holds for the Kilburn experiment. It is not only a means of social control of prisoners; it is also a system installed with the avowed aim of increasing the protection of the rights of prisoners (albeit through the social control of others). In saying this, I do not want to dismiss the extent to which the system introduced at Kilburn is intrusive; it is clearly enormously so. However, in accepting this it would still be very misleading to describe the system simply as some dystopian form of maximum surveillance. This, the closest there is in the UK to the 'electronic panopticon', has more than one face. It holds out the possibility of gain and improvement as well as containing some obvious dangers. This is an important corrective to much current criminology that, in its understandable scepticism about many of the claims made on behalf of CCTV by politicians and policy-makers, has tended to assume that the possibilities opened up by such technologies are generally malign, rather than benign or even advantageous.

In attempting to capture the dual nature of CCTV, Jock Young argued that it:

> is undoubtedly one of the most invidious of inventions. In the wrong hands it can police factories in a minute and draconian fashion ('the boss is everywhere'), it can generate a web of surveillance which far exceeds anything that is historically known, it can invade privacy and make Orwell's 1984 a reality. But it can also, in a different political context, be liberating and protective.
>
> (1999: 192)

Young's description, though it also places much greater emphasis on the negative, is essentially correct. Technologies such as CCTV may, at least in theory, be socially beneficial and well as potentially harmful. Thus, whilst concurring with Young's general observation about the ability of CCTV both to intrude and to protect, I wish also to argue it can do both these simultaneously in the same political context – not merely in different political contexts. Electronic surveillance is multi-dimensional in its functions and capabilities. Thus, as I have already implied, one of the key issues for the Kilburn experiment will be the ways in which the rights to privacy and protection are balanced. Recognising this provides the basis for a fuller and more rounded understanding of the potential of such technologies, and also places at the centre of our concerns the issue of governance. How should such potential be managed and controlled?

The supervisors and the supervised

This brings us to one of the differences between the use of cameras in the Kilburn experiment and their traditional use in town centres and the like – and this concerns the 'watchers' themselves. For in the case of the custody suite the watchers are also the watched (it is not that this cannot and does not happen elsewhere, merely that it is unusual). In this regard, CCTV shares some of the characteristics of other technologies for, as Ericson and Haggerty point out: 'in the very process of using communication technologies to accomplish their work, police officers are subject to the surveillance capacities of those technologies, which are able to monitor and risk-profile officer conduct in greater detail than human supervisors can' (1997: 394). Thus, the introduction of CCTV to the cells at Kilburn is intended not only to allow police officers continuously to monitor suspects in their cells, but it is also intended to record the behaviour of the police officers themselves. Johnston (2000) has argued that under late modern conditions policing shifts from focusing primarily on communities of collective sentiment to *communities of risk*. These are 'not merely [communities] at risk from some external threat...they are increasingly defined, orientated, organised and governed around matters of security and risk' (*ibid*.: 55). One of the early lessons of the Kilburn experiment is that, in such terms, police officers are every bit as much a 'community of risk' as 'suspects'. This is a reminder of Peter Manning's observation 'that the primary, abiding and most persistent problems facing Anglo-American policing from its inception in 1829 have been proper internal control, discipline and supervision' (1983: 169).

In this regard the custody suite differs from many other sites of surveillance. In the custody suite the supervisors are also supervised. Thus in one important respect the officer and the prisoner now have a shared experience of life in the custody suite: they can both be watched. In other respects, however, the generally asymmetrical power relationships that characterise surveillance (Norris and Armstrong 1999) remain largely undisturbed. As Norris and Armstrong (*ibid*.: 5) put it, whilst 'the watcher can see the watched, the reverse is not true'. This also holds for the custody suite. Whilst prisoners are watched by police officers, prisoners cannot watch police officers. Or, more accurately, they cannot do so in real time. There is the possibility they – or their representative – might be able to do so retrospectively. We may assume this possibility is likely to change the nature of relationships within the custody suite. How precisely relationships will change we are currently unsure.

One of the key characteristics of 'late modernity' is held to be the separation of time from space. This 'distanciation' is made possible by new forms of communication, the new 'technologies of life' (Lash 2000). Similarly, watching via CCTV is 'distanciated' – i.e. those watching are removed, spatially, from those being watched. The panopticon no longer requires spatial proximity (Bauman 2000). Indeed, Bauman argues that such distantiation is perhaps the key characteristic of late modernity and, indeed, is what makes late modernity 'post-panoptical'. This has important consequences for social relationships. According to Bauman:

> the end of Panopticon augurs the end of *the era of mutual engagement*: between the supervisors and the supervised, capital and labour, leaders and their followers, armies at war. The prime technique of power is now escape, slippage, elision, and avoidance, the effective rejection of any territorial confinement with cumbersome corollaries of order-building, order-maintenance and the responsibility for the consequences of it all as well as of the necessity to bear their costs.
>
> *(ibid.*: 11):

Though the technology could make it possible, the nature of the custody suite – at least as currently organised – is not yet post-panoptical. For legal and organisational reasons the watcher and watched remain in close proximity. It is the same officers that, under PACE, are required physically to monitor the welfare of prisoners who are tasked with watching the CCTV screens. As such the custody suite in Kilburn resembles, in some important respects, an electronic panopticon; it is something that can 'see constantly and recognise immediately' (Foucault 1977: 200). Clearly, however, it need not remain so. The monitors screening the images from the cells and custody suite could be sited elsewhere. Indeed, in theory the cameras could be monitored by someone other than the police (though this has not as yet been explicitly considered). Retrospectively this already occurs: lay visitors, solicitors and others have access (under limited circumstances) to tapes.

More intriguingly, the technology offers the possibility of 'real time' independent scrutiny: the public could watch the police. To my knowledge this has not been suggested as a possibility. So unusual would the suggestion be that the 'citizen' watch the state that it appears illegitimate – almost impossible. By why should it be so? Moreover, if in Kilburn as elsewhere one of the major concerns relates to perceptions in the local community about the mistreatment of suspects in custody, do not the cameras provide one means of helping directly overcome such distrust? Within the Metropolitan Police one of the current fashions is to appoint 'independent advisory groups' whose role is to advise – and in some ways provide legitimacy for – certain areas of police activity. In this manner it would be possible, in theory, to form an independent advisory committee that would scrutinise, using CCTV footage, activities in the custody suite. This would, in effect, be an electronic extension of the lay visiting scheme. Clearly the installation of cameras in the custody suite opens up a form of police governance that has rarely been considered previously, if at all. In doing so, it demonstrates also the existence of a 'face' of surveillance that has generally remained invisible to criminologists.

Note

1 Some of the arguments in this chapter are based on ideas that first saw the light of day in a paper entitled 'The use of CCTV in police cells: issues of protection and privacy', presented at the British Criminology Conference, July 1999, and written with Oliver Phillips (Keele University).

References

Bauman, Z. (2000) *Liquid Modernity*. Cambridge: Polity Press.

Brown, D. (1997) *PACE Ten Years on: A Review of the Research*. Home Office Research Study 155. London: Home Office.

Cohen, S. (1985) *Visions of Social Control*. Cambridge: Polity Press.

Davies, S. (1998) CCTV: A new battleground for privacy. In C. Norris, J. Moran and G. Armstrong (eds) *Surveillance, CCTV and Social Control.*, Aldershot: Ashgate.

Dixon, D. (1991) Common sense, legal advice and the right of silence. *Public Law*, 233–54.

Ericson, R. and Haggerty, K. (1997) *Policing the Risk Society*. Oxford: Clarendon Press.

Feeley, M. and Simon, J. (1992) The new penology: notes on the emerging strategy of corrections and its implications. *Criminology*, 30(4): 452–74.

Foucault, M. (1977) *Discipline and Punish*. London: Penguin.

Giddens, A. (1990) *The Consequences of Modernity*. Cambridge: Polity Press.

Johnston, L. (2000) *Policing Britain: Risk, Security and Governance*. Harlow: Longman.

Jones, R. (2000) Digital rule: punishment, control and technology. *Punishment and*

Society, 2(1): 5–22.

Jones, T. and Newburn, T. (1998) *Private Security and Public Policing*, Oxford: Clarendon Press.

Judge, T. (1986) The provisions in practice. In J. Benyon and C. Bourn (eds) *The Police: Powers, Procedures and Proprieties*. Oxford: Pergamon Press.

Lash, S. (2000) Technologies of life. Inaugural Lecture, Goldsmiths' College, University of London.

Loader, I. (1997) Thinking normatively about private security. *Journal of Law and Society*, 24(3): 1–31.

Lyon, D. (1994) *The Electronic Eye: The Rise of Surveillance Society*. Cambridge: Polity Press.

Manning, P.K. (1983) *Police Work: The Social Organization of Policing*. Cambridge, MA: MIT Press.

Marx, G. (1988) *Undercover: Police Surveillance in America*. Berkeley, CA: University of California Press.

Morgan, R. (1996) Custody in the police station: how do England and Wales measure up in Europe? *Policy Studies*, 17(1): 55–72.

Newburn, T. and Hayman, S. (2001) *Policing, Surveillance and Social Control: CCTV and police monitoring of suspects*. Cullompton: Willan Publishing.

Norris, C. and Armstrong, G. (1999) *The Maximum Surveillance Society: The Rise of CCTV*. London: Berg.

Police Complaints Authority (1998) *Annual Report*. London: The Stationery Office.

Police Complaints Authority (1999) *Deaths in Police Custody: Reducing the Risks*. London: Police Complaints Authority. http://www.pca.gov.uk/news/deaths2.htm

Sanders, A. (1997) From suspect to trial. In M. Maguire, R. Morgan and R. Reiner (eds) *The Oxford Handbook of Criminology*. Oxford: Clarendon Press.

Spitzer, S. (1987) Security and control in capitalist societies: the fetishism of security and the secret thereof. In J. Lowman, R. J. Menzies and T. S. Palys (eds) *Transcarceration: Essays in the Sociology of Social Control*. Aldershot: Gower.

Uglow, S. (1999) Covert surveillance and the European Convention on Human Rights. *Criminal Law Review*, 287–99.

Young, J. (1999) *The Exclusive Society*. London: Sage.

Chapter 11

The poetics of safety: lesbians, gay men and home

Leslie J. Moran

This chapter explores the experience of safety and insecurity through the relationship between violence, sexuality and space. It draws upon data generated by way of a 30-month project undertaken as part of an Economic and Social Research Council (ESRC) initiative on violence.[1] Let me begin with three snapshots. The first is from the ESRC project data. It comes from the second in a series of six focus group discussions with gay men in Lancaster. In response to a question, posed by the group facilitator, 'So what can and can't you do and where? What about kissing another man?,' one of the gay men replied:

> I suppose I'd be comfortable kissing another man at my home or in their house or...possibly in a gay pub. I wouldn't sort of feel comfortable at all sort of kissing someone in the street or anything like that, because you would always have in the back of your mind, 'Are there any scallies coming to beat your head in?' And you're sort of encouraging [violence].

The second snapshot, again from the ESRC focus group data, comes from an exchange in one of the lesbian group meetings in Lancaster. In response to a question about the relationship between safety and comfort an initial discussion pointed to differences between the two terms. Safety/unsafety was explained in terms of being 'mugged', 'beaten' or 'hit'. By way of contrast one lesbian explained 'uncomfortable' in the following terms: 'Some people can make you can feel uncomfortable by not even saying anything...Just by their body language.' Here the distinction seems to point to the presence or absence of immediate physical violence. However, others in the group talked about the connection between safety and comfort. One participant explained, 'The reason it is uncomfortable is because it doesn't feel safe.' Another added: 'I think sometimes they interlink. If you are uncomfortable it compromises your safety as well, a man walking behind you is uncomfortable but it also compromises my safety because he could attack me.' Here 'safety' and 'comfort' are connected. In the first observation safety is comfort. In the second the relation is one of a continuum by way of violence and the threat and fear of violence.

The final snapshot comes from two recent studies of violence against lesbians and gay men. A study of 'male gay-hate related homicides' (Mouzos and Thompson 2000) found that the majority of the incidents of homicide (62%) occurred in the victim's home. The second study, by the Greater Manchester Lesbian and Gay Policing Initiative, 'Lesbians' Experiences of Violence and Harassment' (1998: 6), found that lesbians 'experience a high incidence of crime and harassment either in their home, workplace or neighbourhood and it is perpetrated by neighbours, family and work colleagues'.

These snapshots address a particular relationship between experiences of safety and danger, security and insecurity and location.[2] They all draw attention to the significance of a particular imagined location, 'home'. They point to the importance of 'comfort', as an attribute associated with 'home', in the generation of experiences of safety or danger, security or insecurity in the face of violence and the fear of violence. 'Home' and its attribute 'comfort' draw attention to the way experiences are generated by way of specific effects produced through particular imagined locations. While 'home' and 'comfort' first appear in these snapshots in the context of the domestic or private sphere their use by the gay man in the first example suggests their significance is not confined to this spatial context. They are also used in the articulation of his experience of safety in a 'gay bar', which might be characterised as a space of civil society and as a public place. Finally, the homicide research and the Mancunian lesbian report problematise the relation between sexualised violence and 'home' as 'comfort' and 'safety'. Far from being a location and effect associated with safety and security from sexualised violence, 'home' is the place were we might be most likely to experience violence and experience it in its most extreme forms. Using the ESRC focus group data, the general objective of this chapter is to examine in more detail the significance of 'home' and 'comfort' and their association with safety and security.

Any attempt to explore 'home' and 'comfort' as intelligibilities and practices of safety and security needs to be situated in the context of

275

feminist scholarship – in particular, feminist criminological scholarship on 'home'. This body of work has developed a critical challenge to the idea of 'home' as safety and security. By way of introduction some of the key themes of this debate will be set out. The focus will then turn to the data drawn from the lesbian and gay focus groups in the ESRC study from the two locations, Manchester and Lancaster. The chapter explores the apparent contradictions of 'home' and 'comfort' both within our data and within the context of debates relating to violent crime, fear of violence and strategies for promoting safety and security. In examining the uses of 'home' and 'comfort' arising from the research, lesbian, gay and feminist scholarship on identity, space and violence will be used to analyse the findings. Finally, the chapter reflects upon the critical contribution the lesbian and gay data on 'home' and 'comfort' might make to policy debates and practical initiatives addressing violence and safety.

Feminist debates on violence, fear of violence and safety: critiques of 'home'

Feminist scholarship has raised an important challenge to any work that seeks to examine the relation between 'home' and safety. In contrast to 'home' as safety and security, feminist work has documented the myriad ways in which women's experience of home has been one of confinement, containment, exploitation and exclusion. Particular attention has been drawn to the way 'home' as security and safety has particular class significance, has been deployed by those associated with a right-wing politics and has had a key place within a reactionary politics of nostalgia and a sentimental domesticity (Bammer 1992; Irigaray 1993). Others have critically examined the ways in which metaphors of 'home', as sanctuary and security, have informed feminist scholarship and progressive politics more generally. In particular, they have examined the way feminism and feminist practice have been understood as 'home', as sanctuary, security, refuge and thereby have (re)produced an experience of 'home' as silence, violence, hierarchy and exclusion (Martin and Mohanty 1986; De Laurentis 1990; Honnig 1994).

Feminist criminologists working on gender, violence and fear of violence have been keen to work against the associations between home, security and safety for good reasons. They have documented the many ways in which 'home' as safety misrepresents the reality of the everyday nature of violence in women's lives (Stanko 1990). Much work has been, and continues to be, done to demonstrate that the home is the primary location of violence against women. Talk of the home as a locus of safety threatens to perpetuate the erasure of this fact. The safe home, it is argued, perpetuates the idea that the major threat to women's safety is the random violence of strangers in public places (Saraga 1996).

In the context of debates about fear of crime feminist concerns have focused upon the way fear of crime talk has contributed to 'the myth of the safe home'(Stanko 1988). It perpetuates the misrepresentation of violence against women in various ways. Attention has been drawn to the way 'safety talk' reproduces the association between gendered violence and the public realm thereby putting women's most common experience of violence (in the home) out of the frame (Valentine 1989, 1992; Pain 1997). In its focus on 'safety strategies' in the public realm the safety literature has been criticised on the basis it merely tells women, and until recently it has predominantly addressed women, what they already know about safety strategies in public places (Stanko 1988, 1995, 1998). At the same time, it fails to offer any advice about those contexts in which women experience most violence and fear of violence – in the home and in other intimate relationships and settings, such as the workplace. Finally, safety talk's focus on victims and its concern with responsible behaviour perpetuates associations between particular gender identities (femininities inflected by class and race) and danger (Madriz 1997; Stanko 1998), leaving out of the picture the gendered behaviour of those who perform the violence (Stanko 1997). In general 'home' as 'comfort' safety and security appears to be implicated in the perpetuation of perceptions, policing policies and practices that sustain and promote gender violence rather than realise safety for those who experience violence.

While Mason (1997a) has drawn attention to the dangers of proceeding on the basis that the nature and experience of heterosexist violence and lesbian and gay experiences of safety are the same as experiences of violence against women, this does not necessarily lead to the conclusion that the feminist challenges to home and comfort as safety and security need not be taken seriously in a lesbian and gay context. For example, the gay-male homicide data and the Mancunian lesbian violence report, referred to above, point to the importance of taking seriously violence against lesbians and gay men in and near the home. This suggests there is clearly a need for caution in reducing violence against lesbians and gay men to stranger violence. There is already some evidence that the 'myth of the safe home' has become part of the police response to homophobic violence, despite the fact violence against lesbians and gay men has only recently come to be taken seriously by the police and the wider criminal justice system (Jenness and Broad 1997; Jenness and Grattet 2001). Stanko and Curry (1997) offer evidence of the ways in which many of the problematic ideas about safety exposed in the context of work on violence against women are being reproduce in this new context. Recent 'hate crime' safety information literature addressing lesbians and gay men produced by the Lancashire Police (1999) works with the assumption that most homophobic crime is violence performed in public by strangers. The leaflet's safety talk urges lesbians and gay men to 'be streetwise, don't be a target'. This slogan reproduces an assumption that lesbians and gay men can choose to be and can choose not to be a victim of homophobic violence. This seems directly to contradict another message in the leaflet, that it is the perpetrator's perception of the sexuality of the object of his violence, rather than the sexual orientation of the one assaulted or abused, that is important in homophobic incidents. When it comes to safety advice, our focus group data suggest that most of the advice is already second nature to our lesbian and gay participants who live with homophobic incidents on a day-to-day basis. In part this is also recognised in the advice in the safety leaflet, which is described as 'common sense' and 'instinct'. All this suggests any work on 'home' as safety and security needs to proceed with caution in order to avoid the further perpetuation of the 'myth of the safe home' and all the problems associated with it. With that firmly in mind, I now want to turn to the lesbian and gay focus group data.

'Home'

An extract from one of the gay men in the Manchester focus group offers some further observations to those in the extract that opened the chapter about the relationship between 'home' and 'comfort':

> I think the expression 'to feel at home' is to feel comforta-
> ble...there's nothing that compares to...being at my own house,
> I just lie there in front of the TV and have my scruffy jumper on and
> that is home to me, it's not being at home, it's not living at home but
> just to feel at home, it's just being comfortable.

In both extracts 'comfort' is a characteristic associated with a particular location, 'home'. Together they draw attention to a relation between experiences of safety and security and 'home' and 'comfort'. In the above extract 'home' and 'comfort' is explained as a very specific relation. 'Comfort' is not merely one amongst many attributes of 'home' but a synonym for 'home'. As one of our participants explains, 'comfort' has a special relation to 'home': 'nothing...compares'. The above extract also draws attention to the way 'comfort' produces location by way of feelings, emotions, effect. Another gay member of the Manchester focus group explained that home is 'where the heart is' and, when asked to explain further, added 'it's about where you feel most comfortable, it's about personal freedom'. While we again have 'comfort' as a synonym for home, at the same time 'comfort' is given different meanings: 'heart' and 'freedom'. One of our Lancaster lesbians associated 'home' with 'real joy'. Other participants have explained it in different ways: the private ('not public') as the place of 'relaxation' and the locus of being 'at ease'. These examples draw attention to the many ways home/comfort might be explained and expressed. Home/comfort is the point of connection and combination of these many different meanings. It is a point of condensation for a chain of other associations. The many meanings are produced by way of metaphor and metonym. Thereby they produce, inflect, re-focus and shift the meaning of home/comfort in a variety of ways.

Another dimension of home/comfort appears in an observation made by one of our Lancaster lesbian group members. Some people, she explains, 'don't want information, they don't want to go...to discos and they don't want to go to all these women's groups, they just want to sit at home, have a pint, have a spliff, you know what I mean, watch the telly or something'. One of the Lancaster gay men explained, '[sitting] at home watching TV [is] easier and it's as rewarding' as a visit to the monthly gay disco'. The positive references to 'home' in these extracts, in contrast to the difficulties of the feminist, lesbian, gay public realm, cannot be reduced to the particular 'problems' of being a lesbian or gay man in Lancaster, a small and in many ways parochial and provincial place with few formal lesbian and gay spaces. One of our Manchester gay men makes similar associations in the following comment:

> [a gay friend] hates 'V' [from our survey Manchester's most popular gay bar] 'cos he says it is too rowdy and noisy...I suppose he doesn't hate it but I just find it is very hard to get him to come out. You know, to even go for a drink say once a month. I suppose in a way he probably does hate it. He doesn't like being there. As soon as he gets there, he wants to go home.

These extracts draw attention to the way in which both male (cf. Sennett 1992) and female participants deploy 'home' as retreat, sanctuary, respite, haven, in contrast with the struggle associated with civil society and the public realm. 'Home' is stability and harmony and a particular sense of peace or certainty with its specific rewards.

The Lancaster lesbian's reference to 'a pint', 'a spliff', 'watching TV' are of particular importance. They are not only signs of 'comfort' but, more importantly, they are practices. They are contemporary practices of 'comfort' that have a metonymic relation to home. They are practices of retreat and sanctuary, implicated in the constitution of the experience of a particular location as 'home'.

Another attribute of 'home' is found in the following extract from a Lancaster lesbian participant: 'You can go home to where you belong and it means nothing to anybody'. Various things are of interest here. The reference to home as a place where life 'means nothing', I suggest, is a reference to anonymity as a characteristic of 'home'. Here that characteristic is made in a very specific context, belonging, which draws attention to another important aspect of home: the relation between home and ontology (cf. Bachelard 1963; Cooper 1994; Forty 1986; George 1999).

The home/ontology relation is explained by one of our Lancaster gay participants in the following terms: 'I think my home is a gay space as well...I live with my partner and...I can be a complete wally there, and just be myself, which is good.' For this gay man 'home' is the locus of ontological authenticity. It is the place of a particular security represented here by reference to a space free from judgement. The located authenticity of the self, in turn, gives a name to the space – 'gay space'. One of our Lancaster lesbians explained:

> If you are happy in your head, you are happy anywhere you want...I'm as happy here as I am in other places and as happy as I will be in other places. If you are genuinely happy and at home with yourself then you will be that wherever you go, won't you?

Of particular interest here is the phrase 'at home with your self'. It captures a particular conjunction of place and ontology. The preposition 'at' draws attention to the importance of 'home' as position. It is a position produced in a very specific context: 'with yourself'. The preposition 'with' suggests home as a place with the quality of proximity, intimacy, nearness, connection to 'self'.

The other side of 'home'

While the focus group data presented so far might suggest a rather one-sided and nostalgic view of 'home' the data portrays another side of 'home'. Reflecting upon her childhood experience of 'home', one

Lancastrian lesbian commented: 'we were kicked out of the house when we came home from school and we didn't go back until half past ten at night. You know that's how I was brought up.' Another member of the group talked of the 'vulnerability' of 'home'. Here, 'home' appears not so much as sanctuary or retreat but as a site of exclusion and an experience of exposure. This is developed by one of our Lancaster gay men, a student. He explained:

> With most of my friends at University [my sexuality] is not an issue. Since about week 2 they've always thought I was gay, so it didn't surprised them. They'll ask me about who I fancy and I'll tell them just like I would if I was straight. But back home I have my parents and they don't understand.

Rather than ontological sanctuary, in this instance, 'home' (as the parental home) is the site where the sexual self is experienced as self that is absent and a self at risk because of non-comprehension. The 'parental home' is in contrast here with 'home' constituted in the wake of departure, the 'home' of choice. More specifically, the parental home is the 'straight home' where 'straight' is marked in the fact that his home of choice is a sexualised location that is elsewhere. As one of our Mancunian lesbians explained: 'You can't go home because of your parents.' 'Home' is a place of exclusion. 'Home' is now not a place of anonymity, where practices 'mean nothing to anybody' but a place that is 'not very anonymous'. A Lancaster lesbian talked of 'home' as an experience of 'constraints' arising out of intimacy and imposed by the 'people who have known you'. It is, explained one of the Mancunian gay man, a place where you are 'criticised, and abused, and condemned and judged and offended'. Here, 'home' is a place of surveillance and judgement by way of particular knowledges. A lesbian mother from the Manchester group spoke of her experience of her home of choice as a permeable space subject to the normative gaze of school officials, children's friends and neighbours. These experiences of 'home' resonate with what Lefebvre (1999) has described as the genitality of home in which the heterofamilial of 'home' comes to the fore. Lefebvre (*ibid.*) suggests the (hetero)genitality of home works to link the home to nature and the natural which, in turn, is implicated in the idea of home as the guarantor (and one might add the beginning) of meaning (*ibid.*: 232). In the context of the lesbians and gay men the straight 'home' as nature is an experience of the homo in the 'home' and the homo-home as the unnatural. As such, 'home' is not a place of belonging, security and sanctuary but the experience of absence, denial and of exclusion.

The ambivalence of 'home'

Far from presenting 'home' in terms of a partial, sentimental or nostalgic place the focus group data suggests lesbians and gay men have a complex and contradictory relation to 'home' and 'comfort'. The close proximity of these contradictory attributes are brought out in the following extract from one of the gay men in the Manchester group. Home, he explained, is: 'a place where you can be free, you know, it's a place where you can look the way you want to look, you can walk about the house butt naked, throw pots and pans, have a tantrum, just be who you want to in your own walls.' While 'home', as freedom, is an experience of self without limit, and an experience of ontological authenticity, that freedom has another dimension. The other side of freedom is the freedom to throw pots and pans and to have a tantrum. This suggests that freedom might be not merely the unruled self and the self free from order but the unruly self, the disorderly self, the violent self.

In the first instance, our data seems to tell us little about how these apparently opposite aspects of home are managed. When the point was directly raised in the Manchester gay men's group the only response evoked suggested that holding these different perspectives on the idea of 'home' was 'not a personal statement'. This explanation offers to distance the speaker from the apparently contradictory associations of 'home' he had deployed earlier in the discussion. Another way of managing the relation between the apparently contradictory meanings of 'home' to be found in our data is in the distinctions drawn between homes – for example, between the parental home and the home of choice. Here, different aspects of 'home' are managed through attempts to distribute particular characteristics to particular sites of 'home': home of choice as good home; parental home as bad home.

If we return to the extract that opens this section, a rather different relation between the opposing aspects of 'home' is suggested. 'Home' as a sanctuary, where you can experience freedom, also appears as its opposite, a sanctuary that is a place of disorder, violence. Far from being an either/or relation this extract suggests the same 'home' is both a sanctuary from violence and a sanctuary for violence. How might we explain this relation?

Freud's essay on 'The Uncanny' (1985) offers a useful insight. He explains (*ibid*.: 345) 'we are reminded that the word heimlich [homely] is not unambiguous but belongs to two sets of ideas which without being contradictory, are yet very different...'[3] He continues (*ibid*.: 346): 'heimlich is a word the meaning of which develops in the direction of ambivalence, until it finally coincides with its opposite, unheimlich.

Unheimlich is.... a subspecies of heimlich.' Applying these insights to our data suggests that 'home' is comfort and discomfort, safety and danger, ontological authenticity and security and threats and challenges to the experience of 'being myself', of insecurity and anxiety. 'Home' is ambivalent.

The ambivalence of 'home' that emerges from the focus group data raises some important challenges to the feminist work that seeks to displace the 'myth of the safe home' by merely substituting the home as violence and fear of violence. This approach to the problem of the 'safe home' suggests a logic of either/or. Carole Vance (1984: 1) draws attention to some of the problems of the either/or approach in the context of feminist work on sexuality:

> Sexuality is simultaneously a domain of restriction, repression, and danger as well as a domain of exploration, pleasure, and agency. To focus only on pleasure and gratification ignores the patriarchal structure in which women act, yet to speak only of violence and oppression ignores women's experience with sexual agency and choice and unwittingly increases the sexual terror and despair in which women live.

Vance's observations resonate with debates about 'home' and suggest there are many problems with the application of the logic of either/or. This logic is at play when critiques of 'home' as safety only offer the home as violence as the appropriate 'correction' to the prevailing myth. In an ironic twist the either/or logic that seeks to promote 'home' reduced to danger also promotes 'home' as safety. What threatens to get lost in the application of this either/or logic in feminist scholarship on violence against women is women's experiences of violence and practices of safety. To apply a logic of either/or to the lesbian and gay experience of violence and safety produced by way of 'home' would be to impoverish, misrepresent and misunderstand the location and the experience of 'home'.

Experiences of violence and practices of safety take place in the context of the ambivalence of 'home'. 'Home' is both danger and safety. Our focus group data provide support for this. At the same time they provide evidence of a desire to manage ambiguity through a logic of either/or. In spatial terms either/or is produced in various forms: the dangers of the parental home or the safety of the home of choice; either the safety of the gay bar or the danger of the family home; either the safety of the home or the danger of the street. In the context of lesbian and gay experiences of

283

violence and safety, the imposition of a logic of either/or and a failure to take ambiguity seriously threaten to misunderstand and misrepresent its complexity and to ignore the experience of violence and safety. The rejection of 'home' on the basis it is a reactionary category and the failure to recognise the importance of 'home' for progressive debates on safety and security may perpetuate the subordinate position that 'home', emotion and femininity has within our culture.

'Home': beyond the domestic and the private

Many of the associations outlined above work with the assumption that 'home' is the domestic and the private. This suggests 'home' has no significance in the context of the civil and the public realm other than as a location that is elsewhere. However, the focus group data suggest such a conclusion is problematic.

Let me illustrate this by way of three extracts. The first is from a gay man in the Lancaster group: 'Starting with my home life, I was working, well sort of working on a YTS and I met someone... in Morecambe.' The second is from the same group: 'So you make yourself in the city, make yourself at home – who you are.' The final extract comes from a gay Mancunian group discussion. One of the gay men explained: 'I think the expression to feel at home is to feel comfortable. You just feel comfortable in 'the Village.'

A feature common to these instances of the use of 'home' is the way it is used to talk about locations and experiences outside the domestic/private realm. In the first, the gay man uses 'home' to talk of his experiences of work outside the domestic sphere and of his amorous experiences in Morecambe, his 'home town'. In the second, 'home' appears as a reference to qualities of life in the city: 'at home in the city'. In both 'home' is a location and experience associated with civil society and the public realm. In the third extract 'home' and its attribute 'comfort' are used to explain the speaker's experience of Manchester's gay Village. One of our gay Mancunian focus group participants explained the experience of 'being at home in the Village' in the following terms: 'I was thinking about "at home" in a pub in terms of the Village. I was thinking about a kind of absence of threat, an absence of judgement and the anxiety that somebody's going to disapprove or that somebody's going to come across and be aggressive or whatever it is.' In this instance 'home' and its many associations are deployed in order to name the experience of safety and security and a lack of insecurity in civil society.

In these extracts 'home' and its attributes are not to be thought of as effects limited to specific space – in particular, the private or domestic space. They suggest 'home' and its attribute 'comfort' have a much wider significance. Many different sites, be they domestic or private, civil or public places, might be imagined as 'home'.

However, there is a need for some caution here. One question that needs to be considered is the relationship between the domestic and private experience of 'home' and the experience of 'home' as a characteristic and imagined location of civil and public society. The data presented so far might suggest a particular relation between 'home' and civil/public space: 'home', as domestic/private, as a prior and autonomous experience; 'home', as a civil/public experience, as secondary and dependent. The data suggest such a conclusion is problematic. This can be illustrated by way of the following extract from the fifth Manchester gay focus group:

> Saturday evening was always dinner at [friends' houses] or they would come to us ... we could all sort of do exactly what we wanted to and there was never going to be the question of getting beaten up or having to spend an inordinate amount of money to enjoy yourself [it's] far easier, far far better at home you know. There was the whole ritual of cooking a meal ... you can choose your own music ... A mini Village at home.

Here 'home' is made up of a range of domestic/familial practices: interactions with a partner, with friends, cooking, entertaining, practices of relaxation and safety. In the first instance these are set up in contrast to the civil/public space of the Village, which is represented as 'unhomely' and a place lacking in 'comfort': as the threat of violence and the high cost of (pink) consumption. However, the reference to 'a mini Village at home' problematises this relation. Here, the 'homely' practices of the domestic are characterised in terms of creating a 'home' associated with a civil/public space, the gay Village. Rather than there being a single hermeneutic, of 'home' as domestic practices of safety security, authenticity and so on, there is a 'double hermeneutic' (Giddens 1990: 15). The practices of home inform the idea of the Village (as unhomely) and the homely practices of the civil/public realm, the Village, such as the music of the gay Village (as 'home') inform the practices and experiences of the domestic as the location of home.

The uses of 'home' as metaphor not only separates 'home' from the domestic and the private but also raises another challenge to feminist scholarship on the 'myth of safe home'. 'Home', as metaphor, has 'an indeterminate referential quality' (Bammer 1992: vii). Thereby 'home' is 'de-essentialised' (Rosaldo 1989). Feminist work on the 'myth of the safe home' tends to reduce 'home' to an idea and set of practices associated with a particular place. As such it ignores the metaphorical deployment of 'home' and fails to recognise 'home' is an indeterminate space. It threatens to (re)essentialise the notion of 'home' and its many attributes such as 'safety'. Thereby it threatens to impoverish our understanding of the nature, experience and significance of 'home' and 'safety'.

It also may leave progressive scholarship with 'no academic language or analysis' (Stanko 1988) to account for safety. It may also impoverish our understanding of the relation between fear and the private/domestic and fear and safety talk in the public realm. In this context, a recognition of the indeterminate referential quality of 'home' suggests fear ascribed to the public realm is not remote from the domestic experience of home and fear and violence within the home but an expression of it. Through a recognition of the metaphorical significance of home the supposed 'gap' between perceptions of fear and the threat of violence in the public realm is transformed into the proximity between fear of violence in public realm and violence in the home.

How might we explain the dominance of the correlation between 'home', the domestic and the private? The tendency to collapse 'home' into the domestic and the private might be explained by reference to the characteristics attributed to 'home'. They have much in common with characteristics attributed to the private, both its positive associations (refuge, sanctuary, security, safety, ontological authenticity) and its negative associations (silence and secrets, isolation, confinement, invisibility, alienation and ontological insecurity).

One explanation for this close relation between 'home' and the private is to be found in the work of Eve Kosovsky Sedgwick (1990). She draws attention to the current cultural importance of the topologies of the private and the public. The public/private binary, she suggests, does phenomenal cultural work in western liberal democratic societies. This is realised through an extensive metonomic chain of associations condensed within the public/private binary. Such is its range of meanings, she argues, it threatens to make it difficult not only to differentiate it from, but also to imagine, alternative metaphors (*ibid*.: 72). However, the reduction of the home to the private might be challenged in various ways.

Historians of the private (Aries and Duby 1989) and of home (Rybczynski 1988) problematise the reduction of 'home' to the private. They have drawn attention to the contingency of the relationship between the private, the domestic and the home. Their work has analysed the ways in which the private emerged as the quality of a place within the home and operated as a set of practices and attributes associated with particular locations within the home. They have mapped the ways in which the relationship between the private and the home differs both over time and at any one point in time. Social class has been an important factor here. While privacy of and within the home does not have its origins in the middle-class home, historians suggest it is in that context that the relation between 'private' and 'home' comes to assume particular importance (Rybczynski 1988; Betsky 1997). This historical work problematises any tendency to reduce 'home' to the private.

The uneasy relationship between the private and 'home' and the private and the domestic is also memorialised in the ambivalence of the 'private' – as both individual and communal. Within the domestic sphere 'the private' retains the trace of this ambivalence in that the private may be a characteristic of the whole house (as a communal space) and a characteristic of a part of house such as a bedroom, bathroom or toilet where it is associated with the individual. In turn, this ambivalence might be read as a reminder of the way in which the private stands as the whole or as the part; as both an essential and a contingent characteristic of home. Another instance of the spatial ambivalence of 'private' is to be found in the relation between private and public. On the one hand, the private is a withdrawal from a particular communal context, the public which stands for some formal institutional communal context, an office or more particularly the state. As that which is against the state, the 'private' is the collective and communal of egoistic market society (civil society). This private is remote from the domestic. On the other hand, at the same time the 'private' is also the domestic, the familial understood as the individual over against the collective/communal understood as civil and/or state society. These differences in meaning provide examples that point to the limits of the reduction of 'home' to the private and draw attention to 'home' as a possible alternative spatial trope. They might also have another significance: pointing to the slippage between the individual and the collective/communal that is a characteristic of the private, and by way of metaphor, a characteristic of 'home'.

This reflection on the relation between the public/private relation and 'home' is significant in the context of our data on 'home' in various ways. While there is considerable overlap between the attributes of 'the private' and the attributes of 'home' there is a need to treat the private/home relation with caution. In particular there is a need to take account of 'private' as metonym of 'home', as well as a synonym of 'home'. 'Home' is both the private and at the same time more than the private. This perhaps has particular significance in the context of the use of 'home' as a metaphor. In part 'home' as metaphor puts into play the ambivalence of the 'private' as individual and as communal (civil) society. At the same time, the deployment of 'home' as a poetics of public space is more than a reference to the communal/collective as private society. 'Home' offers an alternative metaphor.

Lesbians, gay men and 'home'

In this section of the chapter I want to situate the focus group data on 'home' in the context of existing work that addresses lesbian and gay sexuality and space. Spatial concepts such as 'neighbourhood', 'community' and 'nation' have been important in lesbian and gay scholarship (Castells and Murphy 1982; Adler and Brennan 1992; Bell and Valentine 1995; Berlant 1997; Ingram et al. 1997; Cooper 1998; Stychin 1998). Work that directly focuses upon 'home' is rare. While references to 'home' are to be found in various contexts such as oral histories (Cant 1993), literary theory (Jagose 1994) and work on class politics (Raffo 1997), when 'home' does appear it is a term that is quickly passed over. More recent work by Dunne (1997), Carrington (1999) and by a team of scholars working on lesbian and gay families (Heaphy 1999; Weeks et al. 1999, 2001) has begun to explore the idea of 'home' by reference to lesbian and gay family relations. A common characteristic of this work is the reduction of 'home' to domestic relationships and to the private realm, where those relationships are thought of in terms of same-sex couples.

The topology of the public and the private has perhaps been the most pervasive spatial trope in lesbian and gay scholarship. Within that scholarship the private has been both celebrated and criticised. Its multiple positive and negative associations have been excavated and evaluated. For example, the private as refuge, haven, sanctuary, security and as the locus of ontological authenticity has long been offered in juxtaposition to a hostile punitive state (Lauristen and Thornstad 1974; Moran 1996: Chap. 1). More recently, the negative associations of the private have been emphasised. Taking the form of 'the closet' the private takes the form of silences and weighty secrets. It is now a place of isolation and confinement that perpetuates and secures violent exclusion. It is a place associated with invisibility, alienation and 'ontological insecurity'. By contrast, the public is celebrated and advocated by way of 'coming out'; by going public (cf. Mohr 1992; Gross 1993). Here, the public is offered as a place of 'salvational certainty' in contrast to an equivocal privacy (Sedgwick 1990: 71). The public is now the site of ultimate ontological transformation towards authenticity in contrast to the private where it will remain, at worst, impossible and, at best, partially realised.

Lesbian scholarship has inflected the negative associations of the public/private relation in a rather different way, drawing attention to the ambivalence of both the public and the private. For lesbians the private is not so much the locus of a sanctuary from state violence against same sex relations but the very site of interpersonal (state-condoned) and state violence. While the use of criminal law against same-sex relations between women is of less significance due to the relative absence of criminal prohibitions (Majury 1994; Mason 1995; but cf. Robson 1992, 1995) much state action against lesbians has focused upon lesbians as wives and mothers within the private realm. While this might suggest the public as a more viable locus of sanctuary and security, particularly for lesbian women, such a conclusion is problematic (Mason 1997b). Lesbian access to the public needs to be understood in the wider social, cultural and economic context that has (re)produced the public as masculine and the private as feminine and continues to limit women's access to the public (Gluckman and Reed 1997). Lesbian scholarship has drawn attention to the need to take more seriously the ambivalence of both the public and the private (Wilson 1991; Jagose 1994).

I now want to focus on two examples of lesbian and gay work that focus on the theme of 'home'. These examples are of particular significance in that they neither reduce 'home' to the private nor limit it to the domestic. Nor do they examine 'home' merely by reference to 'couples'. Johnston and Valentine (1995) consider 'home' in the context of lesbianism and Aaron Betsky (1997) analyses 'home' in a predominantly gay male context.

Johnston and Valentine's (1995) point of departure is the significance of 'home' in the practices of day-to-day lesbian lives and networking. While they recognise the private as one aspect of 'home' they do not reduce 'home' to the private', even where 'home' is understood as security and sanctuary (ibid.: 100). Their study is significant in the way it brings together both the positive associations of 'home', sanctuary, security, authenticity, origins and the negative, the place of surveillance and exposure, hierarchy, insecurity, violence and exclusion. These negative attributes of 'home' are drawn out in the specific context of 'home' as a (hetero)normative space. With respect to sexuality in general and lesbian sexuality in particular, 'home' is experienced as a place of surveillance, visibility and denial. For the lesbian within the hetero-normative home, being 'at home' is being out of place. At the same time, for reasons that reflect the economic, social and cultural position of women, Johnston and Valentine draw attention to the importance of domestic space for lesbians. They point to the importance of that space as the location of wider lesbian social networks that are central to the production of lesbian identity. More specifically, domestic space as 'home' is implicated in producing an experience of a wider community as 'home' (*ibid.*: 105). In the move from domestic to civil society lesbian practices deploy and transform those associations of security and sanctuary that are an important part of 'home'.

But there is also a note of caution in their analysis. At the same time 'home' is produced and celebrated, Johnson and Valentine draw attention to the ways in which the positive associations of 'home' are contingent. This is highlighted not only in their distribution in various zones within the house (the bedroom in contrast to the parlour) but also evidenced in the potential to 'dedyke' the home when particular, potentially hostile, visitors call.

In Betsky's (1997) work on 'queer space' home emerges as a motif within a different context, that of architecture, interior design and aesthetics more generally. The theme of domestic space is in the first instance understood as 'the closet' rather than the 'home'. The closet has a host of negative associations; it is the place that marks the fact there is no place in the world for lesbian and gay sexuality (*ibid.*: 57). In the contrast between the 'hearth' and the 'closet', as metonyms of home, Betsky draws a contrast between the heteronormative and homonorma-tive home. The 'home as hearth' represents home as the place where the (hetero) family gathers to, 'affirm itself as a unit in the glow of the fire' (*ibid.*: 17). The 'home as closet' represents the homo home as a dark and secret place. At the same time for Betsky 'the closet' is not reducible to the negative of the heteronormative home. It is also to be understood as a container that stores and houses the building blocks, the masks, through which the world, as artifice, is created. Here Betsky draws attention to the ambivalence of the closet. As the 'ultimate interior', it is both the place most distant from the world and the place where the world begins (*ibid.*: 16); where lesbian and gay identity is both denied and born.

Like Johnston and Valentine, Betsky draws attention to the impor-tance of interior decoration as representational practices of the self (Johnston and Valentine 1995: 102; Betsky 1997: 64). However, he goes further than Johnston and Valentine in this respect. First, he draws attention to the challenges men's preoccupation within domestic interiors creates for a gender-normative distribution of spatial preoccupations. It potentially offers a challenge to the correlation between the feminine with the private and domestic interiors and the masculine with the public and with architecture, which is understood as the public aesthetics of space. Secondly, he argues that gay men, who as men were not confined to the home in the same way as women were, took the aesthetic assumptions and practices they developed within the 'home as closet' (fantastical transformations, collecting, posing, resort to masks, the centrality of artifice and the importance of surface) into the public world, reconfiguring and blurring the boundary between an aesthetics and practices of the public and the home.

Various themes are common to the work of Johnston, Valentine and Betsky. First, both draw attention to the ambivalence and contingency of the attributes of 'home' for lesbians and gay men. Secondly, 'home' in both its positive and negative associations is understood as a resource. Thirdly, as a resource for lesbians and gay men 'home' is important in the creation of the self not only as an individual but also as a member of a community. Finally, their work points to the importance of 'home' in the (re)production of lesbian and gay representational (symbolic) space that cannot be reduced to the 'home' as a domestic or private space.

The juxtaposition of these two studies suggests there is a need to approach this work with some caution. The problem relates to the way they tend to reproduce particular relations between gender and space. Iris Marion Young (1997) has drawn attention to the long-standing association between gender and spatial relations. Starting with Heidegger's essay 'Building, dwelling, thinking' (1997) she explores the distinction between building and preservation, which is also a gender distinction between the masculine and the feminine. The gendered dichotomy of building and preservation is a violent hierarchy that has multiple significance. Building and preservation are also a distinction between production and conservation, between the public and the private, of nurture and nature, value and lack of value, labour and lack of labour, of identity and non-identity. Young's study is of significance here as there are elements of this problematic distribution of gender, space and value in the juxtaposition between Johnston and Valentine's and Betsky's studies.

The domestic context of Johnston and Valentine's study tends to reproduce the predominant association of women, 'home', domestic/ private space, albeit in the context of an argument that seeks to point to the capacity of lesbian women to transform that space into a civil and quasi-public space. Betsky's focus on architecture and the professional role of interior designer situates the homely practices of gay men in the context of a relation between men and the public realm: of paid work. The juxtaposition of these two studies threatens to reproduce the gendered distribution of negative (female practices of home) and positive (male practices of home) and a gendered distribution of absence of value (re-production, unpaid labour) and value (production, paid labour). In the distinction between these two studies there is a danger they reproduce and reinforce the gender distinction that represents lesbian women's home-making labour as conservation and preservation in contrast to the men's home-making as labour, production, creation, building. One solution to this problem offered by Young lies in her attempt to problematise the distinction between production and conservation. A key element of this distinction is temporality – of novelty in contrast to repetition – a present, future orientation in contrast to a past present focus. Young's important contribution is to draw attention to the productive and creative features of repetition and to the future orientation of repetition. In short, the dichotomy between building and conservation is a false dichotomy. Young's analysis offers an opportunity to reread the two studies of Johnston and Valentine and Betsky in ways that avoid the reproduction of the problematic gender/space relation.

The focus group data also offer to transcend these limits. The focus group research data gathers information about the everyday use of 'home' and 'comfort' as a set of practices that produce the experience of safety and security, danger and insecurity. As such, the concern is with male and female practices of 'conservation'. It offers important new data about the uses of 'home' by (gay) men. The data suggest 'home' and 'comfort' cannot be reduced or limited in significance to the location of the private or domestic. 'Home' as metaphor de-essentialises that imagined location and thereby problematises the reduction of 'home' as a resource particular to, and limited to, the private and the domestic. The data suggest that as a resource used to make sense of safety and unsafety, security and insecurity, 'home' and 'comfort' are intelligibilities and practices that have significance in the private and domestic context and in the civil and public realm. Furthermore, their significance and use cannot be understood in terms of a crude male/female dichotomy. They offer an intelligibility and a set of practices though which women as well as men produce and experience their gendered and sexualised selves in the civil and public realm as well as the domestic and private sphere. 'Home' as metaphor is a contingent location and experience. It has to be constantly created by way of practices of 'home' that in our data take the form of practices of 'comfort'. Preservation and conservation now appear not so much as making manifest that which lies beneath or at the heart of the place called home but as citational practices that create the very experience of location as 'home'.

Taking home seriously: practical and policy reflections

In this final section of the chapter I want to shift attention to focus on some of the practical and policy issues that flow from the analysis offered so far. Let me begin with an extract from one of our key informants, 'Terry', a gay men's worker for the Manchester City Council. In part I want to use this to illustrate the significance of 'home' in the context of practical attempts to create safer public spaces. I also want to offer an instance of 'home's' analytical capacity and illustrate its significance for the critique of policy and practice. Finally, I want to point to some of the problems with strategies of 'home'.

The following comments were made in the context of a reflection on the Manchester City Council's interventions in 'the Gay Village':

> I think the council's initiatives in improving street lighting and improving the cleaning and taking down of fly posters...we take down fly posters which make the area look bad – that's all about... environmental improvement...if you have safety, cleanliness and environmental improvement all tied together, people feel good about themselves...We would hope to encourage pride and self confidence as opposed to all the self oppression that can be implied by having to occupy a dirty, unkempt, uncared for, dangerous, slovenly space.

Various things are of interest in this extract. Environmental improvements are understood as practices through which lesbians and gay men gain 'confidence' and 'pride'; as such they are practices intimately associated with ontology. They are also practices that seek to bring 'homophobia discrimination, prejudice and anti-lesbian and gay violence' to an end. Of interest here is the correlation between these practices and objectives and 'comfort', 'home' and ontological authenticity; 'environmental improvements' are practices of 'home'.

In our fifth gay men's focus group in Manchester we asked our participants whether these strategies would make them feel more comfortable in the Village. The first response to this question was as follows: 'Well to me everyone's got different opinions and you can't satisfy everyone and I might like one thing, you might like one thing but we're both gay and when you've got different opinions you're never going to have a right or wrong answer.' In response to a further question, 'Would neater, tidier, clearer streets make you feel more comfortable?' the same participant added:

No because the streets would have to be cleaned twenty-four hours a day so you're never going to satisfy somebody twenty-four hours a day...everyone's got a different perspective on how they want it to be kept clean like me and [my partner] are always arguing about the cleaning [laughter]...I've got one way of cleaning which is underneath and he's got one which is on top.

Another group member commented: 'I'd hate to walk down a complete steam-cleaned Canal Street...a few cigarette butts...papers and... boxes! That's all right...That's what makes it feel homely.' These extracts suggest there is no easy relation between policies and practices of public comfort, hygiene and ontological authenticity. As the basis for promoting safer space they are problematic and as likely to be a source of discomfort and insecurity and a site of conflict as they are of comfort and security.

At the same time other techniques of comfort, such as 'lighting', seemed to attract more widespread support. In drawing a comparison between the space of Canal Street as positively represented in the recent gay drama series, *Queer as Folk* (where lighting takes the form of strings of lights and torches), and the current experience of Canal Street (where standard small sodium street lighting is the norm) as the location of a lesbian and gay public realm, our focus group participants draw attention to the importance of aesthetics in the constitution of comfort in public places. 'Lighting' and environmental improvements are not, per se, the totality of initiatives of safety. They are merely a point of departure for a debate about the aesthetics of location and, more specifically a debate about the practice of an aesthetics of public comfort; of home making.

In the extract above the council worker, at best, reduces the aesthetics of comfort to an aesthetics of (total) visibility, hygiene and purity. This approach to an aesthetics of comfort with its focus on surveillance and regulation draws attention to the continuing importance of what Elizabeth Wilson (1991: 152) has described as 'a paternalistic form of planning'. It also raises an important question about the values of comfort and thereby of public space, at work in policy and practice of public safety.

Mary Douglas's (1966) extended reflection on purity and the role of dirt in the formation of experiences of order draws attention to the way purity functions in boundary formation and boundary maintenance as that which is to be excluded (the disorderly). Within the context of the council worker's observations dirt seems to play a similar function. Here the idea of lesbian and gay space as safer space (the space of order) is produced by way of the evacuation of dirt/the unruly. As practices of exclusion, practices of social hygiene are dedicated to the production of space as a purified space. Our research suggests these particular practices of comfort as purity work by reference to violent hierarchies of gender, class, age, race and ethnicity (Moran *et al.* 2001). These practices offered in the name of producing safer space for lesbians and gay men produce danger in the form of 'new' 'strangers' and 'new' 'aliens'. They are environmental policies and practices of safety that institutionalise a certain paranoia (Wilson 1991: 153). They appear to perpetuate an idea of 'home' as a place of exclusion that has been a major theme within recent feminist critiques of home (Martin and Mohanty 1986; De Laurentis 1990; Honnig 1994). They also perpetuate the idea that 'home' is nothing more than exclusion. This is a myth that needs to be challenged if safety is to be a possibility (see hooks 1990; Mohanty 1992; Young 1997).

Purity is problematic in another way. Comfort practices as practices of purity/hygiene need to be situated in the context of the ambivalence of 'home'. Our focus group data draw attention to the practices that seek to deny the ambivalence of 'home' through the production of home as multiple different locations through which the positive and negative of home might be differentially distributed. The extract from our interview with the council worker suggests practices of social hygiene might produce a similar effect. The Village as the locus of security, authenticity, comfort is produced through displacement of danger and discomfort, through the constitution of insecurity and danger as that which lies elsewhere. However, our focus group data and the particular responses to the hygiene strategies suggest this division is neither achievable nor desirable. When put in the context of feminist critiques of 'home', the spatial divisions of safety and danger are positively dangerous. They suggest that strategies that separate safety and danger might make it more difficult to address violence, fear of violence and safety in the Village.

Conclusion

'Home' and 'comfort' emerged as a significant theme in the research data in the context of questions that focused upon lesbian and gay public space, in particular pubs, bars and clubs. From the start, they appeared as ways of imagining place and practices of location intimately associated with safety and security that in the first instance appeared to be out of place. As such, they offered many challenges to understanding safety. They challenge our understanding of way the private and the domestic is imagined and lived as distinct from the civil and public space as safety, security and certainty. The ambivalence of 'home' in general and the ambivalence of the lesbian and gay experience of 'home' challenges any attempt that seeks to put into place an either/or logic of the safe or unsafe home. Another challenge is to be found in the many meanings of 'home' and 'comfort'. The history of the idea of comfort, for example, draws attention to the problem of reducing 'comfort' to the attributes of consolation, physical and mental relief that appear to gain importance with the emergence of bourgeois sentimental domesticity in the nineteenth century. Comfort is also a term that signifies strength and support, incitement to aid and the encouragement of physical, material and emotional well-being. The data on 'home' and 'comfort' provide an important vehicle through which to rethink the relation between violence, fear of violence and safety. A key task that lies ahead is not to abandon the idea of home or to reduce it to a new impoverished myth of the unsafe home, but to complicate the issue of 'home'.

Notes

1 Award no. L133 25 1031. Fellow grant holders on the 'Violence, Sexuality, Space' project are Beverley Skeggs and Carole Truman, working together with three research assistants: Paul Tyrer, Karen Corteen and Lyndsay Turner. As one of the projects in the ESRC Violence Research Programme, this study concentrates on how three specific groups (gay men, lesbians and heterosexual women identified as 'high risk' groups by various crime surveys) produce and make use of space in two contrasting geographical areas in the north west of England. Manchester has an identifiable gay space known as 'the Village' whereas Lancaster had, at the time of the research, no clearly identifiable established gay space. The general aim of the project is to examine the mechanisms by which different groups of people use the experience, perceptions and representations of violence to generate safer spaces. Further details of the research and preliminary findings can be found on the project website: http://les1.man.ac.uk/sociology/vssrp

2 This is not to suggest these extracts from the focus groups can be reduced to the particular themes developed in this chapter (see Moran et al. 2001). Issues of class have been explored in Moran (2000) and Skeggs (2000). Our focus groups were recruited using a snowball technique. While domestic circumstances was not a priority in the process of selection the focus groups were composed of people with diverse domestic backgrounds.

3 The editor notes that 'uncanny' is the English term for the German unheimlich, unhomely (Freud 1985: 339ff 1).

References

Adler, S. and Brennan, J. (1992) Gender space: lesbians and gay men in the city. *International Journal of Urban and Regional Research*, 16: 24–34.

Aries P. and Duby, G. (eds) (1989) *A History of Private Life. Vol. III. Passions of the Renaissance* (trans. A. Goldhammer). London: Harvard University Press.

Bachelard, G. (1963) *The Poetics of Space*. Boston, MA: Beacon Press.

Bammer, Z. (1992) Editorial in 'The question of home.' *New Formations*, vii–xi.

Bell, D. and Valentine, G. (eds) (1995) *Mapping Desire*, London: Routledge.

Berlant, L. (1997) *The Queen of America Goes to Washington DC*. Durham, NC: Duke University Press.

Betsky, A. (1997) *Queer Space: Architecture and Same Sex Desire*. New York: William Morrow.

Cant, B. (1993) *Footsteps and Witnesses: Lesbian and Gay Lifestories from Scotland*. Edinburgh: Polygon.

Carrington, C. (1999) *No Place Like Home: Relationships and Family Life among Lesbians and Gay Men*. Chicago, IL: University of Chicago Press.

Castells, M. and Murphy, K. (1982) Cultural identity and urban structure: the spatial organisation of San Francisco's gay community. In N. Fainstein and S. Fainstein (eds) *Urban Policy under Capitalism*. Beverly Hills, CA: Sage.

Cooper, C. (1994) The house as symbol of the Self. In J. Lang, C. Burette, W. Maleski and D. Vaslon (eds) *Designing for Human Behaviour*. Philadelphia: Dowden, Hutchinson & Ross.

Cooper, D. (1998) *Governing Out of Order: Space, Law and the Politics of Belonging*. London: Rivers Oram Press.

De Laurentis, T. (1990) Eccentric subjects: feminist theory and historical consciousness. *Feminist Studies*, 16(1): 115–50.

Douglas, M. (1966) *Purity and Danger: An Analysis of Concepts of Pollution and Taboo*. London: Ark.

Dunne, G. (1997) *Lesbian Lifestyles: Women's Work and the Policits of Sexuality*. Basingstoke: Macmillan.

Forty, A. (1986) *Objects of Desire: Design and Society 1750–1980*. London: Thames & Hudson.

Freud, S. (1985) The Uncanny. In A. Dickson (ed.) *The Pelican Freud Library. Vol. 14. Art and Literature*. London: Penguin Books.

George, R.M. (1999) *The Politics of Home*. Berkeley, CA: University of California Press.

Giddens, A. (1990) *The Consequences of Modernity*. Cambridge: Polity Press.

Gluckman, A. and Reed, B. (1997) *Capitalism, Community and Lesbian and Gay Life*. London: Routledge.

Greater Manchester Lesbian and Gay Policing Initiative (1998) *Lesbians' Experiences of Violence and Harassment* Manchester: Greater Manchester Police.

Gross, L. (1993) *Contested Closets: The Politics and Ethics of Outing*. Minneapolis, MN: University of Minnesota Press.

Heaphy, B. (1999) Sex, money and the kitchen sink: power in same sex relationships. In J. Seymour and P. Bagguley (eds) *Relating Intimacies: Power and Resistance*. Basingstoke: Macmillan.

Heidegger, M. (1997) Building, dwelling, thinking. In D.F. Krell (ed.) *Basic Writings*. New York: HarperCollins.

Honnig, B. (1994) Difference, dilemmas, and the politics of home. *Social Research*, 61(3): 563–97.

hooks, b. (1990) *Yearning; Race, Gender and Cultural Politics.*, Boston, MA: South End Press.

Ingram, G.B., Bouthillette, A. and Retter, Y. (1997) *Queers in Space.* Seattle, WA: Bay Press.

Irigaray, L. (1993) *An Ethics of Sexual Difference* (trans. C. Burke and G.C.Gill). Ithaca, NY: Cornell University Press.

Jagose, A. (1994) *Lesbian Utopics.* London: Routledge.

Jennes, V. and Broad, K. (1997) *Hate Crimes: New Social Movements and the Politics of Violence.* Hawthorn, NY: Aldine De Gruyter.

Jennes, V. and Grattet, R. (forthcoming) *Building the Hate Crime Policy Domain: From Social Movement Concept to Law Enforcement Practice.* New York: Russell Sage Foundation.

Johnston, J. and Valentine, G. (1995) Wherever I lay my girlfriend that's my home. In D. Bell and G. Valentine (eds) *Mapping Desire.* London: Routledge.

Lancashire Police (1999) *Action against Hate Crime: An Information Leaflet from Lancashire Constabulary.* Preston: Lancashire Police.

Lauristen, J. and Thornstad, M. (1974) *The Early Homosexual Rights Movement (1864–1935).* New York: Times Change Press.

Lefebvre, H.C. (1991) *The Production of Space* (trans. Donald Nicolson-Smith). Oxford: Blackwell.

Madriz, E.I. (1997) Images of criminals and victims: a study of women's fear and social control. *Gender and Society*, 11(3): 342–56.

Majury, D. (1994) Refashioning the unfashionable: claiming lesbian identities in the legal context. *Canadian Journal of Women and the Law*, 7(2): 286–306.

Martin, B. and Mohanty, C.T. (1986) Feminist politics: what's home got to do with it? In T. De Laurentis (ed.) *Feminist Studies/Critical Studies.* Bloomington, IN: Indiana University Press.

Mason, G. (1995) (Out)laws: acts of proscription in the sexual order. In M. Thornton (ed.) *Public and Private: Feminist Legal Debates.* Melbourne: Oxford University Press.

Mason, G. (1997a) Boundaries of sexuality: lesbian experience and feminist discourse on violence against women. *Australasian Gay and Lesbian Law Journal*, 7: 40–56.

Mason, G. (1997b) Heterosexed violence: typicality and ambiguity. In G. Mason and S. Tomsen (eds) *Homophobic Violence.* Sydney: Hawkins Press.

Mohanty, C.T. (1992) Feminist encounters: locating the politics of experience. In M. Barrett and A. Phillips (eds) *Destabilising Theory: Contemporary Feminist Debates.* Cambridge: Polity Press.

Mohr, R.D. (1992) *Gay Ideas: Outing and Other Controversies.* Boston, MA: Beacon Press.

Moran, L.J. (1996) *The Homosexual(ity) of Law.* London: Routledge.

Moran, L.J. (2000) Homophobic violence: the hidden injuries of class. In S. Munt (ed.) *Cultural Studies and the Working Class.* London: Cassell.

Moran, L.J. *et al.* (2001) Property, propriety and entitlement. *Social and Cultural Geography.* 2:4: 407–21.

Mouzos, J. and Thompson, S. (2000) Gay-hate related homicides: an overview of major findings in New South Wales. In *Australian Institute of Criminology, Trends* and Issues in Criminal Justice. Canberra: Australian Insitute of Criminology.

Pain, R.H. (1997) Social geographies of women's fear of crime. Transactions, Institute of British Geographers, 22(2): 231–44.

Raffo, S. (ed.) (1997) Queerly Classed. Boston, MA: South End Press.

Robson, R. (1992) Lesbian (Out)law. Ithaca, NY: Firebrand.

Robson, R. (1995) Convictions: theorizing lesbians and criminal justice. In C. Stychin and D. Herman (eds) Legal Inversions. Philadelphia, PA: Temple University Press.

Rosaldo, R. (1989) Culture and Truth. Boston, MA: Beacon Press.

Rybczynski, W. (1988) Home: A Short History of an Idea. London: Heinemann.

Saraga, E. (1996) Dangerous places: the family as a site of crime. In J. Muncie and E. McLaughlin (eds) The Problem of Crime. London: Sage.

Sedgwick, E.K. (1990) Epistemology of the Closet. Hemel Hempstead: Harvester Wheatsheaf.

Sennett, R. (1992) The Fall of Public Man. New York: W.W. Norton.

Skeggs, B. (2000) Matter out of place: visibility and sexualities in leisure spaces. Leisure Studies, 18(3): 213–33.

Stanko, E.A. (1988) Fear of crime and the myth of the safe home: a feminist critique of criminology. In K. Yello and M. Bograd (eds) Feminist Perspectives on Wife Abuse. London: Sage.

Stanko, E.A. (1990) Everyday Violence. London: Pandora.

Stanko, E.A. (1995) Women, crime and fear. Annals of the American Academy of Political and Social Science, 539: 46–58.

Stanko, E.A. (1997) Safety talk: conceptualising women's risk assessment as a 'technology of the self'. Theoretical Criminology, 1(4): 479–99.

Stanko, E.A. (1998) Warnings to women: police advice and women's safety in Britain. Violence against Women, 2(1): 5–24.

Stanko, E.A. and Curry, P. (1997) Homophobic violence and the 'self' at risk: interrogating the boundaries. In L.J. Moran (ed.) 'Legal perversions', special edition of Social and Legal Studies, 6(4): 513–32.

Stychin, C. (1998) Nation by Rights. Philadelphia, PA: Temple University Press.

Valentine, G. (1989) The geography of women's fear. Area, 21(4): 385–90.

Valentine, G. (1992) Images of danger: women's sources of information about the spatial distribution of male violence. Area, 24(1): 22–9.

Vance, C. (1984) Pleasure and danger: towards a politics of sexuality. In C.S. Vance (ed.) Pleasure and Danger: Exploring Female Sexuality. Boston, MA: Routledge & Kegan Paul.

Walklate, S. (1997) Risk and criminal victimisation: a modernist dilemma? British Journal of Criminology, 37(1): 35–45.

Weeks, J., Heaphy, B. and Donovan, C. (1999) Partnership rites: commitment and ritual in non-heterosexual relationships. In J. Syemour and P. Bagguley (eds) Relating Intimacies: Power and Resistance. Basingstoke: Macmillan.

Weeks, J., Heaphy, B. and Donovan C. (2001) Families of Choice and Other Life Experiments. London: Routledge.

Wilson, E. (1991) The Sphinx in the City. Berkeley, CA: University of California Press.

Young, I.M. (1997) Intersecting Voices: Dilemmas of Gender, Political Philosophy and Policy. Princeton, NJ: Princeton University Press.

Chapter 12

Issues in local community safety: it's all a question of trust

Sandra Walklate

The movement into late modernity is like a ship which has broken from its moorings. Many of the crew cry to return to the familiar sanctuary of the harbour but to their alarm the compass spins, the ship continues on its way and, looking back, the quay is no longer secure: at times it seems to be falling apart, its structure fading and disintegrating. The siren voices which forlornly, seriously, soberly try to convince them that going back is possible are mistaken (Young 1999: 193).

One of the unintended consequences of modern capitalism is that it has strengthened the value of place, aroused a longing for community. All the emotional conditions we have explored in the workplace animate that desire: the uncertainties of flexibility; the absence of deeply rooted trust and commitment; the superficiality of teamwork; most of all the specter of failing to make something of oneself in the world, to 'get a life' through one's work. All of these conditions impel people to look for some other scene of attachment and depth (Sennett 1998: 138).

Introduction

It is now almost commonplace to invoke a conceptualisation of the community as constituting one of the building blocks of effective social life and as being the means by which effective social policy can be put into place. This is the case whether or not one is talking about 'care in the community' in the context of issues relating to health or one is talking about 'community safety' in the context of issues relating to crime. In the latter respect the Crime and Disorder Act 1998 makes it a statutory requirement that local partnerships are formed in order to put crime reduction and community safety plans in place. To summarise a range of developments over the last two decades, the idea of 'community' as a 'good thing' and consequently as the conduit for policy has become deeply embedded both in policy and political rhetoric (Crawford 1997). But what do we mean by community? What kinds of communities are assumed by such policies? What is the lived reality of community life, and why has this notion so captured policy and political imagination?

In some respects the quotations with which this chapter begins capture some elements of an answer to the questions posed above. Late modern capitalism and all its associated uncertainties resulting from rapidly changing structures of work, technology and communications seem to take their toll on human beings in the form of nostalgia. In other words, people routinely look back to what was familiar. They look for some sense of purpose or meaning to their lives, or as Sennett suggests above, 'some other scene of attachment and depth'. Nowhere has the idea of nostalgia been more keenly felt than within the context of understanding the problem of crime. So, for example, the Kray brothers, two offenders of serious proportions in the East End of London during the 1960s, were more celebrated than condemned at the point of their respective deaths during the 1990s. Similar nostalgic constructions of the past can be found in debates on the nature of policework. The question is why? Giddens states that: 'All individuals develop a framework of ontological security of some sort based on routines of various forms. People handle dangers and the fear associated with them in terms of emotional and behavioural formulae which have come to be part of their everyday behaviour and thought' (1991: 44). In the analysis offered by Giddens, managing ontological security is the central problem of late modern society. In part he argues that this is a consequence of the extent to which 'The risk climate of modernity is [thus] unsettling for everyone: no-one escapes' (ibid.: 124) so that as individuals we 'colonise the future' (ibid.: 125) in order to manage (though not necessarily reduce) our anxieties. One way in which we 'colonise the future' is by looking at the past in order to create some sense of continuity, some common thread, between what has gone before, what there is now and what is to come. To use an observation made by Bauman (2000) in a different way, we search for 'biographical solutions to systemic problems'. Such biographical solutions may result in the recasting of individual history or the recasting of collective history in a more favourable light. 'Seeing the world through rose-tinted spectacles', as the saying goes.

However, the desire for ontological security takes us beyond nostalgia, especially in the context of understanding the concept of community invoked by community safety. It is true to say that policies designed to enhance public protection have grasped at the concept of community with both hands and often with a top-down nostalgic image of 'community'. However, such grasping has also occurred with little understanding of how different communities actually might work. Again Bauman asserts:

> The disintegration of the social network, the falling apart of effective agencies of collective action is often noted with a good deal of anxiety and bewailed as the unanticipated 'side effect' of the new lightness and fluidity of the increasingly mobile, slippery, shifty, evasive and fugitive power...Global powers are bent on dismantling such networks for the sake of their continuous and growing fluidity, that principle source of their strength and the warrant of their invincibility. And it is the falling apart, the friability, the brittleness, the transience, the until-further-noticeness of human bonds and networks which allow these powers to do their job in the first place. (*ibid*.: 14)

It is, however, a moot point, as for whom the world is falling apart: for whom is there 'the brittleness, the transience, the until-further-noticeness of human bonds'?

The central purpose of this chapter is to explore an understanding of community safety within the broader context of late modern society and to ask one key question: for whom is social life fragmenting? This exploration will take as central the need to understand the contemporary nature of relationships of trust. Such relationships can be explored in a number of different ways (through the lens of age, ethnicity, sex and place) and may be manifested (or not) on a number of different levels (from the interpersonal, to the organisational, to the social, to the societal). The key variable to be focused on here is place and the key level is the social. In order to engage in this exploration this chapter will, first of all, offer a review of the literature on trust and its relevance for criminology. Secondly, it will offer two case studies, by way of illustration, of the kinds of questions raised by an exploration of trust relationships. Finally it will conclude by offering some analysis of the implications raised by these questions for the relationship between policing and community safety.

Why talk about trust?

The concept of trust has been relatively underexplored in the social sciences. In discussing the question of 'ontological security', Giddens (1991) has argued that trust is most clearly evidenced in traditional societies through kinship relations, local communities or religious commitment. However, he goes on to argue that the absence of these mechanisms in late modern societies renders trust no more than a matter for individual contractual negotiation. Luhmann (1989) presents a similar argument. Gellner (1989) too suggests that urban life is incompatible with trust and social cohesion, suggesting such processes are rooted in rural, tribal traditions. Yet as Fukuyama implies, trust is also an essential part of modern life: 'As a general rule, trust arises when a community shares a set of moral values in such a way as to create expectations of regular honest behaviour' (1996: 153). Here, he is talking primarily about economic relations which, without trust, cannot flourish. These, of course, are also relations that cannot be completely controlled. Trust is therefore essential. However, during the 1990s much was made about the need to reintroduce a sense of morality, associated with 'regular honest behaviour' in the form of communitarianism. Derived from the work of Etzioni (1996), the vision of community embedded in these ideas has been very much embraced in contemporary government policy as the mechanism by which social exclusion might be combated (see, *inter alia*, Social Exclusion Unit 1998; 1999). The kinds of trust that actually exist and work for people, however, may not always be necessarily about creating 'regular honest behaviour', as Fukuyama states and as the communitarians believe. It may just as likely be about creating regular dishonest behaviour. Arguably, it is the regularity or otherwise of the behaviour that sustains or threatens social trust relationships.

In more general terms, Giddens (1991) and Beck (1992) both argue that the increasing awareness of the importance of trust is the concomitant effect of a greater awareness of the possible future damage of risk-taking activity alongside the challenge to universalism posed by postmodernism. As Misztal states:

> By destroying the grounds for believing in a universal truth, post-modernity does not make our lives more easy but only less constrained by rules and more contingent. It demands new solutions based on the tolerant co-existence of a diversity of cultures. Yet although post modernism encourages us to live without an enemy, it stops short of offering constructive bases for mutual understanding and trust. (1996: 239)

In a sense this quotation endorses the view of Fukuyama expressed earlier. It certainly centres the need for understanding the changing nature of trust especially in the context of social relationships that are increasingly characterised by diversity and the celebration of difference. In order to 'live without an enemy' requires trust. But how does trust manifest itself?

Nelken (1994) has explored the relevance of this question for criminological concerns. He raises the value of exploring the question of trust in the context of the importance to criminology of engaging in comparative research. In his review of what might be learned by engaging in a comparative analysis of white-collar and/or corporate crime, Nelken (*ibid.*) suggests a number of questions become pertinent for criminology. These questions are: whom can you trust, how do you trust, how much can you trust and when can you trust? Such questions are relevant not only for the crimes of the powerful. Elsewhere with Karen Evans, I have discussed the way in which questions such as these underpin people's sense of 'ontological security' in two high crime areas (Walklate and Evans 1999). We have suggested that they may be understood through the notion of a 'square of trust' (see Figure 12.1). In

Figure 12.1: The square of trust.

Source: Walklate and Evans (1999: 135)

this square of trust, whom you can trust, how you trust and how much you can trust at an individual level depend upon where an individual is located between the points of the square. For example, based on our fieldwork in one community (which we named Oldtown) it would appear that people trust as much as the local neighbourhood dogma permits whilst simultaneously endeavouring to avoid 'public shaming' (being labelled a 'grass'). This takes the form, primarily, of trusting other local people, because they are local (mechanisms of sociability). This does not mean, however, that other individuals are not trusted. But those others are trusted in a highly individualistic and fragile manner and that trust is dependent upon what those individuals do with the trust invested in them. This may, for example, include trusting individual police officers and individual officials from other agencies, but it certainly does not mean offering generalised trust to those official agencies (the state). The risks of 'public shaming' are too high a price to pay for whatever benefits might accrue from such a co-operative venture. These processes do not mean, however, that the anarchistic politics of the presence of criminal gangs (organised crime) have won the hearts and minds of this community. But it does mean we may have to rethink some of the mechanisms whereby social solidarity is produced and maintained (the organised nature of the community). Trusting relationships look somewhat different, however, in the other community (which we named Bankhill) that was under investigation.

The responses here appeared to suggest that older people were still willing to offer a generalised trust to the 'official agencies' (the state) and that there are friendship and community groups that strive to offer some kind of militation against a totally atomised existence (mechanisms of sociability). However, the belief that 'this area is going downhill rapidly' (the level of disorganisation in the community) and the expressed fears of young people (the disorganised nature of local crime) undermined the sense of belongingness on which the potential for trusting relationships inherent in the call for help from 'the officials' might be developed. Thus there was an absence of social solidarity and a withdrawal from the processes on which such solidarity might be predicated.

For younger people in this community the picture was somewhat different. They know they cannot be seen to be talking to 'officials' (the state), which for them might include older people. They also know that to stay out of trouble of different kinds they have to manage the tightrope of being known (their mechanisms of sociability), but not being a 'grass', nor participating in criminal activity (the disorganised nature of crime). For them, living in their locality was no worse than anywhere else and trust existed between those who know each other, but not much beyond (for a more detailed discussion of these examples, see Evans *et al.* 1996; Walklate 1998; Walklate and Evans 1999).

The different ways in which the questions of whom do you trust, when do you trust, how much do you trust, manifested in the discussion above may be rooted in the different histories of the two areas under investigation. However, whilst that trust may be rooted in history, it is not historical. It is a real mechanism whereby individuals create a way of

305

managing their routine daily lives, which differently situates them in relation to the state, crime, community and social relationships.

As we have gone on to argue, these two research areas were not unusual places. Each urban and increasingly rural area (an issue to which I shall return) has its equivalent location. These are predominantly white areas where the traditional working class has historically co-existed with the 'social scum' along with those who have endeavoured to better themselves as market forces have permitted. As Evans *et al.* have argued:

> ...your place in relation to crime places you in a community of belonging and exclusion... It is consequently important to recognise who is seen to be protecting you and how: for many people it is not the police or the council but local families and/or the Salford Firm. Moreover, it is the absence of confidence in the formal agencies which creates the space for those other forces to come into play.
>
> (1996: 379)

This quotation refers to one of our research areas from which the state has largely withdrawn. These are the locations that have suffered disproportionately as the gap between rich and poor has grown as we have increasingly become a 30/40/40 society (Hutton 1995). But how useful is such an analysis in other locations? Locations that have not suffered at all as the gap between rich and poor has grown? On the contrary, what about those locations that have benefited. What do the issues relating to trust and community safety look like there?

The Blue Lamp Campaign: a case study of rural Cheshire

In August 1999 a Norfolk farmer, Tony Martin, killed a 16-year-old burglar on his property. The rights and wrongs of the punishment subsequently given to Mr Martin for this offence were hotly debated in the press in the months following. However, the significance of this event lies not so much in the particularities associated with it but in the way it brought to the fore some deeply held concerns about crime and policing in the countryside. In the month prior to the Martin incident the National Federation of Women's Institutes published a report, *The Changing Village*, highlighting the lack of 'beat Bobbies' as being a pressing concern for 71% of the villages that took part in its survey. Indeed, in the intervening time there has been repeated coverage of countryside issues. This, of course, has been partly fuelled by other issues, like the debate around fox hunting, the higher political profile given to the Countryside Alliance and the fuel protests in September 2000. However, in amongst all this has been a repeated concern about crime and policing with some evidence to suggest this concern is not just a product of media-led imaginings.

Home Office statistics for 1999–2000 suggest that burglary is rising much more rapidly in some rural areas than urban ones, even if the overall rate of such offences remains relatively low. Changes such as these, along with the slow but sure withdrawal of the police from many police substations, are real enough. So much so that the then Home Secretary, Jack Straw, promised an extra £30 million to rural police forces in his speech to the Labour Party conference in September 2000. The concerns of the 'Blue Lamp Campaign' in Cheshire need to be set against this more general backcloth and is just one example of how some of these wider issues have manifested themselves at a local level.

Moody has stated: 'The countryside is significant in contemporary criminology mainly because of its absence' (1999: 8). Consequently, she goes on to suggest, rural areas become a fertile ground for testing both the empirical and analytical validity of criminological ideas. So with this in mind I was interested to examine the validity of the ideas we had applied as a way of an understanding responses to crime in Oldtown and Bankhill to what appeared to be taking place in rural Cheshire. First, it will be valuable to offer a pen portrait of this particular location.

Cheshire is a very mixed county. On the one hand, it comprise towns like Chester, Nantwich, Crewe, Northwich and Winsford. These towns in and of themselves are very mixed, from the historical tourist attraction of Chester, to the latter-day railway and car-manufacturing base of Crewe and to the Merseyside overspill development of Winsford. On the other hand, Cheshire comprises areas of traditional ancestral wealth, wealth gleaned from the Industrial Revolution and the new wealth of pop stars and sports personalities. The Blue Lamp Campaign originates from that part of Cheshire in the heart of the area known as the Vale Royal – arguably the traditional centre of ancestral farming wealth. The campaign itself centres on the villages of Bunbury, Spurstow, Tiverton, Tattenhall, Eaton and Cotebrook, all of which have as their local commercial centre the small town of Tarporley. To offer a flavour of this area, it is perhaps enough to say that one of the claims to fame of the main hotel in Tarporley is that it is the meeting place for the oldest hunt in the country. Moreover, this hotel is closed to members of the public every November to accommodate the presence of the Duke of Westminster and the Hunt Ball. It was just before Christmas 1999 that this particular part of Cheshire became the focus of concerned local activity.

The catalyst for this activity was the non-replacement of the last remaining permanent policing presence in the area. Until this point of time the village of Spurstow had retained a permanent local constable. However, his removal also meant the whole locality (described above) lost its last permanent policing presence. There was much local concern. This concern was initially expressed by the turnout of over 150 people at the Police Community Consultative meeting held in the village of Bunbury, a village neighbouring Spurstow, subsequent to the non-replacement of the local constable. There was a strong policing presence at this meeting. The response to this local concern on the part of the police was to listen but not accede to the request the local police officer be reinstated.

The refusal to reinstate a local officer and the overall concern about a lack of policing presence in the locality prompted local residents to form what they named the 'Blue Lamp Campaign'. Through the local newspaper, people were invited to join this campaign and it grew rapidly. It comprised 15 signatories at 14 January 2000; this increased to around 200 by 17 March. The key demand of the campaign was for a permanent policing presence in the locality, preferably based in the town of Tarporley where there was a disused police station. The question remains as to why this campaign captured local imagination in the way it did.

The campaign organiser, Leila Potter, expressed this view: 'It gets around the yobs that police stations are closing down in our villages and so they know where to come to cause trouble' (quoted in the *Chester Chronicle* 14 January 2000). The police response to this kind of concern did not appear helpful. The local superintendent stated that: 'The village bobby has gone and I am asking people to accept that because we need to move forward' (*ibid.*). Moreover, he argued:

Seeing uniformed police officers on random patrol might have left you feeling safer but you would not have actually been safer... In almost every category of crime we are below half the national crime rate and people should feel safe with the success we are achieving. There are 2000 fewer victims of crime in this division than there were four years ago because we have been proactive and targeted habitual offenders... These reductions would not have been achieved if we had local beat Bobbies. (*ibid.*)

This is a very similar response to that given by the superintendent of the area in which the Martin killing occurred. He is reported as saying that:

The people in the fenlands are more fearful of crime than in other areas of the county, but their fears are not reflected in our crime figures. Their quality of life is being affected by fear, but they are still much less likely to be burgled than people who live in more built-up areas where crime rates are much higher. The fear of crime is probably psychological. Many of the farmers live in isolated rural areas and they think they are sitting targets (quoted in the *Guardian*, 24 August 24 1999).

Efforts to appeal to the irrationality of people's fears and the rationality of the policing response to crime-related issues, such as these, are understandable given the question of resources must always be upper-most in the mind of any local divisional police manager. However, in the Cheshire case the potential effect of such appeals was largely under-mined by the report of a double burglary of a 91-year-old woman and the local vicar in a village neighbouring the area that was the focus of the Blue Lamp Campaign.

The knowledge of this event had an important impact on the campaign. So much so that, by the beginning of March, Cheshire police reported having established a pilot project to examine rural policing issues. This project was designed to examine the viability of the following issues: whether uniformed officers could patrol rural areas in groups to identify problem points; whether community contact points could be set up in villages; whether the Internet could better facilitate communication; and how liaison with Homewatch and Crimewatch organisations could be improved. A new superintendent was also appointed to the locality in the same month.

Since March 2000 a number of options have been presented to the Blue Lamp Campaign leaders as proposed solutions to their concerns. One of these solutions was the 'Buy a Bobby' plan. It was proposed in the local press that people could join together and jointly invest in their own local police officer. This suggestion prompted the following reply:

Why should the villagers be forced to buy a bobby? It is our right to have the support of our police force, it is our right not to suffer the fear of crime. A local vicar told me the fear of crime is a crime – how true! We need the Chief Constable to show his teeth. We understand and greatly sympathise with his lack of resources but how long do we villagers wait for the government to act and give the police force the resources to train more police officers? Come on, Chief Constable Burgess, The Blue Lamp Campaign completely support you in your efforts to combat rural crime, you need our help and we certainly need yours (Leila Potter, letter to the *Chester Chronicle* 12 May 2000).

At the time of writing the Blue Lamp Campaign is still awaiting a meaningful response (in its terms) to this demand: a permanent police presence in Tarporley.

The question remains: how to make sense of these empirical events. In some respects this campaign constitutes an empirical example of the difficulties confronting individuals faced with the changing nature of society. These difficulties are highlighted in the quotation from Young with which this chapter began. A nostalgia for a past to which there is no return. Indeed one of the struggles facing the local commander in this example was to convince people in this locality the past cannot be re-created in the present. To a certain extent, this was achieved. The letter published from one of the campaign organisers indicates a recognition and acceptance of the difficulties facing the police and calls for energies also to be directed towards central government around these issues. People know the past cannot be re-created in the present. Indeed, in this respect people in this locality still offer a generalised trust to the police and want to work with them towards a resolution of their local concerns. This, in and of itself, reflects an understanding of the changing nature of social reality even if such changes are not well liked. Yet there is more to this than nostalgia. People also know what goes on in their locality. They know that police response times to 999 calls in this locality are in the region of 45 minutes. And whilst such calls may not be frequent, this does fuel local feelings of being excluded: not from jobs or the market-place or access to financial resources, but excluded from services they feel they have a right to. As the front page of the *Chester Chronicle* of 19 May 2000 stated: 'Above all, they [people in rural Cheshire] feel neglected by the police.'

There is, of course, another dimension to this feeling of neglect. The fears and anxieties expressed in this locality about crime also reflect the archetypal response of people in such locations: it is fear of the outsiders. The outsiders are 'the yobs' who know about the lack of police presence and target such areas accordingly. 'Urban crooks target rural communities' read the headline of *The Daily Telegraph*, on the 20 August 2000. The accuracy of such a headline notwithstanding, there are some senses in which this resonates with people's experience of crime (the debate about the invisibility of business crime, etc., notwithstanding). These are not the metaphorical anxieties associated with crime of which Taylor (1996) speaks or those of psychoanalysis associated with the work of Hollway and Jefferson (1997). These are the genuine concerns of people in a highly secure economic environment whose common interests lie in maintaining that sense of security and their economic position but who have had their traditional means of managing these taken away from them. For these people, there are no alternative mechanisms on which to rely, other than those upon which they have historically relied, in order to sustain their sense of well-being. What, then, are the lessons to be learned from applying the conceptual apparatus that seemed to help make sense of responses to community safety in Oldtown and Bankhill to rural Cheshire?

One way of beginning to answer this question is to explore the similarities and differences between the three areas under discussion here. These can be considered along a number of dimensions (Table 12.1 is intended to be suggestive rather than exhaustive).

Table 12.1: Coping with local crime problems

	Cheshire	Oldtown	Bankhill
Understanding the crime problem	Outsiders	Insiders	Insiders
Sense of community	Organised around common interest, fearful but proactive	Organised around kinship, defended	Disorganised, frightened
Social exclusion	Fear of exclusion	Already excluded	On the road to exclusion
Coping mechanisms	No alternative structure	Alternative structure	No alternative structure

Put in the context of trust and trust relationships it is possible to argue that the people of Cheshire trust each other and the official agencies but not outsiders. Their mechanisms for sociability are rooted in their common interests as members of a particular community facing a particular problem and their historical access to influence local decision-making. The problem that concerns them is the intermittent, but nevertheless real, threat of crime from outsiders whom they perceive to be organised enough to have knowledge about the policing dilemma of their locality. Historically, the people in this locality are used to having a good deal of influence in the local context: they are the locally powerful. The informal pressures that have traditionally informed local decision-making in areas like this, however, do not have the same effect as they once did. People here are not used to being socially excluded in this way. This is not the social exclusion of economics but that of politics: informal power and influence. They see themselves as citizens not just with responsibilities but also with rights. Hence a campaign which, to all intents and purposes, was inclusive of all the parties concerned, including the police. A campaign that nevertheless the police were being made to take seriously because of the location in which it was taking place. These trust relationships stand in marked contract to those existing in Oldtown and Bankhill summarised earlier.

So what are the implications of this kind of analysis in general and these case studies in particular for how we think about the question of community safety and how we think about the problem of crime in late modern society? Put another way, for whom are social life and the question of trust fragmenting?

Conclusion

As was stated earlier, trust and trust relationships can be studied at a number of different levels and through a number of different lenses. In this chapter, the concern has been to discuss those relationships through the lens of place and at the level of the social. This is not to say that other levels and lenses might not be equally important as indeed, for example, age showed itself to be in the context of Bankhill. However, overall the implications of this discussion are not dissimilar to those offered by Walklate and Evans (1999). They serve, in one sense, further to challenge the notion that there can be a universally applicable solution, in policy terms, to what can be very local and localised problems; that much is self-evident. There is, however, a deeper message highlighted in this discussion. That deeper message is about historical continuities. It is about understanding *Crime in Context*, to borrow the title of Ian Taylor's (1999) latest book. That historical context arguably takes its toll in different ways, in different geographical areas with different community structures. Some of that context is plain to see in the comparative stories told here.

The Blue Lamp Campaign in rural Cheshire is an ongoing process, the final outcome of which is yet to manifest itself. However, from what has taken place so far it is clear these campaigners have managed to establish a dialogue with local police commanders largely unavailable to the people of Oldtown and Bankhill. People in Cheshire have been listened to. They are having their concerns taken seriously. Whether they will get what they want is a moot point but they achieved in three months much more than the people of Bankhill, in particular, managed to achieve in two and a half years. This tells us something about the locally powerful in each of these locations and their historical relationship with the police.

The police in Cheshire can ill afford to lose the confidence of people in that locality. The voices of these people can be heard in a number of different places, not just in Police Community Forums. It is interesting to note that people in Bankhill endeavoured to be heard in relation to some similar issues but with little impact. People in Oldtown did not even try. They did not need to. Their historical relationships within their community and with policing told them this was a foolish endeavour. So, is this a case of 'plus ça change, plus c'est la même chose'?

In some respects the answer to this last question has to be 'yes'. Those who have always been socially excluded, as the 'dangerous classes', continue to be so. Nothing yet has emanated, in policy terms at least, to convince those at the bottom of the social, economic, educational and health hierarchy that it is in their interests to manage their lives in any other way than the way to which they have become accustomed. Arguably, it is only the introduction of meaningful job opportunities that will achieve this, and then not for all those deemed to belong to the 'dangerous classes'. And those who have always managed to influence local agendas to meet their perceived needs may also continue to do so especially in places like Cheshire.

There are some interesting questions left unanswered by this analysis, not just for the Blue Lamp Campaign but also for the increasing volume of the rural voice. For example, when people call for 'bringing back the bobby on the beat', what are they referring to? For some people, this is more than viewing the past through rose-tinted spectacles. This was their experience of policing in their community where the village bobby lived and that worked for them. They knew whom to trust: not just collectively as 'the police' but as an individual, the local police officer. This was their experience of who would sort things out. How are such gaps to be filled? This is a dilemma facing many police commanders who, with tight resources, can ill afford to lose the support of people for whom such relationships matter and so, by implication, for example, by raising questions about internal policing priorities and external performance indicators. Many other questions may also follow that are not the direct concern of this chapter, but the politics of which may nevertheless prove to be telling for governments who do not heed them.

So, for whom is trust fragmenting? It is fragmenting for those without inherited wealth to rely on, for those in the short-term job market, for those who are over-mortgaged, etc., etc. In this sense, Taylor's analysis of the crises facing late modern society in respect of crime is apt. However, for those left behind there are no crises. They trust whom they always have: family and kinship ties. For those afraid of being excluded there are no real crises: at least, not crises they cannot manage. They have the economic resources and the political access to make sure their voices are heard. In this sense, then, there has been little historical change. It is these relationships, alongside the changing nature of market society, that also form part of the social context of crime and the social context of understanding policy response to crime. It is all a question of trust.

References

Bauman, Z. (2000) *Liquid Modernity*. Oxford: Polity Press.
Beck, U. (1992) *The Risk Society*. London: Sage.
Crawford, A. (1997) *The Local Governance of Crime: Appeals to Community and Partnerships*. Oxford: Clarendon Press.
Etzioni, A. (1996) *The New Golden Rule*. London: Profile Books.
Evans, K., Fraser, P. and Walklate, S. (1996) Whom can you trust? The politics of 'grassing' on an inner city housing estate. *Sociological Review*, 44(3): 361–80.
Fukuyama, F. (1996) *Trust*. London: Penguin.
Gellner, E. (1989) Trust, cohesion and social order. In D. Gambetta (ed.) *Trust: Making and Breaking Co-operative Relations*. Oxford: Blackwell.
Giddens, A. (1991) *Modernity and Self Identity*, Oxford: Basil Blackwell.
Hollway, W. and Jefferson, T. (1997) The risk society in an age of anxiety: situating the fear of crime. *British Journal of Sociology*, 38(2): 255–66.
Hutton, W. (1995) *The State We're In*. London: Jonathan Cape.
Luhmann, N. (1989) Familiarity, confidence, trust: problems and alternatives. In D. Gambetta (ed.) *Trust: Making and Breaking Co-operative Relations*. Oxford: Blackwell.
Misztal, B. (1996) *Trust in Modern Societies*. Oxford: Polity Press.
Moody, S. (1999) Rural neglect: the case against criminology. In G. Dingwall and S. Moody (eds) *Crime and Conflict in the Countryside*. Cardiff: University of Wales Press.
Nelken, D. (1994) Whom can you trust? The future of comparative criminology. In D. Nelken (ed.) *The Futures of Criminology*. London: Sage.
Sennett, R. (1998) *The Corrosion of Character*. New York: W.W. Norton.
Social Exclusion Unit (1998) *Bringing Britain Together: A National Strategy for Neighbourhood Renewal*. London: Cabinet Office.
Social Exclusion Unit (1999) Report of the Policy Action Team on Community Self-Help. London: Home Office.
Taylor, I. (1996) Fear of crime, urban fortunes and suburban social movements: some reflections from Manchester. *Sociology*, 30(2): 317–37.
Taylor, I. (1999) *Crime in Context*. Oxford: Polity Press.
Walklate, S. (1998) Crime and community: fear or trust? *British Journal of Sociology*, 49: 550–69.
Walklate, S. and Evans, K. (1999) *Zero Tolerance or Community Tolerance? Managing Crime in High Crime Areas*. Avebury: Ashgate.
Young, J. (1999) *The Exclusive Society*. London: Sage.

Index

sensitisation of Internet-related
issues, 190-91
mediation agents, 229
migration *see* immigration
money laundering, 82, 119, 123
monopoly of coercion, 52
Multi-Disciplinary Group (MDG) on
Organised Crime, 119
multi-level governance, 3
multisectoral networks, 2-3
murder, foreign nationals involved
in, 172, 173f

National Conference of Villepinte,
216-7, 218
National Crime Squad (NCS), 201
National Criminal Intelligence Service
(NCIS), 201
National High Tech Crime Unit, 201
National Infrastructure Protection
Center (NIPC), 200
NATO
response to TOC, 86
revision of policy agenda, 78-9
natural coercion, 53
netizen groups, 196-7
networked governance, 2-3
constellations of power relations, 5
effectiveness, 5-6
implications for crime control and
security, 3-4
Nice Treaty, amendments to Pillar III,
114-17
non-EU citizens
as bogus asylum applicants, 138-9
crimes committed by, 135-6
human rights, 146
Northern Ireland, compensation for
terrorist property damage, 247
Northern Ireland (Emergency
Provisions) Act (1991), 251
nuclear arms race, 77

ontological (in)security, 28, 301-2

Organisation for Security and Co-
operation in Europe (OSCE), 80
organised crime *see* TOC
Osman v. Umited Kingdom (1998), 255

paedophiles, 65
Palme Commission, 77
parental home, 280-81
partnerships, 3
Pasqua Law, 226
peace-keeping, 79
role of NATO and WEU, 86
penitentiary policies
and crime, 70-73
see also prisons
Pillar III, 88, 96-7, 104
Amsterdam Treaty amendments,
difficulties for enlargement,
109-12
co-operation in areas covered by,
127
difficulties for enlargement, 107-8
moving issues to Pillar I, 106
Nice Treaty amendments,
difficulties for enlargement,
114-17
pillar structure of the Treaties, 104
anxiety over change, 106-7
cross-pillar issues, 108
pluralisation of security, 45-6
Police Complaints Authority (PCA),
262
Police and Criminal Evidence Act
(1984), 261–2
policing, 118
cyberspace, 196-202
disjunctures, 202-4
definitions, 4
developments in European co-
operation, 37, 39-40, 93-5, 109
implications of commercial
security, 46
participation of the public, 228-9
promotion of co-operation in Pillar